PREMISES

MERIDIAN

Crossing Aesthetics

Werner Hamacher
& David E. Wellbery
Editors

Translated by
Peter Fenves

Stanford
University
Press

Stanford
California

PREMISES

*Essays on Philosophy and Literature
from Kant to Celan*

Werner Hamacher

Stanford University Press
Stanford, California

© 1996 by the President and Fellows of Harvard College

Reprinted by Stanford University Press in 1999
by arrangement with Harvard University Press

Library of Congress Card Number: 99-67024

Original printing 1999
Last figure below indicates year of this printing:
08 07 06 05 04 03 02 01 00 99

Contents

Premises   1

Hermeneutic Ellipses: Writing the Hermeneutic Circle in
Schleiermacher   44

The Promise of Interpretation: Remarks on the Hermeneutic
Imperative in Kant and Nietzsche   81

"Disgregation of the Will": Nietzsche on the Individual and
Individuality   143

"Lectio": de Man's Imperative   181

Position Exposed: Friedrich Schlegel's Poetological
Transposition of Fichte's Absolute Proposition   222

The Quaking of Presentation: Kleist's "Earthquake in Chile"   261

The Gesture in the Name: On Benjamin and Kafka   294

The Second of Inversion: Movements of a Figure through
Celan's Poetry   337

Sources   389

Index   391

PREMISES

Understanding is in want of understanding.

The thoughts pursued here cannot be summarized in this proposition concerning understanding without encountering resistance—not in this proposition nor in the three or four sentences into which it can be analyzed and expanded.

That understanding is in want of understanding—a proposition to be read as the principle of understanding, as an announcement or summation, as a demand or complaint—will not have said anything about understanding unless it itself is understood, and unless it is understood that this proposition speaks also of the impossibility of understanding and thus the impossibility of this very proposition.

"Understanding is in want of understanding" means first of all that understanding is not only concerned with understanding things but must itself be understood whenever anything is to be understood. In understanding, something is doubtless made accessible, but it becomes accessible only in the very act of understanding—under its conditions or presuppositions. The object to which understanding refers may exist in the absence of any understanding of this object; but as the subject-matter of understanding, it is already a subject-matter affected by understanding, and as such it remains uncomprehended as long as its understanding is not understood as well. If the determining moments of understanding remain in the dark, if it is not even understood that there are such moments—both historical and structural—then the subject-matter to be understood also remains obscure. Among the structural conditions without which understanding can never take place is there-fore this: in understanding not only something but also the under-standing of this thing must be understood.

That understanding is not only a matter of understanding things and that it, too, wants to be understood means, furthermore, that under-standing produces effects and remains incomplete without the under-standing of these effects. Whether one defines understanding as an oc-currence, a process, or an act, it is never a relation between two already given, immobile entities that somehow remain untouched by this rela-tion; rather, it is a relation in which each term constitutes itself in the first place—the reader turns into the reader of this sentence, the sentence into the sentence of this reader. Understanding is thus a procedure of reciprocal affection and alteration. Unless it is understood that under-standing is this constitutive alteration and indeed the alteration of all sedimented constitutions of the elements involved in its process, then not only does understanding itself remain uncomprehended but also everything that is all too easily called its subject and its object. If, by contrast, it is understood that understanding is change and alteration, then one must also concede that it cannot be arrested in a stable pattern of transformation. Even when understanding exercises control over it-self through reflection, it does not stop transforming its transformative turns and ineluctably becoming another one. "Understanding is in want of understanding" thus also means that however much it may make itself into a theme, it still cannot be stabilized into an essence, a paradigm, or an Idea that would not then be exposed to another understanding, an understanding incommensurable with the first. Understanding wants to be understood by another understanding and wants to be understood otherwise: paradoxically, it is itself only as an understanding exposed to another one and, at the limit, exposed to something other than under-standing.

To understand means "to be able," "to have the capacity," "to take something upon oneself," "to be in charge of it." The proposition con-cerning understanding thus means, in its third version, that under-standing requires the ability to be performed. The dominant philosophi-cal tradition since antiquity has interpreted this ability as *technē*, *ars*, art, and has furthermore taken it for a methodologically controllable proce-dure. This tradition proceeds in principle from an historically invariant analogy between the objects and subjects of understanding. The security of knowledge was based on the correspondence between the structure of the sentence and that of the subject-matter; the "art of understanding" could never go wrong as long as its rules corresponded to those of the "art of speaking." The structural analogy between the possibilities of understanding and the actuality of its objects underwent its first convulsion when it became doubtful whether knowledge had command over its own ground. The dissociation of the possible and the actual unleashed by this doubt—the dissociation between what can be thought and made, on the one hand, and what is given, on the other—did not weaken the faith in techniques and technology, in abilities and powers; rather, it culminated in a philosophy and a praxis of the will-to-power and of the will-to-will that was determined to convert the given into something made and thereby restore the broken unity of the experience of the self. Possibility and ability were defined ontotechnologically as self-enabling and self-empowerment, while understanding was interpreted as self-understanding, the understanding of the already understood, and thus the understanding of understanding itself. An echo of this formula of self-formation—a formula of the will-to-will and the will to self-understanding—may still be heard in the proposition "understanding is in want of understanding."

But the dissociation that was supposed to be healed in the pure self-relation of understanding once again erupts in this very relation. As a self-generating and self-realizing "faculty," understanding was supposed to have been its own unconditioned premise, its absolute autoprotasis, and it was supposed to have drawn from this premise a conclusion about itself. But the proposition "understanding is in want of understanding"—a proposition in which this self-relation is reclaimed—remains valid only as long as understanding is not yet understood, the will to understanding has not yet been fulfilled, no ability has yet secured itself, and no capacity has been saturated in a conclusive experience of understanding. The proposition is valid only under the premise that understanding cannot be fulfilled. As long as understanding still only *wants* to be understood, it *cannot* yet be understood: it cannot yet be enabled and is not yet even possible. The proposition of understanding—a proposition postulating that understanding provides its own possibility—thus touches upon something else, something that does not correspond to understanding and cannot be assimilated to it. The proposition points toward something uncomprehended and incomprehensible, toward an incapacity and an impossibility. Not only is the privilege of technique and technology shaken by this other—by the impossible—but so too is the possibility of regulating and methodologically controlling understanding. And so too is the very possibility of understanding in general, its capacity to find its premises in itself, to understand its own understanding, to stand *before* and thus take charge of this understanding: its ability, in sum, *to be understanding* at all.

The proposition of understanding sidesteps understanding. Precisely what understanding means is supposed to be grasped and comprehended in this proposition; but since this understanding is tied to the unfulfilled and unfulfillable demand to grasp itself and to include itself in its comprehension, this proposition says that understanding must understand itself from its impossibility. That understanding is in want of understanding is, in short, an aporia: the proposition says that understanding—precisely because it is necessary—does not understand. And since the proposition must participate in this non-understanding of understanding, it says that it, the proposition, does not yet say anything. But with this aporetic result at least this much is said, however implicitly: understanding is not a formal-logical relation that must accommodate itself to the principle of non-contradiction; non-understanding is not opposed to understanding but is its inconceivable ground and ungraspable background; and understanding, like non-understanding, moves in an open arena that wants to be understood in terms *other* than those defined by the categories of the understanding and wants perhaps to be other than *understood*.

For it is always another who understands and whose difference from what is understood remains irreducible. Something else is always understood—even when one understands "oneself"—and indeed understood in such a way that a relation to this other, however familiar or well-known it may be, is each time created for the first time or for the first time anew. Hence understanding is indeed a relation, but a relation to something new, however old it may be; it is a relation to another, even when this other would be the nearest and closest to hand; and it is a relation to something that can offer itself only as something uncomprehended, even when it is already considered familiar. It is thus each time another, a new and non-anticipated relation to something uncomprehended and until now incomprehensible. But if it is indeed a relation to something incomprehensible *until now,* then it must also be a relation to something *still* incomprehensible in understanding, for otherwise precisely *this*—the thing uncomprehended until now—would not be understood. If understanding relates itself each time to something strange, then it must be an estranged relation. If it comports itself to another, then it must be a comportment altered by this other and opened to further alterations. Understanding is not therefore a simple relation but an insolubly aporetic one. At the limit, it is a relation to the non-relational, hence a relationless relation: a reference to retreat, hence a self-retreating reference.

Understanding stands off from itself—not just occasionally, because of the constitution of something called its object, or because of the individual incapacities of those who seek to understand. Understanding stands at a distance from itself only because it refers to something un-comprehended. Otherwise it would not be understanding at all: it would be knowledge. Something is understood only in its incomprehensibility. And this incomprehensibility does not simply accompany understanding as an unavoidable evil or a regrettable remnant of finitude that could be cast off under ideal conditions of communication; rather, incomprehensibility is what first grants understanding, discloses its possibility, and preserves it as a possibility. If something is understood, it is only because it stands back from understanding.

It is one of the remarkable features of the movement of understanding that the incomprehensible, the foreign, and the irreducibly other—each of which sets understanding into motion in the first place—can be brought to rest at the end of this movement (but it is precisely this end that is at issue here), can be stabilized into an object of representation, thematized by a subject, and thus made into a cognized, controlled, reduced other of this subject. Understanding does not start by referring to objects; rather, objects constitute themselves in the act of under-standing. Once they are constituted (and this final constitution is, once again, in question) the movement of understanding comes to a halt and turns into a certification of the object and a self-securing of cognitive reason. Perhaps the best place to observe the leap from an understanding that is exposed to the incomprehensible into a self-consciousness that posits its objects is in Hegel's description of Greek "mantics." In his *Lectures on the Philosophy of History* Hegel explains that the mantic, like the philosopher, proceeds from *thaumazein,* from wonder or astonish-ment—indeed, from what Aristotle (in the same section of the *Meta-*

physics to which Hegel refers) describes as an *aporon:* a place without any outlet, an impasse, something incomprehensible.[1] "For the Greeks only *eavesdrop* [*lauschen*] on natural objects," Hegel writes, "and *intimate* these objects with an inward-directed question concerning their meaning. Just as, according to Aristotle, philosophy proceeds from wonder, so does the Greek intuition of nature proceed from this wonder."[2] Not only does an aporia precede philosophy and set it into motion; in every one of its steps philosophy remains bound to it. The relation of spirit *(Geist)* to this aporia consists in a pause, a breakdown of knowledge, a mere "eavesdropping" on something that communicates itself, and as Hegel then indicates, this relation expresses itself in a question about an unfamiliar meaning:

> None of this means that spirit encounters something extraordinary when compared with the usual. . . . On the contrary, Greek spirit, once excited, wonders about the *natural* of nature. It does not relate to it in a dull manner as something given: Greek spirit relates to it as something that is at first foreign to spirit but something to which it nevertheless has the intimating confidence and the faith that the natural bears something within itself that would be friendly to spirit, something to which spirit could relate in a positive manner.   (Hegel, 12: 288; Lectures, 234)

According to Hegel, then, the "natural" of nature, its essence and its meaning, cannot be conceived in wonder as some sort of "given" but must be perceived as a non-given, something that holds itself back, something "foreign" to which spirit entertains no "positive" relation, and that means an absence of any determinate relation of positing: no

---

1. See Aristotle, *Metaphysica,* ed. W. Jaeger (Oxford: Clarendon, 1957), 982b12; *Metaphysics,* trans. W. D. Ross, in *The Works of Aristotle,* ed. R. McKeon (New York: Random House, 1941), 692.

2. G. W. F. Hegel, *Vorlesungen über die Philosophie der Geschichte* in *Werke in zwanzig Bänden,* ed. E. Moldenhauer and K. M. Michel (Frankfurt am Main: Suhrkamp, 1970), 12: 288. Cf. *Lectures on the Philosophy of History,* trans. J. Sibree (New York: Dover, 1956), 234; hereafter, Lectures.

All translations in this volume are new. Whenever possible, I have included references to readily available English translations; but in no case are these translations themselves quoted. —trans.

positing relation at all. The relation to the "natural" is thus at first the aporetic relation to the relationless. By relating itself to the "natural," spirit refers to something that is not given to it, something that it does not posit, and something that it therefore cannot make into an object of representation. "Nevertheless," Hegel writes—and this "nevertheless" marks the turning point from the aporia to representation and spirit— spirit has "the intimating confidence and faith that the natural bears something within itself, something that would be friendly to spirit, something to which it could relate in a positive manner." The foreign, the non-given, is not recognized as friendly but is, instead, "intimated," not known but believed. Whatever the natural is supposed to "bear in itself" must therefore already be *presupposed* in order for spirit to be able to enter into a "positive" relation to it. It is this *supposition* of faith that turns the foreign into something friendly, the non-given into a given, and makes that which withdraws from every determinate position into something positive.

Hegel does not dissolve the aporia of understanding. On the contrary, for him, the aporia constitutes the resistance from which experience must rebound and turn back on itself. By supposing that the incomprehensible has a meaning, spirit understands it as its object and understands itself as its positing. Hegel describes the leap from aporia to representation—or the contraction of difference into position—in the following terms: "Yet the Hellenes did not remain immobile before these feelings [wonder and intimation]; rather they brought out [*herausstellten*] the inwardness about which their intimation asked, making it into a determinate representation [*Vorstellung*], an object [*Gegenstand*] of consciousness" (Hegel, 12: 288; Lectures, 234). To suppose that the foreign would be something friendly is essentially to suppose that an interiority inhabits that absolute exteriority which hitherto could be experienced only as an aporia, something impossible to experience. It is to presuppose an interiority that can be "brought out" and placed in the hands of knowledge as a "determinate representation" and thus as an "object of consciousness." The positing of spirit brings itself out in this bringing forth of representation, and from the aporia something is brought to light that ought no longer be aporetic at all: positionality itself. The "natural" of nature, its essence and meaning, is only the positing and self-positing of spirit. And this positing consists in the

movement from wonder to mantic supposition and semantic explication, a movement leading understanding to representation, concept,
and philosophy.

Positing, setting into place, position—these are always, for Hegel,
placing together, co-positing, inaugurating a synthesis of spirit with
itself in its other. Even in wonder, where spirit does not understand and
does not understand itself, it can still consolidate its powers of cognition
by presupposing an inwardness, a meaning, or a significance, and
thereby achieve knowledge and self-knowledge. The path of spirit is in
every case circular: it leads spirit from its presupposition of an absolute
other to this other as the other *of itself,* and in this way it returns spirit
to itself. Hegel thinks the course of autoposition not only as the path of
thinking but also as the way of song, poetry, and literature:

> Similarly, the Greeks listened to the murmurings of the springs and
> asked what was the meaning of this. . . . The Naiads, or springs, are
> the external inception of the muses. Yet the muses' immortal songs are
> not what one hears when one listens to the murmurings of springs;
> they are the productions of spirit in its capacity for sensible hearing,
> which produces [them] in its eavesdropping on itself.   (Hegel, 12:
> 289; Lectures, 235)

Spirit does not simply listen in astonishment, thus caught in an aporia;
it hears "sensibly," *sinnig,* in a reasonable manner. Spirit thus listens for
the sense and meaning of a murmuring that, as "something foreign at
first," must have lacked sense. In this way, it can produce "in its eavesdropping" the song of meaning "in itself." The work of spirit is the
appropriation of the foreign, the semanticization of the asemic, the
positivizing of the aporetic. The song of the muses is not the mere
murmuring of the springs but only the "sensibly" heard murmuring, the
murmuring heard with a sense for its sense. Spirit hears itself singing in
the spring as its muse. Song—and thus art in general—is not incomprehensible nature but a representation of spirit that perceives and understands itself in nature. Every muse is already the muse of the mantic and
thus the muse of speculative auto-semanticization:

> The interpretation and explanation of nature . . . the demonstration of
> sense and significance in nature—this is the activity of subjective spirit

to which the Greeks gave the name *manteia*. . . . Both the material and the explicator who brings out what is significant belong to *manteia*. . . . Nature answered the questions of the Greek: this is the sense in which the statement that man obtained answers to the questions of nature from his spirit is true. (Hegel, 12: 289–90; Lectures, 235)[3]

Wherever this speculative inversion of question and answer takes place there must be a circular path between spirit and nature. Its logical form is the self-presupposition of spirit in its other—and "spirit" is nothing but this self-presupposition. Interpretation, as the "bringing out" or understanding "of sense and significance," is for Hegelian spirit— whether in its subjective, objective, or absolute state—always only a "bringing forth" of something previously put into place, a laying out of something earlier laid down, an understanding of a previous positing. The hermeneutics of the *mantis* is autohermeneutics. It is self-under-standing and, more exactly, the understanding of understanding itself as position.

But the aporia remains uncomprehended. In the aporia—and in the astonishment that responds to it—the Greeks, according to Hegel, do not simply stand still. On the contrary, "Greek spirit, once excited," spirit that has "the natural only as incitement" (Hegel, 12: 288–89; Lectures, 234), takes the only path that the blockage of the aporia leaves open: a path back to itself. Something is then understood, to be sure, but it is understood only by turning away from that which, as incom-

3. Other passages from the same context point in a similar direction: "Thus the Delphic priestesses, without consciousness and without reflection, in the rapture of enthusiasm *(mania)* uttered unintelligible sounds from themselves, and only then did the *mantis* lay down a specific meaning for these noises" (12: 290; Lectures, 236). And: "*manteia* in general is poetry—not arbitrary fantasizing but a fantasy that puts spirit into the natural and is meaningful knowledge" (12: 291; Lectures, 236–37). Interpretation *(Auslegen)* is, one could say, a putting inside *(Hineinlegen)*. It obeys the mechanism of projection that Goethe ironically recommended in the "Tame Xenien II": "Im Auslegen seid frisch und munter,/ Legt ihr's nicht aus, so legt was unter" (In interpretation be fresh and cheerful; if you don't lay it out, lay something down) (Goethe, *Werke*, Hamburger Ausgabe, ed. Erich Trunz [Hamburg: Wegner, 1964], I: 329). How little the Hegelian presentation grasps the peculiarity of Greek mantics becomes clear in Jean-Luc Nancy's commentary on its first philosophical discussion in Plato's *Ion;* see J.-L. Nancy, *Le partage des voix* (Paris: Galilée, 1982); cf. "Sharing Voices," trans. Gayle L. Ormiston, in *Transforming the Hermeneutic Context*, ed. G. L. Ormiston and A. D. Schrift (Albany, N.Y.: SUNY Press, 1990), 211–59.

prehensible, first demands comprehension, whether it "excites" or "incites." It is thus understood at the cost of not understanding the very excitation to which the further course of understanding owes its impetus. The significance is grasped but not the *mania:* the *Sinn* (meaning) is understood but not the *Wahnsinn* (de-mentia)[4] that undoes the production of meaning. For de-mentia is not supposed by spirit nor posited in its representations and concepts but is, rather, whatever lies in advance of all positings and presuppositions and thus precedes every possible understanding. It is an other that is not the other *of* spirit and not the other *of* understanding but is other than any other still susceptible to semanticization and ontologization—an other that offers no point of support for the hermeneutic reduction to sense and enters into the horizon of self-positing only as its disruption.

The aporia incites understanding, but it remains incomprehensible—and with this abyss of understanding, so too does understanding itself. Understanding cannot, therefore, as Hegel proposes, obey the matrix of a thoroughgoing dialectization; rather, it obeys a double law—one could call it the law of dia-lecture,[5] double reading: the law of hermeneutic reduction whereby a stable semantic position is attained, on the one hand, and on the other, the dismaying law of de-posing under which no position, no understanding, and no mantic, semantic, or hermeneutic reduction are possible. If understanding understands itself, it has already forgotten the devastation, the astonishment, the wonder, and the eavesdropping from which it took its point of departure. Since, however, it does not understand its provenance, it does not understand. If, by contrast, it remains in astonishment, it does not understand yet again. Something is "understood" in every case only because it is not "understood." Understanding is possible only between these two impossibilities of understanding—the hermeneutic parousia of spirit in its autoposition and de-posing *sans phrase*—only *between* them, hence only insofar as the movement of self-positing must always be exposed and once again discharged by another understanding, and thus only insofar

4. See Hegel, 12: 290; *Lectures,* 236.
5. See my study, *pleroma—zu Genesis und Struktur einer dialektischen Hermeneutik bei Hegel,* in G. W. F. Hegel, *Der Geist des Christentums: Schriften 1796–1800,* ed. W. Hamacher (Berlin: Ullstein, 1978), 7–333. My work does not discuss premises but rather the structure of the dialectical "pre" and the speculative mass. I also make the suggestion that one should speak of diaporia rather than aporia—of an impasse in the passage itself.

as its standing suspends itself in this unposited, groundless "between." There is understanding, including self-understanding, only from the aporia—and the aporia is what asemantically, alogically, and adialectically grants understanding, including dialectical understanding, by refusing it. When understanding fails, so too do philosophy and art.

With his interpretation of understanding as dialectical self-presupposition, Hegel does not simply react to the Platonic-Aristotelian aporia; he also links up with Kant's thesis on Being as absolute position. Kant first set down this formula for the fundamental thought of modern metaphysics in his treatise of 1763, *The One Possible Basis of Proof for a Demonstration of the Existence of God:* "Existence [*Dasein*] is the absolute position of a thing."[6] He then comments: "The concept of position or positing [*Position oder Setzung*] is completely simple and is the same as the concept of Being. . . . If a thing is considered posited in and for itself, then Being [*Sein*] is as much as existence [*Dasein*]." This position is absolute in the Kantian sense because it refers purely to the existence of "a thing in and for itself" regardless of all relations to possible predicates. Just as the positing of Being cannot be the copula in the predicative judgment, this positing cannot be a predicate, since every predication must already presuppose the existence of its logical subject.[7] And this absolute, pre-predicative presupposition, as the unconditioned fiat of Being, does not become any less absolute because it must still entertain one relation: that of the subject to this positing. In the *Critique of Pure Reason* Kant explicitly defines the modalities of Being—being actual, being possible, being necessary—in such a way that they are said to "express the relation to the faculty of knowledge" (A 219;

---

6. Immanuel Kant, *Gesammelte Schriften*, ed. Königliche Preussische [later, Deutsche] Akademie der Wissenschaften (Berlin and Leipzig: Georg Reimer [later, Walter de Gruyter], 1900–) 2: 73. There is a reprint of the Akademie edition of this treatise alongside an English translation entitled *The One Possible Basis for a Demonstration of the Existence of God*, trans. Gordon Treash (New York: Abaris, 1979). All subsequent citations of Kant refer to the Akademie edition, hereafter "Ak," except citations of the *Critique of Pure Reason*. In accordance with scholarly tradition, all citations of this work refer to its original editions (A, B).

7. Kant explicitly writes: "The relations of all predicates to their subject never indicate something existing, for the subject must have already have been *presupposed* as existing." And "if the subject is not already *presupposed* as existing, it remains in every predicate undecided whether it belongs to something existing or merely to a possible subject. Therefore, existence cannot itself be a predicate" (Ak, 2: 74; emphasis added).

B 266).[8] Being thus consists in a positing with respect to the subject of knowledge, and this positing—whether it be a pure synthesis of transcendental apperception or, as in Fichte, a primordial "enactment"— is the original act of the cognitive subject. In this act the Being of the thing is posited along with the Being of its knowledge in the subject. The absolute positing of Being is a positing of knowledge. Because this positing, as a transcendental act, is absolutely foundational and because it conditions both conceptuality and intuition, the "supreme principle" of experiential synthesis resides in it: "The conditions of the possibility of experience in general are at the same time conditions of the possibility of the objects of experience" (A 158; B 198). The essence of knowledge, like the essence of the object known, is conceived as an original act of positing, as a dictate of subjective consciousness in which it dictates itself and affects itself.[9] Kant's ontology and that of his speculative followers can thus be characterized as autotheseology and ontotheseology.

Existence must be based on the transcendental positing of the self if knowledge is to have "objective reality," that is, if knowledge is supposed to refer to existence in such a way that, according to the *Critique of Pure Reason,* it can find in existence "meaning and sense" (A 155; B 194). If the criterion of existence—of its objectivity and reality—is "meaning and sense," if positing always posits an existing entity by simultaneously positing meaning, then ontotheseology is possible only within a logic of Being as meaning: only as semontology. But ontotheseology is at the same time only possible if the agent that posits Being

8. Kant's thesis on Being should be compared to an essay of Martin Heidegger from *Wegmarken* (Frankfurt am Main: Klostermann, 1967), 273–307; cf. "Kant's Thesis on Being," trans. Ted Klein, Jr., and William Pohl, *The Southwestern Journal of Philosophy,* 4 (1973): 7–33. For Kant's later theory of positing, see Eckart Förster, "Kant's *Selbstsetzungslehre*" in *Kant's Transcendental Deductions,* ed. E. Förster (Stanford: Stanford University Press, 1989), 217–38.

9. These positio-ontological premises are universally valid and are thus even valid for things in themselves, hence for things with no relation to our modes of thinking and sensing—albeit with an important distinction. These premises have, for Kant, transcategorial validity. In a very important section of the *Critique of Judgment,* § 76, Kant says: "But our entire distinction between the merely possible and the actual rests on this: the merely possible means the position of representation of a thing with respect to our concept and the ability to think in general, whereas the actual means the positing of a thing in itself (apart from that concept)" (Ak, 5: 402).

and meaning posits itself in what it has posited, if it posits and knows itself as meaning. The fact that the existential position of the subject posits itself *as* positing immediately makes this position into a reflection. After Fichte's *Wissenschaftslehre,* this is most clearly expressed in Hegel's *Science of Logic:* "Existence [*Dasein*] is only being-posited [*Gesetztsein*]; this proposition expresses the essence of existence."[10] Since, however, being-posited originates from the "absolute presupposition" in which positing bends back on itself and reflects itself, Hegel can conclude: "Being-posited is thus a determination of reflection." And furthermore: "Being-posited is a relation to other, but to reflectedness-in-itself" (Hegel, 6: 33; Science, 407). As being-posited, Being is, for Hegel, other; but the absolute premise of this other—precisely the premise that it is posited unconditionally and thus posited as something unconditioned—refers the other back to its positing and turns its existence into reflectedness. Reflection takes being-other back into itself and is the very unity of itself and the other; more exactly, it is the other as self. The circle of position is thereby closed: the experience of the other has shown itself as an experience of the same, reflection as expanded position—or reposition—and the premises of theseology are once again secured, this time under the sign of speculative dialectics. In every relation to the other the original positing returns to itself, understands itself in this other as a form of its understanding, and is in this process of self-comprehension the unity of subject and substance, knowledge and meaning, thesis and semiosis. It is ontotautology—but therefore aporetic.

And yet the fundamental aporia—the aporia of positing, of founding itself—remains uncomprehended once again. A positing that is supposed to be unconditioned must be a positing without presupposition and thus a subjectless positing. It must purely posit itself; but by positing itself, *it* already posits *itself,* and so the positing that it is first supposed to perform must already *allow* itself to be presupposed. But such an allowance, admission, or concession of a presupposition can no longer be thought according to the logic of positing. It must be other than a presup-position and other than a positing of a prior support; on the contrary, in the very act of positing it must be precisely the opening that remains independent of the positing, an opening onto another that itself

10. Hegel, 6: 32; cf. *The Science of Logic,* trans. A. V. Miller (New York: Humanities Press, 1969), 406; hereafter, "Logic." (Miller translates *Dasein* as "determinate being.")

withdraws from the power, the faculty, and the possibility of positing. But if a positing can be a positing only by allowing something other than itself—other than its thetic Being—then an original positing cannot be performed. It is in need of a difference with respect to itself that can under no condition be reduced to a thetic act. Only by allowing something other than itself can it then grant admission to itself—and grant admission *to* itself, in turn, merely as that which it is not yet and never will have been, as the mere promise of a position, never as this position itself. But this is to say that any position is essentially defined from a distance from itself, and since this distance remains, for it, unmeasurable, it means that positing is an ineluctably aporetic act, the act of a non-action, an act of omission. And it means that positing, affected by something other than Being understood as position, never *is*—never "is" according to its own sense of "is," according to the sense of thetic Being. Philosophical negligence cannot then be held accountable for the fact that the aporia of positing is not understood, never analyzed, and has not been made into a theme. The aporia, as a displacement of every positing, *is* not—and therefore cannot be a theme for understanding. Making possible every theme and making every one impossible, it must be an *anathema* to understanding in every possible sense.

If positing must give leave to a non-positing; if positing, exposed, must break down in order for it to be a positing in the first place, then the structure of positing must be determined by a twofold leaving: by a leaving out (an ellipsis) and a letting in (the disclosure of a possibility). It must not be able to be what it must be able to become. It can claim to be only in the form of a demand for Being, not as a thetic Being but only as an imperative "Be!" And yet, since it is an aporetic claim, it must place this dictate of its fiat under this reservation: it cannot be pronounced and cannot be performed. Finite reason cannot ground itself; it can posit itself only by letting this positing be given out as an apodictic but unfulfillable imperative. And this not only applies to the transcendental act of theoretical reason—an act that posits the thing in itself in pure self-affection as an appearance of an appearance[11]—it also applies,

---

11. In one of his last notes Kant wrote about the thing in itself as *ens per se:* "It is an *ens rationis* = x of the position of itself according to the principle of identity wherein the subject, as self-affecting, hence according to the form, is thought only as appearance" (*Opus postumum,* Ak, 22: 27).

a fortiori, to the law of practical reason, a law that can demand self-consistent, autonomous action and Being only because it, under the conditions of finitude, never offers this action and this Being as actual. It was Schelling who, in his *Philosophical Letters on Dogmaticism and Criticism,* gave the structure of the Kantian aporia of positing its most pregnant formula: "Be! That is the supreme demand of criticism."[12] The ontological imperative that Schelling deciphers in Kant's work transforms the principle of Being as position into the unfounded demand for a Being—unfounded because it first demands a foundation for any position. Demanded in this way, Being cannot persist as a result, a fact, or even only as a being. The imperative testifies to this: from its inception positing is exposed to something else, something that is neither realized nor even conceivable in this positing. Indeed, the imperative indicates that positing is exposed positing; abandoned by itself, it is thus ex-position. Since ontotheseology understands Being and language in such a manner that it can find an autonomous foundation only in the command that there be a foundation and only in the promise of a grounding, it itself must be constituted in an ex-thetic manner. It cannot be concerned with Being and the meaning of this Being as givens but only as tasks given out, as assignments demanded and omitted. And for its part, it can only be an ontotheseology that gives up. The principle of ontotheseology is a leap; its form—if it can still be called a form—is the aporia.

To the ontological imperative Schelling discovers in Kant's theory of position there corresponds the "hermeneutic imperative," whose existence Friedrich Schlegel asserts in one of his fragments: "There is a hermeneutic imperative."[13] The imperative "Understand!" does not simply mean "You must understand" but also "You do not yet understand—and you do not yet understand that you must understand." The hermeneutic imperative explicitly states that understanding is necessary, and it implies that understanding cannot be actual as long as it still must be demanded; indeed, it states that understanding is impossible as long as its possibility must be first disclosed in the imperative demand. Only in

12. F. W. J. Schelling, *Sämmtliche Werke* (Stuttgart: Cotta, 1856), 1.1: 335; cf. *Philosophical Letters on Dogmaticism and Criticism,* in *The Unconditional in Human Knowledge,* trans. Fritz Marti (Lewisburg, Pa.: Bucknell University Press, 1980), 192.

13. Friedrich Schlegel, *Fragmente zur Poesie und Literatur,* in *Kritische Friedrich-Schlegel-Ausgabe,* ed. Ernst Behler, Jean-Jacques Anstett, and Hans Eichner (Paderborn: Schöningh, 1958-), 16.1: 69; section 4, "Zur Philologie," II no. 95. Hereafter, KA.

the not-yet and never-once of understanding can something be understood. Like Kant's and Schelling's ontological imperative, Schlegel's hermeneutic imperative thus expresses the aporia of position. There must be communication and understanding, but there can be communication and understanding only in view of them as *another* communication and *another* understanding—as a communication and understanding that are not and never will be given, as a communication and understanding of something other than the subject. In the imperative, whether ontological or hermeneutic, it thus becomes clear that there can be a position—and thus Being, subject, language, and understanding—only from the ex-position of this position: only, therefore, from what is precisely not an understanding of Being as position, not a subject, not a language, and not an understanding—and is, moreover, not a negation of any of these but the opening of every one. Only as an ex-posed, abandoned subject is there a subject in the first place, and only as ex-posed, disrupted language and understanding is there anything like language or understanding at all.

Schlegel captured this insight with the formula of philological self-affection: "Reading," he notes, "means to affect oneself philologically, limit, determine oneself philologically" (KA, 16.1: 68; no. 80). His plan for a "deduction of philology," which is perhaps not without irony, makes an effort to conceive of philology "as a logical affect and a subjectively necessary condition for the fulfillment of the logical imperative" (KA, 16.1: 72; no. 121).[14] The term "logical imperative" is here to be understood as an imperative of logic, but also as an imperative that demands a logic and a logos in the first place. Accordingly, the hermeneutic imperative is the one that will have commanded understanding from the position of an always only futurial hermeneutics. Like hermeneutics, philology is a "logical affect"—*philia* of the *logos*—as sheer self-affection of the logos, a logos that consists in nothing other than pure self-affection. The imperative that philology gives itself must therefore be understood as the self-affection of the logos—but for this reason as

---

14. See KA, 16.1: 36; no. 14: "Not a deduction but TOWARD the deduction." In "On Incomprehensibility," he brings up the Idea of "constructing for the reader . . . as it were, before his eyes another new reader to my liking, indeed . . . even to deduce him" (KA, 2: 363). A translation of the last quotation can be found in "On Incomprehensibility" in *'Lucinde' and the Fragments,* trans. Peter Firchow (Minneapolis: University of Minnesota Press, 1971), 260. All citations of Schlegel have been newly translated for this volume.

affectio in distans, for otherwise it would not be an imperative. The riddle of the logical and hermeneutic imperative leads back to the structure of logical and hermeneutic self-affection, which is to say, the aporia that the self can affect itself only as another. Understanding is self-affection, but affection only of a self that is unable to be affected in its otherness. Its homogeneity must be in itself heterogeneous; its temporality the torn temporality of asynchronicity and achronicity; its topic atopia. But this means that there is no understanding *itself,* and there is no language *itself* in which understanding could develop itself. There is, Schlegel insists, a hermeneutical imperative; but there can be such an imperative only when it refuses the very understanding and language that it makes possible—and even refuses itself in granting itself. The hermeneutic imperative is as little a part of actuality as any understanding that stands under this imperative, but it is hardly a projection of actuality either, since a teleological project can open itself up from this imperative alone. Neither substance nor presence nor even a project, the imperative—whether hermeneutic or ontological—is a mere admission of understanding and of Being without any of the conditions for their actualization. And this admission, this opening up, this unarrestable gift of understanding must be thought as the disclosure of the possibility of understanding and thus as itself incomprehensible.

Or, as Schlegel says in his essay "On Incomprehensibility," it must be thought as irony. Irony is, for him, neither the rhetorical figure that allows self-sufficient subjects to take flight to other meanings of their discourse, nor an occurrence within a tropologically well-defined and already constituted language. Rather, it is the structure by virtue of which language is possible but its complete constitution—as something like a *characteristica universalis* or a closed system of tropes—is impossible. Instead of being an inner-linguistic figure, for which it is often mistaken, irony is, for Schlegel, the limit figure of affiguration: the interminable opening of the domain of figures, always at their margin, noticeable in every particular figure as the quivering of its contours, and at the same time their de-figuration. At once making language possible and making it impossible, irony—like the apodictic imperatives "be" and "understand"—is the aporia of its acconstitution: constitution and nonconstitution of language in one. Schlegel can thus write the following fragment about Socratic irony, a fragment he first published in the the *Lyceum* and later cites in "On Incomprehensibility": "It contains and incites a feeling of indissoluble antagonism . . . between the impossibility and the necessity of a complete communication," and as a version of the categorical, logical, and hermeneutic imperative, irony is in turn the law of freedom, for, as Schlegel writes in the same fragment, it "is the freest of all licenses, for by means of it one posits oneself way beyond oneself, and yet it is also the most lawful, for it is unconditionally necessary" (KA, 2: 268; Incomprehensibility, 265). The self does not posit itself in irony; rather, it posits itself *away*—way beyond itself. Irony is not a position but an excess beyond the form of subjectivity, and it thus cannot be reduced to a comprehensible thing: it is the incomprehensible, the "impossibility . . . of a complete communication." But it is just as much the necessity of this impossibility, for only in this excess— only by acceding to another—does the subject have the chance to constitute itself. Irony, incomprehensibility, is thus "the form of paradox" that must precede every form and every communication in order for them to be able to become form and communication. It is the necessary impossibility that inscribes itself in every possibility of language, and since it is also the form—without form—of unconditioned admission, "the freest of all licenses," it allows communication without limits and thus eclipses, leaves out, and leaves in the dark this giving-leave. It is the limitless admission of communication: "Indeed, the most precious thing human beings possess . . . depends in the final analysis, as anybody can easily know, on some such point of strength that *must be left* in the dark, but that nevertheless carries and supports the whole, and this force would give out at precisely the moment when one wanted to dissolve it through comprehension" (KA, 2: 370; Incomprehensibility, 268, italics added). This force left in the dark, Schlegel implies, is a non-force; it is the impossibility of complete communication, the impotence, incapacity, and inability to understand and to make comprehensible—"as anybody can easily know" from, for example, a passage in Aristotle's *Metaphysics* where he speaks of a force that is essentially a non-force in relation to the same thing for which it is a force: *dunamis adunamiai,* force non-force, possibility impossibility (1046a31). As the medium of the possibility and impossibility of communication, language—and that is in every case the language of irony—is always a broken, fragmented language, a language distanced from itself. It must offer itself in always other meanings, in an uncontrollable flight of allosemies and allegories, as always other than meaning, always other than language, and only thereby as language "itself": as exposed, disrupted, abandoned language, language without language.

Reason is not autonomous, only the demand that it should be so. The given—and thus retained—ground has given way to the movement of grounding ever since Kant's *Critiques;* but since this grounding in an injunction that language should lay down its own ground is infinite, it remains exposed to an irreparable abyss. If the imperative that there should be a self-grounding language, a language of reason, and therefore language as such is the absolute, unique, and unconditioned premise of language, then it will never have grounded itself: there will never have been *a* language and never a *language.* The apodictic imperative, language as the claim that there should be a language, always means this as well: there is not even one language, there has never been one, and none could ever be given. And so it, almost, has no meaning. In this imperative, the movement of semiosis remains exposed to an uncontrollable anasemiosis. By indicating a direction, it goes astray and becomes aberrant: every imperative is also an imp*errative,* its operation an ope*rration,* its reference re*ferrence.* If the imperative of a rational, autonomous language is the premise of understanding—for only a thoroughly rational language can be understood, strictly speaking—then understanding will never have secured a ground and will never have come about. It remains in falling apart. "Premise" no longer means ground and presupposition but *Aussetzung:* ex-position, exposure, interruption, abandonment. In its premises language misses itself and thus misses its understanding. Only what goes astray and foregoes itself is promised in language.

The non-understanding—or incomplete understanding—that was decried or simply denied by rationalists who did not investigate the *ratio* of their own rationality is in truth what makes understanding possible. Non-understanding does not belong to the pathology of linguistic Being; it belongs to its logic. A rearticulation of this logic, which became necessary after the Kantian discovery of an apodictic aporia of action, demanded that the dominant lexicon of "understanding," which had suggested such a pathology, a deficiency, or even a degeneration of understanding, be subjected to a displacement and transformation. And this affected the entire vocabulary by which the concept of understanding had been defined: not only the vocabulary of thesis, position, positing, *Setzung, Gegenständlichkeit, Stellung, Vorstellung,* and *Darstel-*

lung but also that of substance, constancy, and consistency.[15] All these concepts have their place in the topology of a metaphysics that essentially conceives itself as ontotheseology. Wherever the possibility of a non-understanding is no longer perceived as a contingent but as a structural devastation of the system of positings and emplacements, the axioms of these concepts are forfeited. This happens in Friedrich Schlegel's essay "On Incomprehensibility," in his theory of irony and fragmentary discourse, in the thought that whoever stands—or understands—can also fall, in his citation of Goethe's line, "Let everyone see where he stands / And let him that stands not fall."[16] This happens in Hölderlin's remark "Daß sich krümmt der Verstand daß nimmer das Forschen / Aufgeht."[17] It happens in Kleist's "Earthquake in Chile," where knowledge collapses under the weight of accidents. It happens in a note Kierkegaard wrote for *Fear and Trembling:* "Write for the dead, for those in earlier times whom you loved.—Will they read me?—No."[18] It is for this reason that Kafka's Odradek, another Hermes, roams in hallways, staircases, corridors, and lofts, between life and death, where he is not

---

15. Positing *(Setzung)*, objectivity *(Gegenständlichkeit)*, placing *(Stellung)*, representation *(Vorstellung)*, presentation *(Darstellung)* all refer in German to a certain stance or to the act of taking a stand.—Already in his earlier work Heidegger referred the tradition of these concepts, which he later collected under the title *Ge-stell,* back to Greek philosophy and its language. In his *Introduction to Metaphysics* he thus writes: "But this erect standing-there, coming to a stance [*zum Stande kommen*] and enduring in a stance [*im Stand Bleiben*], is what the Greeks understood by Being" (Martin Heidegger, *Einführung in die Metaphysik* (Tübingen: Niemeyer, 1966), 46; cf. *Introduction to Metaphysics,* trans. Ralph Manheim [Garden City, N.Y.: Anchor, 1961], 49). "'Being' meant for the Greeks *constancy* in a double sense: 1. standing-in-itself as emergence [*Ent-stehung*] *(phusis)* 2. 'standing' as such, that is, enduring, lingering *(ousia)*" (*Einführung in die Metaphysik,* 48; *Introduction to Metaphysics,* 52). Heidegger's terminology of "decline" *(Verfallen)* indicates that he does not simply have a critical relationship to this tradition and indeed lets it persist in its "destruction" through "fundamental" ontology.

16. Friedrich Schlegel, *Charakteristiken und Kritiken I* in KA, 2: 372: "Sehe jeder wo er bleibe, / Und wer steht daß er nicht falle."

17. Friedrich Hölderlin, *Sämtliche Werke,* ed. F. Beißner (Stuttgart: Kohlhammer, 1943–1985), 2.2: 606 (late variant to "Bread and Wine"): "that the understanding writhes that research never / arises."

18. Søren Kierkegaard, *Papirer,* ed. P. A. Heiberg, V. Kuhr, and E. Torsting, rev. ed. N. Thulstrup (Copenhagen: Gyldendal, 1968–1970), 4: 244 (B 96 1b); cf. *Fear and Trembling—Repetition,* trans. and ed. Howard V. Hong and Edna H. Hong (Princeton: Princeton University Press, 1983), 244.

at home, cannot be placed, and cannot be arrested by understanding. It is for this reason that *Finnegans Wake* writes itself as "a fadograph of a yestern scene"[19]—as a writing not of saturated phenomenality but of aphanisis. And it is for this reason that Celan speaks of the "unreadability of this/ world."[20] Something is readable only in its unreadability, comprehensible only in its resistance to comprehension—at the place where understanding writhes or falls, where its object slips away from it, and where its addressee is missing. The literature of recent centuries has indicated this with greater passion and honesty than its institutionally bound theory. Literature pursues the movements of language in which every stance starts to oscillate, quiver, or collapse. It is only from distance and difference, from the unattainable "before" *(Vor)* of understanding that understanding *(Verstehen)* is henceforth to be "understood."

It is from here—from the distance of understanding to standing, placing, and stating, from the distancing of a language that is infinitely addressed and claimed but never given and never fixed—that the following becomes clear: understanding can never be a passive absorption into a vessel of concepts or expectations; understanding must, instead, be a process in which the self and other are altered—and altered in ways impossible to anticipate. Understanding must be a standing-before-itself-toward-another-language, hence an exposure and ex-position of language. Understanding stands toward language—not simply toward a specific language, but in every language toward what is not yet said in it. It remains true to language, and in every language true to what is already thematically fixed in no language. In every one of its places it can be dispossessed by the theme of another language and indeed dispossessed by this other language. Understanding stands up to language: it allows speech and fosters further speaking. For this reason, its turning—and understanding is once again essentially a turning toward another—must be a turning toward what is unsaid, toward silence, speechlessness, and muteness. Before it can be the transition from one language to another, it must already be the transition to what no longer speaks or does not yet speak or will never be able to speak. Understanding is thus

---

19. James Joyce, *Finnegans Wake* (London: Faber and Faber, 1975), 7.

20. Paul Celan, *Gesammelte Werke,* ed. Beda Allemann and Stefan Reichert in association with Rolf Bücher (Frankfurt am Main: Suhrkamp, 1983), 2: 338: "Unlesbarkeit dieser / Welt." Hereafter, GW.

never without tension and pain; hence its strange pathos and apathy. What never stirs is touched upon in understanding: the apathetic itself. And it is for this reason that death and the dead obtain an outstanding place, a boundary position, in all attempts to think understanding: facing that which no longer understands and no longer lets itself be understood but which still defines all understanding as its limit. Thus Euripides writes in *Heracles*, after the hero of culture has murdered his children: "There inside is the horror./ You need no other interpreter."[21] Death itself gives the unsurpassable interpretation; in every surpassable one it must already be at work. It is what the journeyman in Johann Peter Hebel's story understands when "Kannitverstan," the supposed owner of limitless capital, presents himself as a corpse. And Kierkegaard tells himself in a note for *Fear and Trembling* to write for the dead, for those who will not read. Speaking is always also imparting to the dead and parting with them. Whoever speaks, whoever understands, dies— and, prosaically enough, does not stop dying. To use a word that was important to Nietzsche, Kafka, and Benjamin, one could say: whoever speaks, whoever understands, "outlives" and is "outlived."

Not even so-called "life philosophy," which has been reputed—not without justification—to promote the ideology of immediacy like no other, could deny the part played by the mute, the departed, and the incomprehensible in understanding. The bourgeois mentality expressed in the relevant reflections of Dilthey may have led to the tenacity with which the hermeneutics of empathy and reliving took hold of the question of understanding, and it may have contributed to the long-held view of hermeneutics as a technique of methodical identification with the author, the contexts of his life, and his intentions. The ideal of this comfortable identity of I and Thou that continues to flourish in consensualist theories of language and society even today was defined by Dilthey as a grounding form of understanding, and in a programmatic gesture he accorded it the status of an axiom to which the methodology of the "human sciences" had to conform. In his "Drafts for the Critique of Historical Reason" he writes: "Understanding is a rediscovery of the I in the Thou. Spirit finds itself again at ever higher levels of

---

21. Euripides, *Heracles,* ed. G. W. Bond (Oxford: Clarendon, 1981), ll. 911–12; cf. *Heracles,* trans. William Arrowsmith, in *Euripides* (Chicago: University of Chicago Press, 1956), 2: 93–94.

connectedness. This identity of spirit in the I, in the Thou, in every subject of a community, in every system of culture, finally, in the totality of spirit and universal history makes possible the successful cooperation of different processes in the human sciences. Here, the knowing subject is one with its object, and at all levels of its objectivation this is the same."[22] Using these words to announce its right to "universal history," the hermeneutics of the "human sciences" *(Geisteswissenschaften)* understands itself as the rediscovery of the I in the Thou, the subject in the object, spirit in its objectivations—and thus the same in the same. But if it is the same spirit that everywhere rediscovers itself and, like the hedgehog in the fairy tale, is already there whenever it, as a hare, reaches its goal; if spirit is always already understood and can never be understood as anything other than the same, then understanding is not only an exclusively reproductive process and not only a process that is superfluous in principle: it is also an impossible process. For it can no longer be understood; it can only have been understood. And the same goes for language: if it must already exist as an objectivation of "spirit" at the spot where the very same spirit should rediscover it, then all language is a mere reproduction of language; everything has already been said, and further speaking is superfluous, indeed impossible; there is no further speaking that does not for its part already belong to the stable stock of language. *Wir erleben Bestand:* "We experience stability" (Dilthey, 3: 195). In these words the hermeneut of "life philosophy" makes a statement that must be restated by anyone for whom understanding is the rediscovery of the I in the Thou, hence an understanding of what is already understood or is comprehensible in principle. But the ideal of language would then consist in the loss of language, and the ideal of understanding would be its renunciation.

"We experience stability"—this also means for Dilthey that we never experience life itself. "Lived experience," *Erlebnis,* is never the experience of life itself but always only an experience of its fixed stock of forms: "And if one wanted to try to experience the flux of life by means of any particular kind of effort . . . then one falls prey to the law of life itself yet

22. Wilhelm Dilthey, "The Construction of the Historical World in the Human Sciences" in *Gesammelte Schriften* (Leipzig: Teubner, 1927), 7: 191; cf. Dilthey, *Selected Writings,* ed. H. P. Rickman (Cambridge, England: Cambridge University Press. 1976), 208. All citations of Dilthey refer to the collected works.

again, a law according to which every moment of life that is observed . . . is a remembered moment, no longer flux. . . . And so we cannot grasp the essence of this life itself. What the young man of Saïs unveils is a statue, not life" (Dilthey, 7: 194–95). Life does not let itself be grasped as "lived experience." By saying this, Dilthey also acknowledges that only those things that are not alive and have thus departed from the "structural connectiveness" of life can be grasped as "lived experience." Since, however, to understand is to experience life, it is impossible to avoid the conclusion that only the fixed and dead forms of life, not life itself, can be understood. Understanding would not be the rediscovery of the self in the other; it would not be empathy and reanimation but sobriety before the image of Saïs. The continuum of life would not be universalized in understanding: it would be interrupted—and only something incomprehensible would ever be understood. But Dilthey avoids this obviously aporetic conclusion, for it means that the "sameness of spirit in the I, in the Thou, in every subject of a community" is only to be found in its otherness; spirit, subject, and society only in their collapse; identity only in difference. If Dilthey had yielded to his insight into what he called the "law of life," he would have had to admit that understanding cannot be the narcissistic "rediscovery of the I in the Thou" but only a "rediscovery" of what has never been before.

"The present never *is*" (Dilthey, 7: 194)—from this, his most pregnant formula, Dilthey avoids drawing the conclusion that there is never any past-present and no future-present either. He thus misses an opportunity to conceive of time as something other than a continuum and to think of understanding as something other than a process of homogenization. Instead of holding onto the experience of selfhood, he would have had to concede that this selfhood only constitutes itself in the medium of alteration—and that it cannot as a result ever stop deconstituting itself. The law of which he would have had to speak is not that of life but, instead, the law of life's law: a law of missed selfhood, of non-return, of ever-otherness. It is the law of delegation under which only another can ever be understood: a law under which the law must give leave to another and cede its rights to this other; a law—of the de-legation even of the law—under which the law itself must break down. It would be the law of a priori manifolding: a law commanding that there always be more than *one* law and always something other than the *law,* each one isolated and standing together with others only in its isolation. It is thus the law of a whole that converges in—and does not emerge out of—separation and division. Only where understanding stands under this law of delegation is it *itself* and yet open to *another.* It is understanding only when it touches, in itself, upon something incomprehensible.

"Rediscovery," repetition, returning to oneself and to the self are not simply obsessively cited and recited topoi of the philosophical tradition. Under the title "hermeneutic circle" the theorem of return holds an axiomatic status in all hermeneutic theories, regardless of whether they make universal claims or limit themselves to regional investigations into scholarly domains of historical philology. The "circle" in understanding is an expression of a difficulty that can be characterized as the paradox of presupposition, for this circle is at once demanded and prohibited. There is a demand that all understanding of a part be grounded in the understanding of a supposed whole, but it is forbidden that the whole be anticipated and set down as a formal structure in advance of the understanding of the part. The model of an organic connection among all individual phenomena lies at the basis of the demand, whereas the prohibition arises from the belief in demonstrative certainty; in order to achieve such certainty, no one is allowed to turn a proposition to be demonstrated into a premise of the demonstration. In his "Second Academic Discourse," Schleiermacher paraphrases the "founding proposition of hermeneutics" as the principle "that all parts can be understood by means of the whole and therefore every explanation of the particular already presupposes the understanding of the whole."[23] But this presupposition of the whole—and on this point Schleiermacher leaves no doubts—is a presupposition of something that is never given as a consistent phenomenon but always only as an ideal of understanding. The presupposition, the circle, and thus the "principle of hermeneutics" have the structure of a project, a prolepsis toward that which is not yet and never will be given: they are ground, principle, and premise only when they forever forestall every factual stance and every form of phenomenal consistency. The premise is a promise. This promise, it should be emphasized, is not founded on secure knowledge of particular states of affairs that it intends to complete in the future; rather, it is the only

---

23. Friedrich Schleiermacher, *Hermeneutik und Kritik,* ed. and intro. Manfred Frank (Suhrkamp: Frankfurt am Main, 1977), 328. Hereafter, HK.

possible grounding of such knowledge, and thus a promise that not only precedes all acts of cognition and understanding but also, for this reason, precedes every predicative use of language, every predicative promise. If the ground (and thus the whole) is structured as a promise, then everything that was grounded in this whole, hence every part, must have functioned as its fulfillment. But in the same academic discourse Schleiermacher concedes that "non-understanding will never entirely disappear" (HK, 328). He thus admits that the whole of understanding, its ground, and its presupposition remain out of reach, and so the part, far from redeeming the promise of totality, must participate in the structure of promising, in the impossibility of its fulfillment.

Understanding remains an unfulfillable promise, always behind and ahead of itself at the same time. The objection lodged by formal logic against the "circle"—it takes for its premise what could only be its result—is in this way untenable: from the perspective of formal logic, the whole, which is precisely the result, is a conclusion whose certainty is in principle compelling; for understanding, by contrast, the whole remains a necessary but unredeemable project. Yet the notion of a "circle"—not a logical one, of course, but a hermeneutic one—is still justifiable. For understanding cannot do without an understanding of the whole and is understanding in an emphatic sense only when it can no longer be refuted by a single uncomprehended detail. The anticipation of its totality, the anticipation of *itself,* is thus constitutive of understanding; it consists essentially in *being* its own premise and thus being—being toward—that which it is not yet. No longer, then, is a "presupposition" the *propositio maior* from which subsequent propositions can be derived for the understanding according to consistent logical rules; rather, understanding, structured as ahead-of-itself, is nothing other than "presupposing." Understanding cannot therefore succumb to the objection of a *petitio principii;* as an aporetic prolepsis, it is itself the *principium petitionis principii.*

In *Being and Time* Heidegger tried to defend the hermeneutic circle along similar lines. He took his point of departure from a concept of understanding that is not limited to the understanding of texts, discourses, or actions and does not allow the conventions of any particular science to proscribe its horizon: "In ontic discourse we use the expression 'to understand something' to mean 'to be in a stance of control over something,' 'to be capable of coping with it,' 'to be able to do something.'

That which can be done as an existential in understanding is not a 'what' but rather Being as existing. The mode of Being of *Dasein* as being-able [*Sein-können*] lies in an existential manner in understanding."[24] Understanding thus means to be able, and as an existential it is, according to Heidegger, "the most primordial and the final positive ontological determination of *Dasein*" (SZ, 143–44). As a primordial and indeed as "the most primordial" mode of being-ahead-of-oneself and standing-in-advance-of-oneself, understanding is, once again, the "final positive determination of *Dasein*." It is for this reason that, as Heidegger always underlines, *Dasein* is "free for *its* possibilities" (SZ, 144). "What it is *not yet* in its ability-to-be, it *is* existentially" (SZ, 145). And by understanding in this way, *Dasein* is always already its own "not-yet": it stands ahead of itself where it does not yet stand, and it thus understands in its "not" each time itself, each time understands in another *its* other, and each time understands possibilities as *its* possibilities. There is no "there" of being-there that would not be a "before," and there is no "before" that could not be its own "before." *Dasein* does not therefore make any presuppositions; rather, as understanding, it *is* "the most primordial 'presupposing'" in which it "relates itself solely to itself" (SZ, 228).[25] Without any presuppositions, it is itself the performance of "presupposing" in which it understands itself as understanding—as premise and project. And this movement of Being called "understanding" is, according to Heidegger, related solely to itself, grasped as a circular self-relation.

The terminology of throwing, projection, and thrownness that Heidegger mobilizes in this context still moves within the horizon of a standing and a "positive" determination, even if it is a "final" one. However much *Being and Time* may reclaim a pre-positional and pre-

24. Martin Heidegger, *Sein und Zeit* (Tübingen: Niemeyer, 1967), 143; cf. *Being and Time,* trans. John Macquarrie and Edward Robinson (New York: Harper & Row, 1962), 183. Since the English translation includes the pagination of the German text in its margins, all citations refer to the German edition; hereafter "SZ." All translations of Heidegger are new.

25. This formulation from § 44 (on the "Presupposition of Truth") reads in context: "What does it mean to 'presuppose'? To understand something as the ground for the Being of some other entity. . . . Thus to presuppose 'truth' means to understand it as something for the sake of which *Dasein* is. But *Dasein* is already—this lies in its being constituted as care—ahead of itself in each case. . . . The most primordial 'presupposing' lies in *Dasein* being constituted as care, in its being ahead of itself. . . . This 'presupposing' that lies in the being of *Dasein* relates itself . . . solely to itself."

propositional structure for the Being of *Dasein,* it nevertheless conceives of *Dasein* in its "before"—to the extent that it is *its* "before"—as a position and thus grasps *Dasein* within the horizon of ontotheseology. Heidegger is never more consistent than when he redefines the autonomy of *Dasein* as standing-on-its-own *(Selbst-ständigkeit),* which is to say: "the standing of the self in the sense of having achieved a stance" and "in the double sense of consistent standing-firm" (SZ, 322).[26] And Heidegger is equally consistent when he attempts to secure the status of the self-relation of understanding as a "circular Being of *Dasein*" (SZ, 315). The circle is the basic figure of the horizon of positionality: there is no position that would not stand in the horizon of self-movement, no horizon that would not be circular, no circle in which the position would not relate to itself by being out ahead of itself and would not therefore close in on itself. Thus Heidegger can write: "The ecstatic character of the primordial future lies precisely in the fact that this future concludes one's ability-to-be; that is, it is closed [*geschlossen*] and as such it makes possible the resolute [*entschlossene:* disclosed] existentiell understanding of nothingness" (SZ, 330). Understanding is conclusive; it is the closing and coming to an end of understanding. Thus the original finitude of understanding. The circle designates the figure of all possible figures, the primordial figure of the authentic, existentiell pre-position in which *Dasein* as understanding encounters itself as the end of understanding. The "presupposition" in which *Dasein* discloses itself is at the same time the conclusion in which it closes in on itself.

The "circular Being of *Dasein,*" the "ontological circle-structure" (SZ, 330) of an entity that is concerned with its own being and with Being as its own, is not, for Heidegger, a deducible and further reducible phenomenon; on the contrary, it is the phenomenon that precedes all phenomenality and inscribes itself in every other phenomenon, including the "phenomenon" of phenomenality itself. For the very possibility that something will show itself *as* something—whether in the apophantic or hermeneutic mode of the "as"—is already "circular," since something can show itself only to a *Dasein* that therein understands one of its own possibilities and thus understands itself in anticipation of itself.

---

26. The connection between "running ahead" or "anticipating" *(Vorlaufen)* and "standingness" *(Ständigkeit)* is made explicit in the following sentence: "Standing-on-one's-own means existentially nothing but resoluteness running ahead" (322).

In this way Heidegger draws all talk of a "circle" away from its restrictive use in regional hermeneutic investigations and reclaims it for a fundamental hermeneutics, and he likewise dismisses the charge lodged by formal logic against the circle—the charge that is is a *circulus vitiosus* and should therefore be banned from all further proceedings: "But to see a *vitiosum* in this circle and to be on the look-out for ways to avoid it, even if one only 'senses' it as an unavoidable imperfection—this is to misunderstand understanding from the ground up" (SZ, 153).[27] The circle of understanding cannot be avoided because it is an "expression of the existential fore-structure of *Dasein* itself" (SZ, 153). Avoiding this circle would then be nothing less than suicidal. Yet at the same time Heidegger insists that precisely this "circle" must be avoided if *Dasein* is to be characterized in an ontological manner. At the very end of § 32 ("Understanding and Interpretation"), having formulated the "ontological circle-structure" of *Dasein,* Heidegger offers without further commentary the following sentence: "Nevertheless, if one notices that a 'circle' belongs ontologically to a kind of Being that is present-to-hand (subsistence [*Bestand*]), we must altogether avoid using the phenomenon to characterize in an ontological manner anything like *Dasein*" (SZ, 153). The "circle" thus *cannot* be avoided, and yet it *must* be avoided; it is not a vicious one, and yet it is one after all. This flagrant contradiction between the unavoidable and what is to be avoided "nevertheless"—the contradiction between understanding as event and advent of Being and

27. In the same vein, the section devoted to the "hermeneutic situation" and the "methodical character of existential analysis in general" (§ 63) speaks of the unavoidability of the "circle": "A 'circle' in proof can never be 'avoided' in the existential analytic, because such an analytic does not do any proving at all according to rules of the 'logic of consistency.' What common sense wishes to eliminate in avoiding the 'circle,' on the supposition that it is satisfying the loftiest rigor of scientific investigation, is nothing less than the basic structure of care. Because it is primordially constituted by care, *Dasein* is always already ahead of itself" (315). At the point where the "idea of existence" begins, "pre-supposing" has "the character of interpretive projecting" (314)—and so, one could add, runs for precisely this reason in a circle. Heidegger adds that the "project" does not somehow prejudice that which is to be understood; rather, it discloses it by "indicating [it] in a formal manner" and "allowing" it "to come into speech for the first time" (315). The circle thus discloses, but it discloses as a formal indication that already has a determinate structure and by means of this structure determines the "word" of that which is disclosed for understanding. This "word" is spoken only as a word predisposed by the "circle"—of care, of understanding, of being-able, and being-able-to-be-oneself.

understanding as a securing of something subsistent—gives rise to the suspicion that even authentic understanding is resistance to under-standing. Indeed, it gives rise to the suspicion that the project of a fundamental-hermeneutic analysis is afflicted in its entirety by a deficient understanding, and at the same time it indicates the possibility of an opening up of the hermeneutic horizon toward an understanding that is not simply an understanding of itself and thus not simply an under-standing of the Being of *Dasein:* it is the possibility of an opening of understanding to something other than a phenomenon, to another "be-fore"—or something other than a "before"—and thus to another exis-tential premise or something other than a premise.

Heidegger's analysis of the problem and metaproblem of under-standing, being-ahead-of-oneself, projection, and *Dasein* becomes ex-plosive at the very moment it reaches the *locus classicus* of hermeneutics and its question concerning the premises of understanding: the mo-ment, that is, it sets out to analyze the whole. According to Schleier-macher's formulation, an understanding of the whole must be "presup-posed" for the explanation of the part. In accordance with the fundamental-hermeneutic deregionalization of this question carried out in *Being and Time,* such an understanding must refer to the "possible being-whole of *Dasein*" and this being-whole can only have the structure of a Being *toward* the whole, which is to say, the structure—*a limine*—of a being-toward-the-end, a being-toward-death. "This end," Heidegger writes, "which *belongs* to being-able, i.e., to existence, limits and deter-mines the possible wholeness of *Dasein*" (SZ, 234).[28] Heidegger poses the question concerning the possibility of being-whole as a question concerning the possibility of death, hence as a question concerning an understood death, a death *Dasein* is in a position to die. Thus it is the question whether death "belongs" to being-able. Heidegger seems to answer this unequivocally in the affirmative whenever he speaks of the anticipation of death and the unbroken circularity of understanding—for example, in the following sentence, where the word "belonging" is underlined: "*Dasein* always already exists in just such a manner that its 'not-yet' *belongs* to it" (SZ, 243). Or, to take another example, when he

28. This comes from the opening of the "Second Section" of *Being and Time* ("*Dasein* and Temporality"), which integrates the "Results of the Preparatory Fundamental Analy-sis of *Dasein.*"

asserts: "Just as *Dasein* already *is* as long as it is constantly its 'not yet,' likewise it *is* always already its end" (SZ, 245). This being-already of the "not-yet," this being-beforehand of *Dasein* forbids the interpretation of death as "outstanding" *(Ausstand)* and thus as a mode of "subsistence" *(Bestand)*.[29] For death is never an actuality in the sense of the objectivity of something present-to-hand; it is always a futurial possibility of *Dasein*. And this possibility is from two points of view "distinguished" from all others: it is the most extreme possibility and thus the only one from which the ontological analysis of being-able can attain its completeness; but as this, the most extreme possibility, it is at the same time the one in which being-possible runs up against the end of all possibilities. In view of this "distinction," which represents an existential premise of Heidegger's entire existential analytic, the question concerning the possibility of being-whole, the horizon of *Dasein*, the structure of understanding and its "before," and finally the question whether the end "belongs" to *Dasein* must all open themselves to something other than a merely affirmative response.

Heidegger presents the aporia that death, as the possibility of the end, is at the same time the end of the possibility of *Dasein* in one of the most decisive and subsequently most famous passages of *Being and Time:*

> The closest proximity of Being to death as possibility is as far removed from anything actual as possible. The more this possibility is understood without any veiling, the more purely does understanding penetrate into possibility as the possibility of the impossibility of existence as such. Death as possibility gives *Dasein* nothing that could be "actualized" and nothing that *Dasein* could ever actually *be*. It is the possibility of the impossibility of every way of comporting oneself toward . . . , of every mode of existing. In the anticipation of this possibility, it becomes "greater and greater"; that is to say, the possibility unveils itself to be such that it knows no measure at all, no more or less, but signifies the possibility of the measureless impossibility of existence. (SZ, 262)[30]

29. See Heidegger's analysis in § 48, "Outstanding, End, Wholeness" (SZ, esp. 242–246).

30. In a more elliptical fashion than here, I commented upon this decisive thought of Heidegger in an earlier work. See my "Peut-être la question" in *Les fins de l'homme—A partir du travail de Jacques Derrida*, ed. Philippe Lacoue-Labarthe and Jean-Luc Nancy

That understanding, as Heidegger writes, "penetrates into possibility as the possibility of the impossibility of existence as such" means that it "penetrates" into and anticipates this possibility, that it understands, is able and capable of this possibility as the dis-abling of precisely its ability. Hence understanding must always be an understanding of non-understanding if it is ever understanding at all. Insofar as it is understanding, it always already understands this understanding as an understanding of non-understanding; understanding still understands this non-understanding, the impossibility that is—never actual—death. This is to say that *Dasein* still grasps "the absolute impossibility of existence" (SZ, 265) as a possibility and indeed, as Heidegger emphasizes, makes it possible in the first place. But it also means that there is thus absolutely no limit and no measure for the possibilities and understanding of *Dasein:* it is always dying, and by dying in this way it is infinitely finite. *Dasein* still understands its end, and by still understanding, it is the infinite finitude of understanding. It still—and precisely here—understands itself in its Being toward death and *is* thus itself essentially the understanding of the absolutely incomprehensible. *Dasein* is understood, enabled death.[31]

The possible being-whole of *Dasein* as understanding would indeed be reached, the completeness of the hermeneutic situation would be attained, and the fundamental-hermeneutical circle would be closed

---

(Paris: Galilée, 1981), 245–363. In this essay I pursue the structure of the apophantic and hermeneutic "as," the possibility of self-understanding in Being-toward-death, the possibility (the "perhaps" and "peut-être") of the impossibility of one's "own" death and one's "own" understanding, namely, being-able, and finally the possibility—of the impossibility—of the question of Being. A few sentences from this fragmentary commentary: "This possibility that bears the name death cannot be grasped or conceived under the schema of the 'as.' It is just as little possible to speak of death *as* death, to speak of death *as such* as it is to say that it *is*" (356). "Nothing can assure me that I die my own death, that I properly die, that I do not die the death of another" (362). "By virtue of its not-yet structure, its apo- and para-structure, authentic understanding compels its own inauthenticity" (363). The motifs of possibility and the possibility of the impossibility of existence as such are further pursued and questioned in Giorgio Agamben's essay "La passion de la facticité," in *Heidegger—Questions ouvertes* (Paris: Osiris, 1988), 63–84, and in Jacques Derrida's *Aporias,* trans. Thomas Dutoit (Stanford: Stanford University Press, 1993).

31. "Der verstandene Tod" (Understood Death) is the title of Dolf Sternberger's "Untersuchung zu Martin Heideggers Existential-Ontologie" of 1932–33; it has been reprinted in D. Sternberger, *Über den Tod* (Frankfurt am Main: Insel, 1977).

with this "most extreme and ownmost" possibility. If the possibility of impossibility still "belongs" to the circuit of possibilities—which is the circuit of understanding as being-able—then there is nothing more that could withdraw from understanding, oppose itself to understanding as something exterior, or determine it from the outside. If the "absolute impossibility of existence" constitutively "belongs" to the possibilities of *Dasein,* if *Dasein* has from the beginning cut out the circle of its ability and understanding, if it has always already enabled its own not-being-able, then it not only never stops understanding itself and understanding itself as understanding, but, in making possible its own impossibility, it comes to the summa of its existence, to itself as ability. Death, the end of understanding, is understood; the end of being-able is enabled; the end of enabling is still enabled. And so death as a possibility and a capacity of *Dasein* is the absolute of its self-appropriation.

But Heidegger's formula—"the possibility of the impossibility of existence"—has another side. Death, Heidegger writes, "is the possibility of the impossibility of every way of comporting oneself toward . . . , of every mode of existing" (SZ, 262).[32] And death is, accordingly, the possibility of the impossibility of this very possibility. If finite Being is comportment toward the end of Being, then it is comportment toward the impossibility of this very comportment. Understanding—since it means being-able—must be structured as an understanding of the non-understanding of this understanding itself. It can understand itself only as possible non-understanding, and since this possibility does not remain exterior to it but rather determines it from the outset, it can understand itself likewise only by not understanding itself—and by not understanding itself as understanding. Making-impossible must then

---

32. Heidegger's formulation reaches its peak in the paragraphs concerned with the "ability-to-be-whole of *Dasein* in an existentially authentic way as anticipating resoluteness" (§ 62): "We conceived of death in an existential manner as the characteristic possibility of the *im*possibility of existence, that is, as the absolute nothingness of *Dasein*" (306). It should be noted that Heidegger does not write that death is conceived "as a *possibility* of the absolute nothingness of existence" but "as the absolute nothingness of existence"—and that he thus conceals the double sense of this possibility: on the one hand, this possibility is itself already a nothingness and, on the other, nothingness is always still a possibility of existence. These distinctions stop sounding "sophistic" when one is clear about the degree to which the meaning of "possibility" and "*im*possibility," "nothingness," "being-guilty," "conscience," "self," and *Dasein* in Heidegger's work depends upon them.

"belong" to the structure of making-possible; non-understanding must still "belong" to the most authentic and "the most primordial" under-standing. And this affects every possibility of *Dasein,* including the pos-sibility of ontology, phenomenology, and hermeneutics. The postulate that "death is, as long as it 'is,' essentially always my own" (SZ, 240), becomes untenable: the "ever mineness" *(Jemeinigkeit)* of death with-draws into ever otherness *(Jeandersheit).* Death, the end, the most ex-treme and "ownmost" limit of *Dasein* and its possibilities, insofar as it is non-comprehended death, cannot be one's *own* death without at the same time being *another* death, a death impossible to appropriate. Wher-ever understanding is supposed to be "the most primordial," it must turn into an incomprehensible, other understanding. The project of a fundamental hermeneutics of understanding thus collapses at its limit, at the very place where it was supposed to have secured the completeness of understanding and therefore its own wholeness. The "not-yet" of the end, as a "never-once," does not always "also belong" to *Dasein;* in the absence of every phenomenologically graspable marking, it marks the non-appurtenance, the non-belonging to *Dasein.* Whenever the horizon of understanding is affected by incomprehensibility, there is no longer simply a "hermeneutic situation"[33] that would allow an adequate onto-logical analysis. Whenever it is no longer possible to have, see, or grasp anything, the three forms in which interpretation unfolds—fore-having, fore-seeing, and fore-grasping *(Vorhabe, Vorsicht, Vorgriff)*[34]—are bound to fail; whenever understanding no longer grasps its "before" as its *own,* no longer grasps it as *its* possibility, and is no longer able to rediscover itself in this "before" and thence return to itself, the hermeneutic circle remains open.

Every "anticipation" of understanding, every understanding as being-in-anticipation-of-itself, must be an anticipation of its incomprehensi-bility. There is no "before" that would not also be its making-impossible and thereby de-structure the fore-structure of *Dasein.* The premise of understanding must also be a premise of its impossibility and thus

33. The first paragraph of the chapter that concerns "The possible being-whole of *Dasein* and Being toward death" (§ 46) begins by calling attention to "The insufficiency of the hermeneutic situation from which the preceding analysis of *Dasein* has arisen" (235). But this situation remains "insufficient" and thus never turns into a "situation" at all.

34. See Heidegger's analysis in § 32, "Understanding and Interpretation" (SZ, esp. 150).

dismissed: the making-impossible of every premise. "Before" is the prefix of the disappropriation and de-authentication of understanding. Every phenomenon is crossed out by this "before" and its movement of aphanisis.

Heidegger does not pursue this other side of the formula of the possibility of impossibility; nowhere does he analyze it and never does he draw out its consequences. The impossibility of understanding—of *Dasein*—continues for him to "belong" to the domain of understanding; it remains an understood, enabled impossibility and thus an existential of appropriation. He no longer understands, one could say, what he himself had indicated in his description of the "phenomenon" of being-toward-the-end, because he understands this mode of being only within the parameters of understanding *itself*. But his phrase concerning the "possibility of measureless impossibility" also indicates the impossibility of appropriation, thus the collapse of being-whole, the fall of every stance that understanding is supposed to be able to attain in its most extreme possibility, and the opening onto an other—and this other can no longer be understood according to the measure of the self, no longer according to the measure of the understanding, and no longer according to the measure of ability. The measureless understanding toward which Heidegger's phrase points—an understanding without stance and without standard—would have to be understood in the absence of every measure and thus in the absence even of understanding *itself*. Something, including understanding, would have to be understood always in such a way as if there were no understanding at all. For if understanding is supposed to understand *another*—and only then can it it be called understanding at all—then for the sake of this other it must give up even its most minimal premise, namely, the premise that it is understanding. This hyperbolic demand, request, or hope defines—and undefines—every moment of understanding. Without it, understanding would be an imposition. What Heidegger's phrase thus discloses—and Heidegger's interpretation of this phrase immediately forecloses—is the possibility of thinking about understanding no longer as an archi-eschatological self-appropriation, no longer as a making-present, as a presentation or appresentation, but as an always singular alteration and thus an alteration of the very concept of understanding, even the most "radical" one. Only an understanding that was free of understanding would be a *free* understanding.

The "before" does not therefore "belong" to understanding: it ab-

solves itself of understanding in the movement of its "presupposing."
No longer—always already no longer—a "pre-" of positing, the self
cannot understand or grasp itself in this "before," recognize itself as its
other, and thence return to itself. Exposed to this "before," understanding breaks the circle that it itself draws. It always "belongs" to
another that does not belong to it, to others to which nothing can
belong.

Heidegger never denied the movement of understanding in the direction of the other, but he placed this movement under the sign of
being-oneself and the possible wholeness of the self. One of most remarkable statements devoted to this motif in *Being and Time* reads: "As
non-relational possibility, death individualizes—but only in such a manner that, as the possibility not to be surpassed, it makes *Dasein* as being-
with have an understanding of the being-able of others" (SZ, 264).
Accordingly, being-with only becomes comprehensible within the horizon of the "ownmost" possibility of *Dasein* itself; "others" become
comprehensible only in *Dasein*'s own "being-able" and thus on analogy
with its "final positive" characteristic—without Heidegger even noting,
much less discussing, this homogenization of the self and the other.[35] If,

---

35. Being-there *(Dasein)*, for Heidegger, is doubtless "equiprimordially" being-with
(Mit-sein), but this being-with—if it is "primordial," which is to say, "authentic"—is
always a being-with with another *Dasein* in its "ownmost" being-able and is thus *Dasein*
understanding itself in its being-toward-death. The analogy between *Dasein* and *Dasein*-
with in *Being and Time* is, so far as I can see, never relinquished. It is this analogy that
allows Heidegger to conceive of *Dasein* constituted as being-with but not as co- constituted by *another*—and that means constituted as other than *Dasein*-with as well. It
becomes free *for* another by becoming free *from* it. (Michael Theunissen points this out
in his analysis of "authentic being-with-another" in *Being and Time;* see M. Theunissen,
Der Andere—Studien zur Sozialontologie der Gegenwart [Berlin: de Gruyter, 1965], 181; cf.
The Other: Studies in the Social Ontology of Husserl, Heidegger, Sartre, and Buber, trans.
Christopher Macann [Cambridge, Mass.: MIT Press, 1984], 192.) And *Dasein* becomes
free *for* another by submitting this other to the model of its "own" *Dasein*. For the
Heidegger of *Sein und Zeit,* each one gains freedom out of what is most proper to it, not
out of what is impossibly its own, not out of that which neither "belongs" to *Dasein* nor
to *Dasein*-with. But doesn't *Dasein,* by relating itself to *Dasein*-with, relate to the possibility of its *im*-possibility and thus to an immensely other relatum and to this other in
another manner than mere relation? If this relation—this irrelation—is constitutive for
every being-with, then must it not also be constituted as being-without-with and thus
irreducibly de-constituted? The point is to think through the relation to the other not
only as constitutive but as deconstitutive as well.

by contrast, the possibility of not-being-able already had to be admitted as one of the determinants of *Dasein,* then it cannot be considered any less constitutive—and deconstitutive—of being-with and must even be thought of as the opening of every access to another. But the fact that it is not only *my* death that I die, not only *my* other that I understand, means that the other, death, can be experienced neither according to my measure nor on analogy with a self. The fact that I am not simply *with* my death, that it does not simply "belong" to my being-there, my *Dasein*—this devastates the with-structure of my relation to another. Being with another, I am already without the "with" that secures my commensurability with it. Only in this with-without-with, only in an understanding-without-understanding, is another "understood" in such a manner that it is not subjected to the measure of *my* possibilities, and I in turn do not fall prey to its tyranny but, instead, experience the "measureless" possibility of the impossibility of our relation. Horizons can be fused only if they are analogical specimens of one and the same geometrical structure. As an analogue to the self, the other is always understood only as another self, never in its otherness, never from the perspective of its difference—and so precisely misunderstood. Not the "fusing of horizons" recommended by a diplomatic hermeneutics of mediation,[36] but only the draft of aporetic distancing and the disappropriation of the horizon allow for something called understanding, admit understanding from its withdrawal, and free up access—the aporia—to the other.

The fact that understanding must be free in order to be understanding at all means that it must open up and keep open a space that just as little

---

36. In *Truth and Method* Hans-Georg Gadamer makes the fusion of horizons of understanding into the very form of hermeneutic acts in general. Despite his constant appeal to Heidegger, despite the claim that he continues the fundamental-ontological project, he thus falls back upon a position that can best be characterized as a doctrine of diplomatic moderation. "Historical consciousness," Gadamer writes, brings "together once again that from which it has kept itself apart in order to mediate itself with itself in the unity of the historical horizon that it thus acquires for itself" (*Wahrheit und Methode* [Tübingen: Mohr, 1965], 290; cf. *Truth and Method,* 2nd rev. ed., trans. J. Weinsheimer and D. Marshall [New York: Crossroads, 1989], 306). Unity and completion are the results of a diplomatic—not dialectical—mediation at the end of which it becomes clear that it has been the mediation of the self with itself. The other comes into consideration, for Gadamer, only insofar as it has already entered into the horizon of a common sense and thus shed its otherness in favor of commonality.

"belongs" to it as to anything else that could arise therein as a possible object. Something is understand*able* only when it is set free from understanding. Heidegger does not describe this movement of laying bare, setting free, and opening up in *Being and Time,* and when years later he does so in the essay "On the Essence of Truth," he does not use the terminology of understanding and anticipation but that of letting, leaving, and ex-posing: "As this letting-be, it exposes itself to beings as such and transposes all comportment into the open. Letting-be, that is, freedom, is in itself ex-posing [*aus-setzend*], ek-sistent. Seen from the perspective of the essence of truth, the essence of freedom shows itself as exposure [*Aussetzung*] to the unconcealment of beings."[37] With this ex-posure to an open arena where another can first appear, understanding abandons its ontotheseological horizon: no longer is it subordinated to a praxis and a theory of "position or positing," and no longer does it go in search of a certain stance, the constancy of objects, or the consistency of representation. As the ex-posure of positing—the *Aussetzung der Setzung,* the interruption of every positional act, the exposition of every possible position—it draws on an opening, an unposited space, and a place impossible to posit. Whatever still appears in this opening as an object of representation and comprehension must be tinged by its openness and cannot therefore, as Heidegger insists, simply appear *as* such an object. Just as ex-posure—this immemorial "premise" of understanding, a premise in which every act of communication and understanding is disclosed—can no longer be thought in accordance with the logic of positing and that of Being conceived as position, it is no longer possible to think of the "pre" of this "premise" simply as something that still "belongs" to positing and could be referred back to understanding; the "pre" of this "premise" can be thought only as something that no longer "belongs." Along with the exposure of understanding comes the ex-position, abandonment, and loss of its "before."

Even the most defiant positivists cannot deny that this insight into the paradoxical structure—this de-structure—of understanding does not thrive on the soil of fundamental ontology alone. The peculiar crossing

37. Martin Heidegger, *Wegmarken* (Frankfurt am Main: Klostermann, 1967), 84; cf. "On the Essence of Truth," trans. John Sallis, in *Basic Writings,* ed. D. F. Krell (New York: Harper & Row, 1977), 128.

of understanding's possibility and impossibility is also found in the work of the most vehement critic of this ontology, namely Adorno. And in Adorno's writings this crossing of possibility and impossibility is formulated in less hidden, more categorical, and much more aggressive terms than in Heidegger's intricate phenomenological aporias. In his essay "Trying to Understand *Endgame*," Adorno says of Beckett's play: "Understanding it can only mean understanding its incomprehensibility, concretely reconstructing what it means that it has no meaning."[38] Concerning Rudolf Borchardt's "Position of the Poet," he writes: "He was 'cornered,' to use English, the language he loved: his work was an impasse, aporetic. That it gave shape to its own impossibility is the true seal of its modernity" (Notes, 553; 2: 208). In his "Speech on Lyric Poetry and Society," Adorno speaks of something that "suddenly flashes out, something in which the possible surpasses its own impossibility" (Notes, 64; 1: 50), and a little later he says: "the chimeric longing of language for the impossible becomes an expression of the insatiable erotic longing of the subject who discharges himself of himself in another" (Notes, 67; 1: 53).[39] Longing for another must mean longing for something "impossible," since this longing strives to break through the categorial forms of subjectivity that dominate every experience of the

38. Theodor W. Adorno, *Noten zur Literatur*, ed. R. Tiedemann (Frankfurt am Main: Suhrkamp, 1981), 283; cf. *Notes on Literature*, trans. Shierry Weber Nicholsen (New York: Columbia University Press), 1: 243. Hereafter, "Notes."

39. Any time the disclosure of possibility and the impossible are discussed in connection with language and understanding, a discussion of affect is sure to follow. In every case it is a privileged or even grounding affect, never a fleeting feeling. In Kant (and among his successors in Schlegel) it is a pure self-affection, more exactly, pain. In Nietzsche it is the pathos of distance, as in the aphorism from *The Gay Science* that bears the title "Toward the Question of Comprehensibility" and begins with the sentence: "One does not only wish to be understood when one writes; one wishes just as surely *not* to be understood" (*Fröhliche Wissenschaft*, in *Werke*, ed. K. Schlechta [Munich: Hanser, 1954], 2: 256; cf. *The Gay Science*, trans. Walter Kaufmann [New York: Vintage, 1974], 343; § 381). In Kierkegaard it is despair; in Heidegger anxiety or boredom; in Adorno erotic longing; in Bataille hate. In the foreword to the second edition of his book *L'impossible* (perhaps named in honor of "L'impossible" from Rimbaud's *Une saison en enfer*) Bataille explains in the first sentences why the first chapter bears the title "The Hatred of Poetry": "It seemed to me that only hate leads to real poetry. Poetry has power and sense only in the violence of revolt. But poetry achieves this violence only by evoking the *impossible*" (George Bataille, *L'impossible* in *Oeuvres complètes* [Paris: Gallimard, 1971], 3: 101; italics added).

other and distort every other into a replica of the self: the other must be the impossible, the one beyond all possibilities of the subject—the *other* other—if the I is going to be able to discharge itself of itself in this other and come free. The language that turns itself toward this other can no longer conform to the communicative codes in which an egologically structured society comprehends itself. Indeed, this language must be impossible, incomprehensible—and in its incomprehensibility it must allow, as Adorno writes, that "sudden flash" that in language itself, under the conditions of its impossibility, is other.

In an essay entitled "Presuppositions" Adorno comments, referring to texts of modernity, that "The harsh light of the incomprehensible such artworks turn toward the reader renders customary comprehensibility suspect of being stale, shallow, thingly—preartistic" (Notes, 431; 2: 95).[40] In the same essay Adorno denounces any attempt to limit the principle of incomprehensibility to modernity and to the domain of art, or to a merely "aesthetic" concept of understanding, and this denunciation is undertaken with enough energy to make it clear that he does not conceive of the collapse of comprehensibility only as a regional and historically circumscribed phenomenon. Thus he writes: "In art—and, so I would like to think, not in art alone—history has retroactive force. The crisis of comprehensibility . . . drags even older works into itself" (Notes, 432; 2: 96). It is the incomprehensible—and incomprehensible in principle—that is torn open by the "crisis of comprehensibility" in modernity. And thus it is an aporia, a self-denial of both rationality and the course of history, that breaks through all the borders between epochs, institutions, and genres, between theories and practices, between conscious and unconscious acts. By "surpassing its own impossibility," the possible testifies to a language that no longer obeys the distinctions of subjectivity, and it testifies to an understanding that would have leaped clear of the categories of rational construction and leaped into another understanding—not an understanding that is somehow "irrational" but one that consists in the freeing of the *ratio,* the emancipation of an altered *ratio.* It is this event of the impossible that matters in the end—and matters not simply because it discloses an understanding that no longer conforms to conceptual and social forms of understanding

40. Adorno's discussion then takes issue with an "aesthetic concept of understanding" (Notes, 433; 2: 96).

but, most of all, because only in the arena of this other understanding is it possible to experience *what* understanding, language, and society could be—and *that* they could be at all. More exactly: what and that they could *perhaps* be.

In a speech entitled "The Meridian," Paul Celan spoke of the paths of poetry and language: they are "paths of a voice to a perceiving You, creaturely paths, perhaps projects of existence [*Daseinsentwürfe vielleicht*], a sending oneself out toward oneself, in search of oneself . . ." (GW, 3: 201). One can understand Celan's progression of phrases in this way: the paths are not only toward a You; they are also toward oneself, toward another and toward an I, hence toward the other as an I or toward the I as another; they are paths, finally, in search of themselves. Indeed, there is no guarantee that they are paths; they move in the mode of "perhaps," more exactly, in the mode of suspending all modalities: "projects of existence *perhaps*," Celan says. There is, for these paths, no certainty, not even that they could have taken their point of departure from "art as something given in advance and something that is supposed to be unconditionally presupposed" (GW, 3: 193). This alone is certain: "The poem is in want of another, it needs this other, it needs an against to work. It seeks it out, it gives itself over to it in speaking" (GW, 3: 198). But neither this other nor the path—which is to say, the art or the language able to lead to it—are presupposed or given in advance of the poem. A poem without presuppositions, even without the presupposition that it is a poem, is something that "sends itself out toward itself"— but toward a "self" impossible to secure, a merely virtual "self." It is a prolepsis into an other. "Perhaps," Celan writes, "here, with the I—with the *here* and estranged I set free *in this way*—perhaps here an other becomes free?—Perhaps the poem is from that point itself . . ." (GW, 3: 196). It is not from its own point of view but only from that of this other, the non-given and non-presupposed—an other who is without methodological guarantees of understanding and has thus "perhaps" become free—that the poem is then—but once again "perhaps"—"itself." Its language speaks from the place of a "perhaps," a possible other; but this possibility is impossible to secure, and so the language of the poem can speak only "perhaps."

By describing the path of language and poetry in this way, Paul Celan describes the path of understanding as well. Understanding does not so much set out in search of the other as set out *from* it. Celan does not deny the "darkness" with which poetry is reproached, and one can doubtless understand this "darkness" as incomprehensibility; rather, he offers this by way of clarification: "the darkness assigned to poetry from a—perhaps self-projected—distance and foreignness for the sake of an encounter" (GW, 3: 195). If the poem is an apostrophe to an other, then it must speak in such a way that it is comprehensible to this other according to the measure of its otherness; but since this measure is uncertain, the poem can hope for comprehensibility only in its estrangement from comprehension. The poem is incomprehensible for the sake of *another* understanding. In its darkness the otherness of its addressee already speaks too: the one addressed is the one who addresses. And this otherness speaks in a language other than that of commodious communication, in a language that is never already common language, never already language at all, and can therefore never be certain of its comprehensibility. The poem can be written only from something other than the poem; understanding—"perhaps," if it comes to the poem—can only come from something incomprehensible.

Celan called the path that he himself forged in his speech "this impossible path, this path of the impossible" (GW, 3: 195). The path was impossible, and so too are the paths of language, one can surmise, because "what is claimed and what is turned into a You, so to speak [*gleichsam*], by the act of naming brings its otherness along" on this path (GW, 3: 198). The path of what is called a You "so to speak" and what must no less be called an I "so to speak" leads out into the open—and is thus an impossible path and a path of the impossible. "We are," Celan says, "if we speak with things in this way, always in the space of a question about their whence and whither: in an 'open-ended' question, a question 'coming to no conclusion,' a question pointing toward the open and empty and free—we are far outside" (GW, 3: 199).[41] Far out-

41. Just as Celan lets the movement of the poem proceed from a question, Emmanuel Lévinas lets the movement of understanding proceed from a "primordial" question that is always also a request and a prayer, and he characterizes this question as "a relation to the other that refuses thematization and therefore always also an assimilation to knowledge because of its irreducible difference. A relation that therefore does not make itself into a correlation. Hence a relation that strictly speaking cannot express itself as a relation, since under its terms there is an absence even of that commonality of synchrony that no relation is allowed to refuse for its terms. And yet to the other—relation. Relation and non-relation" (Emmanuel Lévinas, *De Dieu qui vient à l'idée* [Paris: Vrin, 1986], 168–69).

side, in a question pointing toward the open, not at a site definable by temporal and spatial parameters, not in a given or presupposed rhetorical topos, but at a site to be projected, a non-site: "u-topia" (GW, 3: 199). The path of language goes toward the otherness of one "turned into a You, so to speak," and it thus goes out into an opening that cannot be occupied or invested by methods and topics: the impossible. It goes to the otherness of language and is therefore, "perhaps," already the path of another language. It is the path of understanding toward the siteless, the unsecurable, toward the "otherness" of understanding—toward an understanding of Being other than as position—and is therefore, once again "perhaps," already other than understanding.

On March 26, 1969, Celan wrote this about poetry: "La poésie ne s'impose plus, elle s'expose" (GW, 3: 181).

And so, too, does understanding. It ex-poses itself.

HERMENEUTIC ELLIPSES

Writing the Circle in Schleiermacher

"What a catastrophe! Then there will be readers who can read."
—Friedrich Schlegel, "On Incomprehensibility"

I

In accordance with the strange logic by which witnesses for the prosecution can strengthen the case of the defendant against their own will, those who plead for the universalization of hermeneutics and for its emancipation from the doctrines of both divine inspiration and enlightened rationalism cannot stop arguing, implicitly or explicitly, for the other side in the dispute. The man who carried out the most complete and, because of its eristic mode of argumentation, the most effective attack on the positions of a hermeneutics that tried to secure the apparently steadfast architecture of theological dogmatics or to stabilize the canonical systems of rationalism was Friedrich Schleiermacher, for he submitted the discipline of hermeneutics to the transcendental turn initiated by Kant's critique of reason and developed by the theoreticians of German romanticism. Whereas hermeneutics had hitherto understood itself as an appendix to the particular disciplines of theology or philology and was satisfied with the establishment of a heuristic canon by means of which certain "dark passages" from the Bible or from classical literature could be clarified, Schleiermacher's hermeneutics for the first time systematically put into question the conditions of understanding texts and discourses in general. Through methodical reflection on the transcendental and historical conditions of understanding, he intended to emancipate hermeneutics from the "corners in a parenthesis"[1] of a theological or philological treatise and indeed "to secure still another place" (311) for hermeneutics as a discipline. It deserves a place in a general system of dialectics that would accord it the rights due any genuine discipline—a place where it, as "the science of the unity of knowledge," would be located alongside ethics as the "science of history" and across from physics as the doctrine of the "natural" side of human experience (76–77). Yet Schleiermacher's emancipation of hermeneutics from one of the corner positions that are forever overshadowed by already accredited philosophical disciplines still operates—and not by accident or by virtue of some strategic error but from the pressure of its transcendental mode of questioning and thus from the instruments of its own emancipation—with arguments borrowed from the arsenal of the opposing party. Within Schleiermacher's formulation of the concept of universal hermeneutics, these arguments on loan from dogmatic theology and rationalism constitute the residue of the representationalism he had subjected to a thoroughgoing critique. The various distortions of Schleiermacher's theory of interpretation that mark the course of its historical reception—as the cases of Dilthey and Gadamer demonstrate with unmistakable clarity—were capable of claiming a certain plausibility only when they appealed to that moment within the development of his theory in which the tradition of generally valid and historically invariant truths of reason survives intact. In order to elaborate not only a general but also a *literary* hermeneutic—an elaboration in which the relation of the general to the literary must itself be questioned—it is therefore of particular importance to comprehend this residue in a precise manner, to define its function within the economy of a new hermeneutics, which can also claim to be a hermeneutics of newness itself, and thus to dissolve a whole series of limitations that, issuing from classical transcendental philosophies, oppose the analysis of the process of understanding and work against the development of a useful organon of philological knowledge.

1. Friedrich Schleiermacher, *Hermeneutik und Kritik,* ed. and intro. Manfred Frank (Frankfurt am Main: Suhrkamp, 1977), 313. Further citations of this edition throughout this chapter will be indicated in parenthesis in the body of the text.

II

In his lectures "On the Concept of Hermeneutics in Relation to F. A. Wolf's Suggestions and Ast's Primer," Schleiermacher emphasizes that the definition of hermeneutics found in Friedrich Ast's *Outlines of Grammar, Hermeneutics, and Critique*[2]—"Hermeneutics is the art of discovering the thoughts of a writer from his discourse with the necessity of insight"—represents a definite achievement. No longer is the field of hermeneutical operations reserved for classical authors or the Bible, and once hermeneutics no longer shies away from texts written in the vernacular and written recently—be they only newspaper articles, scientific treatises, or "advertisements"—the field is open for everything that, as "foreign," works against unmediated comprehension (313–14). After praising the vastly broadened domain of objects susceptible to hermeneutical operations—a broadening that is doubtless announced in Ast's definition but not in a pronounced manner—Schleiermacher rejects this definition on two counts. On the one hand, he censures the still too restrictive treatment of speech and thus the implicit suppression of the manifold difficulties spoken discourse can impose on understanding; on the other hand, he protests against the decisive phrase through which hermeneutics is defined: "the thoughts of an author are discovered with the necessity of insight" (317). The process of understanding in the discipline of literary scholarship does not proceed according to the logic of deductions or dialectical syntheses, as Ast, a student of Schelling, implies. And it ends up in a mode of certainty that is altogether unlike the certainty of a mathematical solution. Neither the sheer "reproduction or reconstruction of the already constructed,"[3] nor even the positivistic "collection, coordination, and weighing of minute historical moments" (318)—a positivism often practiced to this day—can adequately grasp the stylistic peculiarity of a text. For the mimetic "reconstruction" of a literary production that Schleiermacher, like Ast (although for en-

---

2. Friedrich Ast, *Grundlinien der Grammatik, Hermeneutik und Kritik* (Landshut: Thomann, 1808); partially reprinted in *Philosophische Hermeneutik,* ed. Hans-Georg Gadamer and Gerhard Boehm (Frankfurt am Main: Suhrkamp, 1976), 111–30; cf. *The Hermeneutic Tradition,* ed. Gayle L. Ormiston and Alan D. Schrift (Albany, N.Y.: SUNY Press, 1990), 39–56. Excerpts from Schleiermacher's discussion of Ast can be found in *Hermeneutik und Kritik,* 309–46.

3. Friedrich Ast, *Grundlinien,* § 80.

tirely different reasons), considers indispensable must first fashion a solid historical and grammatical basis in this process of "collection" and "coordination" if it is to avoid the trap of sheer arbitrariness. Yet on this basis alone it is not possible to reconstruct the "individual way an author makes a combination, which, otherwise articulated in the same historical situation and in the same form of address"—and therefore under the same initial historical and linguistic conditions, including those specified by a genre—"would nevertheless have yielded a different result" (318). The meshes in the nets of communication, which are as tightly woven by language and history as they are rigorously reconstructed by linguistic and historical disciplines, are never so narrowly knotted that the individuality of an author could not succeed in slipping through. What presents itself as the strength of language is the fact that it is not simply a generally valid and codified linguistic *system* but is also, by virtue of the individuality of its speakers and their specific *usage* of language, always a "primordial productivity" (326). But this strength must count as a weakness of hermeneutics so long as it is unprepared to place alongside its historical archives of words and invariant rules of grammar a form of understanding that complements this productivity. Schleiermacher calls such a form of understanding the "divinatory procedure." As an operation of "guessing" (318), this procedure concerns both the irreducibley individual elements of a text and the entirety of its composition, and since it also demands the engagement of the interpreter's individuality, it cannot be regulated according to any preconceived method. Since, however, this operation belongs to the "complete" interpretation of any given work and indeed prescribes the interrogative interest and the "manner of posing a question" (314) to grammatical interpretation— that is, "the manner of posing a question" to the mode of interpretation that seeks to structure a foreign linguistic system and to translate this system into one more familiar to the interpreter and his "cognitive community" (375)—no hermeneutic operation can in principle have the "necessity of insight." Its field is not one of necessity but one in which possibilities are realized, and none of these realizations can claim to be the sole representative of truth: "as long as one such possibility has not been entirely cast aside, all talk of necessary insight is impossible" (317).

The point of Schleiermacher's critique of a postulate in which necessity plays a decisive role is that necessity unavoidably dissolves the hermeneutical circle. For the hermeneutical principle consists in a postulate of another sort altogether: "just as the whole is understood from the part, the part can only be understood from the whole" (329). This circle, however, can be seen as closed only when the totality of a linguistic system is completely present in every one of its moments and in every one of its actualizations of possible linguistic usage—without any remainder. Only one circumstance allowed Ast to maintain such a seamless continuity between the whole and its parts: the construction of a "hermeneutics of spirit" in which "the hermeneutics of letters," whose aim was to clarify words and topics, and "the hermeneutics of meaning," whose aim was to ascertain the intention of an author in the context of his times, joined one another to form a unified whole.[4] The speculative hermeneutics of spirit propagated by Ast did away with the real and concrete aporias that result from the construction of the hermeneutic circle.

At this point emerges the first connection between Schleiermacher's critique of the exclusion of "living discourse" from the domain of objects under study in hermeneutics and his critique of the suppression of the practical aporias generated by the postulate of the hermeneutical circle. Because difficulties can arise even during an "intimate conversation" with a "friend" whose way of life and mode of thinking are familiar to the conversation partner and indeed far more familiar than the linguistic and historical conditions that have to be laboriously reconstructed for the interpretation, say, of ancient Greek texts; because, in other words, understanding still faces difficulties even when the totality of the linguistic, historical, and personal factors is already "given," the claim that all particularities and all parts can be completely clarified through an appeal to a given whole is untenable. A segment of the conversation that falls out of any given horizon of comprehension and thereby breaks the consensus among communicators oriented toward the ideal of a preestablished harmony that operates like a game of ping-pong (Schleiermacher speaks of the "almost spiritless and entirely mechanical" activity in which "spoken discourse becomes rule-bound, like a ball that is caught and then thrown back" [309])—this segment is, once again, the "individual combinatory mode" that remains peculiar to every speaker: "I catch myself very often in the middle of an intimate conversation performing hermeneutical operations when I am not

4. Friedrich Ast, *Grundlinien*, § 82.

satisfied with the usual level of understanding and am trying to figure out how my friend made some transition from one thought to another, or I do the same when I try to trace what views, judgments, and intentions are bound up with his discussion of some topic in precisely this way and not another" (315). The individual mode of expression and the specific "this way and not another" of its combination cannot be frozen into a body of invariant rules of a particular linguistic community. For the sake of its production of self-activated individuality and its hermeneutical clarification, it needs an effort on the part of the "faculty of divination" to reflect on the rules but not to fix them once and for all. From the context of Schleiermacher's allusion to the conversational situation, at least two things are sufficiently clear: the "living expression" in the "immediate presence of the speaker" (316) is closer to the free productivity at the basis of linguistic usage than written expression could ever hope to be, and writing favors the forgetting of its genesis, the amnesia of "free self-determination" (184) by its use of signs, thus inducing the mechanistic conception of the circular character of the hermeneutic operation. Yet the extraordinarily complex connection between the principle of hermeneutics, which Schleiermacher seeks to establish in opposition to the mechanical contraption of Ast, and the problem of writing—the solution of which must be counted among the most pressing tasks assigned to any *literary* hermeneutics—requires still further clarification to make out its contours.

To broaden the field of hermeneutical operations beyond the limits of theological and rationalistic canons of writing and even beyond the reaches of fixed and already codified writing, Schleiermacher called upon an old, long-standing ordering of priorities, one that Plato had postulated and that is rarely questioned even to this day—the priority of living discourse over writing. He mobilized the far older and more powerful discipline of philosophy, conceived as a general and fundamental science, in order to weaken the grip of an antiquated tradition of regional hermeneutics on the discipline of hermeneutics, and he suppressed the fragile distinction between written and spoken usages of language in favor of an abrupt hierarchy so as to make hermeneutic techniques capable of distinctions fine enough to take into account the individual stylistic nuances of a person. Primacy and privilege are reserved for the spoken word—up until the present. Gadamer, for example, in the "Fundamental Characteristics of Philosophical Hermeneutics" that he developed under the title *Truth and Method* does not hesitate to hypostasize conversation as the model of the "hermeneutic phenomenon"[5] and indeed leaves no doubts that he also wants to conceptualize the act of reading in accordance with this model: "Written tradition . . . as long as it is deciphered, is pure spirit, so much so that it speaks to us as though it were altogether present."[6] The peculiar semanticism of this conception of hermeneutics—a semanticism that rests on an apodictic principle according to which the representation of discourse and its object reside in a historical continuum of meaning—inevitably results in this postulate: "the actual and authentic hermeneutic task" is the "backwards transformation" of writing into speech.[7] Such a "backwards transformation" can take place only on the condition that, regardless of all historical and empirical points of determination, writing be conceived as an ideal form of spoken language generated by an abstraction, an ideal form whose conceptual character guarantees that every reduction will, without further mediation, arrive at meaning. Not only is conversation the model; it is the very matrix of all other linguistic articulations and, in particular, that of writing: "The sign-language of writing refers to the actual and authentic language of discourse."[8] Nowhere is this characterization of writing more striking—and nowhere more ironic—than in one of the basic theses Gadamer draws from his misunderstanding of Heidegger: the thesis of the "prejudgment-structure" of understanding. "Speech" is "actually" language; it is language proper. Writing, by contrast, consists of signs that have been derived from speaking and refer to *it,* not to the objects with which spoken discourse is concerned. Writing is a secondary sign, the sign of a sign or, as Aristotle maintains in a passage of *De Interpretatione* that sets the standard for the theory of writing up until Gadamer: "Spoken words are the symbols of affections in the soul and written words are the symbols of affections in speech."[9] Instead of submitting this conception of writing proposed by Aristotle

5. Hans-Georg Gadamer, *Wahrheit und Methode,* 2nd ed. (Tübingen: Mohr, 1965), 360; cf. *Truth and Method,* 2nd ed., trans. Garrett Barden and John Cumming (New York: Seabury Press, 1975), 340–41.

6. *Wahrheit und Methode,* 156; *Truth and Method,* 145.

7. *Wahrheit und Methode,* 371; *Truth and Method,* 354–55.

8. *Wahrheit und Methode,* 370; *Truth and Method,* 354.

9. Aristotle, *De Interpretatione,* ed. L. Minio-Paluello (Oxford: Clarendon, 1949), 16a3–7; cf. *On Interpretation,* trans. E. M. Edghill, in *The Works of Aristotle,* ed. R. McKeon (New York: Random House, 1941), 40.

and the comparable one developed in Plato's *Phaedrus* to an analysis of their controversial function in the context of ontology, Gadamer reissues them in an affirmative and foreshortened form—and does so under the sign of continuity. Contrary to Gadamer's suggestion, these conceptions of writing are not simply subject to continual enrichment in the course of linguistic theory and hermeneutics; they undergo and thus underlie certain radical alterations, and never more so than in an epoch inaugurated by the transcendental turn.

However much Schleiermacher emphasizes the homogeneity of spoken and written discourse with regard to their sign-character and however strongly the Platonic-Aristotelian tradition exerts its influence on his view of writing, his definition of written discourse differs from this tradition at one decisive point. While formulating this definition, Schleiermacher speaks of a "state of discourse fixed for the eyes through writing" (315), and this reference to a "fixation" drives the homogenization of spoken discourse and writing to a point where the latter is no longer seen as a subordinate sign but is characterized as an aggregate state of the former. Writing is arrested, fixed, and firmly held speech; it is speech in which speech ceases to be present before the ears in a procession of sounds and becomes, as image and shape, an object for another organ of sensibility—the eye. Once the traditional borders between speech and writing have been opened up in this way, all of the hermeneutical principles acquired in association with spoken discourse—and in particular the conception of language as "act," as "a moment when life bursts forth," and as divinatory attention to its stylistic singularity—can now be legitimately reclaimed for an adequate understanding of writing. Thus Schleiermacher's urgent advice to the

editors of written work to practice diligently the interpretation of more significant conversations. For the immediate presence of the speaker, the living expression that announces the participation of his entire spiritual being, the mode in which thoughts develop from communal life, all these things—far more than lonely meditation on an entirely isolated piece of writing—entice one to understand a sequence of thoughts as a moment when life bursts forth and as acts bound up with many other kinds of acts. It is precisely this side of understanding that is most often slighted and for the most part entirely neglected whenever a writer is explained. (316)

The *function* of expanding the domain of objects studied in hermeneutics and redefining the relation between written and spoken discourse announces itself here in a precise, encapsulated form. This expansion and redefinition support the effort to model the interpretation of altogether isolated and lifeless writings in such a way as to give both communal constraints and "lively expression" their due. This helps secure for the interpretation of written texts an understanding of the central point at which all perspectives on language converge: an understanding of the "moment when life bursts forth," the "resolution of the conception" (184), and the activity of speaking subjects as they actually found and constitute meaning. But a *consequence* of this expansion and redefinition is announced with corresponding clarity: when writing is characterized as an aggregate state of spoken discourse, the latter—however much it may be distinguished as lively, immediately present, and social—must also bear the mark of the negative evaluation under which writing was conceived; it, too, must be affected by absence, by death, by isolation. The generalization of the hermeneutic operation under the signs of phonocentrism and logocentrism corresponds step by step with a counter-movement—the decentered outbreak of a graphematics that withdraws from the regime of logocentrism. Not only is the historical continuity dominated by the paradigm of spoken discourse syncopated; this paradigm disarticulates itself. The moment of language—the "moment when life bursts forth"—shows itself as one already traversed by traces of a mortifying movement of writing.

This conflict between the paradigms of living discourse, on the one hand, and an already departed and exterior script, on the other, becomes particularly virulent whenever Schleiermacher solemnly asserts their essential identity in the midst of discussing the problems and tasks arising from the fundamental principle of the hermeneutical circle. The hinge between these two forms of linguistic articulation is formed by memory. In mechanical memory—*hypomnesis, Gedächtnis*—the character of speech and that of writing are so intermingled that they become an impermeable amalgamation. For memory, like writing, is given the task of "holding fast" the particular passage, so that one might be able to return to it from the sequence of other passages, each of which is comprehended in the course of understanding a given whole. By definition, then, understanding is achieved—which is to say, achieved insofar as the understanding of particular passages is determined by the whole and the whole by the particular passages—only in the course of running through the particular textual or discursive elements twice. A preliminary effort at understanding can actualize only the meanings deposited in the general repertoire of the language; but neither the syntactical nor the semantic system of rules in which such meanings are embedded can give any information whatsoever about the particular and utterly non-preformed composition of the determinate whole. Only the possibility—prepared by memory and writing—of breaking off a preliminary and incomplete understanding of the whole, which is oriented toward the compendium of linguistic conventions, and returning to its component parts allows for the adequate comprehension of their specific functions within the composition of a discourse that at the limit is independent of rules. In this sense, every act of divination that seeks to encircle the irreducibly individual stylistic gestures of a spoken discourse, a textual series, or even an epoch refers *a priori* to the fixing and holding fast of a discourse in the medium of memory or writing. These operations are the conditions of possibility for divination and hence understanding. Without the possibility of a return from the whole to the parts, neither the specificity of the whole nor that of its particular moments could be understood; without a memory trace in the mind or a written trace on paper, there is neither understanding nor comprehension but only the pre-understanding and pre-comprehension that take up residence within the confines of lifeless linguistic conventions.

Once the function of "fixing" speech and "holding it fast" has been shown to reside at the foundation of meaning in general, the double deficit common to writing and memory appears dangerous to the entire hermeneutical project. Schleiermacher clearly acknowledges it:

> There certainly must be an understanding of the whole . . . merely through the part, but this part will necessarily be only an incomplete one if memory has not held it fast, and if we, after the whole has been given, could not return to the part in order then to understand it more precisely and more completely in relation to the whole. Thus the difference between that which is perceived by the ear and that which is before our eyes in the form of writing once again disappears altogether, since, in order to serve the former, we are able to utilize, in memory, all the advantages that apparently belong exclusively to the latter—so that, as Plato already said, the usefulness of writing consists only in

remedying the deficiencies of memory. But this is an ambiguous remedy since, having been founded on the corruption of memory, it promotes again and again the very same corruption. (333)

The Egyptian myth of the origin of writing recounted by Socrates in the (written) dialogue entitled *The Phaedrus* entertains no doubts about the fatal flaw of writing. The inventor, Theuth, god of the underworld, is instructed by Ammon, the sun-god:

> If people learn this, it will set forgetfulness in their souls; they will no longer care for memory because they will put their trust in writing, no longer remembering from within themselves and by means of their own power, but outside themselves by means of external marks. What you have discovered is a remedy not for memory but for reminder. You do not offer your disciplines true wisdom but only its semblance.[10]

As a means of healing and helping memory, writing, for all its "ambiguity," contributes to the disease of memory, to its corruption and loss. Yet Schleiermacher, like Plato, could not deny its necessity. For memory is finite and limited, however much it might brace itself against the successive loss of the present moment in its capacity as a faculty of ideas, notions, representations. The deficiency of memory is in need of a remedy if something like understanding is to be possible in the first place: the re-presentation of something now absent, the remembering of something forgotten, the guessing of something foreign, the reviving of something dead. Writing—and all exterior forms of archiving life—furnishes understanding with such a remedy: "speech must become writing" (98) whenever the reach of memory does not suffice to guarantee comprehension and, along with comprehension, homogeneity within the community and continuity in the course of history. Yet this indispensable supplement, this necessary aid, and indeed this *telos* of the living organism of spoken discourse as it comes to understand itself—

---

10. Plato, *Phaidros* in *Opera*, ed. J. Burnet (Oxford: Clarendon, 1901), 275a2–7; cf. *The Phaedrus*, trans. R. Hackforth, in *Complete Dialogues*, ed. E. Hamilton and H. Cairns (Princeton University Press, 1961), 520. (It should be remembered that Schleiermacher produced unsurpassed German translations of this and other Platonic dialogues.) On the interpretation of this text, see Jacques Derrida, "Plato's Pharmacy," *Dissemination*, trans. Barbara Johnson (Chicago: University of Chicago Press, 1981), 61–171. My analyses are linked to this and other works of Derrida.

telos, for Schleiermacher could not otherwise write about speech "having to become writing"—is always and irreducibly a poison, a recipe for the kind of "corruption" that dismembers and dissociates this organism. The thing that is supposed to make the life of spirit, if not infinite, then at least complete, is in the same stroke the radical finitization of this life, its deprivation, and its falling prey to decay. Writing is at once the condition of possibility and the ground of the impossibility for any authentic understanding of oneself among speaking subjects; it is the foundation for the hermeneutic reconstitution of another person's discourse in the context of the various grammatical and semantic conventions of language that this discourse has inventoried, and at "one" with this, it is the destruction of any and every form of constituting meaning, hence of every hermeneutics. No wonder Schleiermacher, in his discussion of the concept of hermeneutics, does not want to expose this concept to any dangers and thus seeks to banish the infection emanating from the ambiguity of writing—an infection that threatens his entire hermeneutical endeavor. And it is no wonder he takes refuge in the words of Plato downplaying the function and violence of writing and limiting its utility: the usefulness of writing is supposed to consist in remedying the failures and deficiencies of memory—and nothing more. It is understandable, finally, that after singling out memory and writing as constituent elements not only of communication but of all historical and social life, he then makes the following remark in a marginal note to his "Outlines for a System of Moral Doctrine": "But communication through writing alone, without living dialogue, always turns into death" (386).

III

Schleiermacher's attempt to ground and justify the possibility of understanding and the possibility of hermeneutics shows them to be systematically bound up with their own failure. The unstoppable shaking of their foundations appears in an even more glaring light when one considers how often not only understanding and hermeneutics but also the theories of language and subjectivity that are enlisted in their service must forfeit their firmly held positions in response to the necessary eruption of the destructive forces of writing into the field of meaning. Schleiermacher takes his point of departure—and here he anticipates

Saussure[11]—from the double character of language. On the one hand, language is a grammatical-semantic system that "conditions all thought of particulars . . . if one considers the particular human being as only a locus for language" (78–79), and, on the other, it is linguistic usage "from which every new act of speaking emerges" and then "returns to the individual" (80). The term "linguistic usage" *(Sprachgebrauch)* should not be understood as the merely mechanical-repetitive actualization of either the grammatical system or the rules of social relations— only apparently invariant—through which a "cognitive community" defines itself and which are deposited in the grammatical system. Without this mechanical side of actualization by means of which pregiven schemata are realized, language could not be used, for it allows all speaking individuals continually to objectify the determining factors of their social life. Under the rubric of "linguistic usage,"[12] however, Schleiermacher's theory of language emphasizes the predominance of the generative aspect of each discursive action and thus the overall ability of individuals to constitute language and grant meaning in a society they themselves found. These two aspects of language—as linguistic system and speech act—do not therefore relate to one another in a symmetric manner: if under one aspect speakers present themselves as products of a pregiven language, under the other they present themselves as its producers. But how language is generated, and how an already given language is both modified and transformed—these become the principal points of interest for any hermeneutics concerned with the *differentia singularis* of individual linguistic acts. The hermeneutic technique responsible for this realm of knowledge goes by the name of "psychological interpretation" in Schleiermacher's work. This name lets one forget all too easily that the technique it designates deals precisely with constructions that owe their existence to the "untranslatable peculiarity" of linguistic productions (372)—"untranslatable peculiarity" because of the *natural* determinacy of finite reason. Schleiermacher's conception of

11. Peter Szondi was the first to notice this connection; see "Schleiermachers Hermeneutik heute," in Peter Szondi, *Schriften* (Frankfurt am Main: Suhrkamp, 1978), 2: 118; cf. *On Textual Understanding and Other Essays,* trans. Harvey Mendelsohn (Minneapolis: University of Minnesota Press, 1986), 104.

12. Friedrich Schleiermacher, *Hermeneutik,* ed. Heinz Kimmerle (Heidelberg: Winter 1959), 39; cf. "The Aphorisms on Hermeneutics from 1805 and 1809–10" in *Hermeneutical Theory,* 58.

"psychological interpretation" has nothing to do with psychology, however it may be articulated, and it especially has nothing in common with *psychologia rationalis*. Psychology in Schleiermacher designates the logic by which language and literary works are produced, and is therefore no closer to physis than to the psychic processes through which the naturally conditioned particularity of a linguistic utterance—however untranslatable it may be—is mediated through a "faculty" that remains identical for all speaking beings.

Every linguistic production that is more than a mechanical imitation and execution of already given socio-grammatical rules—and there is none that would not be more than this—presents itself as a "differential" between physis and psyche, between exteriorization and interiorization, between an "inner speaking" from which knowledge emerges and an outward-oriented discourse that turns toward other speakers (376). As the differential in which language is constituted and knowledge founded, it realizes a "determinate identity of the transcendental and the empirical" (381); that is, it realizes the identity of a generally valid schema and a unique affective modification. Whereas the schema makes possible the formation of the most general concepts and guarantees that particular speakers will be able to comprehend one another, the affective modification is a concern of the individual and indeed of each individual throughout the manifold of circumstances in which it becomes active. If, however, the transcendental is supposed to become a sensible experience, as the notion of an identity with the empirical implies, then the process of semiosis must include a constitutive factor that works toward the identical schematism against the background of the empirical. For everything general needs to be posited within the empirical and is nothing outside of this positing, just as each individual moment has to produce the general out of itself in order to find in this, its product, the guarantor of its determinacy. The constituent factor in which the transcendental and the empirical—and with them, nature and spirit, individual and society, inner and outer—are mediated with one another and thus reciprocally produce themselves and their determinate identity is, once again, memory.

In memory language finds the condition for its ability to constitute both the subject and its society; but insofar as memory cannot exist without language, it remains a secondary phenomenon despite its mediating status. Only memory—and not spontaneously produced linguistic behavior—"is the necessary condition for communication outside and inside oneself" (385).[13] For the self to be able to relate to itself *as* itself—and this alone is what "communication with oneself" means— the self requires a bond that, on the one hand, is not immediately itself (for then it could not be aware of itself in the mode of *as*) but, on the other, does not present itself as sheer exteriority (for then it could gain no access to itself as a *self*), and yet this bond must still link the self with itself. Memory puts such a bond at the disposal of the I, but not without a cost: caught in a movement of irrevocably delayed action, the self, always "thinking" only of itself, slips away from itself. The I is no longer present to itself in memory, however deeply its trace may have left an impression on itself, and only in this dis-membering, de-presenting distance does the I find a continually withdrawing and yet never com- pletely withdrawn point of support for its awareness of itself *as a self*. Self-consciousness and self-comprehension are thus characterized as in- conclusive hermeneutic events in which a still indeterminate I overrides the temporal difference opened up by its being fixed as a memory trace; this override is accomplished when the I posits an equivalence with this fixed linguistic shape and experiences itself as a self determined by this shape. This process is inconclusive, because every act of self-comprehen- sion includes a temporal index that refers to the fact that the self does not simply posit an equivalence with something unequal, for this pos- iting takes place in the *medium* of inequality. The hermeneutics of the self—the hermeneutics of "communicating with oneself" or "imparting something to oneself"—is the hermeneutics of an inconclusive self-divi- sion, self-partition, and self-imparting: it is the hermeneutics of a self that is not its own foundation, a hermeneutics of the interruption of hermeneutics.

By means of its mnemonic linguisticity, self-consciousness is singled out as radically finite, as a mode of consciousness that cannot consoli- date itself into a conclusive figure, not even the one envisaged by specu- lative theories of reflection. That the I, as linguistic and memory trace, can achieve a certain objectivity but at no point and at no time can become present to itself and thereby turn into an indubitable self—this intrinsic duality of every self-relation marks a fundamental deficiency in

---

13. Cf. my *pleroma—zu Genesis und Struktur einer dialektischen Hermeneutik* in G. W. F. Hegel, *Der Geist des Christentums,* ed. W. Hamacher (Berlin: Ullstein, 1978), 9–333.

the very concept of subjectivity. Schleiermacher interprets this deficiency (and so supplements it) as the result of an "absolute dependency"[14] upon a transcendent authority and thus upon an Other that, according to his theological mode of understanding, must be placed outside this self-relation in order for it to put a halt to its ineluctable, irreducible ambiguity. But it is clear that Schleiermacher's theological *interpretation* of the heterogeneity within the phenomenon of self-relationality only exports one moment from the double structure discovered by *description,* and that this moment of irreducible exteriority only receives a cogent explanation from the internal tension between the I and itself. Anyone who does not wish to reproduce Schleiermacher's hermeneutics of self-understanding—his hermeneutics *itself*—within its theologically oriented framework and tries, instead, to understand this hermeneutics must derive the hypostasis of an altogether Other from the intrinsic heterogeneity of the self and treat this hypostasis as one more attempt to relieve interpretation of the immanent tensions characteristic of every self-relation.[15] Only as the memory of God would memory be a place capable of safeguarding the self and guaranteeing its capacity for self-comprehension; as finite memory, as writing, by contrast, it is the place of a possible forgetting, a place that is still "within" the self and still includes within itself the forgetting of God.

14. Friedrich Schleiermacher, *Der christliche Glaube nach den Grundsätzen der evangelischen Kriche* (Reutlingen: Macken, 1828), § 3–5.

15. Schleiermacher's hypostasis of the other into an entirely other is reaffirmed by Manfred Frank's interpretation; see his *Das individuelle Allgemeine* (Frankfurt am Main: Suhrkamp, 1977); cf. the introduction to his edition of *Hermeneutik und Kritik.* This becomes clear when Frank writes that the other is the transcendent foundation from which the subject experiences its "imprinting" and thereby finds access to itself. The fact of imprinting cannot be denied, of course, but the possibility of such imprinting already belongs to subjectivity. Yet this is inconceivable if immediate self-knowledge gathers around a point of "feeling," as it does in a number of Schleiermacher's reflections, or around an immediate self-possession of any sort. Only in the *stamp* of imprinting—a stamp for which the structure of subjectivity lends its support at the very least—does the other become actual *as* other. Its transcendent position is thus conditioned by the structure of subjectivity. But under these circumstances there can no longer be any talk of one-sided "dependency." This dependency would reduce the instance of the other to a moment of a hierarchical, bipolar structure and would indeed remove from this instance the sense of opening, the sense of an inaugurating self-understanding as such. Subjection to this dependency would hardly amount to a "protestant" hermeneutics and certainly not to a hermeneutics of singularity.

Memory is also the "necessary condition" for "communication out-side of oneself," since every conversation between two different persons excludes simultaneity and is in this way no different from the conversa-tion with oneself from which Schleiermacher develops his conception of subjectivity. Not only must an individual's discourse gain inde-pendence from the time of its production, it must be countermanded and held back—in memory—as long as the other continues to speak. Thus does memory, which forms the foundation for the linguistic com-bination of words into sentences, become the foundation for social—in Schleiermacher's language ethical—"combinations" (381) as well. On the basis of memory two individuals can gather to speak, for memory posits at the origin of one discourse the acknowledgment of another, just as self-comprehension had posited the acknowledgment of the al-terity of the self in advance of all empirical otherness. Memory so econo-mizes its alterity that it no longer seeks refuge in abstract disparity. The ineluctable non-simultaneity that installs itself in memory is therefore the necessary condition for all forms of linguistic, self-referential, and social relations. Only in its medium can the "identity of the transcen-dental and the empirical" be realized; but for this very reason it can be realized only as a "determinate"—and that means precarious and un-translatable—individuality.[16]

The identity with which Schleiermacher is concerned and which is indispensable not only for every form of self-comprehension but for all efforts to understand someone else as someone other than oneself—this identity does not have the closed, final, and synthetic shape that specu-lative dialectics attributes to it. It takes place as a movement *between* the transcendental and the empirical, a movement that Hegel would doubt-less place under the polemical label of "bad infinity." Yet this identity is supposed to take place within the framework of the transcendental and the empirical and according to the regularities they impose on it. Schleiermacher's concept of the precarious relationship between the general and the individual, in whose movement all linguistic and lan-guage-generating acts manifest themselves, is called the "schema of os-

---

16. It is almost unnecessary to indicate that Schleiermacher's concept of "transcenden-tal" and "empirical" stems from a Kantian vocabulary, and yet his usage of this terminol-ogy, as his discussion of an "identity of the transcendental and empirical" shows, remains decisively non-Kantian.

cillation between general and particular" (374). Not without reason does the term "oscillation" claim an exalted position in Schleiermacher's text. If the relation between the particular and the general is not one in which the particular, having become a mere particle of the general, is subsumed by it and deducible from it, this relation can be adequately grasped—and then at the cost of renouncing the logic of concepts—only as a quantitative relationship and in the form of a metaphor that does not participate in the repertoire of logical relations dominated by the ideas of subsumption and deduction. Thus the relation of particular to general can be grasped only as a swaying, a hovering, and a pendulum movement between the two poles of the relation. Besides the sense of swinging, swaying back-and-forth, and shuttling to-and-fro—movements in which textiles and texts are woven together—Schleiermacher, who was a philologist of ancient writings after all, may have had in mind a further meaning when he chose the concept of "oscillation," a meaning that retains a closer relationship to language: *oscillum* is a derivative of *os* (mouth, face) and means "little mouth," "tiny face," and "mask." Understood in its etymological context, oscillation designates the "original" linguistic movement, the movement in which language is imparted to someone or something without language and without a face, without an intuition and without a concept.[17] Every assertion, every representation is "an oscillation between the determinacy of the individual and the indeterminacy of the general image. . . . The identity of the individual and the species is posited in this oscillation" (458). Although indispensable for all communicative acts, conceptual generalities can be retrieved from the chaos of individualities only by an abstraction, and yet each abstraction is detrimental to the determinacy and thus the

17. For the meaning of the word, see the fascinating study of Karl Meuli, *Altrömischer Maskenbrauch,* reprinted in *Gesammelte Schriften* (Basel: Schwabe, 1975), esp. 1: 261–64: "The word is clear linguistically: *oscillum* goes back to *osculum* and then to *os,* 'mouth,' 'face' . . . *Oscillum* thus means 'little mouth,' 'diminutive face'; glosses translate it as *stomation, prosopon, prosopeion,* 'mask.' One should not think of face masks; the *oscilla* are rather *pilae*—small, round balls made of wollen shreds or threads. . . . Macribius accurately calls them *capita,* 'heads'; onion or poppy heads were used to make them as well. . . . They must have been ugly in order to ward off evil; according to Varro, one would hang *oscilla* wherever someone had hanged himself. Whoever has been hanged, like anyone who dies a violent death, is a dangerous ghost who returns from the dead, and the *oscilla,* according to widespread practice, evidently have the task, as *apotropaion, probaskanion,* of keeping the uncanny at a distance from the living" (262–63).

communicability of the individual. For this reason the process of abstraction needs a corrective: it needs a supplementary individual that is given to this process in the subject of abstraction and that makes *a priori* every generalization into an individual generalization belonging to a linguistic and cognitive community or even to a particular speaker. If an abstraction were to be complete, it would no longer be communicable, and in every abstraction something incommunicable is posited along with the determinacy of the individual: "we can never express an individual through language" (466). Between these two poles of individual and general—neither of which belongs, strictly speaking, to the domain of language—language oscillates. In a labile, paradoxical, and always incomplete manner, language constitutes itself in the very interval between these two impossibilities and constitutes itself *as* oscillation: as oscillation between terms that experience their determination only *from* this oscillation and *in* its movement to-and-fro. If general concepts are not *given* to memory but must, *qua* abstractions, first be *generated* by memory, as Schleiermacher so impressively demonstrates in his "Dialectic" lecture on schematism and language (498); if, therefore, inscription in memory is *the* operation through which language and understanding are constituted, then his description of the emergence of language—which contrasts with his idealistic tendency and thus with his desire to grant the general an autonomous power[18]—must lead to the following conclusion: there cannot be a general schematism of designation and signification; there cannot be a schematism that would somehow be historically and culturally invariant and would not be tinged by particular historical and social conditions. Schleiermacher himself emphasizes that a purely individual linguistic gesture developed without reference to another instance—even if this other instance was precisely the one in which the I recognizes itself as a determinate self—is impossible. As the schematism through which language is formed and developed, memory neither submits to the rules of a code nor operates idiomatically in its generative acts. The traces fixed and held fast by memory can be neither absolutely indecipherable nor transparent to all. The specific mode in which memory functions withdraws from these two polar concepts—

18. For one example among many, see Schleiermacher's defense of the correspondence theory of truth and the "system of innate concepts" against the possibility of a "difference in intellectual function" (462).

not, however, because they are oxymoronically amalgamated, but because they take their leave from memory itself. The "schema of oscillation between the general and the particular" cannot, therefore, be characterized as a movement of mediation between two given quantities; rather, this schema, by oscillating, first produces such quantities as its always varying, ever trembling margins. General and individual, transcendental and empirical are functions of this oscillation, and whatever is incommunicable in their abstract constructions and singular events casts its shadow of incomprehensibility over the interpolar region of oscillation—an always different, always changing shadow.

IV

This much is clear: Schleiermacher's postulates concerning the philosophy of subjectivity and language can be understood as complements to his hermeneutics, and they serve, in particular, to specify the process of linguistic formation and thus the object of any psychological-technical interpretation; but these postulates do not remove the difficulties that hermeneutics encounters when, in trying to grasp more extensive linguistic constructs or ones that have become historical, it has to make reference to writing. On the contrary: what at first glance appeared as a difficulty encountered by a special branch of hermeneutics—*literary* hermeneutics—shows itself to be a much broader problem whenever one examines the general conditions in which language and thus all social interaction can arise. The problem besets any hermeneutics that refers to linguistic constructions—regardless of whether they are concerned with self-consciousness, linguistic phenomena such as semantics or referentiality, graphic presentations, behavioral codes, or any other symbolic system, including ethics. None of these hermeneutics—and they must be differentiated from one another if they are to take account of the diversity of their domains—can disregard the minimal conditions necessary for the constitution of their objects, for these conditions are at the same time their very own conditions: "memory," which is said to be the "necessary condition of communication outside and inside oneself" (385); the temporal difference posited with memory; and the possibility of forgetting. Schleiermacher makes it clear in his considerations of dialogics, ethics, and aesthetics that none of these hermeneutics can disregard the constitutive defect in the structure of their objects and in their specific sets of procedure, which can be supplemented only by means of a problematic remedy—by means of writing or something that substitutes for the capacity of script to hold fast and fixate.

Writing in its widest—if you will, its "metaphorical"—sense has the advantage of elevating merely subjective acts of linguistic creation, which are always bound to a spontaneous moment, into the ranks of objectivity. Only in this way can the language of the I (or of any other, more complexly structured institution of selfhood) encounter itself and others as something relatively whole; only then can it maintain its specificity and at the same time be the object of observation undertaken according to rules: "Inner speaking is the language of memory; writing is the memory and tradition of language through which it first becomes fully objective and by means of which communication is first posited independently of its time of production" (382). But this advantage of the graphic supplement[19]—which singles it out as the installation of "the determinate identity of the transcendental and the empirical" and as "the schema of oscillation between general and particular"—remains inextricably linked to grave disadvantages: the supplement corrupts the memory it had enabled; it corrupts the identity of the general and the particular which it had realized; it corrupts the identity of the transcendental and the empirical; and it even corrupts the possibility of understanding and thus life itself. "Communication through writing alone, without a living dialogue, always becomes death" (486). Against the ruinous double function of writing in the production of signs and meaning, it can be argued—and this argument has been advanced with considerable persuasive power—that writing is, according to Schleiermacher's apt formulation, only a "necessary" condition for the unification of the general and the particular, not their *causa per quam*. This qualification, however illuminating it may appear in the context of rhetorical distinctions made for the purposes of metaphysical investigations, does not withstand Schleiermacher's description of the function and effect of writing. Living dialogue does indeed owe its life to the

19. The term comes from Jacques Derrida. Manfred Frank has also attempted to indicate and reconstruct the concept of the supplement as it was developed by Derrida in his readings of Plato and Rousseau (cf. *Das individuelle Allgemeine,* 119–20). But Frank remains more faithful to Schleiermacher than Schleiermacher was to himself: by essentializing this concept, he relieves it of the tensions he had noted.

fixing and holding fast of a combination of memory traces, and in order to remain a "living" dialogue and to totalize itself in history, it must refer to the material grapheme and its particular domain—and this domain is not immediately subjected to the command of the intellect and its categorial functions. Intellectual spontaneity in the act of founding signs and constituting meaning, which is the only "act" that could in any case claim to be a *causa per quam,* cannot attain the status of a sufficient condition. Every *causa* of this kind is traversed by the aporetic trait of *conditiones sine quibus non:* necessary conditions provided by writing and its set of implications. Whatever is living in a system of signs imperceptibly ends up in a position diametrically opposed to Schleiermacher's own proposals: dialogics turns into a supplement arising from writing, a supplement that makes up for a deficiency in writing, although writing was supposed to be nothing more than a supplement of speech. But such a radical inversion in the framework of functions—ranging from primary to derivative, from the act of instituting meaning to the establishment of this institution, from inner to outer, from life to death—is possible only if both terms of the opposition, each of which is incomplete in itself and incomplete with regard to the other, are alloys of writing from the very beginning. In the field of writing, meaning no longer *is* and is not yet; it is not life and is yet not death either; ·it is neither the power of a pure self-positing nor the sheer passivity of something deposited into a stable position—but always both at the same time and never entirely either one. No linguistic praxis, no praxis mediated by language, and no hermeneutic operation can mask this indeterminacy or overdetermination of its medium and its object without becoming blind to its own conditions.

From the irreducibly double effect of writing in all systems of signs and in all operations lying within its reach, at least three consequences can be drawn for the theory of hermeneutics.

The status and functional mode of graphic articulations can no longer be understood according to the model of "living" discourse as soon as one acknowledges that the necessary intervention of writing subverts the validity of any such model. Writing can claim a relative autonomy with respect to spoken discourse not only because it withdraws from the logic of objectifying self-presentation—and even shows this logic to be an effect of its ambiguity—but also because of its material shape. Along with Hamann, Schleiermacher is, to my knowledge, one of the first theorists of language to proclaim that writing has a right to its own history:

> For criticism, writing is also, outside of language, something for itself, and it has certain positive aspects that, when abstracted from writing, do not appear in speech. . . . Writing has its own history. Alterations occur in it that are independent of the alterations in speech. But these alterations are nevertheless essential moments in the totality of linguistic history. (262–63)

When one thinks of the baroque pattern poetry, Mallarmé's *Coup de dés,* or Hölderlin's "Look, Gracious Sir, a Comma!" and when one considers the values a writer like Francis Ponge can give to punctuation and typeface, it becomes clear how great a role the material aspect of scriptual articulation would have to play for a specifically *literary* hermeneutic—and yet does not play even to this day. The imagistic character of writing cannot, of course, make the business of interpretation and of the theory of reading any easier. It may be easier to abstract from the materiality of the phonetic sign than from that of the graphic, but even the graphic sign is transparent to the eye—"the schema of all sensuous activity" (455), according to Schleiermacher—*as* a sign oriented toward its meaning only because the "intellectual function" and with it "memory" intervene. With greater force of resistance than any other complex of signs, however, writing opposes the compulsion of reason to idealize its objects, and in some boundary region between an "organic" and an "intellectual function," it must remain, in a strange chiaroscuro, a scandal for every hermeneutic effort (459–60, 465).

Although *literary* hermeneutics is a regional one, it can still claim a special status within the sphere of a general and fundamental hermeneutics on the basis of its specific domain—and this would be the second consequence one can draw from the double effect of writing. If, as Schleiermacher indicates, writing functions as a problematic instituting and necessary condition of every system of signs, including the molecular system in which the subject relates to itself, then any hermeneutics concerned with the literal constitution of texts and oriented toward the specific forms of fictionality on which linguistic constructions depend can raise the ironic claim of staking out the foundation for every fundamental hermeneutics and, although still a regional hermeneutics, staking out the field for every general one. Literary hermeneutics would be in an outstanding position to show that writing—or more accurately, scripturality—is the constantly self-decentering structure of every conceivable form of articulation and experience. This claim would be ironic because the activity of such a hermeneutics would undertake the permanent dismantling of the hermeneutic paradigms of (self-) presentation, (self-) objectification, and living discourse—without, however, being able to replace these paradigms with any others. In accordance with Schleiermacher's argument that the experience of a generality can only be acquired through an inconclusive approximation by way of the particular, such a hermeneutics would be the critique of the principal insufficiency of principles and paradigms of understanding. Wherever it has its specific powers in view, a literary hermeneutic linked to Schleiermacher operates on the edge between a regional hermeneutic and a meta-hermeneutics. As it oscillates between the two, it lays bare the general conditions of understanding, on the one hand, and the particular, material, and historical modifications that traverse every pretension to general validity, on the other.

In the course of the transcendental turn that it undertook under Schleiermacher's direction, hermeneutics comes across a structure on which the project of transcendentalism itself breaks down—and this is the third consequence. Hermeneutics poses a question concerning the most general and perpetually valid forms—forms whose rules first made possible the development of every system of signs and every corresponding act of understanding. An answer is found in a medium that connects transhistorical universals with sensible representations—and to this extent takes on the task Kant assigns to transcendental schematism—and yet this medium can carry out the business of mediation only at the cost of a radical historicization and thus only insofar as it breaks its promise of generality. Memory traces and graphic fixations are—always at "once"—the conditions of possibility for a transcendental schematism and conditions of its impossibility. Writing, as organon of transcendence, detranscendentalizes. This does not simply mean that no speaker and no interpreter can be certain of the truth of a given topic of discussion or a given text, since every connection established in transcendental schematism is necessarily marked by the disruptive irregularity of writing; it also means that from the perspective of its dependence on writing, truth itself turns into a finite and transient institution, a conventional realization of certain possibilities of meaning dependent on empirical constellations of power and thus alterable according to its economy.[20] By instituting the "schema of oscillation between general and particular," writing slips away from this and every other dichotomy: the dichotomy of life and death, addition and subtraction, communication and untranslatability, nature and culture, sensibility and intelligibility, inner and outer, truth and fiction, remembering and forgetting, unity and difference. . . . Between the individual terms of an opposition—indeed within each term—writing marks the difference from which each emerges, but it is a difference that at the same time stamps each one with the mark of incompleteness. Writing (de)generates the series of oppositions, including the one between writing and speech. Neither a logic of opposition nor a logic of dialectical opposition, which remains bound to the former in any case, can serve as the plumb line for any hermeneutical operation seeking to account for the differential function of the graphic supplement. Hermeneutics need not orient itself toward the logic of concepts, the derivative character of which Schleiermacher, despite his inclination toward a philosophy of identity, never tired of emphasizing; on the contrary, hermeneutics has to orient itself toward a logic—if this is still a logic—of the linguistic forms that withdraw from the regime of the concept and its inventory of rules. Although methodological reflection on the transcendental conditions of understanding in general is necessary for every interpretative discipline unwilling to succumb to a crude positivism, something else is just as indispensable: a systematic analysis of the genesis as well as the paradoxical function of those conditions. The example of writing offers the opportunity for an abstract sketch of such an analysis. When Schleiermacher proposes the statement "interpretation is an art" (80), he draws a consequence from the relaxation of the transcendental obligations to which hermeneutic theory had been committed until his time, and this statement can serve as a gesture toward the logic that hermeneutics—and especially literary hermeneutics—would have to work out.

"Interpretation is an art" because none of the rules registered by grammar can simultaneously contain the rule for its application in lin-

---

20. With this interpretation we have only drawn out a line whose mathematical equation, so to speak, is contained in Schleiermacher's texts.

guistic *usage*. Neither complete knowledge of the linguistic system nor complete familiarity with the individual ways in which a writer makes combinations is therefore possible. Both could be achieved only on the premise that a transcendental grammar could extend its competence into the finest ramifications of its various actualizations. Understanding must leap into the breach that opens up between linguistic system and linguistic usage, but an understanding on the verge of this leap cannot then follow either a grammatical calculation or a sheerly subjective act of the interpreter; on the contrary, such an understanding must mobilize those moments that were effective in the process of language's emergence and in the process of self-understanding: "The whole business of hermeneutics should be seen as a work of art—not as though the execution resulted in a work of art, but so that the activity itself bears the character of art in itself, because the application is not also given with the rules, i.e. cannot be mechanized" (81). The activity to which Schleiermacher here attributes the character of art—and does so not only in the sense of technique but also in that of artistry—is the same activity at work in every original act of self-understanding. Schleiermacher characterizes this activity as a rhetorical one: "Thinking is made complete by inner discourse, and to this extent, speech is only thought that has come into being. But whenever anyone who is engaged in thinking finds it necessary to fix his thoughts, there arises the art of speaking, transformation of the original thought, and henceforth interpretation also becomes necessary" (76). This "art of speech," or rhetoric, is the form of language through which a thought "fixes" itself in view of its combination with other thoughts, the self-understanding of the one engaged in thought, and its communication to potential interpreters. Both the mnemotechnical function of this fixing and the effect of the alteration of the "original" thought through the medium of rhetorical or grammatical tropes turn rhetoric into a functional equivalent of writing. But rhetoric has something else in common with writing: although introduced for the sake of understanding, it hinders understanding and requires a special theory of art for the clarification of its obscurities, namely hermeneutics. The twistings and turnings to which a literal meaning is exposed through the violence of rhetoric and writing ought then to be straightened out through an inverse movement carried out by the art of understanding—and indeed straightened out in such a way that the specific forms of distortion are taken into consideration as moments of that "literal" meaning. Schleiermacher's conception of the relation between rhetoric and hermeneutics can seek support on this point from the late-classical and Protestant traditions of these disciplines: "The correlation of hermeneutics and rhetoric consists in the fact that every act of understanding is the reversal of an act of speech, for the thought that was at the basis of the spoken discourse must enter into consciousness" (67). If one still takes Schleiermacher's thesis concerning the artistic character of hermeneutics seriously, then one has to conclude that rhetoric not only has its place within the sphere of objects surveyed by hermeneutics but also constitutes an integral component of every hermeneutic operation. Every step in an interpretation corresponds to a rhetorical—or grammatical—figure. And the same can be said of the general rules (or, as Schleiermacher prefers to put it, the bits of advice) hermeneutics gives out. Only by virtue of the close alliance between hermeneutic and rhetorical operations does *literary* hermeneutics legitimate its title: as a theory of the *art* of understanding, a theory that reflects the structure and function of the *scripturality* as well as the *rhetoricity* of its objects and procedures.

V

Schleiermacher does not immediately thematize the rhetoricity of hermeneutical operations. But it emerges from the systematic connection through which and in which these two—rhetoric and hermeneutics—are located. And it comes out of the context of his descriptions, especially when he discusses the most precarious problem of hermeneutic praxis. This problem is nothing less than the principle of the hermeneutical circle: "the whole is understood from the part, just as the part can only be understood from the whole" (329). Now, Schleiermacher seldom fails to mention that this figure—the contours of which are defined by the reciprocal presupposition of the whole and its parts—is only an *apparent* circle in understanding. The emphasis falls on "apparent" not because he finds in this circle an inadmissible mixture of deductive and inductive modes of procedure; on the contrary, knowledge, according to Schleiermacher, has a scientific character only when it is acquired through the synthesis of these two operations. He calls it an "apparent" circle because he starts from the premise that there are two structurally different readings of a work, and the relation between these two readings is not that of circular dependence; for this reason, the circle can never become a vicious one. The task of a "cursory reading" of a given work is to facilitate a rough pre-comprehension of the whole on its grammatical level alone. The point of a second reading is then to grasp, in accordance with this grammatical pre-comprehension, the relation of the parts to the whole, the individual gestures of composition, and the determinate meaning that emerges from the relation of all the details to one another and to the text as a whole. This second reading can be brought to a successful conclusion only on the condition that the divination of a text's own logic of production always accompany the analysis of its compositional techniques.

Just how problematic in principle the assumption of a naive first reading can become—a reading that does not yet proceed synthetically and thus would be completely disinterested in the law of composition—becomes evident in Schleiermacher's advice for the cursory structuring of the grammatical exterior of literary works. This structuring, he informs us, should proceed according to a schema of substitution that allows the reader to formulate an overall notion for a closed sequence of sentences, a notion in which all the elements of this sequence are thought to be contained. Such a substitution takes place in all interconnecting sentences of a text and does so in such a manner that, after having structured the entire text according to the model of substitution, one does not come up with an incoherent series of abstract notions but a genuine whole—a whole like that of a complete sentence. In Schleiermacher's formulation:

> For every articulation of sentences that are joined together with some degree of exactitude . . . there is in some manner . . . a main concept that dominates it or, as we could also put it, is the word for it; and just like an individual word in an individual sentence, this word can receive its fully determined meaning only if it is read in connection with all other, similar words; that is, every articulation of sentences, be it larger or smaller, can be correctly understood only from the whole to which it belongs. (331)

Substituting a main concept for a text segment is one of the two fundamental operations of hermeneutics; together with the second—the combination of the substitutions into a sequence having the form of a sentence—it presents the condition for the construction of the entire text from its parts and the condition for the understanding of each part from the whole. Yet both of these fundamental hermeneutical operations follow from rhetorical models: the substitution is executed according to the pattern of selecting a concept from a given syntagmatic chain, and this substitution then represents a *pars pro toto*, a metonymy that functions as a metaphor; the combination of the individual conceptual paradigms into a new syntagmatic series inverts the first model and may be described economically as the metonymization of metaphorical substitution. The hermeneutic syntagm achieved through both operations then relates to the text it transcribes as a metonymy meant to fulfill the function of metaphor.[21]

The rhetoricity of these fundamental operations of hermeneutics corresponds to the rhetorical procedures that Schleiermacher sees at work in the origin of language. The interpretative reference to texts is not in principle different from linguistic reference to the world of experience. It represents only an elongation of the rhetorical interpretation of the world and the self into the sphere of historical and philological disciplines. At the basis of Schleiermacher's conception of linguistic constitution lies the assumption later developed by Nietzsche that no historically invariant categories prescribe rules for the relation of language to objects; on the contrary, all forms of linguistic articulation—within the bounds set by "the schema of oscillation"—spring from an always individuated intuition and its rhetorical transformation. Only from the standpoint of the "logic of concepts"[22] can it be maintained that the "literal" meaning is also the original one. From the standpoint of a theory of schematism that accentuates individual initiative, it is "folly to posit a literal meaning chronologically before the tropaic one—[as in the case of] white and snow-white."[23] One should proceed in reverse—

---

21. This exercise in structuring is oriented toward Roman Jakobson's model in which two axes of language are singled out; cf. Roman Jakobson, *Poetik, Ausgewählte Aufsätze,* eds. E. Holenstein and T. Schelbert (Frankfurt am Main: Suhrkamp, 1979); *Selected Writings* (The Hague: Mouton, 1961–), vol. 3 ("Poetry of Grammar and Grammar of Poetry").

22. Schleiermacher, *Hermeneutik,* ed. Kimmerle, 58; *Hermeneutics: The Handwritten Manuscripts,* trans. James Duke and Jack Forstmann (Missoula, Mont.: Scholars Press, 1977), 71.

23. *Hermeneutik,* 35; *Hermeneutics,* 72.

from the assumption that "the tropaic meaning is dissolved into the literal one,"[24] and that the origin of the literal meaning in the rhetorical transformation of intuitions is simply forgotten in the language of concepts. The examples of such transformations Schleiermacher discusses in the drafts for his hermeneutics are metaphor and metonymy. On the theme of the emergence of language he notices "that we regard a particular case as the entire range of the original meaning only because it is the usual one. This is often the case with metaphor and everywhere with metagony,[25] e. g. a) movement and shape are identical for language where it can pursue the shape genetically: *planto, serpens.*"[26] As in the case of *serpens,* which designates self-entanglement, a movement is substituted for the shape; a dominant trait is projected from the syntagmatic axis of combination onto the paradigmatic axis of resemblance and functions there as a "representative" of the entire shape. Nothing changes in Schleiermacher's second example: "That the content of intuition is limited to a specific sphere already given by the context. Aspects of the speech act falling under the formula *continuo pro contento . . .* belong here. The sphere in which the connection of the *continuo* with the *contento* falls is already given, and the whole is only to be regarded as an ellipsis of whatever in the part is already presupposed as known in the whole."[27] In the case of this metonymy as well, a part is selected from the whole and used in the "speech act" as its index.

All the figures that constitute language and all the figures that proceed according to the model of selection and distribution receive their meaning at the cost of an eclipse: at least one element may be given in the immediate context—although there, too, only problematically—but in the further course of the linguistic tradition, as Schleiermacher emphasizes, it is eclipsed, falls prey to forgetting, and can no longer be actual-

24. *Hermeneutik,* 39; *Hermeneutics,* 76.

25. A photocopy of Schleiermacher's manuscript convinces me that everywhere Kimmerle reads "Metagonie," one should read "Metonymie."

26. *Hermeneutik,* 58; *Hermeneutics,* 72. In his treatise "On Truth and Lying in an Extra-Moral Sense," Nietzsche refers to the same figure and the same example to show the rhetorical character of language: "We speak of a 'snake': the designation concerns nothing but self-winding and could therefore also apply to a worm" (Nietzsche, *Werke,* ed. K. Schlechta [Munich: Hanser, 1954], 3: 312). Nietzsche radicalizes the consequences drawn from his observation to the point of ironically relinquishing the very concept of truth.

27. *Hermeneutik,* 58–59; *Hermeneutics,* 72 (in context).

ized. The ellipsis provokes the loss of at least one element in a given chain of signifiers, thus allowing a particular verbal representation gained in this process to combine with other verbal representations; the result of all these combinations would then be a total conception. Ellipsis thus lies at the root of the two rhetorical-grammatical figures that are the foundation of language in the first place, and so it lies at the root of the fundamental operations of hermeneutics. Ellipsis is the rhetorical equivalent of writing: it depletes, or de-completes, the whole so as to make conceptual totalities possible. And yet every conceivable whole achieved on the basis of ellipsis is stamped with the mark of the original loss.[28] Like writing, it withdraws from the alternatives of presence and absence, whole and part, proper and foreign, because only on its ever eroding foundation can conceptual oppositions develop: it withdraws from its own concept. Ellipsis eclipses (itself). It is the "figure" of figuration: the area no figure contains.

The ellipsis that prescribes a course for the two fundamental rhetorical-hermeneutic operations of substitution and combination de(com)pletes any totality that could be constructed with the help of these same operations. But the "principle" of the hermeneutic circle proves to be fractured not only at its rhetorical foundation; fractures appear in every interpretative practice grounded in it. While attempting to give a plausible account of the hermeneutic demand that any explanation of a part must emerge from a consideration of the whole, Schleiermacher can outmaneuver his own problematic only with great difficulty: "And just as everything small is conditioned by something large, which is in turn something small, so it follows that the part can be perfectly understood only through the whole" (331). Progressing from a small part to a momentarily larger one, the hermeneutic operation grasps the word in the sentence, the sentence in the discourse, the discourse in the genre, the genre in its history and in the history of other literary productions, literary history in the context of social history, both in relation to the interpreter and his "cognitive community". . . . And in this way, in increasingly wider contexts, the strict relation of what is for

28. To assess more precisely the extent and intention of this essay, it would be necessary to undertake a more exact presentation of Schleiermacher's concept of the sentence and especially an analysis of his "dynamic" concept of the copula; even this element of the sentence, a combinatory one in the strict sense, can be understood as an ellipsis; see *Hermeneutik*, 41–44; *Hermeneutik und Kritik*, 120–23.

a time relatively whole to its constitutive parts dissolves; but it was precisely this relation, constructed in all its concreteness, that was supposed to be the central concern of interpretation. As the progressive dilutions of the bond between the parts and the whole give way to ever greater unities, only one thing makes itself known—the consequence of loosening the connection between the parts of a text and the larger organizational schemas: "for the explanation depends only on the clear view that this part of a text is really a whole in relation to the word that lies before the reader. . . . To the extent that this is not ascertained, however, the application also becomes uncertain" (329–330). Neither the application of the hermeneutic principle nor this fundamental principle itself can be secured, since the mutual interconnection of each element with every other—the interconnectiveness that first make them into a common whole—can be shown only by comparing these various elements, and yet the result of this comparison needs to be legitimated by further attempts at comparison. The "comparative procedure" (325, 341) Schleiermacher introduces in support of the grammatical one leads to an infinite regress, and this regress is as incapable of restoring the originally eclipsed textual elements as of constructing the totality. Yet without this totality it is impossible to understand with any degree of certainty a part as a part of a specific whole or to understand the whole from its specific parts.

Since the grammatical procedure of hermeneutics transgresses the syntagmatic linkages it first produces—linkages made up of main concepts serving as substitutes—and since it must continually do so if the ideal of perfect understanding is to be approached, it is clear that both the category of substitution and the category of syntagm are incapable of giving adequate contours to the relation between the whole and its parts, the general and the particular. The category of substitution cannot serve that function because every substitution is based on an abstraction that has to prove itself in connection with other substitutes for textual segments; the category of syntagm cannot do it because every sentence-like connection has to legitimate itself through its connection to every other. And the reason for this duel incapacity is also clear: it lies in the two ellipses that condition these categories. The hermeneutic operation thus succumbs to a movement of displacement that is in principle impossible to stop, for it can check itself only with reference to a provisionally final term. This movement traverses the two most important operations of hermeneutics, selection and combination, the corresponding concepts of part and whole, and so the very ideal of an adequate representation of a text in its interpretation. There is no last court of appeal before which the partiality of the part and the totality of the whole could prove themselves, for this court itself would then be in want of—and at the limit be incapable of—legitimation. The part is never demonstrably part of *its* whole, the whole never the whole of *its* parts. The hermeneutic circle thus opens up and makes every closure into a hermeneutic fiction—a heuristically useful fiction, no doubt, a fiction capable of economizing on a deficit in understanding, but a fiction that can neither accommodate itself to the ideal of perfect understanding nor redress the loss, constitutive of language and understanding, which the ellipses themselves introject. Understanding cannot keep itself within a circular economy whose limits are defined by the whole, for this whole is the result of rhetorical-grammatical tropes and is, for this reason, a subcode of a language-game that is itself incapable of codification. The tropes imprint it with the mark of a linguistic difference that no epistemological exertions, however strenuous, are able to fill out or even control. Every hermeneutical operation proliferates ellipses, multiplies its expenditure in the production of meaning, and accelerates its fragmentation in the production of totalities.

Schleiermacher could not hide from himself the principal deficiency of the grammatical procedure in interpretation. The opening in the hermeneutic circle designates for him the gap in the repertoire of syntactic-semantic rules stored in a "linguistic system." The provenance of these rules is seen as the free initiative of speaking subjects, and the rules, for their part, keep a space open not only for linguistic innovations but for individual hermeneutic acts of divination. "A perfect knowledge of a language" is as impossible to attain through the grammatical procedure of hermeneutics as is "a perfect knowledge of human beings" (81) through its technical and psychological procedures. And yet, according to Schleiermacher's presentation, it is reserved for the latter to fill up the gaps in the stock of positive knowledge by means of an ungovernable divination on which meaning is founded, however revocable each effort at filling up gaps may be. Divination is the method that poses questions to the grammatical procedure of comparison and thereby condemns this procedure to inconclusiveness; yet at the same time it is supposed to be the operation that solves the puzzle of the phenomenon of the new—the phenomenon most in need of understanding:

> For what are we to do whenever we come across a passage where an ingenious author first brings to light a phrase, a constellation in the language? There is no other procedure here than in a divinatory manner to take our point of departure from the state of mind that gripped the author and then to ascertain how the needs of the moment could have affected the linguistic thesaurus that hovered in all its liveliness before his mind—to imitate the creative act. And here, again, there will be no certainty without the application of a comparative procedure on the psychological side. (325)

Even the divinatory mimesis of the logic according to which a text is produced—a mimesis that amounts to another form of substitution—is not sufficient to secure an interpretation of a linguistic usage that has not yet been registered into the linguistic system. The advice offered by Schleiermacher—that divinatory and grammatical-comparative procedures should supplement each another so that "the procedure of interpretation appropriate to the art might reach its final goal" (326)—disregards the fact that even the connection of both procedures is incapable of "perfect knowledge" of their respective objects. The divinatory substitution of the productivity of the interpreter for that of the object under interpretation, which is the most seductive and least mediated substitution that Schleiermacher includes in his catalogue of hermeneutical operations, doubtless rests on grammatical comparison and must rest there if divinatory substitution is going to proceed with the secure knowledge that it is the substitution of precisely *this* object of interpretation; but grammatical comparison, as a mechanical calculation, is in no position to account for the *novum* in linguistic usage and cannot therefore help a divinatory metaphor attain any degree of certainty or completeness. The category of the new, which Schleiermacher emphasized like no other, is a scandal to understanding—like writing and like ellipsis. Nor is divination immune from the impertinence of the new, for, like the first, "cursory" reading, the second reading, which is the only one concerned with the irreducibly individual moments of a composition, refers to conflicting rhetorical figures. This conflict among figures bars interpretation from ever attaining completeness and certainty.

Schleiermacher tried to accommodate the inconsistency of the hermeneutic "principle" by correcting the thesis of the circle, which aims for absolute synthesis, with the thesis of hermeneutic approximation. Understanding executes its task—and does so not only in the comparative procedures about which Schleiermacher is quite explicit—in such a manner that "we always bring some related, already understood part closer to something that is not yet understood, and we thus enclose noncomprehension within ever narrower boundaries" (324). Whatever is "still" foreign and new should be joined with the something "already" understood with the following result: in everything that has been understood, the motivating forces behind whatever remains uncomprehended (and indeed is the reason for its incomprehensibility) come into view. The hermeneutics of approximation not only offers "to find out the concealed addition of, as it were, lost suggestions" (317), but also seeks to understand the concealed *as* concealed, the foreign *as* foreign: the other as other. Its result, in turn, can only be ambiguous.

Because the "appropriation" (320) of the other that divination accomplishes under the sign of substitution not only falsifies this other by making it identical with itself but betrays the "untranslatability" of individual productions to the general system of language by seeking a translation, divination necessarily fails. And the hermeneutics of approximation draws the following consequence from this failure: whenever the other is interpreted, it can be maintained and "given back" (466) *as* other only when it is overlooked as *other*. If the other were to remain purely outside of the regulatory system of grammatical operations, it would be absolutely unrecognizable and could hardly be understood as their modification; but if it were to be translated into an already established register of linguistic usages, it would abandon its untranslatable alterity and would thus cease to be understood as a modification of this register. The foreign can be understood *as* other only if it is overlooked as *other*; it becomes comprehensible as *other* only if it is not comprehended *as* other. It is necessarily understood as other only if it is understood otherwise than it is and when the rules of understanding concerning its otherness themselves alter. The foreign, the other, slips away from any understanding that proceeds not only according to the oppositional logic established by the terms "alterity" and "identity" but also according to the very rhetoric of substitution and combination. The foreign, the other, is only accessible to a process of interpretation that itself incites active interpretation and, activated in this way, never ceases to alter the other and, beyond this, to alter in always unprogrammable ways the rules of understanding.

The hermeneutics of approximation paradoxically follows the logic of distancing or de-stance, the logic of *Ent-fernung:* with every movement toward the other, the other retreats farther, and every step that leads away from the other draws it nearer. In order to proceed in a non-reductive manner, hermeneutics must resist the temptation to dissolve the other into the same; in order to proceed in a non-mystical manner, hermeneutics must refuse to hypostatize the other into the altogether Other, into a theological *negativum.* Between these two forms of reduction, in the interval between the same of the other and the other of the same, a certain kind of understanding operates: an understanding that mobilizes dissent in the very production of consent, that alters with every iteration, that can stand to withstand understanding, that allows for *Verstellen* (dissemblance) in *Verstehen* (understanding)—and that reads a hermetics of the new in herm*en*utics itself. This hermeneutics sides with the doctrine that correct understanding is the agent of incomprehensibility. Friedrich Schlegel, who was a friend of Schleiermacher's, wrote the ironic laudatory address to such incomprehensibility. Only in this way does hermeneutics accommodate itself to the fact that "nonunderstanding will never entirely dissipate" (328); but hermeneutics can do this only at the cost of acknowledging its inability to ground and justify its basic operations. It is no longer a theory of art concerned with an understanding that is not immediately comprehensible to itself and becomes an understanding that, at the limit, does not itself understand.

Schleiermacher is not the "veil-maker"—the *Schleiermacher*—whom Nietzsche, his most important successor in the theory of interpretation, once attacked.[29] His attempt to formulate the conditions and rules of understanding is one of the few that energetically criticizes and successfully avoids both unreflective grammaticism and the synthesism of speculative dialectics. At a time when the framework for hermeneutic inquiry is nearly exhausted by the narrow-minded alternatives of scien-

---

29. Nietzsche, *Werke,* 2: 1149; cf. *On the Genealogy of Morals—Ecce Homo,* trans. and ed. Walter Kaufmann (New York: Vintage, 1969), 321.

tistic formalism and journalistic semanticism, Schleiermacher's hermeneutics gives lessons on how to take leave from both. That this hermeneutics needs a critical para-theory to discuss the effects of the scripturality and the rhetoricity not only of its objects but also its own efforts
at understanding follows from Schleiermacher's insights. Critique and
supplementation are functions of elliptical paraphrase in which every
understanding of an object and every self-understanding gives up something in order "to give" it—itself—"back"—otherwise.

THE PROMISE OF INTERPRETATION

Remarks on the Hermeneutic Imperative in Kant and Nietzsche

If by the end of the eighteenth century nearly everything pertaining to the process of understanding and the constitution of its objects became problematic for hermeneutics, the theoreticians of this discipline would nevertheless speak of one issue so fleetingly that it seemed as though they feared that discussing it would topple its very premises, and yet this issue had to be understood before all else: the demand that understanding must take place; the imperative of understanding itself, the obligation to perceive, hear, and understand every message *as* a communication even before its content has been communicated. If the hermeneutic operation occupies the place where understanding, to use Schleiermacher's words, can no longer "go without saying," then the question arises whether all understanding does not hold its breath in the face of that which—as a linguistic fact or a fact mediated by language—withdraws from immediate understanding, from self-evident comprehension, and in the end from understanding as such. If hermeneutics is, as Schleiermacher elsewhere defines it, "the art of correctly understanding another's discourse, especially a written one,"[1] and if correct understanding entirely grasps the discourse of another in its individual-

---

1. The definition of the "scientific concept" of hermeneutics as the "art of correctly understanding another's discourse" can be found in the companion notebooks to Schleiermacher's lectures on hermeneutics of 1826, here cited according to F. D. E. Schleiermacher, *Hermeneutik und Kritik,* ed. Manfred Frank (Frankfurt am Main: Suhrkamp, 1977), 75. Schleiermacher speaks of an understanding that "goes without saying" *(sich von selbst versteht)* in his treatise "Über den Begriff der Hermeneutik mit Bezug auf F. A. Wolfs Andeutungen und Asts Lehrbuch" *(Hermeneutik und Kritik,* 333).

ity, then hermeneutics lives off the failure of its own project: "for every [soul] in its particular existence is the non-existence of the other, and so non-understanding will never be entirely done away with."[2] The boundary by which every individuality is separated from every other is at the same time the limit to understanding—not only a limitation on things that are "obvious" and "go without saying" or on understanding in general, but, in addition, a limit on the effort to come to an understanding about the matter of understanding itself. As long as the "individual being" of "the other's discourse" is not understood—and, according to Schleiermacher, it is never "entirely" understood—understanding itself is not understood, for understanding, by definition, could be understood only when non-understanding is "entirely" done away with. This fundamental dilemma of understanding—it already has to be what it is not yet and will never be "entirely"—has a single yet problematic solution: the lack of understanding must also be understood as a demand and, therefore, as a stimulus to understanding.

Schleiermacher's attempt to give a methodological justification for hermeneutic operations solves the problem of the necessity of understanding in the form of a paradox: from the very point where there can be no understanding arises the obligation to understand. The paradox is unavoidable within the framework of Schleiermacher's basic conception of hermeneutics. It states that all understanding plays itself out within the dynamic polarity between general rules of language and individual acts of linguistic creativity. Only the rules can be considered to have been understood, whereas the particular linguistic utterances from which these rules were drawn are genuine acts, the very generation of language, and thus can never be entirely reduced to rules; as a result, they must remain inaccessible to a mechanical understanding garnered from linguistic conventions. "Another's discourse," if it is to be understood as precisely the discourse of *this* other, cannot be disclosed by the application of a universal norm, a common precomprehension, or only a common interest. Schleiermacher tried to settle the conflict between comprehensive knowledge according to generally valid laws of language and the demands of individual and, in particular, of artistic performance in language through recourse to the ancient conception of *divinatio*. In divination, interpretation is not located on the side of an already constituted linguistic system, nor on the side of its individual alterations,

2. Schleiermacher, *Hermeneutik und Kritik*, 328.

but between the two—at the point where they diverge. As an agent of "another's discourse," divination continues the process of individualization introduced by this discourse, testing, as it were, the system of conventions and thereby trying to transform the singularity of the other's discourse into general rules and likewise to transform these rules into their singular alterations. The vanishing point of this divinatory movement of mediation—a movement that cannot be controlled by any technique because it starts up at the point where all techniques fail—is the precise instant when, at the end of history, "another's discourse," free of compulsion, makes the transition into the discourse of the first one. The interpreter is never in a position to bring this instant about. Still, it must be thought, and this task makes hermeneutics into an aporetics.

If understanding is not to harden into a mechanism of identifications and projections, it must allow itself to be moved by what escapes identity and withdraws from assimilation. "Another's discourse" can be understood only in an interpretation that makes room for its alterity in the very act of understanding: room for silence, interruption, and methodic self-criticism; room for the infinite capacity of interpretation to be revised and thus the impossibility that interpretation will ever be saturated. In all these forms—in the development and application of which the early romantics showed a still unmatched resourcefulness—understanding points toward another understanding, one that would be more adequate to "another's discourse." Understanding thus offers itself as the infinite, historical approximation to a text it itself cannot reach if this text is to preserve its absolute singularity. But the approximation can be historical only because it is at first semiotic: an interpretation already points toward its own inability to present the other and thus evokes *ex negativo* the possibility of a proximity to "the other's discourse," a nearness that transcends the merely formal commonality of a general rule of substitution. This *pointing* whereby an understanding refers to another understanding that would alone be the understanding of the other is to be understood in effect as a "pointing out," a "pointer," an instruction, an order, indeed as a "hermeneutical imperative"[3] that demands the infinite unification of universal and individual, of the discourse of the

3. This phrase does not come from Schleiermacher but from Friedrich Schlegel, who employed it in 1797 for his notes "Zur Philologie" (Toward Philology). The formulation is concise: "There is a hermeneutic imperative" (*Kritische Friedrich-Schlegel-Ausgabe*, ed. Ernst Behler, Jean-Jacques Anstett, and Hans Eichner [Paderborn: Schöningh, 1958-], 16,1: 69).

one and that of the other. Since, however, there is no understanding without this order, and since there is no language that is not already subject to the demand that it communicate itself and make itself understood, all language must be thought to stand under this hermeneutic imperative and all understanding must be thought as an attempt to correspond with it. This imperative is not actually pronounced in "another's discourse," since it issues the command to listen to this discourse in the first place, nor is it spoken in the discourse of the interpreter, since this discourse only arises in response to the imperative; it arises only in the movement through which every discourse heads for another as the *a priori* altering of itself, this side of universality and individuality, in an interminable process of universalization and individualization.

"Understanding" is thus, as Schleiermacher says, a "task" and indeed an "infinite" one: a task that precedes all positive acts of understanding and is incapable of a conclusive resolution because it seizes hold of finite beings—beings incapable of totality—and makes them place themselves under the form of universality.[4] It is a task that *seizes hold:* a task that arrests the fleeting movements of expression in any regulated language, but does so only by subjecting language to the command of a universality whose actuality is found nowhere else than in this very command. Hermeneutics does not therefore set out to arrive at an adequate description of someone else's already functioning discourse—such would be the object of an epistemology—nor is it concerned with the modalities of aesthetic judgment, which in any case could only refer to given phenomena. The concern of hermeneutics is not even with the structure of a given language but, rather, with a language that gives itself—and gives itself to be understood—as language independently of empirical data and pregiven categorial rules, each time singularly and yet always as a language capable of universalization. Hermeneutics is therefore concerned with the giving of language, not a given language, and with the giving of understanding, not pregiven rules of comprehension. The

4. Schleiermacher uses the Kantian formulation of the "infinite task" in his lectures on hermeneutics: "The task can only be expressed in this way—'first to understand the discourse as well as the author, then to understand it better.' . . . Thus put, the task is an infinite one, because at the moment of discourse we want to see the infinitude of the past as well as the future. This art is therefore just as capable of enthusiasm as any other" (*Hermeneutik und Kritik,* 94). Such "enthusiasm"—or divination—emerges at precisely those places where understanding becomes aware of its own finitude and simultaneously sees itself thrown beyond the limits of objective reconstruction.

concern of hermeneutics is, in short, an autonomous legislation of practical reason as linguistic reason. By using the formula of the "infinite task" of understanding, Schleiermacher alloted a field to hermeneutic reflection that he himself never cultivated but one that nevertheless circumscribes the horizon of his entire work. With this formula, then, he expressed his conviction that the problems of hermeneutics could not be appropriately handled in the domain and with the methods of epistemology, nor in the domain of aesthetics or historiography, but only in the field of ethics: these problems demand, in other words, a critical theory of praxis.

Kant's Imperative

Kant points out the connection between understanding and ethics with even greater energy than Schleiermacher, who was already entrenched in the ontology of mediation developed under the auspices of speculative Idealism. In a short treatise of 1791 entitled "On the Failure of All Philosophical Attempts at Theodicy," Kant proceeds from the assumption that "the world, as God's work," could be viewed as a "divine announcement of the intentions of his will" for which there was only a single "authentic interpretation."[5] This interpretation is undertaken by practical reason, which is itself legislative and which, prior to all experi-

5. Immanuel Kant, *Gesammelte Schriften,* ed. Königliche Preussische [later, Deutsche] Akademie der Wissenschaften (Berlin and Leipzig: Georg Reimer, later, Walter de Gruyter, 1900–); 8: 264; hereafter, "Ak." All citations of Kant's texts will refer to the Akademie edition with one exception: references to the *Critique of Pure Reason,* according to scholarly tradition, will refer to the pagination of its original editions (A, B). Reliable English translations of Kant generally incorporate references to the Akademie edition in the margins. An English translation of this essay, unfortunately without Akademie-edition pagination, can be found in Michael Despland, *Kant on History and Religion* (Montreal: McGill-Queen's University Press, 1973), 281–297.

The passage from Kant's essay on theodicy quoted above corresponds to certain remarks he makes in § 42 of the *Critique of Judgment:* "One will say that these interpretations of aesthetic judgments in view of their affinity with moral feeling look too studied for them to contain the true interpretation of the cypher-writing through which nature speaks to us figurally in its beautiful forms" (Ak, 5: 301). These remarks correspond even more accurately to the passage from the essay on theodicy in Hölderlin's paraphrase, which can be found in the motto to the second version of his poem, "Hymn to Beauty": "Nature speaks to us figurally in its beautiful forms, and moral feeling has lent us the talent for interpreting its cypher-writing" (Friedrich Hölderlin, *Sämtliche Werke,* ed. F. Beißner [Stuttgart: Cotta, 1943–1985], 1: 152).

ence, postulates the concept of God as the author of the announcement. This interpretation of the divine will by a "power-wielding practical reason" can be called "authentic" only because this reason is itself "the immediate declaration and voice of God" and because God's will, in turn, interprets itself by means of a mediator, namely practical reason. Since, however, the concept of God can be developed in full only when the moral law is already effective, "authentic interpretation" defines itself as the self-interpretation not of the divine will—this can only be postulated—but of finite reason and, furthermore, as the self-interpretation of a purely rational law. Understanding Kant's remarks on "authentic interpretation" thus depends on a prior understanding of what authenticity—hence *autos,* self, and law—means in the context of his philosophy of praxis.

Interpretation, insofar as it deserves to be called authentic, does not expound an already given text but is itself the attestation, proclamation, and communication of this text. Because the only place for the proclamation of the law is in its interpretation and because this interpretation is the only place where the law is *given,* it is authentic: it is the interpretation the law *itself* gives of itself. The peculiar self-relation in which, for Kant, the tension between text and interpretation and thus the entire problem of hermeneutics is recapitulated seems to erase the singularity and alterity of "another's discourse," whereas it is singularity and alterity that make interpretation necessary and set hermeneutic reflection into motion in the first place. But Kant makes a point of not erasing this alterity; rather, he shifts it into the self-relation of the law. If the law can experience itself only in its interpretation, then this experience can take place only in its singular announcement and thus only in its alterity. It is a law only insofar as it can experience itself as another, as another self, as the other itself. The same goes for the reverse proposition: if interpretation is the experience of the law and thus the experience of the law of interpretation, it is interpretation only insofar as it is the experience of another, the experience of itself as another and, therefore, the experience of a certain inadequacy with respect to the law. Both the law and interpretation are themselves—and the same—only when they are exposed to the alteration that plays itself out between and within them: an alteration that does not consist in mere change but in becoming another, being otherwise.

Because the law of reason—the moral law—can do no more than

demand prescriptively the reality for which it vouches, it is sharply distinguished from empirical norms, physical rules, and conventions of behavior, all of which can be the objects of constative statements. Drawing on an equivocation in the concept of *law,* Kant maintains that the law in the form of an *imperative* commands an action through which it ought to appear as though it were a physical *rule.* The law commands that it ought to be the actual norm of action. The law demands the law. And indeed it does not exhibit its demand as an agent of another power, in view of a higher law or already determined ends, for this higher power—and not the law—would then be the law. The law makes its demands without presuppositions, unconditionally, only from itself and in view of itself. The law alone demands the law. This not only means that the law is essentially alone, and alone with its demand to be alone; it also means that in every matter where demands can be raised, these demands must at first be raised from the law *itself* and at first addressed to the law *itself.* The faculty of raising demands is called the will, and it is a faculty to which Kant, following a long philosophical tradition, accords a certain privilege. The unprecedented, absolutely fundamental—fundamental because self-grounding—law must be a will that demands itself, wills itself, and wills itself only for the sake of itself: such is the law of the will, its principle, its essence, itself; it is, in other words, practical reason. Before there can be any talk of a particular purpose in volition or an occasion for voluntary action, there must already be this will, and the character of this will—the will itself—must lie in a striving or a demand that is itself only by having itself as its sole end and sole ground: in a demand, therefore, that determines itself as itself and is thus autonomous. If the will were not its own law, it would not be a will. Self-determination, however, is its own law not just in the sense that determination is its structure but likewise in the sense that in its autonomy the will performs its own universalization. By determining itself, the will—it alone—conjoins itself with itself, forms in an *a priori* synthesis a community that not only precedes every association of individual wills but in the constitution of the will gives each association its possibility and its criteria. The will is, therefore, universal in itself. The internal universality of the will to will—and nothing else—is its autonomy: in this universality it demands itself as the law.

The autonomy of the will, its freedom to determine itself in its absolute singularity as a universality, has no positive reality but only the imposing reality of a demand, the reality of a will *to* will. This is the decisive point. The will does not determine itself; it determines itself for self-determination. It is not autonomous; it imposes on itself the demand for autonomy. It is not already the subject of its actions; it demands of itself that it be the subject. Unlike the will in Hegel's system of speculative idealism, the will in Kant does not transcend the limits of finite reason but *is* finite reason insofar as it is the *demand* for reason. It is not the autonomous will that decrees the law but the will in view of its autonomy, and the law it decrees only demands the law. It is therefore the law of the law—a law that it is not yet the law commanded in this law, a law that it is not yet, and never will be, the law *itself,* and a law that there is such a law, the law itself, only insofar as it is yet another one. "The law demands the law" thus means: the law demands itself as *another* law; it refuses and conceals itself as another and is *itself* only insofar as it is the law of the *otherness* of the law—the law of the absolute singularity of the law, the law of the incommensurability, non-fulfillment, and finitude of the law. It is autonomous only insofar as it is still autonomous with respect to autonomy, insofar as it demands autonomy and infinitely demands only this. It is the law of freedom insofar as it is still free from freedom: it makes freedom possible, and it can be saturated by no positive reality.

Since the law has no positive, institutional or, as Kant say, "statutory" reality and is only a demand for a positive rule and therefore a law of an unfulfilled and unfulfillable law, it can express itself only as an "absolute command," as a "principle" according to which actions "ought to be done," and as a categorical imperative that immediately claims its own lawfulness. "There is only one categorical imperative, and it is this: act only according to the maxim by which you can at the same time will that it should become a universal law."[6] But this absolute principle of practical reason implies something else: since you ought to act according to the maxims of the lawfulness of your will, you do not in fact do so, and you cannot yet act in this way as long as this imperative must still command you. The imperative is always an imperative of *finite* practical

6. This formulation of the categorical imperative and the characterization of the law as a "principle" according to which actions ought to be done—"that is, an imperative"—can be found in the *Groundwork for the Metaphysics of Morals* (Ak, 4: 421). In the same place he speaks of an "absolute command" (Ak, 4: 420). Kant discusses "statutory" laws in *Religion Within the Limits of Reason Alone* (Ak, 7: 102–109).

reason and thus of an incomplete will, a will that does not freely dispose over itself and does not autonomously regulate itself. And this also applies to "authentic interpretation" or the self-interpretation of the law: it is not formulated by an autonomous subject but assumes a form in view of autonomous subjectivity; it does not contain an assertion about a positive state of affairs but an injunction for a mode of acting that could satisfy the form of the law. "Authentic interpretation" makes a demand—it is imperative—on every text, whether this text be nature or the world, and the demand is: act in language, or in speech, so that there could be a homogeneous continuum of understanding, comprehension, and agreement—and thus a universal language. It demands that an interpretation should be possible. Since, however, it is merely the imperative of this interpretation, it also contains the following concession: such an interpretation has not yet come into being, and under the conditions of finitude it never can and never will. It is an interpretation on the way to itself, to its own law, and as a finite interpretation, it is at the same time the block that keeps this law at a distance, keeps itself as law at a distance—is its own de-stancing, its own undoing of stances and distances, its own *Ent-fernung*.

The preceding remarks should have made clear that Kant's episodic comments on "authentic interpretation" contain in miniature a transcendental hermeneutics. Such a hermeneutics is concerned neither with the application of a given method of interpretation to a given text, nor with the exposition of certain technical procedures that would do justice to "another's discourse," nor even with bridging the historical or structural distance that separates an interpreter from whatever text is to be interpreted. Rather, the concern of this transcendental hermeneutics is exclusively with interpretation *itself*, with the law of interpretation, and therefore with the demand that there be a law of action, the law of self-determination (and thus autonomy), and also precisely this law of interpretation. Interpretation, which is always a matter of a relation, must be determined as such; as interpretation, however, it can be determined only if it corresponds to its own law: this law lays down the condition of possibility for interpretation in general. But—and this is the decisive Kantian discovery, the discovery of finitude—a law is not only the essence and ground of a thing but is just as much the demand for this thing, an imperative. If interpretation is founded on its law, it is founded on a transcendental imperative that only makes one demand:

it ought to be an interpretation. But this imperative cannot secure that any interpretation is in fact—or ever will be—an interpretation, and so this imperative becomes the index of the impossibility that interpretation is ever itself. As long as interpretation must be commanded, there is no interpretation. The transcendental law of interpretation thus dictates that there ought to be an interpretation, but it also stipulates that there neither is nor can be interpretation. It is the law of interpretation as an autonomous act, an act that must have its condition in itself, and it is at the same time a law that there is no autonomous interpretation precisely because its "ought" is not a sufficient reason for its "being." By demanding the law, the law forbids the law. By dictating a non-existent rule as an imperative, the law marks an unlawfulness inherent to the law itself: because it is a law it is also its counter-law, the law-without-law, the law of the finitude of all laws. And this law is not only the law of the will and its actions but also the law of interpretation. Kant's transcendental justification for the possibility of interpretation discloses in the imperative structure of the law the basis for the impossibility—the abyss—of interpretation. It is a theory of finitude, a theory of the transcendental uncertifiability of understanding. It could draw its title from Kant's short treatise on theodicy and call itself "On the Failure of All Philosophical Attempts at Hermeneutics." But it would be a misunderstanding to see in this a naive attempt to destroy hermeneutics. Rather, the double structure of the law—command and rule, the command that there be a rule, hence unregulated command and law without law—this bi-struction or di-struction of the law is precisely what Kant discloses as the sole possibility of an understanding that does not depend on alien premises, nor on the presupposition of a given structure of comprehension, but constructs itself alone and is therefore the only structure that can be called "understanding," "interpretation," or "exegesis."[7] Because

7. The discussion of the bi-struction and di-struction of the law—this doubling of its structure or its internal deviation—recalls a passage in the *Groundwork for the Metaphysics of Morals* where Kant expressly characterizes the "prescription of the will" as a "paradox": "And here lies precisely the paradox: that the mere dignity of humanity as rational nature without any end or advantage to be gained by such dignity, and thus respect for a mere Idea, should nevertheless serve as the inflexible prescription of the will, and that the sublimity of the maxims consists precisely in their independence from all such motivating drives" (Ak, 4: 439). The paradox, in short, is that independence from prescriptions ought to be a prescription, independence from a precept a precept, and independence

of the finitude and freedom of interpretation, it is always still outstanding, and it can be thought only from the perspective of a hermeneutics of unreadiness, failure, and miscarriage. Only the possible miscarriage of understanding or its simple failure to show up, as a moment of its structure, allows for something like understanding at all.

Only the ex-position of the law in the law, only the interruption and breakdown of the "laying down" that makes up the law give rise to the possibility of interpretation. Such would be a concise formulation of the principle secured by Kant's critique of the pure will. All the features that characterize the concept and experience of interpretation can be read from the structure—or bi-structure—of this pure will. If the law of interpretation is always a double law that forbids what it commands, if the autonomy of interpretation is always an antinomy and therefore an unresolvable paradox, how can one even talk of interpretation and speak of a sense it brings to language? Kant concedes to "authentic interpretation" the capacity "to make sense of the letter of creation." Far from being the result of an exegetical effort to discover or produce the meaning of a text and then to trade this outcome over the counter of knowledge, the sense made of the letter of creation—its significance—lies in the following imperative: in any particular act of understanding conduct yourself according to the universalizability of this very understanding. Interpreting the letter of creation from practical reason does not make sense of this letter in the same way a lexicon secures the significance of a conventionalized sign; interpretation, rather, gives itself to this letter, remains nowhere but in the space of this giving, and gives nothing but the gift of possible meaning—and does not even *give* it, but "is" precisely this giving. Kant characterizes "authentic interpretation" as an interpretation "of power-wielding practical reason, which, insofar as it is absolutely *commanding,* without further grounding in legislation [*Gesetzgeben*], can be seen as the immediate explanation and voice of God through which he makes sense [*einen Sinn giebt*] of the letter of his creation."[8]

---

from laws a law. This paradox corresponds to the "circle" of freedom and autonomy later discussed in the *Groundwork* (see Ak, 4: 450). Kant finds the resolution of both this paradox and this circle in the unity of the pure spontaneity of reason. But one could add that this spontaneity is nothing less than a code name for the paradox of a lawless law, a law that gives itself as the law.

8. Kant, "On the Failure of All Philosophical Attempts at Theodicy" (Ak, 8: 264).

Absolutely commanding, the law gives itself as a ground, gives itself as the letter of creation, and in its command gives this letter "immediate explanation and voice": it gives meaning to—and therefore makes sense of—the letter of creation. But the immediacy of this giving, its unmediated character, turns the letter of the law (of creation) into its meaning, turns the meaning and voice into a mere letter of the law. And because the law and its meaning are nevertheless different, because Kant could not even conduct an inquiry into meaning or pose a problem of hermeneutical theodicy unless the law and interpretation were separated from each other, the meaning and the letter, the law and the interpretation, reside in no other place than in the giving of this law and this interpretation. They do not reside in anything given—whether given in intuition or given as a feature of the categorial endowment of the understanding—but reside solely in the giving of the letter and its meaning. Neither the meaning nor the letter are, for Kant, given facts. Both letter and meaning take place only in the event of their interminable giving, a giving without results. And just as they are never data, they can never be simply received and do not simply belong to receptivity. Even their reception must be retained in this giving if this reception is to be the in-ception of a giving, not of a gift, and the re-ception of a law-giving, not of a law already laid down and firmly established. According to Kant's formulation, reason "commands without further grounding in legislation," and this means: insofar as reason gives and commands itself—which is to say, the law—it has not yet received itself, the law; it has not yet received its own ground and will never do so. The law lies in the giving and the commanding of the law: it is a law of the giving of the law and not a given law, a law laid down—although this is after all what "law" means, "things laid down." The law lies, rather, in its groundless laying down—groundless because ground-giving and ground-laying. If, therefore, Kant speaks of the meaning of the law or the sense of creation, and if creation is still understood in a theo-theseological manner as a positing from pure reason, this meaning is nothing but meaning in the absence of its self-giving; it is nothing but the project of meaning, nothing but giving—not an already received, meaningful gift. The sole "authentic" interpretation is one that appears on the way between reason and itself or, more exactly, nothing but this very movement of reason toward itself, without beginning and without end. Creation and its meaning, the book of nature and its interpretation, are never *natura naturata* but always *natura naturanda* and correspondingly open to the possibility of never becoming, in a strict sense, creation, interpretation, or nature. The last ground of interpretation and meaning, which, for Kant, would have to be a self-giving ground, is *der aufgegebene Grund* in every sense: the ground that gives up; the ground as a task given out; the basis that is never given and therefore the abyss; the grounds one has to give, the commanded ground, and so the never completed, always outstanding ground. The skeptical question addressed to Kantian transcendentalism in hermeneutics would be: under the conditions of the imperative to understand, what gives the possibility of meaning? And the answer would be the law of law-giving; or the law of legislation gives this possibility, but the actuality of meaning is itself never given. There is a possibility of meaning only on the horizon of its impossible actualization: this, and nothing else, constitutes the finitude of meaning. If Kant's nature is *natura naturanda* — nature only in view of a still outstanding nature — then the "authentic interpretation" of which he speaks is always only an *interpretatio interpretanda,* an interpretation only in view of a still outstanding interpretation: an interpretation out of the difference to itself, out of its "own" inter-.

The project of practical reason — the project in which reason grounds itself and thereby grounds a homogeneous, universal interpretation — must remain a project, and thus groundless, as long as its legislation, its law-giving, has not yet turned into the gift of reason and its command is not automatically fulfilled. Kant tries to bridge the gulf in practical reason — the gulf in the will itself — by introducing the Idea of the "pure spontaneity" of reason.[9] Yet the Idea of spontaneity is, in turn, nothing but a law stipulating that there ought to be a law. Not only is this Idea not already the fulfillment of this law, it cannot even represent it as a positive fact. Kant emphasizes in the section devoted to the "Legislation of Pure Reason" in the second *Critique* that the phrase "fact of reason" does not refer to something given but to a sheer giving: "Yet in order to regard this law without any misinterpretation as *given,* one must duly note that it is not an empirical fact but the sole fact of pure reason, which thereby proclaims itself as originally legislative *(sic volo, sic iubeo)*."[10] The only thing "given" is a giving, a *Gesetz-geben,* a legis-lating. And since

9. See Kant, *Groundwork for the Metaphysics of Morals* (Ak, 4: 452).
10. Kant, *Critique of Practical Reason* (Ak, 5: 31). Kant underlines "given."

only a giving and not something given *announces* itself in the fact of reason, it is also—and here Kant again and again uses the word "break"—a taking and a taking-away of all positive facticity available to empirical consciousness.[11] The law of the will does not even assume a positive shape in the form of a rational Idea toward which finite action could orient itself. For the law does not exhibit itself as a command but rather commands that a command is to be assumed: it is the command of a command, which can never be represented as such and escapes every effort to make it into the object of a constative sentence. The thought of a possible universal legislation is doubtless *apodictic* insofar as it commands unconditionally; but this thought is nevertheless *problematic* to the degree that it concerns a mere possibility, a possibility incapable of a positive actualization. It is, in short, the thought of the apodictic character of a project to which not a single fact within the horizons of representation can completely correspond.[12]

It would be erroneous to represent the rational law of the will as an Idea or as an Ideal of a future community of the will—the Ideal, for

11. Despite Kant's insistence on a distinction between freedom and the unconditioned practical law, what he says of the former goes for the latter: "we can be neither immediately conscious [of freedom], since our first concept of it is negative, nor can we infer it from experience, since experience lets us know the law of appearances alone and consequently the mechanism of nature, which is the exact opposite of freedom" (*Critique of Practical Reason,* Ak, 5: 29). Knowledge of the practical law is a knowledge of pain, which, in turn, makes us aware of our deviation from the law; it is thus never the positive knowledge of a some object or state of affairs (cf. the chapter of the second *Critique* on the "Motivating Drives of Pure Practical Reason"). One could say that this knowledge is not the knowledge of a *positum* but the apodictic knowledge of a *ponendum.*

12. "The *a priori* thought of the possibility of giving a universal law, which is thus merely *problematic,* is unconditionally commanded as a law without borrowing anything from experience or from any external will" (*Critique of Practical Reason,* Ak, 5: 32; emphasis added). Whereas in the second *Critique* the thought of a purely rational law is characterized as "merely *problematic,*" in the *Groundwork* this thought is distinguished from hypothetical imperatives, which always function as means, and is called an "apodictic" principle (Ak, 4: 415). In the chapter of the *Critique of Pure Reason* devoted to the "Regulative Use of Ideas," Kant contrasts the "apodictic" use of reason with the "problematic" use; the latter is related only to a "projected unity that one must regard not as given but only as a problem" (B 675, A 647)—as a problem, therefore, in the sense of a project, a throwing ahead or a plan. Despite these unmistakable distinctions, there is no contradiction when Kant sometimes characterizes the categorical imperative as apodictic, other times as problematic, meaning hypothetical. The riddle of this double characterization cannot, of course, be solved by interpreting the apodictic character of the

example, of a limitless communicative community—and then to interpret this law as a command to correspond to this Ideal. For the law of the autonomy of the will, the law of the unconditionedness and self-grounding of practical reason, forbids every recourse to a ground that would precede and determine it. Reason cannot base itself on the hope of a coming harmony of languages, because it alone is the unconditioned and thus purely self-relational coming of the law of harmony. If it raised hopes for something else in the future, it would renounce its own capacity for autonomy, become a means in service of an optimistic doctrine of historical progress, and, finally, degrade itself into an instrument in the service of a regime ruled by a tyrannical consensus. The principle of the will cannot be adequately thought as a future fact but only as the advent of the will that announces itself and makes itself known in every *hic et nunc.* This advent of the will—and therefore of language and understanding as well—expresses itself in the apodictic command that every act of the will convene with itself and, by coming together in this way, agree with itself. The command is the sole mode of this convention and advent of the will; it is the will as it comes to itself, to its unity and internal universality with itself. This also means that the law of the advent of the will, as it expresses itself in its imperative, is the law of its non-arrival. There is no will unless it is distinct from the fulfillment of the very acts it wills and remains distinct from its identity with itself. Only because the will does not fulfill the demand for unity and universality at any particular moment and from any particular perspective, can it express itself in the form of a demand. But for this reason it must also express itself in the form of a demand that cannot be fulfilled. Every imperative of the form "Act so that . . ." implies "You cannot act so that. . . ." Practical reason can only be experienced as an incomplete and never to be completed coming to itself, and it is nothing other than this coming that never arrives. The will has its finite autonomy only under

---

imperative as a mere hypothesis but only if the imperative is understood to be problematic in an apodictic manner. That is, the project is an unconditioned one, related to nothing outside itself; it is not even the project of its own unconditionedness but the unconditioned project that offers itself apodictically, the absolute problem, autonomy in projection and as this very projection. If, however, this law is the will, and the will is another name for practical reason itself, then law, will, and reason are nothing but the project in its apodictic character.

the following conditions: that it not be purely itself; that it not be a "holy will," which would already be its own fulfillment;[13] that it not base itself on the presupposition of anything else, which would make it heteronomous, unfree, and thus no will at all; but that it presuppose exclusively itself as its ground. Yet, in pre-supposing itself, the will is its own ever prevented "pre," the ever subtracted "sub" of its presupposition. The will is autonomous; language (along with its understanding) is autonomous only as a relation to its receding "pre"—an absolute project, a positing never brought to a standstill in a perfected position, an ex-position.

In the *Groundwork for the Metaphysics of Morals* Kant clarified the specific form of the self-relation in which the will gives itself its universality by drawing attention to an example that illuminates not only his entire theory of action but also this theory's latent conception of language. Kant often invokes this example because it lets him examine each variation in the formulation of the categorical imperative: it is the example of promising.[14] Promising presents itself as an example of—indeed as a paradigm for—the self-relation of the will, because it is a linguistic act that represents a plan or a rule of the will whose realization is still outstanding but which, as a prescription, binds the will and obligates it to accomplish certain actions in the future.[15] In promising, the will gives itself a law. Even before it promises something to someone

13. Cf. Kant, *Critique of Practical Reason* (Ak, 5: 32).

14. The most detailed inquiries into promising can be found in the *Groundwork for the Metaphysics of Morals* (Ak, 4: 402–403, 419, 429–30).

15. By choosing this paradigm, Kant may have been following the example of Hume, who had carried out a detailed analysis of promising in Book 3, section 5 of *A Treatise of Human Nature* ("Of the Obligation of Promises"). See also Hume's essay "Of the Original Contract," where he refers to Plato's *Crito* as one of the first investigations into the theory of promising. The decisive features of Hume's skeptical-empirical analysis of promising were set in opposition to the expositions of promising among rationalist theoreticians of the State, particularly Hobbes in *De Cive* (especially book 2, sections 5–11) and in *Leviathan* (part 1, chapter 14), but also Locke in *Second Treatise of Government* (e.g., § 117). In all these cases—Hobbes, Locke, Hume—the problem of promising is the problem of an original social contract whose binding power coincides with the free renunciation of natural rights. It is in this social contract that the ground for a general ordering, an alliance, and a law is established. Kant is the first explicitly to pose the question of the self-relation of the law in the act of promising and thereby to turn the empirical problematic of the association of already constituted wills into the transcendental problematic of the constitution of the will itself.

else, a promise promises itself: it promises to be a promise, and insofar as it is, before anything else, such a promise—a promise of itself—it is an utterance of the unconditionedness and autonomy of the will and its language, an utterance of language *tout court*. A promise is in fact more than just another example of the autonomy of practical reason: it is the legislation of linguistic reason itself, a speech act in which language gives itself a law and thus constitutes itself as language in the first place. This act does not have a merely empirical character but is constitutive of every will and every language—a transcendental speech act. Performative acts defined by conventional rules are not therefore under discussion here: rather, the discussion concerns a fundamental linguistic operation. This operation can ground conventional performatives but only in such a way that the language of the promise convenes exclusively with itself as this singularity enters into a minimal social contract with itself, and lends itself consistency and existence. In every promise, the promise makes a promise to itself to be a promise. Only insofar as a promise is an *a priori* autosynthesis and thus autonomous, can it also be the discursive synthesis that binds any given word with a future one, any word with an act, each word and each act with every other. A promise lets the will conclude a contract with itself. If I want to make a promise, if this is my will, I must at the same time will that this promise be valid for me as a law and the rule of this promise be capable of conforming to a universal law. My subjective will must be willing to be universalized in order for it—subjective and isolated as it is—to gain any consistency whatsoever. If my will were not to place itself under a universalizable will, it would have to destroy itself. For, under a universal law to lie or to make mendacious promises, there could be no such thing as promising, neither actual promises nor the concept of the promise as such.[16] A promise is a

16. Kant writes: "I am soon aware that I could indeed will the lie but not a universal law to lie. For according to such a law, there would in fact be no promises at all, because it would be pointless to reveal my will with regard to my future actions to those who do not believe my words or, if they overhastily did so, would pay me back in my own coin; the result of all this would be that my will, as soon as it was made into a universal law, must destroy itself" (*Groundwork,* Ak, 4: 403). Kant's assumption that it would be possible to will a lie or a mendacious promise involves a certain inconsistency, since every will, to be itself, must will itself and therefore must will its universalizability. A will is a will only under the maxim that brings it into law and, hence, into the good. The will to lie must immediately *destroy itself* and must even destroy the possibility of willing. This, however, is precisely what Kant means by "radical evil"—a will that destroys not only its own existence but the very possibility of its existence.

promise only insofar as it gives itself the law and gives itself *as* the law—insofar as it gives itself a ground and gives itself *as* the constant ground. By thus giving itself a law and ground, it is a transcendental speech act, a speech act that grounds a universal law of language and speaking. Only the individual will that posits itself as its own presupposition and thereby turns into its own ground can be a will that indeed *wills* and thus a will that is at once subjective and universal. This will alone comes into existence. Only in the law is the very existence of the will posited.[17] If Kant defines Being as "absolute position or positing [*Setzung*],"[18] then it can be said of the law that it is the *a priori* gathering of positings, the collection of *Setzungen*. Law, *das Gesetz,* is the original

17. Compare Kant's interpretation of natural law as the law of existence in the *Groundwork:* "what is properly called *nature* in the most general sense (as to form), that is, the existence of things so long as it is determined according to universal laws" (Ak, 4: 421). The following variant of the categorical imperative derives from this definition of nature as existence according to universal laws and the implicit definition of existence as posited existence: "act as if the maxim of your action were by your will to become a universal law of nature" (Ak, 4: 421). But this means: act so that your action is a law for itself and, therefore, so that your action comes into existence, which is to say, as an absolutely posited action and an action that, because it altogether accords with itself, *is*. Certain questions then arise in connection with this onto-theseological determination of action: if action fulfills itself only in the law and in positing, if action *is* itself only as positing, in what sense does a law that is not a positing but a demand *exist*? In what sense *is* there a law that is not positive but imperative? In what sense is there a law that is not a representation but a project, not a given but a giving and a task? And furthermore: in what sense *is* a finite action? In what sense does an action that does not (yet) correspond to the law *exist*? Under the conditions of finitude, hence under the conditions of the mere *imperative* of the law of action, can one speak in a strict sense of "action" at all?

18. See Kant's treatise of 1763, *The One Possible Basis of Proof for a Demonstration of the Existence of God* (Ak, 2: 73) and also the *Critique of Pure Reason* (A 598; B 626). Cf. Martin Heidegger's lucid study of the problem of Being as positing in Kant, "Kants These über das Sein" in *Wegmarken* (Frankfurt am Main: Klostermann, 1967), 273–307; "Kant's Thesis on Being," trans. Ted Klein, Jr., and William Pohl, in *The Southwestern Journal of Philosophy,* 4 (1973): 7–33. Heidegger, who does not enter into a discussion of Kant's practical philosophy and indeed deliberately avoids such a discussion, restricts himself to the determination of the Kantian thesis on Being as a position in relation to the transcendental unity of original-synthetic apperception. He thus remains within the definition of Being as the Being of transcendental subjectivity. This presentation of Kant does not lose its validity because of its orientation toward his theoretical philosophy, but it will still always suffer a certain displacement when the law is no longer determined as a rule but as an imperative and thus as an always incomplete positing. The onto-theseo-logy of subjectivity is suspended by this determination, which is to say, by "self"-determination.

collection of all Being under the form of the demand. But no longer as a law of theoretical reason; as a law of practical reason, this collecting and placing together, this original synthesis has the characteristic form of ex-position *(Aus-setzung)*: Being, as demanded, is not an actual position; it is never actualizable and is therefore absolutely impossible to posit. The fact that it is an apodictic imperative means that it is given up, ex-posed Being—and is thus a Being that *is* not.

The categorical imperative is not at first an imperative of the "good will" but of the will as such. It is an imperative of identity and existence. Only what has existence in the mode demanded by the imperative—the mode of positing—can lay claim to the predicate "good." And only something in unity with itself in this positing can be called "true." Kant doubtless treats promising as an example of one of the acts—or speech acts—that are subordinated to the categorical imperative to the extent that this imperative alone delivers the criterion of morality; but it also becomes clear that this example, more than any other, shows that "the concept of action contains in itself a law for me." For in every promise a law of action is given.[19] The deepest affinity between the imperative and the promise does not, however, consist in the fact that both are speech acts but in the fact that they are the kind of speech acts that speak prior to what is supposed to come: they are both pre-mises, pro-missions, binding pro-clamations. The categorical imperative is characterized by its example, the promise, as an unconditional pronouncement, as an absolute pre-announcement and premise, without temporal conditions, which gives rise to the representation of time as a future whence the will can return to itself as the past of that future. The fore-structure of the imperative is determining in every sense not only for language but also for the will and its temporality. Since the speaking of the imperative must absolutely precede every action, every speech act, every act of understanding—and must precede in order to determine each of these—none of these actions can overtake it: a will that first

19. See Kant, *Groundwork* (Ak, 4: 402). That the very concept of action already contains a law also clearly implies that there is no example of the law in general—or that there are only examples. Every action, insofar as it is an action, must already correspond to the law and can always be more than a mere example. Since, however, finite actions always stand under the imperative of their lawfulness, without ever being able to be altogether lawful, none can be more than an example for the imperative and thus for the necessary possibility of action.

becomes a will when addressed by this imperative cannot perform this unprecedented speaking; an understanding that stands under the dictates of this imperative in every one of its gestures cannot reach it; and a language whose every moment is beholden to its demand cannot correspond to it. If the categorical imperative provides the condition of possibility for an internally homogeneous will and thus for the will in general, then it, as an absolutely prior speech act, holds out this possibility as one that cannot correspond to anything actual and so offers this possibility only as the possibility of its impossibility.[20] What is expressed in the categorical imperative is not only a demand constitutive of the rational will—a demand without which it could be neither a will nor rational—but at the same time an absolutely excessive demand, an overdemand under which the will not only suffers the "infinite disruption"[21] of its natural modes of relating to itself but also devalues its intentions and humiliates its instinct for self-preservation. And this goes for language as well: since the promise exposes it to its own absolute anteriority, there is always the possibility of a universal language that conforms

20. This formulation has been chosen with some care, for it—like many others, including the discussion of the fore-structure of understanding and the structure of the task the will gives to itself and, in so doing, gives itself up—makes it possible to see a certain affinity between Heidegger's "existential project of an authentic Being toward death" and Kant's doctrine of the categorical imperative. In terms of Heidegger's analysis, being-ahead-of-oneself, which is constitutive of all *Dasein,* culminates in the possibility of death and determines this possibility "as the possibility of the impossibility of existence as such." See Martin Heidegger, *Sein und Zeit* (Tübingen: Niemeyer, 1967), 262; *Being and Time,* trans. John Macquarrie and Edward Robinson (New York: Harper & Row, 1962), 307; all citations refer to the German edition, the pagination of which can be found in the English translation. Because this formulation is so close to Kant's definition of the moral law as a "disruption" of all merely subjective aspirations and simultaneously as the ground for the possibility of practical subjectivity—hence as the ground of *Dasein* that is never given but always given up as a task—it is possible to suggest that Heidegger's projection of an "authentic Being toward death" is an ingenious transformation of Kant's theory of practical reason. Heidegger also speaks in this context of the task *Dasein* gives itself as "the most extreme possibility of existence . . . to give itself up" (*Sein und Zeit,* 264). On the relationship between understanding and being-toward-death in Heidegger, cf. my essay "Peut-être la question" in *Les fins de l'homme: A partir du travail de Jacques Derrida,* ed. Jean-Luc Nancy and Philippe Lacoue-Labarthe (Paris: Galilée, 1981), 345–63.

21. See Kant, *Critique of Practical Reason* (Ak, 5: 74). Compare the series of symptoms of "pathological feeling" that testify to the effectiveness of the law as they are laid out in the chapter on the motivating drives of pure practical reason in the second *Critique* (Ak, 5: 71–89).

to the law; but since the absolute anteriority of its speaking is unattainable by any particular, finite language, there is language only as promising—and therefore always as an already broken promise. Forgettable but unacceptable, the excessive demand of the law makes the will aware of its finitude. Unable to be either renounced or attained, the promise *traces* the horizon of both language and its understanding. It determines language and reason as infinitely finite.

The absolute anteriority of the imperative thus grounds the possibility of the will's self-relation and at the same time withdraws this possibility into an unreachable distance. The will draws out its self-relation *(Selbstbezug)* only by with-drawal *(Selbstentzug)*. The will can strive toward existence as will only in a proleptic relation to the law that precedes and proposes it. But insofar as the will wills the law for the sake of the law alone, it cannot will *itself.* Only where all subjective intentions are disrupted does the will enter into its freedom, "sublimely" above all finite forms. The fore-structure of the imperative as the absolute promise thus gives rise to a specific ethical consequence: the will that wills itself cannot and does not want to will itself. And this is the extremity of the will's *Selbstaufgabe:* its task lies in giving itself up. Those who assign a law to their will by making a promise can no longer recognize in this law a self-assigned goal of action; they can only recognize a still heterogeneous demand before which their will must falter. In giving one's word—and the concept of promising and the concept of language demand this gift—giving itself is exposed, interrupted, broken down. A word can really be given, and a word can really be kept, only if it is given away without reserve, abandoned so completely that it is no longer recognizable as the gift of any given subject. If it is to be a free gift, given without conditions, a given word can no longer be recognized as something anyone has ever given—neither seen as a piece of property nor considered a possession. It must withdraw itself not only from all positive knowledge but from the dialectic of self-knowledge—a dialectic of "the other of the self" which speculates on the restitution and raising of the self in the other, and therefore a dialectic that conceives of the gift, the promise, the imperative, or the law as rational cunning by way of which subjectivity is completely universalized. But the given word, the promise, must—this injunction comes from the logic of giving itself—stop being a given word; it has to give up its status as a given. In the law the subjective act of positing must break down, and positing must ex-pose itself to this breakdown. The given word is given up, and so, too, is giving itself. The act of practical reason—"pure spontaneity," pure origination—must have turned into an act of omission if this act is to be pure: it must have let itself out, deleted itself in a pre-original ellipsis.

Action deserves to be called "rational" if the imperative to which it submits itself is not *given* but unconditionally *perceived,* and therefore conditioned by no gift whatsoever. Yet the per-ception that brings about reason in this way—this *Vernehmen* that brings *Vernunft* to itself—cannot be the perception of an actual datum, a positive present that could enlarge or even produce a pleasure.[22] Paradoxically, this perception must be the perception of a withdrawal of all the premises on which empirical subjects have staked their existence. It must be the perception of an abandonment in which all forms and figurations that could guarantee the stability of sensuous experience are given up. And so this perception must be the inception of an "infinite disruption" of subjective and objective existence. If such a perception—the perception that bears the name "reason," the *Vernehmen* that makes up *Vernunft*—is to correspond to the logic of promising and its law, it can be a perception only *before* the perception of anything in particular, a perception *before* the perception of Being understood as positing. It must therefore be a perception of nothing and a non-perception. Just as the autonomous giving of the law in promising, which takes place without conditions and presuppositions, can never result in a positive gift, the presuppositionless and autonomous perception of promising and the law can never be the perception of something received but always only the perception of something not yet perceived and never perceived, hence something imperceptible and unacceptable. In the face of the imperative, the faculty of representation fails, for the imperative makes everything standing within the domain of representation tremble.[23] Only this trembling—

22. The connection between *Vernunft* (reason) and *Vernehmen* (perception, interrogation) is not an arbitrary one. It was emphasized with great regularity by the philosophers of German Idealism, although seldom so explicitly as in this passage from Schelling's *Philosophy of Mythology:* "The great hearing [*Verhöhr*] or interrogation [*Vernehmen*] from which reason [*Vernunft*] gets its name and into which it intends to draw everything conceivable and actual" (*Philosophie der Mythologie,* in *Werke,* ed. M. Schöter [Munich: Beck and Oldenbourg, 1927–1954], 5: 502).

23. Compare the metaphorics in § 27 of the *Critique of Judgment* on the "Quality of the Delight in the Estimation of the Sublime": "In the representation of the sublime in

the vibration of finitude, so to speak—communicates itself in the "fear-some voice" of conscience, communicates itself therefore in the failure of the "faculty" of representation and the power of imagination. In a section of the *Metaphysics of Morals* Kant writes about that—and thereby defines man as a rational being:

> Every man has a conscience. . . . And this power watching over the law in him is not something that he himself (arbitrarily) *makes,* but some-thing incorporated into his very being. It follows him like his shadow when he thinks to flee it. He can indeed numb himself by pleasures and distractions, or by falling asleep, but he cannot avoid awakening . . . and when he does, he immediately perceives its fearsome voice. . . . He cannot avoid *hearing* it. . . . Thus, for all duties, man's conscience will have to conceive something *other* (than man as such), that is, than himself as the judge of his actions; otherwise, conscience would be in contradiction with itself.[24]

What man as a rational being cannot avoid hearing and perceiving, what thus marks an absolute limit to his powers and faculties—and defines him by this inability—is a "fearsome voice": a non-human voice, not his own voice, not the autonomous voice of himself but the voice of some-thing "other (than man as such)." The voice of nemesis, of a shadow, the shadow of a voice—something other than voice in general, its "infinite interruption"—is perceived. The voice that is perceived from reason and the voice that in this per-ception *(Vernehmen)* makes reason into reason *(Vernunft)* in the first place (it is "incorporated" into human beings) is "fearsome" only because it is a voice beyond and before all voices, a voiceless voice and thus an imperceptible and unacceptable voice. Reason is the perception of the imperceptible and unacceptable, the perception of the absolutely unacceptable, which, for its part, is "incorporated" into reason as something altogether different, as some-thing thoroughly incompatible with reason. As something impossible

---

nature the mind feels itself *moved.* . . . This movement (especially at its inception) may be compared with a convulsion, that is, with a rapidly alternative attraction and repulsion produced by the very same object. The effusiveness of the imagination (toward which it is driven in the comprehension of the intuition) is, as it were, an abyss in which it fears to lose itself" (Ak, 5: 258).

24. Kant, *Metaphysics of Morals,* "Doctrine of Virtue" (Ak, 7: 437).

to assimilate that thereby convulses the body, it determines reason as bodily reason and the body as the body of reason.[25] The imperative that speaks this "fearsome voice" is therefore a presentation of the unpresentable, a manifestation without object, without subject, and without semantics, a demonstration that articulates itself only negatively, in the denial of every mimetic, representational, or signifying form.[26] Anything that can be the object of language, anything that exists, including language itself, draws its validity from the excessive existence of the law, an existence that stands neither under the conditions of objectivity nor under those of a presentational, expository language. Just as the injunction brings out the imperative function of the moral law, the voice of conscience brings out its condemning function. For every effort of the will to correspond to it—and thus to itself—is shown to be insufficient, to be finite in the face of this law. If, for Kant, the truth of propositional knowledge is subordinated to the principle of correspondence, then the truth of practical reason is subject to the principle of absolute incommensurability and therefore to a principle that states: the language of propositional knowledge in its entirety and thus the language of judgment in general must fail. In the categorical demand of the law as well as in the "fearsome voice" of conscience, the presentational function of language—a function that exhausts itself in propositions—gives way to a linguistic occurrence in which nothing other than the other (the other of "man as such") is articulated: not assertions, judgments, or communications about given states of affairs but, instead, the objectless, subjectless, propositionless saying, imparting, and speaking of language itself.

Conscience is not science. It does not reside in an aggregate of cognitions concerning facts and rules; it is not con-science in this sense but

25. On the complex of the unacceptable in the process of incorporation and incorporation as the unacceptable itself, see my *pleroma—Zu Genesis und Struktur einer dialektischen Hermeneutik bei Hegel* in G. W. F. Hegel, *Der Geist des Christentums,* ed. W. Hamacher (Berlin: Ullstein, 1978), 11–333.

26. Kant discusses the "presentation of the unpresentable" as a "negative presentation" in the Analytic of the Sublime and connects it with the representation of the "moral law and the capacity for morality in us" (*Critique of Judgment,* Ak, 5: 274). On the connection between the moral law and art in the feeling of the sublime, see Jacques Derrida, "The Colossal," in *Truth in Painting,* trans. Geoff Bennington and Ian McLeod (Chicago: University of Chicago Press, 1987), 119–47. Cf. "The Quaking of Presentation" in this volume.

is, rather, the active consciousness of a disparity between the law and those who stand under the law: a disparity, therefore, between the law and everyone whose existence consists of standing under the law; a disparity between the law and everyone whose Being is defined as be-ing-posited with respect to the transcendental unity of self-conscious-ness. From the perspective of its "fearsome voice," language determines itself as terrible, in a strict sense, as *ent-setzlich*: as the terrifying ex-posi-tion of positing itself. On this point Kant is emphatic: "this power, which watches over the laws in him [in man], is not something that he (arbitrarily) makes": it is not something made and not something in which the consciousness or the self-consciousness of the subject as a maker would ever be active; it is, in short, not a positing, not an act of any subject. If the voice of conscience can still be called a "speech act," it is one that proceeds from something "other (than man as such)," as the other of acting in general, and therefore as an action before and beyond every action that could be defined anthropologically in terms of intention, will, or purpose: an "action" that, by opening up the horizon of possible actions, exceeds every action.

If conscience follows human beings "like a shadow" when they dare think of fleeing it, it is because conscience is the force of the difference between every act and its law and is thus an excessive act, a positing beyond all epistemologically controllable and voluntarily regulated po-sitings, an ex-position, an ex-action.[27] Conscience is consequently never the consciousness of the self but consciousness of the difference that splits the self of the "moral person" off from the empirical self. This consciousness of the difference—Kant speaks of a "doubled self" and the "two-fold personality, which is how the man who accuses and judges himself in conscience must conceive of himself"[28]—cannot then appear as my *own* consciousness but only as the consciousness that someone else has of me, and this "someone else" cannot be reduced to another egological consciousness.[29] The voice of conscience cannot be heard as

27. In Latin *exactio* means "driving out," "expelling," "collecting" (of taxes and or tributes), "supervising." In English the word "exaction," like the French *exigence,* means not only compelling and demanding but also an exorbitant, excessive demand, an over-demand. In every case action is driven to, and beyond, its extremity. Ex-action would be the "action" in which the horizon of acting is exceeded.

28. Kant, *Metaphysics of Morals,* "Doctrine of Virtue" (Ak, 7: 438).

29. See Kant's explication of the metaphor of the tribunal in § 13 of the "Doctrine of

a human voice but solely as the voice of something "other (than man as such)," as a non-human voice. If the law of pure practical reason expresses itself in conscience, and if the will to the existence of the will speaks in conscience, such an existence cannot be captured and stabilized in an affirmative assertion; it is only demanded in a claim that the will makes on itself. The language of the law is not that of correspondence, agreement, reproduction, or representation; it is, on the contrary, the language of disparity and assignment, of dissociation, dissent, and remonstrance, not merely the language of demand but of excessive demanding, of overdemanding. The language of the law is not therefore a constative language; it is not a language in which something is stated, but it is also not a positive, positing, performative act. The language of the law is, in short, an ex-formative act. In this mode—which is not really a mode but is in every language the absolute of its speaking—being does not communicate itself: it imparts a claim of being alone, a claim that disavows everything incapable of corresponding to the claim. The principle of moral self-consciousness is not, therefore, "I am"; it is—and for this reason self-consciousness is "categorical," which is to say, accusatory—"I owe myself an 'I am,' I ought to be myself." It is not a consciousness of being, of positing, but of something other than being, and is thus, strictly speaking, other than conscious*ness*, other than being-conscious.

Although no finite action can ever correspond to the claim of conscience, the site at which a corresponding response takes place is occupied by responsibility. "Responsibility, probity, uprightness"—these are

---

Virtue." The critique of this metaphor undertaken by Schopenhauer in his Prize-Essay on the *Foundations of Morality* (§ 9) rests on a fundamental misunderstanding. In particular, the moral self-consciousness that Kant designates as conscience is not, as Schopenhauer impressively suggests, a "prosopopoeia" for a voice of reason activated in a conventional or utilitarian manner; in accordance with its thoroughly *a priori* and thus non-anthropological argumentation, moral self-consciousness is the representation of "something other (than man as such)"—therefore precisely not a prosopopoeia but its disruption. If Kant continues to speak of a "representation" in this context—namely, the "representation of a duty"—this is nothing other than the representation of representing itself ("which reason itself creates") and thus the pure form of representation that bears all empirical representations. Where they do not correspond to it—they never correspond to it—it interrupts them all. Conscience is therefore not a science but an awakedness—openness to that which cannot be assimilated into the form of representation.

the virtues in which Kant finds the "authentic interpretation" of the world "expressed allegorically" in the story of Job.[30] This authentic self-interpretation of practical reason is imperative. The will interprets in the form of the law, and its interpretation—because it is imperative and categorical—is a verdict of guilt: the interpretation is different from, and does not measure up to, its imperative. The probity of the interpretation—and probity *is* interpretation—thus consists in letting the difference of the law, the other, and the "other's discourse" enter into discourse. The "incapacity of our reason"[31] to satisfy not only reason pure and simple but also, for this reason, the law of "authentic interpretation" expresses itself in the probity of discourse: *die Redlichkeit der Rede*. The concern of this probity is not truth but truthfulness in the admission that truth cannot be reached. And since the pure, saturated discourse of the law (as the universal rule of every manner of acting) can never be reached and is always only vindicated by the law (as command), the inception of the probity of finite language and finite modes of action lies in the following admission: *die Redlichkeit redet noch nicht;* probity does not yet speak; probity has not yet proved itself; probity does not yet correspond to the rule of universalizable language and thus to something other (than "man as such"); there is not yet a common language and so, strictly speaking, there is none at all. The inception of probity lies, furthermore, in letting this other, which is other than every empirical other, come into discourse—letting into discourse what has no language and letting it be said that there is no universal language and never can be.

The language of the law—and so the language of the law of interpretation as well—is the language of the difference between every given language and the language of giving; it is the language of the difference of language, language *before* the law of language, language as *pro*mising language. Since every interpretation testifies to this difference and is, as a result, a testimony to something other than language—a path of language, a leap of language—"authentic interpretation" must admit, above all, that it does not yet, and never will, speak the same language as the "other's discourse," that it does not, and never will, speak a

30. See Kant, "On the Failure of All Philosophical Attempts at Theodicy" (Ak, 8: 264–67).

31. Kant, "On the Failure of All Philosophical Attempts at Theodicy" (Ak, 8: 267).

universal language, and that it never speaks language itself. The probity of "authentic interpretation" does not consist in claiming a degree of authenticity for itself or its text but only in claiming authenticity for something else altogether, something toward which both text and interpretation are heading. The probity of such interpretation—and probity is its only authenticity—consists in writing the allegory or, as Kant writes, the allegorical expression of "the other's discourse," and so probity consists in writing the allegory of language as such. Only as an allegory of this kind, only by speaking of itself and others in another manner and thereby altering both itself and everything else, is probity a promise of interpretation and an experience of finite autonomy—of autonomization—and of finite freedom—emancipation. Only insofar as allegory is self-altering and other—and other than a mere allegorical "figure"—does it take part in the otherness of the other, in its alteration. Understanding stands for another understanding and still another, for an understanding of the other that it releases it from itself and frees it for another. The foundation of hermeneutics toward which Kant points with his cursory remarks on its relationship to ethics offers only one transcendental condition of understanding: the imperative of autonomization. He provides only a single law: a law is commanded. And he lays out only a single ground: there must be one. It is less a sketch of some transcendental hermeneutics than the outlines of an attranscendental one—on the margin of the ground, not this ground itself. It is not a hermeneutics; it is an ahermeneutics and anahermeneutics in which it is said that there must be a hermeneutics but cannot be one, and that it is always possible only as something other than a hermeneutics: as its—and not merely *its*—alteration.

Nietzsche's Promise

Kant's efforts to relate ethics and hermeneutics and, more exactly, to think through the foundation of hermeneutics in a theory of practical reason were not, of course, ignored. There was no lack of *aperçus* among the early romantics—Schleiermacher, Schlegel, and Hardenberg—nor was there a failure on the part of Schelling and Hegel to pursue this foundation in a systematic manner. But the only one who placed the precarious connection between ethics and hermeneutics at the focal point of his philosophical attention was Nietzsche. He never stopped referring his efforts to those of Kant, whether implicitly or explicitly, consciously or without accounting for this filiation. It is uncertain how far his familiarity with Kant exceeded the distorting lenses of a Schopenhauer or a Kuno Fischer and whether this familiarity went much further than an intensive study of the second part of the *Critique of Judgment*, a study undertaken in conjunction with a dissertation on "Teleology Since Kant" he had planned to write in 1868. But these questions are relatively insignificant in view of his attempt to investigate the systematic connection between moral philosophy and the theory of interpretation according to their changing historical formations. For it is quite certain that Nietzsche's earliest notes on the theory of rhetoric and interpretation stand in an informal but hardly accidental proximity to his notes on the problems of ethics. It is also certain that a text like "On Ethics" of 1868 suspects ethics of being grounded on aesthetics and entertains the possibility of grounding it on "ugly and unethical truth."[32] And it is no less certain that a text like "On Truth and Lying in an Extra-Moral Sense" interprets morality as conventional behavior and recommends viewing it, like truth, as a formation of life-sustaining misinterpretations the interpretive character of which is simply forgotten. Nietzsche's considerations of morals and morality, which always place them under the optic of their historical emergence, are woven into all his texts, and they entangle the various threads of *Beyond Good and Evil* and its "expansion and clarification" in *The Genealogy of Morals*—the metaphysics of the will, the history of morals, the theory of interpretation—into a tight knot. In a section of the preface to *The Genealogy of Morals* that was written after the completion of the book and was probably dropped from its published version for reasons of economy, Nietzsche places great emphasis on the universality and the determining status of the problem of ethics. He points toward "an enormous and not entirely undiscovered fact," a state of affairs that even he only "slowly, slowly grasped: up until now there were no more fundamental problems than moral ones; all great conceptions in the realm of morals up until this time owe their origin to the driving force of these problems." He then specifies these "great conceptions"—"everything that is commonly called 'philosophy,' down to its final epistemological presuppositions."[33] The history of moral problems is to be written with a view toward

32. Friedrich Nietzsche, *Gesammelte Schriften* (Munich: Musarion, 1922), 1: 405.

33. Friedrich Nietzsche, *Sämtliche Werke: Kritische Studienausgabe,* ed. Giorgio Colli and Mazzino Montinari (Berlin: de Gruyter, 1980), 14: 378; hereafter, "KSA."

"problems still more fundamental than moral ones," for only the genesis of these problems can clarify on which ground they rest and how this ground not only has determined but can determine philosophical conceptions and their epistemological presuppositions. Although Nietzsche does not explicitly state that the concepts of genesis, foundation, and morally justified grounds must become problematic, the problematic character of these concepts is nevertheless implied in the comparative formulation: "still more fundamental problems."

Yet at first, and for long stretches of his argumentation, Nietzsche remains loyal to a moral suggestion, which, for him, can only mean a conventional one—the suggestion, namely, that it is possible to write a history of morals. Whereas Kant understood moral consciousness as a consciousness of a self-effective law that is not grounded on anything empirical—a consciousness that makes possible a history and historical alterations independent of the experiences available to historiography, and thus a consciousness through which human beings distinguish themselves as rational—Nietzsche inquires into the historical conditions for such a moral consciousness and thus turns his attention toward the genesis of the human being as a being capable of autonomy. Nietzsche does not inquire, as Kant does, into the structure of free will but into its history, and so his questions no longer concern an *a priori* genesis but the historical conditions of history. But this history of history cannot be told as a history—on this point Nietzsche leaves no doubt, however often he also yields to the rhetoric of historical discourse: the history of history is, strictly speaking, pre-history and "nature"—whatever Nietzsche may have meant by this latter word. But it is indeed a "paradoxical" nature to the extent that it, as the realm of chance and mechanical causation, is supposed to produce the very sphere that takes on the appearance of a free realm of the autonomous individual, the "master of the free will."[34] A freedom produced by nature can only be an acci-

34. Friedrich Nietzsche, *Zur Genealogie der Moral* in *Werke in drei Bänden,* ed. Karl Schlechta (Munich: Hanser, 1966), 2: 801; cf. *The Genealogy of Morals,* trans. Walter Kaufmann and R. J. Hollingdale (New York: Vintage, 1969), 59; hereafter, "GM." Whenever possible, citations of Nietzsche's writings refer first to the Schlechta edition (volume number, page number) and then to a readily available English translation. In addition to the translation of the *Genealogy of Morals* mentioned above, this essay will refer to the following English editions of Nietzsche's writings: "BGE" = *Beyond Good and Evil,* trans. Walter Kaufmann (New York: Vintage, 1966); "GS" = *The Gay Science,* trans. Walter

dental freedom, not a freedom *from* accidents; it would be as though nature itself were already the realm of freedom or an order of necessity that had its telos in human freedom. But nothing is further from Nietzsche than this assimilation of nature and autonomy under the concept of teleology. As early as his notes on teleology of 1868, he took issue with Kant's postulate that organic causes had to be represented as effective ends and, instead, pointed to the "coordinated possibility"[35] that these causes could be understood as incalculable accidents. The possibility of teleological organizations, as he argued in later writings, applies to those places where chance and mechanical causation no longer determine the play of the world but where the autonomous will—departing from nothing but accidents and mechanical causation—has developed into the capacity to effect actions according to the representation of their ends and purposes. The central concept of ethics, the self-relation of the will, can be used only for the interpretation of nature, never for insight into its workings. On this point Kant and Nietzsche agree, but Nietzsche contests the exclusive claim of this one interpretive schema, for the very exclusiveness of this claim elevates it into the ranks of natural lawfulness and thus threatens to conjure away the difference between interpretation and insight, between knowledge and its objects. If one cannot speak of the historical emergence of the autonomous will in terms of final causation, then sovereign self-determination must be determined by accidents. The history of its emergence cannot therefore be a teleological one: paradoxically, it must be a history that cannot exclude chance; it must be a history of chance. In terms of the structure of the will, these historical reflections on its contingent origin give rise to an aporia that is not unlike the aporia of a will under the categorical imperative. If the will purely wills itself, then with respect to its provenance, which does not lie within its power, it must will what it has not willed, what it does not and cannot will: it must will itself as chance— and its autonomy as contingency.

Kaufmann (New York: Vintage, 1974); "TI" = *Twilight of the Idols* in *The Portable Nietzsche*, trans. and ed. Walter Kaufmann (Harmondsworth: Penguin, 1976); "WP" = *The Will to Power*, trans. Walter Kaufmann and R. J. Hollingdale (New York: Vintage, 1968); "Z" = *Thus Spoke Zarathustra* in *The Portable Nietzsche* (see above). All citations of Nietzsche are newly translated for this volume.

35. Nietzsche, *Gesammelte Schriften*, Musarion-Ausgabe, 1: 412–13.

Nietzsche pursues the collision between heteronomous history and autonomous subjectivity in a variety of forms throughout *The Genealogy of Morals*. The result of this collision is nothing less than the dissolution of the traditional concepts of both history and subjectivity. According to Nietzsche as well as Kant—and here Kant perhaps exercises a certain influence on Nietzsche's formulations—moral consciousness is bound up with the capacity to make promises: "To breed an animal *with the right to make promises*—is this not the paradoxical task that nature posed with respect to man? Is not this the real, the proper problem *of* man?" (2: 799; GM, 57). The "memory of the will" (2: 800; GM, 58) is the condition for a will that can be a law unto itself. Such a memory of the will conceives of the word given for the future as a possible obligation, as a commitment of the past to the future and as a binding connection between past and future wills. Only when a word is given, only when a promise is made, does there arise the possibility of a continuum of the will. Only by means of promising can the will consolidate itself as will, and only in the act of promising does the will—and nothing else— promise and promise itself as the will. Promising—as the mode of discourse in which one speaks ahead of oneself in view of oneself—dictates the structure of the will. The will can be ahead of itself only if it maintains itself in this "ahead"—in other words, only if it has a "memory." The "memory of the will" is the memory of the promise of the will, the memory of the future, and the promise of this memory. Only as the promise of itself, only in this always open distance from itself—open to interruptions, distortions, and accidents—*is* there a will, and only under this condition, only as long as the will is open to itself and to the other, is it a will at all. As a promise, the will is, strictly speaking, a "problem— the real, the proper problem *of* man": it is something thrown ahead, a pro-ject *of* man and, in an ablative sense, something thrown from man, ahead of him and foreign to him, and only in this way "proper" to him. Thus, the problem is a "paradoxical" task: whatever is supposed to be promised of man himself—namely, the will—must already exist in order for him to make this promise himself. The promise can aim teleologically at man as such, if he—ateleologically, in a way that remains open to contingencies—has not yet reached himself and if his promise is neither fulfilled nor even *his*. The will cannot promise itself if a promise makes it into a will in the first place. The will cannot anticipate itself in a teleological manner if teleology is an effect of a promise—a promise, however, that the will cannot accomplish. The will can only open up the contingent possibility of its autonomy and autoteleology, leaping toward itself, anateleologically and prototeleologically. It can only speak in advance of itself and promise itself in retrospect—or in retro-speak—to a self that is never and nowhere given. The will enters into a promise and thus into its own domain only to remain before this promise and to step back away from itself: not to take it over and carry it out but to remain before even the "before" through which teleology and intentionality are defined: before *its* "before," before *its* promise and ahead of *its* language. Ahead of itself and behind its "before," the will is the step over the threshold and is itself the threshold that separates it from itself. If the will, as Nietzsche assumes, must first be brought or forced to preserve "itself" in memory, and if it can be a will only as a promise of its "memory of the will," then the question must remain open—for it is necessarily a question of contingency—whether there can be a will that preserves itself in memory, maintains itself as a will, and is capable of keeping—and willing to keep—its word, which is to say, itself. Promising also means not yet, and perhaps never, being able to promise. Willing means not yet, and perhaps never, being able to will.

If, as Nietzsche demonstrates, the possibility of the will depends on the open structure of promising in the transition from necessity to autonomy, if it is always a promise of the will and a promise of a kind of will that paradoxically is a will only insofar as it is not yet this promise and only wills itself as a will and wills the will insofar as it does not will and cannot yet willingly want itself, then it is precisely in this paradoxical structure that the possibility opens up for a history that would be neither absolutely contingent—for that would not be a history—nor altogether mechanical, which is not a history either. In short, promising opens up both the will and history. By making promises, the will experiences itself not as something self-identical and uniform, something independent of temporal conditions; it does not think itself under a rule to which it has to correspond; and it does not make itself into a consciousness that, secure in its freedom, declares itself independent of time. By giving its word to itself—without there being a given self—it first gives itself time, history, and a future. The "self"-relation of the will in its memory generates time. But the teleological time of the will's "self"-anticipation in its promises is not a phase within an already teleologically determined temporal continuum: "no one would have had a right to promise it"

(2: 802; GM, 60). Promising cannot be promised. As a speech act, it posits a new fact the anticipation of which must have already been the production of this fact. Even though it cannot be promised, promising—and with it, the "self"-relation of the will, time, and conscience—was "prepared for" by "the monstrous work . . . the actual, the proper work of man upon man" (2: 800; GM, 59). The will cannot be promised, and it cannot be anticipated. Nature does not provide for it, and it has not been dictated by some supernatural power. For if any of these things were true, the will would have to stop being a will, the will to will itself, the will to will autonomously. But precisely at the point where it—the unpromised will—can promise, aim for, and anticipate, its promise must be a mere "out-ahead," a project, and an intention that has not yet found its fulfillment and whose actualization can be thwarted by another resolution, an accident, or "active forgetfulness," that "counter-capacity" to the ability to make promises (2: 799; GM, 58). Even a will capable of promising would always remain a mere promise of an unsecured future will, unable to turn into the actual will itself. Being ahead of itself in the promise, the speech act of the will falls short of being an act and is not even linguistic in any conventional sense. Rather, the performative of promising is merely a pre-performative, the event of an opening of the will, the disclosure of the possibility of an auto-thetic act and a consistent language: an event that has neither ground nor goal and whose form cannot be stated or stabilized in the will. Exposed to promising as condition of its possibility, the will—like the promise—remains revokable, breakable, unperformable: a promise prohibited for the sake of the promise.

The Genealogy of Morals is a genealogy of the human being, of humanity in the sense of autonomy, and thus of the will. The central problem it poses to its historiographer is to construe the passage of will from its eccentric position—where it is not yet the voluntary will, but merely an arbitrary willfulness—into the center of itself. But it must not appear as though it were under the power of this will to accomplish the passage on its own. For this reason, the *petitio principii* in the formulation "work of man upon man" is placed under the sign of absolute exteriority: this, "the actual, the proper work" of human beings and therefore work in which they are already at home with themselves is a "monstrous work" in the sense of being huge and because it makes each human being confront himself in an inhuman, uncanny, foreign way. The properness of each productive "self"-relation lies in an ineluctable, unsublatable foreignness with respect to itself: its "self"-appropriation cannot be appropriated; it is not assimilation but alteration. Philosophical historiography, no less than nature, faces a "paradoxical task" whenever it tries to present the provenance of the will, for not only do the pre-historical premises of the will withdraw from the will and are thus unavailable to any rational construction of history that would be the will's own history, but the very relation of the will to "itself"—which is affected by these pre-historical conditions—is also withdrawn from the will. If one can say of Hegel that he wished to write the autobiography of absolute knowing in the *Phenomenology of Spirit,* one must say of Nietzsche that he wrote a pre-biography of the will that never stops being haunted by what it is not and therefore can never arrive at the point of writing its own history.

Since chance can befall the constitution of the will, and since the will is at first never anything but chance, its constitution as law is at the same time its deconstitution, and its genesis is always also its degeneration. The pre-struction and de-structure of the will and its history—if it still makes sense to speak of structure and history, of prehistory, nature, and history—means that the project of genealogy cannot positively describe a constituted subject in its historical modifications but must actively participate in the constitution of this subject and therefore in the dissolution of its merely contingent forms. Historiography stands under the imperative that it make history. But it cannot then avoid acknowledging those moments that are not subject to the authority of the will. A historiography that understands itself as performative and seeks to participate in the production of a sovereign legislative will cannot deny the contingency that threatens it, for it would then have to deny itself and its will to history. It must, instead, make room in every feature of this history for whatever could not correspond to the will. But this means that it must in a certain sense take leave of the illusions of objectivity for the sake of its own objectivity. It can no longer proceed from the premise that it only reproduces a given state of affairs—the "other's discourse," for example—in which it would have no stake and take no part; instead of desiring to be a description, it must confess that it is an interpretation. As a procedure of manifestation and activation not only of the will but also of what is not the will, as a procedure that thus entails all the dangers of chance and corruption to which the will falls prey because of its contingency and its imperfection, this "interpretation"—to use Nietzsche's word—could just as well be called transformation, fabrication, and falsification. Nietzsche legitimates his radically interpretive historiography with reference to the prehistory of the will, for the latter cannot either relate or refer to itself before it is interpreted *as* a will. And this interpretation issues the promise through which the contingent will seeks to bring itself into a secure relation to itself and thus tries to secure its autonomy. Understanding is a promise—the promise that the will will be able to understand itself in its history and context. This promise of interpretation would not be "enormous" and its task would not be "paradoxical" if it were effective as an activity of an already constituted subject or as an action of the will with regard to itself. Just as genealogical historiography has to separate itself from the illusions of objectivism, it must take leave of the fiction of subjectivism, the activism that always accompanies subjectivism, and hermeneutic performativism as well. It must take leave of them if only to think what it means "to act," to clarify what it means "to make history," and to make clear the specific structure of the events called "historiography," on the one hand, and "interpreting," on the other. For interpretation does not simply *make* history but "makes" it possible to think the making of history. Interpretation is therefore just as little subordinated to the category of autonomous, self-determined action as is the promise that sets up the possibility of a genuine action without being such an action itself.

Nietzsche develops the thought of the interpretation of the will in a story about history with almost mythological dimensions. This story concerns the world-historical struggle between two "races" and may well be among the most scandalous writings in the philosophical literature of modernity. But Nietzsche's description of the struggle between prototypes and races must also be read—and this reading mitigates the moral and political scandal without doing away with it—as an allegorical staging of a *gigantomachia peri tēs ousias*. For the conflict is then read as a struggle over the will and its power to decree itself as law. If the presuppositions of the free will include that it be "calculable, regular, necessary" (2: 800; GM, 58), then those who seem to enjoy Nietzsche's favor—the so-called "noble races"—are the ones least likely to possess such a will. For they are characterized as "mad, absurd, sudden," and their undertakings as "uncalculable, the improbable itself" (2: 786; GM, 41). By contrast, the counter-type to the "blonde beast"—namely, the man of *ressentiment*—stands in the closest possible relationship to the "memory of the will": "he understands how to keep silent, how not to forget, how to wait, how to make himself small and humiliate himself in anticipation" (2: 784; GM, 38). If the noble ones are "replete with power and consequently active men by necessity" (2: 783; GM, 38); if they are the ones whose spontaneity immediately expresses itself in action or, if blocked, is immediately forgotten; if they are, therefore, "forgetfulness incarnate" (2: 802; GM, 60), the very incarnation not only of the necessity of will and deed but also of the lack of distinction between deed and will—an identity that Kant grants God alone but that Nietzsche, who is not so far removed, reserves for the good, the Goths, and the gods—: if all this characterizes the "noble ones," then the man of *ressentiment* is the prototype of detour and delay. He is the type that does not forget but develops a "memory of the will" and learns to promise; he is the type that has "need of a freely choosing 'subject'" (2: 791; GM, 47) and thus distinguishes himself from his deeds. In this way, the Idea of freedom has its origin among those who are not free. The will emerges at the precise place where it is lacking. The capacity to give one's word owes its existence to those who withhold their word and falsify its original meaning—a meaning it could have only in the instantaneous unity with its verbal sign.

Using a striking example, Nietzsche demonstrates the capacity of *ressentiment* to transform a fact whose power it cannot withstand and to translate the independent unity of this fact into the language of differential references. His example is "the lightning bolt flashes":

> For just as people separate the bolt of lightning from its flash and take the latter for a deed, for the effect of a subject called lightning, so popular morality separates strength from the expressions of strength, as if there were an indifferent substratum behind the strong one that was free to express strength or not to do so. But there is no such substratum; there is no "being" behind the deed, the effect, the becoming; the "doer" is a mere fiction added to the deed—the deed is everything. People at bottom double the deed when they allow the lightning to flash. That is a deed of a deed: it posits the same occurrence first as cause and then again as its effect. (2: 789–90; GM, 45)

Language separates the occurrence from itself, if only by sheer doubling. It dissolves an event into imaginary constituent parts, disintegrates it into a grammatical relation between a subject and a predicate, into a complementary relation of cause and effect. In this way, language not only leads away from the actual occurrence and its traumatic experience, it leads astray. The "seduction of language"—a recurrent argument in Nietzsche's epistemological reflections—conceals and distorts every possible event. The sentence "lightning flashes" cannot in principle claim to be adequate to its object: whereas lightning as event is the nonreferential, meaningless identity of its appearance and its being, the sentence is an articulated structure that, as an appearance, is supposed to refer to something outside it. By splitting the event into a subject and a predicate, language suggests that behind this world there is a second one, an immobile and ideal world, the stable realm of grounds and essences. Language immobilizes becoming into being, and degrades the operations of becoming into mere appearances. In short, grammar sets apart what belongs together; it lays out, or takes apart, and as ex-egesis, ex-plication, or inter-pretation—as *Aus-legung* (laying out)—grammar fabricates what does not exist.[36] Freedom, for Nietzsche, has as little substantial being as lightning; it gains the appearance of being only by way of grammatical dissociation, by way of a language that does not operate but rather delays, breaks up, and distorts every operation: a language that does not act but dissolves action and invents a subject of action and an action of this subject. Freedom thus comes to light by way of "this sublime self-deception that interprets weakness as freedom and its mere being-so-and-so as merit" (2: 791; GM, 46). Laying out, taking apart, ex-egesis, inter-pretation—this grammatical laying asunder and setting apart—makes possible the subject of a deed and the deed as a deed of this subject; it first gives rise to the voluntary will, hence to the possibility of autonomy. Neither interpretation nor language act on their own. Each is only the block on which the event breaks. But if the event did not break apart, there would be none at all.

The grammar of language introduces into the absurd, unaccountable, subjectless, and thus actionless "deed"—of lightning, for example—the substantializations, idealizations, and mythologizations that constitute the idealism of language. However arbitrary this idealism may be, it is the awkward ground on which *ressentiment* builds its world. With the help of grammar and "of the basic errors of reason ossified in it," *ressentiment* can articulate its No. "Whereas all noble morality grows out of a

---

36. See Nietzsche, 2: 598–601, 615–16; BGE, 45–48, 66–67. See also 2: 959; TI, 482–83.

triumphant, self-affirming Yes, slave morality from the outset says No to an 'outside,' to an 'other,' to a 'non-self': and this No is its creative act" (2: 782; GM, 36). The lightning bolt exemplifies this "doing, acting, becoming" (2: 790; GM, 45) as well as the immediate, "self-affirming Yes." But it also exemplifies the agents in Nietzsche's pseudo-history, namely "any pack of blonde beasts of prey": "they come like fate, without cause, reason, regard, or pretext; who are there as lightning is there, too terrible, too sudden, too convincing, too 'different' even to be hated" (2: 827; GM, 86). Against the lightening bolt of this Yes and the sheer alterity of appearing and disappearing, a No must be raised that impedes, delays, and defers the Yes: a No *must* turn against the Yes, lay it out and set it apart, if this bolt of lightning is to be something in the first place and if everything, in turn, is not to disappear at a single stroke. The speculative grammar of *ressentiment* is the apotropaic inter-pretation and ex-egesis of the stroke of lightning; its sentence is the articulated and articulating No to the essentially unarticulated, undifferentiated Yes of the will. In a mode of transcendental immediatism, incapable of either meaning or significance, the "self-affirming Yes" (2: 782; GM, 36) refers immediately to itself and never to an exterior object. It is a linguistic event *par excellence,* an event that glows and fades in the punctual intensity of lightning because it has no room for the difference between doer and deed, deed and effect, outside and inside — because it allows for no reserve and no precondition, no precaution and no model. By contrast, the No doubles the Yes in setting it apart; it splits the Yes into a Yes of a Yes, a "deed of a deed." By removing it from its acts, the No makes the Yes into a stable subject-substratum and makes its acts — its flashes — appear as exchangeable masks. In this way the Yes, which, strictly speaking, cannot belong to language as a conventional system of signification, dissolves into a linguistic relation whose discrete elements are furnished with stable functions and meanings. But for this very reason, language fails to strike the things of which it speaks. The disjunction between the will *(Wille)* and the act of willing *(Wollen)* reduces the willing that is already the act itself to a mere possibility of willing. Having been brought into language, the will is a will that only may be willing.

But the will does not will. It is the simple tautology of willing, without subject, intention, or object. If language makes the act of willing into the mere predicate of the will, and if willing — which always implies intentionality and aspiration — becomes a predicate that can be affirmed or denied of the will, if willing becomes willingness, then language is not the site of the will but of *ressentiment* against the will. It is language that isolates the will from willing, *Wille* from *Wollen*. And by means of an interpretive fiction, language lets the will become independent of itself as willingness. Neither free nor unfree, language first frees the will. And only where the will is free of its own volition can it raise itself as will into the law and subordinate itself freely to this law. The free will is therefore the will of *ressentiment*. By taking the will apart, *ressentiment* interprets its incapacity to be the unity of will and deed as its ability to will or not to will this identity: it has a choice—and so has the possibility of deciding between alternatives—only when it also has the possibility not to will, when it can maintain itself in its volition and be the pure possibility of willing in a virtually infinite retention of the will. Only the inability to will, only this infinite reserve of the will, only nonwillingness brings the will to itself. The epitome of the paradox is: only the possibility of the impossibility of willful action gives rise to the possibility of willing. Nietzsche leaves no doubt that the will is an effect of the grammatical structure of language and thus of inter-pretation. Before it can be an art of correctly understanding "the other's speech," the hermeneutics of grammar is the art of interpreting the absolute otherness of the act of willing as the will pure and simple, splitting apart the movement of willing and even turning the deficiency of the will into the will itself. This inter-pretation, without subject, and this side of the alternative between freedom and unfreedom, is the invention of the subject, of freedom, and of meaning. But just as interpretation betrays the lightning bolt of the will, which immediately disappears into itself, the inter-pretation of the will—its being taken apart—preserves it: "the will itself was saved" (2: 900; GM, 162). With this statement Nietzsche summarizes the intervention of grammar into the will. Language—the language of taking the will apart and laying it out as a relation of subject to predicate—is the prevolitional and transvolitional power that inhabits the will from its inception: a power that tears the will apart and preserves it in these parts, a power that shatters the will by making it into a substance, and that saves it in its shards. The will—which appears "all of sudden," without substance and without consistency, and immediately disappears—emerges as "itself" only by virtue of its interpretation and therefore only by virtue of its deferral, its splitting apart, its disposal, its grammaticalization and depotentialization as subject and substratum. It is an effect of its difference from itself; it is itself by virtue of being another; it is its "own" disowning. In his "interpretation"—as Nietzsche calls it—of the traditional characteristics of the will and of those who are able to will, he not only asserts that the will proceeds from its self-interpretation, from taking itself apart and laying itself out; he also asserts that it *is* its taking apart, its auto-analysis and alteration, without this "is" being simply substantial Being. And so he claims that "the will" means paradox of the will, will-contra-will, a will sick of itself. Each of these assertions arises from an interpretation, more precisely, an etymological analysis of the word *bonus:* "I believe I am allowed to interpret the Latin *bonus* as 'the warrior', provided I am right in tracing *bonus* back to an earlier *duonus* (compare *bellum = duellum = duen-lum,* which seems to me to contain *duonos*). Therefore *bonus* as the man of strife, of division *(duo),* as the man of war: one sees what constituted the 'goodness' of a man in ancient Rome" (2: 777; GM, 31). Strife, the division of the will, is therefore good; good, too, is the will as it is taken apart, the will no longer one with itself, the pathos of distance—the good is not the identity of the will but its immediate alteration, its immediacy *as* alteration. If in the triad of the highest categories—*unum, verum, bonum*—*bonum* must be understood as *duonum* and *duellum,* then the other two are likewise split at their core, or rather have a split *as* their core, *verum* no less than *unum.*

When Nietzsche divides the world into active and reactive—a world of the Yes and a world of the No, the one inhabited by noble beasts of prey and the other by a dull herd—the suggestiveness of his rhetoric obscures certain traits of this division: that the Yes is no more a self-sufficient, independent quantity than the No, that the reaction is no less active than the spontaneous act, and that a loathsome aversion to the will belongs to the very structure of the will. Yet all this becomes sufficiently clear in central passages of his treatises and fragments. At the arithmetical center of *The Genealogy of Morals,* in the eighteenth aphorism from its second and central section,[37] Nietzsche interprets the act of violence by which, according to the preceding aphorism, the "master race" organizes the as yet unformed "raw material of people and half-animals" as an act of "self-violation," a self-rape by a "soul willingly at

---

37. The 18th aphorism of the section section of *The Genealogy of Morals* is the 35th of the 70 that make up the book.

odds with itself that makes itself suffer out of the pleasure of making suffer" (2: 828; GM, 87). The terms of this self-relation relate to each other as spontaneity and receptivity, as Yes and No. But in contrast to the preceding and following aphorisms, the actors in this drama present themselves as figurations of one self, or a single "soul." This self-relation is outdone by still another one: a self-relation in which the No, contradiction, *ressentiment,* relates to itself. And this self-relation of passivity— of a passivity before all passivity—first gives rise to affirmation, the Yes, and the will. For it is the "pleasure in making suffer," the *ressentiment* of the will against itself, that "brings to light an abundance of new, strange beauty and affirmation, perhaps even beauty itself. . . . For what would be 'beautiful' if the contradiction had not first become conscious of itself, if the ugly had not said to itself: 'I am ugly?'" (2: 828; GM, 87–88). Beauty, which in the "aristocratic" value-equation stands next to power, happiness, and the good (2: 777; GM, 32), does not arise from a self-sufficient positing, nor from an immediately positive self-relation of the will to power, nor even from the effect of this will on extraneous material. On the contrary, beauty arises from the self-negation of the No, the crack in the ugly, the self-affection of mere receptivity.

The same can be said of Being, reality, and truth. For beauty is nothing more than an example of the will to power as organizing artistic instinct: "the word *esthlos* coined [for the noble race] means, according to its root, one who *is,* who has reality, who really is, who is true" (2: 776; GM, 29). If Being can be attributed to the good, the true, or the beautiful, this attribution is not the result of a simple self-affirmation, as the example of the lightning bolt in which Being and appearance are immediately identical would lead one to believe; the attribution of Being to the good, the true, or the beautiful owes its origin, rather, to the self-affection of what does not exist. Whatever "noble" may mean, it arises from the self-negation of *ressentiment:* the Yes arises from the No that doubles and turns against itself. And Nietzsche indicates clearly enough that even the will is not to be regarded as something given but as the outcome of the self-negation of a deficiency of will. "The active force . . . of precisely that instinct for freedom (spoken in my language: the will to power) *delights* in giving a form to itself as a heavy, recalcitrant, passive material, and in branding itself with a will, a critique, a contradiction, a contempt, a No" (2: 828; GM, 87). According to this asyndeton, the will is the No, the very contradiction that the will opposes to itself; it is the form that delimits it, the critique that splits it off from itself, and the contempt that makes it into a pathos of distance. The will gives itself a will; the will brands itself with a will. And because the will still means what it meant previously—sheer willing—the act of willing is not a willing act unless an opening of distance has separated it from itself, unless this splitting tears it asunder and so delimits, forms, stamps, and makes it into a type—unless, in other words, the act of willing is taken apart, laid out, inter-preted. By hating itself, ugliness brings forth beauty. By denouncing non-being, nothingness turns into reality, into Being. By saying No to itself, by saying No to No, the No brings to light and into the world every Yes and every Yes to the Yes: "One already understands me: this ascetic priest [hence the prototype of *ressentiment*], this apparent enemy of life, this *denier*—precisely he belongs to the altogether great *conserving* and *Yes-creating* forces of life. . . . The No he says to life, his No, brings to light, as if by magic, an abundance of tender Yeses; yes indeed, even when he *wounds* himself, this master of destruction, of self-destruction—it is henceforth the wound itself that compels him *to live*" (2: 862; GM, 120–21). Without the intervention of interpretation there is neither a will nor a pure alterity of volition. These two propositions—"the will to power brands itself with a will," and "I am ugly, therefore beauty exists"—are variations of one and the same structure that generates the Yes from the self-negation of the No. The discord in the will thus cannot be thought as a vague relation between two already constituted wills or two modes of willing but only as the difference from which both terms in this relation arise. The will becomes will only by being taken apart.

The discord in the will—the split, crack, break, or breech that allows the will to come into being—is at bottom articulation, the linguistic event of an irreducible difference. This difference precedes the will, hollows it out, and transcends it. Nietzsche brings out the decisive linguistic trait of the self-relation of the will not only in his remarks on linguistic history but also in his reflections on the critique of language and in the metaphorics of writing and language by which he characterizes the constitutive acts of the will. He emphasizes this trait when he writes of the ugly having "*said* to itself 'I am ugly,'" and when he considers the delight of "*branding* a *contradiction* . . . a *No*" into oneself. At each moment the discord opens up in the form of speaking or writing, etching, branding, stamping—in all those forms of psychic and physical torment that Nietzsche counts among the "mnenotechnics" of the will: not only quartering, breaking on the wheel, flaying, and castration but all the forms of marking through which "a few ideas" are supposed "to be made inextinguishable, ever-present, unforgettable, 'fixed'" (2: 802–803; GM, 61). Speaking and writing could appear here as interruptions of a physical and psychic continuum. But if the question still concerns the genesis of a not yet and never completely constituted will, they must have another status than that of a foreign body in a homogeneous context or that of the wound in a previously uninjured body. If we can say that the Yes is generated from the self-negation of the No, then we can likewise say that speaking and writing constitute the wounds that precede the body, the thorn in the flesh that awakens to life, an interruption from which the continuum results. To cite once again Nietzsche's characterization of the "ascetic priest," the prototype of *ressentiment* and the misleadingly termed "reactive" feelings: "The No he says to life, his No, brings to light, as if by magic, an abundance of tender Yeses; yes indeed, even when he *wounds* himself, this master of destruction, self-destruction—it is henceforth the wound itself that compels him *to live*" (2: 862; GM, 121). The word against life compels him to live. As long as the will articulates itself in a linguistic manner and as long as it would not be a will without articulation, the will is nothing more than an effect of its interpretation—an effect of the analysis, spatialization, and temporalization that every mode of marking, not only a narrowly conceived linguistic one, exercises. But what is stamped into the will by language and writing, by mutilation and castration, by these and other mnemotechnic markings, including the threat of death—what, in short, is stamped into the will by its promise are "five or six, 'I will not's,' in relation to which one had given one's *promise*" (2: 803; GM, 62). The will brands itself with a will by stamping itself with an "I will not." The will that is capable of making law, the will that can make promises by articulating itself as language, is a will that does not will *itself* but wills its inter-pretation, its being taken apart, its promise, its law: it is a will that wills *not* to will. In its law, it does not will a particular law, a particular moral convention but the law of lawfulness itself, the law that, as in Kant, first presents the conditions of possibility for moral legislation and for the possibility of willing itself. It is in this law of the will that Nietzsche formulates one of those "problems even more fundamental than the moral ones" to which he turns his attention in the unpublished paragraph of the *Genealogy*. But this law of the will, the will *itself*—what in the will lets it be a will—is the promise in which it projects itself in view of itself, appeals itself to itself, places itself under its own word, and by standing under its word as law, no longer wills.

In order to be a will and in order to be *as* a will, the will must renounce willing. Furthermore, it must will its own nothingness. *Aus-legung*, inter-pretation, ex-egesis, as the taking hold of and displacing the will outside itself, is the mode in which the will realizes this not-willing, this dislodging and disconnecting of the will from its hinges in the modal categories of necessity and accidentality. The word Nietzsche uses again and again is "unhinging" (2: 799 and 860–61; GM, 58 and 118–19). As displacing and unhinging, not-willing realizes itself in a promise that is an inter-pretation—an *Aus-legung*—not only in the sense of a taking apart and a displacing outwards but also in the sense of a filling and a filling out. Thus Nietzsche writes in the last of the fragments devoted to answering the question "what do ascetic ideals mean?": "If one looks away from ascetic ideals, man, the *animal* man, up until now makes no sense. His existence on the earth contains no goal . . . The *will* for man and earth is missing." What offers this will and this meaning is, according to Nietzsche, the ascetic ideal, the ideal of *ressentiment,* and in a more sober, less idealistic and less psychological manner, grammar. Grammar offers human beings this will by way of interpretation, for interpretation is the self-displacement of the will toward a goal: "In it [the ascetic ideal] life was *interpreted* [*ausgelegt*]; the enormous emptiness appeared to be filled out [*ausgefüllt*]; the door was shut on all suicidal nihilism" (2: 899; GM, 162). Interpretation fills out nothingness by unhinging the will and displacing it outwards. When the will no longer senselessly disappears in a singular Yes but turns toward itself in making itself a promise, nothingness is lost—and something is won: a sense of direction, sense as such, meaning and significance, and constant will. This will is, to be sure, a will *against* life, a will *against* the will, a will to *nothingness,* but still a will that this counter-will against itself, this disgust with itself as will, alone keeps alive and keeps willing. The door is shut on all suicidal nihilism—such is the ineradicable paradox of the will, its interpretation, and its promise: it is nihilism that shuts the door on nihilism; life preserves itself by a permanent suicide; everything living gains a direction and sense by executing a maneuver toward its execution; the will saves itself in willing nothingness. By taking aim at itself as a *pudendum* or *castrandum*, the will—this conserving and salvational power *par excellence*—preserves itself as will. Indeed, the will, this absolute oblative power, places itself in life by putting itself to death.

The last and the most emphatic sentences of *The Genealogy of Morals* describe the movement of the will and thus the law of its interpretation: "This longing to get away from all appearance, change, becoming, death, desiring, from longing itself—all this means, let us venture to grasp it, a *will to nothingness*, a counter-will, disgust, and aversion to life, a rebellion against the most fundamental presuppositions of life, but it is and remains a *will!* . . . And, to say once more in conclusion what I said in the beginning: man would rather will *nothingness* than *not* will. . ." (2: 900; GM, 162–63). What Nietzsche said "at the beginning"—more exactly, in the opening aphorism of the third section of *The Genealogy of Morals,* which is devoted to the question "What Do Ascetic Ideals Mean?"—had a slightly different wording: "it [the ascetic ideal] would still rather will *nothingness* than *not* will" (2: 839; GM, 97). This principle is developed throughout the third section of the *Genealogy,* and in both of its versions it presents an echo and interpretation of Leibniz's question: "Why is there something rather than nothing?"[38] Leibniz's "rather something" becomes in Nietzsche "rather will nothingness," "nothing" becomes "not will," "something" becomes "willing something" (even if this "something" is nothingness), and "nothingness" becomes "not-willing." Leibniz's metaphysics of force reaches its pinnacle in Nietzsche's metaphysics of the will—the point where Being comes forward as will and where, for this reason, the will to nothingness proves to be an affirmation of Being, more precisely, a preference for the will as opposed to not-willing. In Nietzsche's formula the place of Being—the place of being "rather," of possibility, ability, faculty, hence the place of that force which maintains itself even in its annihilation—accrues to the *will* to nothingness. The formula of nihilism thus proves to be the final consequence of the principle of Being established by Leibniz. If, however, this will is a will to *nothingness*—and it must be so if its force is to maintain itself even in the face of nothingness—then it cannot be so unless it is therein tinged by nothingness. This is less clear in

---

38. Gottfried Wilhelm Leibniz, "Principles of Nature and Grace, Based on Reason" (§ 7) in Leibniz, *Philosophical Papers and Letters,* ed. and trans. Leroy Loemker (Dordrecht: Reidel, 1969), 639.

Nietzsche's explicit formula than in the section of the *Genealogy* that it opens and closes. For it becomes clear in this section that the will that wills nothingness must have already not willed in order for it to have a chance of becoming a will. History—for Nietzsche, the history of the will to nothingness and thus of nihilism—is secretly exposed to a not-willing (this is the insight that ties Nietzsche most closely to Kant), and this not-willing is no longer capable of offering a point of support for the subjectivity of the will and its project of self-grounding, for history and its endogenous nihilism. Nietzsche pinned his hopes on the possibility that his discovery could turn this history around, turn it away from a history of annihilation and into one of salvation—the salvation, more exactly, of not-willing, of incapacity, and impossibility, and thus the salvation of that which is not and cannot be.

What Nietzsche attempted to formulate and to detail in *The Genealogy of Morals*—and not only there—is a law to which the will is subordinated when it interprets itself toward the law: a law of the law; a law of the possibility of—and the suspension of—the law of the will. This law can only be aporetic if it includes both the erection and the collapse, both the genesis and the decline of the institutions of the will. Nietzsche formulates the law in this manner: "In order for a sanctuary to be erected, *a sanctuary must be destroyed:* that is the law—show me the case where it is not fulfilled!" (2: 835; GM, 95). This law of building by dismantling, of dismantling in building—one could call it the law of erecruption—is the law of the law itself, the law that disrupts itself and is immediately a law without law. Nietzsche calls it "the law of life," but he leaves no doubt that it is also the law of death and of the self-sublation of the law. He writes: "All great things collapse by themselves, by an act of self-cancellation: this is what the law of life wills, the law of the *necessity* of 'self-overcoming' in the essence of life—the lawgiver himself always comes across the call in the end: *patere legem, quam ipse tulisti*" (2: 898; GM, 161). If the lawgiver must erase his law, then he stands under a law that is more powerful that he himself: he stands under a *lex delegationis* that he, as the one whom he delegates, merely executes. His law is defined as a *legat* of another law before which it is untenable. But legislative power is here "the law of life," its very "essence," and it commands, in absolute autonomy, this law and thus sublates itself. The *lex delegationis* is thus at once a law of the affirmation and negation of the law, the law of the breach of law and the ex-position of the law. As a law of delegation to another, it is at the same time a law of de-legation, of self-dissolution. And the will no less than its exposition, promising no less than its interpretation, obeys, in turn, this logic of de-legation.

The law of the de-legation and de-position of every positing means that the will gives itself only insofar as it retains itself in this very giving: that it wills and wills itself insofar as it does not will but rather wills its nothingness; that it wills itself as a will to the failure of the will and as a will to the breakdown of the law of will. Therefore, it is a will of something other than the will, autonomous only in being heterono-mous—and thus essentially "its" auto-heteronomization. In terms of the promise in which the will dispenses its law, this law of the law means that the will is both posited in its law and omitted, given up, made into a task, and suspended: that the promise *of* the will—subjective as well as objective genitive—is the promise *of* not-willing; that the promise and indeed every promise does not promise; that it can be given only as a promise of a not-promising and of an un-promisable—and thus can be given only as a promise retained.[39]

Nothing is promised. In every promise there must be a non-promise if it is to be and remain a promise. For promising—and thus language in its entirety—directs itself toward this "not," the wound in the speaking of every language—and it is kept as a promise only when it is kept in the "not." Nothing would be more erroneous here than to speak of a "performative contradiction." Contradictions arise only within an al-ready established linguistic system of rules and therefore only where language has already established itself as a disposable instrument with which particular operations, each one regulated by certain conventions,

---

39. As early as *Fear and Trembling,* Kierkegaard had developed the paradox and irony of promising with even greater explicitness than Nietzsche. *Fear and Trembling* can in fact be read as one of the most honest and most subversive contributions to post-Kantian hermeneutics, which it to say, to the understanding of incomprehensibility. In one of the passages Kierkegaard later deleted, he writes: "One of the gospels tells the parable of two sons, one of whom always promised to do his father's will but did not do it, and the other always said 'No' but did it. The latter is also a form of irony, and yet the gospel commends this son. . . . A man of any depth cannot be unacquainted with this modesty. It has its basis partly in a noble distrust of oneself, for as long as a person has not done what is demanded, it is still possible for him to be weak enough not to do it, and for that reason he will not promise anything" (Søren Kierkegaard, *Fear and Trembling—Repeti-tion,* ed. and trans. H. V. Hong and E. H. Hong [Princeton: Princeton University Press, 1983], 253).

could be performed: they are contra-*dictions*. In the thought of Nietzsche and Kant, by contrast, there is no language before the act of promising, and there is certainly no language regulated by conventions. Promising is, according to both of their accounts, an inaugural event, each time singular—pre-singular—an event from which a language, a linguistic law, and thus action oriented toward specific ends, is projected. And such action is not projected or promised according to rules that are capable of contradiction, and does not reside in a "performative" speech act that could either fulfill or violate a given code of action. There is no law of action or speech act—and therefore no "performative" either—before there is a promise, and only by virtue of promising is there the kind of law that is open not only for other "linguistic" initiatives but at first open for *itself*—the always promised, still outstanding law, the always still unspoken language. In order for it to be a promise, it must be an infinite, unsurpassable promise, hence a non-promise; in order for it to be an originary performance, it must be a performance of its interminable beginning, of its non-performance. The law of promising is a promise of the law: exposition and ex-position, delegation and de-legation of the law, neither an action nor a nonaction but the opening up of action, its laying out, its being taken apart and displaced toward an action. Since this action is unattainable *as such,* opening up is the only "action." The outcome is at once worse than the logical crux of a "performative contradiction" and better, for it remains open to the future: language is a promise of language, language without language, infinite inconsistency of speaking.

Action under this law of action can only be a beginning, and thus an opening toward something other than the action itself. In this opening of the self, action is access to another, to the opening of another self, hence co-action, co-language, and communication with others: interpretation. Interpretation is never the interpretation of a given other—whether it be a text, a person, a fact, an event, or a history—but is always the laying out of what lays itself out in view of something else entirely. Interpretation is always co-interpretation, common displacement-outwards, synekstasis. Its law requires that it bring the other to itself, to interpretation; that it bring the other, itself, into interpretation and hold it there, in its opening. Interpretation, *Auslegung,* then appears in several ways: as analytic separation, as a filling out that saturates an empty space, or as original displacement-outwards. But it is always an "unhinging"—a dissolution of fixed placements and fixed statements—and it is always an alteration of oneself as well as another, alteration of an alteration and co-alteration. Whenever the will is in play, interpretation is the infinite opening of its possibilities and at the same time—for this opening, the making of promises, means nothing else—its infinite suspension. Interpretation suspends the will in projecting something other than the will: the pre-first, an-archic paradox and anadox of the will's task, its *Aufgabe*, as both destination and disruption—the only freedom this side of the autonomy of the subject.

This structure—or destructure—of the law, of inter-pretation, and of the will's promise allows a series of consequences to be drawn concerning Nietzsche's most often misunderstood utterances about the relation of will and interpretation. "The will to power interprets," reads a now famous note in Nietzsche's unpublished papers (3: 489; WP, 342). Interpreting is therefore not an accidental but a necessary predicate of the will to power; wherever a will is at work, it appears as interpretive activity, and the will to power is not some sort of will to (the power of) interpretation but is itself immediately this activity of interpreting. Nietzsche's cursory characterization of the "essence of interpretation" as "violating, adjusting, abbreviating, omitting, padding, inventing, falsifying" (2: 890; GM, 151) does not constitute an attack on philological probity, faithfulness, and precision. For the question here has nothing to do with philological procedures but with the *essence* of philology, with the *essence* of interpretation and therefore with the *essence* of the will as inter-pretation, as taking apart and laying out. If Nietzsche characterizes interpretation as "violation" and "padding" and "inventing," this is because he applies the principle of philological probity to the procedures of philology itself—and so inquires into its ground. After finding this ground in unreliable conventions and in the peculiarities of linguistic structures, Nietzsche is forced to draw the conclusion that even the most faithful and precise interpretation is in principle unreliable. And he must draw still further conclusions: the final instance, the last power that is supposed to guarantee the security of self-conscious action according to the metaphysical tradition—the will, in other words—is not transparent to itself; it gives no guarantee of epistemological security; it is not even given as a will and does not give itself but is in all events given up (to itself as its task). Although effective, the will is not, strictly speaking, a practical power—which is to say, an auto-teleological capacity—but is a non-saturated, uncontrollable interpretive occurrence, an event that can find no point of support in itself. "The will to power interprets" thus means that the activity of interpretation, which is the will to power, relates to itself primarily as "self-violation"; interpretation relates to itself first and foremost as to another. As the activity of taking apart and laying out, interpretation is the dismemberment to which the will is exposed, for interpretation exposes the will to the law under which its law operates and thus to something over which, as will, it has no say.

The first consequence to be drawn from the interpretive structure of the will runs counter not only to the account of his work Nietzsche tried to promote but also to any account that, like the Heideggerian one, hypostatizes the will into a transcendental subject. Because the structure of the will is interpretive, the will cannot be a subject of its interpretations. The idealism that stylizes the will into a position where it would be a subject of interpretation is an exegetical effect of the grammatical calculus and of the paradoxical logic that give rise to the activity of interpretation in the first place. For whatever is raised into the position of a subject in control of itself can only reach this sovereign position if it is cut off from its predicates, if it is depotentialized at the height of its potency. God is God only when he is dead. Nietzsche has to carry out a Copernican turn whose center is no longer the will but, as it were, the turn itself, alteration and decentering. In *Twilight of the Idols* he writes:

> It is no different here than with the movements of the sun: there our eye is the constant advocate of error, here it is our *language*. . . . It [language] everywhere sees a doer and deed: it believes in the will as the overall cause; it believes in the "I," in the I as being, in the I as substance, and it *projects* this faith in the I-substance upon all things— only thereby does it *create* the concept "thing." Being is everywhere projected as cause, thought up and *pushed underneath*. The concept of "being" follows, and is a derivative of, the concept of the "I." In the beginning there is the great disaster of an error that the will is something effective, that the will is a *faculty*. Today we know it is only a word. . . . I am afraid we are not rid of God because we still believe in grammar. (2: 959–60; TI, 483)

It is not the will that interprets: it is grammar. For grammar distinguishes between doer and deed, subject and predicate, active and passive, and thus grammar offers its not altogether arbitrary but nevertheless indemonstrable distinctions in order to justify the substantialization of these virtually fictive entities. But to speak of grammar as the agent of interpretation is no less deceptive, for grammar "itself" cannot be considered a subject to the extent that particular grammatical structures first suggested the possibly erroneous notion of the subject. Grammar would then be a subject of a subject and would have to be subordinated to a meta-grammar that would have to regulate not only the relation between grammar and world but also their non-relatedness, their agrammaticality and unregulatability—an aporetic rule of rulelessness. Such a paradoxical rule—a rule that disengages itself from its hinges—is, for Nietzsche, the *belief* in grammar: it is a grammar of agrammaticality. This belief no longer has a subject but is itself the discreditable and *a priori* discredited subject of interpretation: a relation that is in principle modifiable and is even capable of being suspended, a relation whose suspension is no less expected than the unhinging of the entire "metaphysics of language" (2: 959; TI, 483).

If it is no longer assumed that grammar and the entire order of linguistic mechanics is in any way representative of the "objective" constitution of the world; if grammatical structures no longer are understood as analogies of objective structures; if, therefore, world and language fall asunder and the grammatical interpretation of the world is seen precisely as an *interpretation*—not as a reproduction of the world—and if, finally, there is a grammar of the disjunction between grammar and world, then the words "grammar," "world," "language," "interpretation," and "will" all miss their mark. None of these misnomers can correspond to their "own" structure, their "own" essence, or their "own" function. "Today we know that it [the will] is merely a word. . . ." Indeed, it is a word without an objective correlate, a word that designates nothing, not even, as in the modern tradition of practical philosophy, the source of language, the substance of the word—a word for the disjunction from the word. This incorrigible failure to reach the target, to hit upon the self, bears in Nietzsche the much-interpreted misnomers "exegesis" and "interpretation." They do not foreclose—and indeed they even suggest—the possibility that the question concerns their agents or them as agents, and so these misnomers demonstrate that desubjectivizing concepts are always susceptible to a subjectivist reappropriation. Interpretation generates the representation of the will as a substantial power, as an active and self-effecting ground, as a subject of interpretation; it thus gives rise to the representation of Being and of God. As a genealogical category of this sort, interpretation should be immune to subjectivist modes of interpretation. But since it is not, Nietzsche has to give an explicit answer to the question he poses: "One may not ask: 'who after all interprets?' Rather, interpretation itself, as a form of the will to power, has existence (not as a 'being,' but as a *process, a becoming*) as an affect" (3: 487; WP, 302). This means that no doer stands behind the doing: there is no one to whom the grammatistic question—of "who" the interpreter may be—could be referred. But if the one who activates interpretation is "unhinged," so too is the interpretation as act. Interpretation is not a performative; it is not an act in the sense of a praxis performed by a subject, nor is it the deed of an empirical or transcendental doer, whether this doer is called will, grammar, or faith. Rather, interpretation is the aporetic—the self-missing— premise of every possible performation, a pre- and mis-performation. It has no Being, is not a transhistorical substance but a becoming without ground and goal, at the limit of "itself," neither act nor fact, but—with all the unresolved tension this concept connotes—an *affect*. Interpretation is, in short, the word for the aporia of interpretation: for the experience of the aporia of a nonsubjective process turning into a subject. And this experience is itself an aporetic one—hence an *affect*—because only at the point where a subject *is* not yet and will never *be* is it possible to undergo the experience of a still outstanding experience, the experience of an impossible experience and thus the experience of the impossibility of the aporia of experience. But finite autonomy means nothing else—autonomy even with respect to the will, the law, and the self. Promising means nothing else—a promise of the mere possibility of making promises. And speaking a language means nothing else than speaking as one who does not yet have a language.

The second decisive consequence of the interpretive structure of the will—and one that distinguishes Nietzsche's theory from all previous hermeneutics—concerns the relation of the will to the realm of objects and to the objectivity of the objects toward which it refers. Whereas the rationalist hermeneuticians of the seventeenth and eighteenth centuries—and even Schleiermacher—took their point of departure from the premise that every interpretation must refer to linguistic or semiotic facts and interpretive activity consists in reconstituting the meaning embedded in these facts, Nietzsche's concept of interpretation designates the process in which the will, perceptual consciousness, and its perspectives are first generated as such along with the objects to which they refer. Interpretation is not the process of reconstituting an object but the process of constituting one. No sublimated subjectivism lurks behind the thought that the objective realm is not immediately disclosed to understanding but must always be sketched out anew in historically varying forms. On the contrary, with the pathos of the philologist Nietzsche insists that it must be possible to read a text "as a text . . . without an interpretation getting in the way." But with the ethos of a philosopher he insists in the very same sentence that the capacity to grasp an object or to have an experience without perspectival distortions is "the latest form of 'inner experience'—one that is perhaps scarcely possible. . ." (3: 805; WP, 266). Experience free of interpretation is itself the product of the history of interpretation. It cannot arise until reason has reached the point where it entertains doubts about its ability to conceive of reality as it really is. In the absolute skepticism of reason turning against itself, Nietzsche sees "the ability to exercise control over one's pro-and-contra, to unhinge them and to put them back on their hinges, so that one knows how to enlist the variety of perspectives and affect-interpretations into the service of knowledge" (2: 860; GM, 119). The "objectivity" of knowledge increases to the degree that the will's perspectives and its interpretive forces multiply. But it can increase only because every particular perspective can be disavowed, dissolved, and replaced by another, because no perspective is the correct, adequate one, because every one is only an instrument in the service of a cognition, an intellect, or, in the final instance, the will. Yet this very will must be capable of being "unhinged" if it should be capable of becoming the vanishing point for its perspectives, the instrument for its cognitions or acts. If the will and its interpretation were to be eliminated, knowledge would surpass its subjectivist limitations. At the very instant when a text can be read *as a text* without perspective, "through which seeing alone becomes seeing *something*" (2: 861; GM, 119)—the will would disappear along with its realm of objects. The pure will, the "ability to exercise control over its pro-and-contra, to unhinge them and to put them back on their hinges," is the will that is true not to the will and not to the will itself; a will that can*not* will and can*not* will itself; a will that recedes into the sheer potentiality of willing. The object, when it purely appears, would not be an object posited by a will, and it would be a free object—

just as the will is perforce free—only when it is released from its positings and perspectival armatures. Its reading would then no longer be
reading something, for the text on which it could be focused spells itself
out as subjectless and objectless reading, as sheer relation without relata,
as a giving that is absorbed into none of its gifts and can, therefore, alone
be called free—even free from itself. If reading is a perspectival operation
and thus an unfree one, then altogether free, aperspectival reading
would be a non-reading. It would not only follow, it would itself be the
lex de-lectionis, the law of un-reading. For this reason, Nietzsche calls his
experience "one that is perhaps scarcely possible. . . ." In this "scarcely"
the experience of interpreting touches, "perhaps," its impossibility.

The interpretive structure of the will gives rise to a third consequence:
the thought of totality, which is bound up with the concept of knowledge, can no longer be maintained. It, too, is "unhinged," if we can no
longer proceed from the assumption that knowledge has an immediately
accessible world at its disposal, that it is homogeneous with this world
because it shares its origin, and that it stands in a relation of analogy
with its objects. If these assumptions are not fulfilled, two contradictory
consequences arise, both of which dislodge the concept of totality from
its moorings. On the one hand, knowledge thereby becomes monothetic
or monoperspectival: it forces its objects into forms of appearance that
are not forms of these objects themselves, and it can therefore no longer
count as knowledge but only as a violent imposition. On the other hand,
since knowledge has no secure access to the "things in themselves," it is
no longer possible to decide whether knowledge forces its forms onto
the "things in themselves" or whether the forms of things—which may
be completely heterogeneous with respect to one another—force themselves onto human knowledge. In the face of this undecidability, it is also
no longer possible to talk of knowledge. A fragment from *The Gay
Science,* which Nietzsche entitled "Our New 'Infinite,'" can be read with
this thought in mind:

> How far the perspectival character of existence extends or indeed
> whether existence can have any other character; whether existence
> without interpretation, without "sense," does not become "nonsense";
> whether, on the other hand, all existence is not essentially an *interpret-
> ing* existence—this cannot in fairness be decided even by the most
> dutiful labor and the most painfully conscientious analysis and self-

examination of the intellect; for in the course of this analysis the human intellect cannot help but see itself under its perspectival forms and *only* see in them. We cannot look around our own corner: it is a hopeless curiosity that wants to know what other forms of intellect and perspective there *might* be. . . . (2: 249–50; GS, 336)

It has not been decided whether "all existence is essentially *interpreting* existence," nor has an answer to the question whether there is existence other than merely interpreting existence been secured. Yet neither possibility can be excluded either. One cannot exclude the possibility that there is existence without interpretation and, accordingly, without "meaning," and so one must concede the possibility that our knowledge, our "meaning," is tinged by that meaningless existence, that existence without interpretation. Nietzsche concludes that: "The world has once again become 'infinite' for us: insofar as we cannot dismiss the possibility that it may include in itself infinite interpretations" (2: 250; GS, 336). These "infinite interpretations" are not, however, interpretations that would be available to knowledge and would have expanded the closed universe of knowledge into a world of polyperspectival interpretation. Since the thought of an infinitude of possible interpretations cannot be dismissed, the interpretation that is possible for human beings cannot claim a privileged access to the world, an access that would allow it to unite all possible interpretations of the world into a world of worlds and thereby attain the totality of knowledge denied to every particular interpretation. There is still less reason if, as Nietzsche emphasizes in this fragment, non-interpretations or interpretations that allow for no decision concerning their status as interpretations can also belong to the infinity of interpretations. It is no more possible to have a closed totality of interpretations than a closed unity of cognitive forms. Every particular cognition, every particular perspective, and every interpretation comes across the "coordinated possibility" that it could be a non-interpretation, a non-perspective, and a non-cognition—at the absolute limit of their meaning, at the limits of their determinability and self-determinability. To the degree to which the world has become infinite for "us," it has also become ineluctably, irreducibly, infinitely finite, incapable of presenting itself as a *world* at all. The infinite is the indefinite and therefore something that cannot be completely determined by a finite or an individual faculty of knowledge. In a later remark concerning the attempt to arrive at a complete characterization or definition of an object, Nietzsche puts it this way: "A thing would be characterized if all beings had first asked about it and come up with answers. Supposing a single being, with its own relationships and perspectives for all things, were missing, then the thing would not yet be 'defined'" (3: 487; WP, 301–302). As long as possibilities of interpretation other than those realized by conscious perception are still conceivable—and these possibilities include the liminal possibility of an interpretation that is not one—perpetual interpretations remain incapable of realizing the world and attaining a complete concept of the activity of interpreting itself. The possibility of infinite interpretations makes every particular interpretation and therefore the very concept of interpretation contingent. The possibility that the world, the perspective of the will, and interpretation could always be another one and, *a limine,* none at all—this potential of other possibilities that interpretation can never exhaust—inscribes an uncontrollable alterity into the very concept of interpretation and forbids, strictly speaking, all talk of interpretation *itself.* Tinged by other interpretations and non-interpretations, every interpretation must also be capable of being something other than interpretation and, *a limine,* no interpretation at all. Every interpretation is exposed to its other and to its Not: each one is from the beginning an ex-posed, interrupted interpretation.

The fourth consequence of Nietzsche's theory of interpretation concerns the traditional concept of truth as *adequatio intellectus et rei.* It makes sense to speak of measuring an exegetical assertion against its object only if the object of the assertion is already given. An interpretation can be said to correspond to the *interpretandum* or not to do so only if this *interpretandum* has a reality independent of every possible interpretation and the interpretation, in turn, has a reality independent of every possible *interpretandum.* The fundamental, diffundamental hermeneutics that Nietzsche sketches in his texts cannot have anything to do with given objects; it must concern itself with the constitution of its objects, on the one hand, and with the constitution and—since this constitution can only be infinite—the inconstitution of the activity of interpreting, on the other. This "hermeneutics" cannot construct a theory of truth as correspondence but must set out the conditions of possibility for, the genesis of, and the imperative demand for such a truth. If all knowledge is interpretation, and if interpretation, as Nietzsche understands it, is a form of the will to power, then his theory must give an account of the provenance of the theory of truth as *adequatio* and at the same time try to explain the possibility of another truth and exhibit this possibility in the very structure of the will. In a fragment dating from the time he wrote *Twilight of the Idols*, Nietzsche remarks: "'willing' is not 'desiring,' striving, longing for: it distinguishes itself from these by the affect of the commando."[40] The truth of interpreting is imperative. The command of the will—the "commando" in which it alone is will—is thus to be understood as the way in which the truth of the will, the truth of its interpretation, interpretation, and the will itself all occur. Interpretation, being imperative, is not a constative statement but the performance of truth, the truth itself as performance. But because the performance of the truth of interpretation—of this interpretation, which posits itself as truth and, positing itself as truth, performatively comes true—occurs in the precarious form of the imperative,

---

40. Nietzsche, KSA, 13: 54. Heidegger laid great emphasis on the command character of the will in the lectures on Nietzsche conducted in 1939 as well as in his essay of 1943, "Nietzsche's Word 'God Is Dead.'" See Martin Heidegger, *Nietzsche* (Pfullingen: Neske, 1961), esp. 1: 606–48; *Holzwege* (Frankfurt am Main: Klostermann, 1950). In the latter he writes: "The will is not a desire and no mere striving for something; rather, willing is in itself commanding. . . . Willing is the self-collecting in the task to be done. . . . As commanding, the will puts itself together with itself and that means: with what it wills" (216–17). Both the lectures on Nietzsche, especially the section on "Truth as Justice," and the essay on the statement "God is dead" engage in a thoroughgoing identification of the will with its imperative. That is, Heidegger places the will, as unconditioned synthesis, *together* with this imperative instead of seeing the will placed *under* the imperative. By speaking of the will's self-collecting, Heidegger denies the will's interpretive structure. From this he arrives at an exegesis of Nietzsche's philosophy as the completion of the metaphysics of subjectivity. To invoke *Auslegung* (taking apart, laying out) as an objection to Heidegger would obviously not matter very much if it were a matter of taking apart and laying out already available constituent parts of the will. But this is just what cannot be the case if taking apart, laying out, inter-pretation, and *Aus-legung* are always modes of an *impossible* self-relation of the will as well, if interpretation touches upon the possibility of a non-interpretation, if the world has "once again" become "infinite" in interpretation—which to say that it has become uninterpretable, impossible to will—and if therein the will concedes its inability to will or, rather, is free not to will. The will can *collect* itself only by being its own overpowering force, its own increase in power, its own self-transcendence. The will is thus auto-synthetic, becoming itself, and as this form of formation, it is the constitution of willing. Interpretation, by contrast, means inconstitution of the will, inconsistency of its form and self-formation, infinitude of its fragmentation.

and thus in the very form of an unfulfilled command; because it is, accordingly, not a perlocutionary but an illocutionary speech act; and because the language it commands has not yet come into being, the imperative occurs as a *pre*-locutionary "speech act." The will is what never fulfills itself, what resists itself as non-willing and never-willing, what infinitely slips away from its own performance and "unhinges" its per-formative, its command, the imperative of the truth of interpretation and self-interpretation as well. Without this failure—without a *Fehl*, an absence, a "without"—there would be no command, no *Be-fehl*.

The performative and *a fortiori* the sui-performative of imperative truth can accomplish itself only under the condition of its possible failure. This does not mean that there are no performatives, nor does it mean that there cannot be a will, the performative *par excellence*. But it does mean that the will can ground itself only if something of the will withdraws from it—something that is not itself, not yet itself, and never will be itself, and yet something that is still the basis of the will's fulfillment. Only if the will is exposed to its ex-action—its exformance—can it posit a ground for itself. The "ground" of the ground for the unconditioned auto-performance of the will in its imperative is this withdrawal of every ground—not only the withdrawal of the will but the withdrawal of everything it wills. The ground of the truth that establishes the will as the site of pure self-grounding is freedom from—or toward—the ground; the ground is thus freedom from—or toward—every truth, including the truth of correspondence. But only where the will is imperative and commands itself as will, only where it therefore does not yet stand in unison with itself but, positing itself as a "commando," first calls itself to this unison, only where the possibility remains that it does not correspond to itself, to its imperative, and that the imperative itself does not correspond *to itself*—only there can the will be the performance of its own truth, an always unfulfilled, retarding, retreating, withdrawn performance. The condition for the independence of the will thus lies in whatever in the will desists from willing, what in the will is released from the will and is therefore released *to* the will. In *Zarathustra* Nietzsche writes: "To stand with slack muscles and with unharnessed will: that is the most difficult for all of you, you sublime ones!" (2: 374; Z, 230).[41]

41. In the episode of *Zarathustra* that bears the title "Of Redemption" and concerns "the revulsion of the will against time and its 'it was'"—that is, representation of the will's

The will must be "unharnessed." It must be "unharnessed" and released, above all, from the will—from the will to self-redemption, from the will not to will and the will to will nothingness. Otherwise, the will— "slack," in repose—will not be able to enter into the freedom to will and thus into the freedom not to will. But this release from the will occurs in the imperative; it takes place in the very movement of the will as it interprets itself in this imperative, lays itself out and displaces itself toward something that can never correspond to it. The imperative of the will, its law, is its *Auslegung,* its displacement toward what is not and can never be posited or placed. The will is its release from itself, and this release occurs when the will lays itself out in the direction of something else—something independent from it—and when it reclaims for itself precisely what it never was: the unrepeatable, the unappropriable, its "own" alteration.

The will is the promise of itself. But it is such a promise only insofar as it does not have itself as the promised one at its disposal; only insofar as it withdraws itself from this promise of itself; only insofar as it—its "own" promise—is unfulfilled and is therefore not the will at all.[42] In its imperative the will is ahead of itself as another, as an unwillable will,

---

vengeance and self-redemption—Nietzsche writes in the same vein: "Is the will already unharnessed from its own foolishness?" (2: 395; Z, 253)—from the foolishness, that is, of being able to redeem itself by a willful non-willing. The meaning of "unharnessing" thus comes close to that of "unhinging" in the *Genealogy*. In Kafka, who was one of Nietzsche's best readers, one finds a note that could be taken for a reminiscence of Nietzsche's metaphorics of disjunction and, in particular, the metaphor of "unharnessing": "The more horses you harness up, the faster it goes—not the ripping of the block out of its foundation, which is impossible, but the tearing up of the straps and thus the empty, joyous ride" (*Hochzeitsvorbereitungen auf dem Lande* [Wedding Preparations in the Country] [Frankfurt am Main: Fischer, 1980], 66).

42. These considerations, which issue from the structure of the self-relation of the will in promising, find a pendant in Heidegger's *Nietzsche,* but astoundingly enough, *not* in his commentary on Nietzsche's texts. In one of the passages devoted to the "unthought" of Nietzsche, Heidegger writes: "Appealing to itself in this way, and holding itself in reserve by staying away, Being is *the promise of itself.* To think an encounter with Being itself in its staying away means: to become aware of this promise as the promise that 'is' Being itself. But it is by staying away, by failing to arrive, which is to say, insofar as nothing is going on with it" (Heidegger, "Nihilism Determined According to the History of Being," *Nietzsche,* 2: 369; cf. Heidegger, *Nietzsche,* ed. David Farrell Krell [San Francisco: Harper, 1991], 4: 226.).

"unharnessed" and "unhinged." Insofar as the will is ahead of itself, it is a will for another will and, perhaps, something other than will: a will that is not an object of willing but something absolutely impossible to will, something altogether non-intentional, not the gift of the will but a task it was never given. So long as the will is ahead of itself, it is something that does not belong to the will but is, rather, the absolutely un-bonding, dis-banding, un-belonging, un-longed-for. Ahead of itself, promised to be something it can never be, it is whatever remains impossible to promise. Because—and as long as—the will is the promise of itself, it remains precisely what cannot be promised.

Because—and as long as—promising sets out in the direction of the consistent, autonomous language of a will in accord with itself, the act of promising and thus language itself remain impossible to promise, impossible to pronounce, impossible to speak. "Promise" is a word for the aporia of the word and of language. It speaks of language as something that has not yet come into being, and merely by promising, this word says that it does not yet speak. "Promise" says that it does not yet say anything; it speaks of its non-speaking, hence of its incomprehensibility, and thus of the impossible premise on which every possible understanding rests. A promise sets out in the direction of what alone offers the possibility of, or the chance for, interpretation, namely the uninterpretable. The interpretation of the will is thus its excess, its taking apart, the exposition of every one of its positings, exposition *in* the very act of positing. Exegesis can no longer be understood as commanding execution (*exēgeomai*) of what already is but, rather, as a leading outward of whatever is and whatever is projected: it goes to and beyond the limits of the imperative will's hegemony, touching upon precisely what takes away its power and what the power of the will therefore always misses: the anexegetical.

This missing is the premise of promising and thus the premise of language in general. Missing is the self-withdrawing ground of this premise. Without a prior failure of language—without a *Ver-sagung*—nothing could ever be premised, nothing promised, nothing *versprochen*. The possibility of the Idea of autonomy, the possibility of what Kant calls reason, the possibility of a language that, because it is universally responsible, could measure up to its own criteria—each of these possibilities lies in this self-receding foundation, in a ground that is never given to the will and never given by itself: in a missing, a taking-away, an interdiction, a *Versagung*. Missing is the truth of promising. If something promises—promises promising and thus promises language—it is missing. Missing releases the promise from promising, and it alone lets it go out freely. But the freedom of promising, as freedom *to* autonomy and freedom *to* the self, is then freedom *before* the self as another: freedom *to* the other and *before* it. And as a *letting* out, as a freeing up, the freedom of promising is itself the alteration. If the truth of promising lies in this alteration and thus in something other than promising, then no correspondence can measure up to such a truth. Truth is not "correctness"—for it does not consist in the correspondence between given entities—and hermeneutics is not the "art of *correctly* understanding another's discourse," as Schleiermacher defines it. Hermeneutics is the releasing, the setting free of "another's discourse," and being itself discourse in its alteration, it is ana- and allo-hermeneutics. No will governs the conditions under which a promise could be fulfilled, and indeed the will cannot even raise the claim of giving promises *itself* and *giving* promises at all. Whenever there is a promise, something other than the promise and something other than language—or simply another language—is also spoken. What is promised is always something other than understanding, other than another understanding, and other than an alteration of understanding alone. Something unpromisable. "With slack muscles."

"DISGREGATION OF THE WILL"

Nietzsche on the Individual and Individuality

"Individuality" is a diplomatic word. By designating singularity, it treats it as a universal. It divides the indivisibility of which it speaks and imparts it to a generality from which singularity is supposed to withdraw.

Determined to mediate between the generality of what it asserts and the specificity of what is meant, the concept of individuality already speaks of a commonality of the word in whose sphere the claim to individuality becomes faint and dies away. The concept of individuality—even where it seeks to grasp its substance through mediation—"betrays" individuality. It betrays individuality by abandoning its claim of immediate singularity to the power of general language and generally comprehensible usage of language, yet at the same time in a way that perhaps lets it indicate its specific structure in relation to itself and in relation to generality as such. The ambiguity of the concept of individuality has left its traces in every system dedicated to its determination. When—entering this history at a relatively arbitrary point—Leibniz insists that every individual is individuated throughout its entire being (*omne individuum sua tota Entitate individuatur*[1]) and therefore comprises an infinity of determinations, each of which corresponds to the infinity of the universe and so escapes all finite modes of cognition, he must henceforth characterize individuality as the representation of a

---

1. Gottfried Wilhelm Leibniz, *Die philosophischen Schriften,* ed. C. J. Gerhardt (Berlin: Weidmann, 1890), 4: 18.

totality from which it must nevertheless be distinguished. A complete cognition of the individual is possible, according to Leibniz, only for a being that gathers the totality of necessary determinations into itself and is, as a result, no longer subjected to the conditions of its representation. The individual is therefore a monadological unity of an infinity of determinations, a unity that only an infinite faculty of cognition—that of God—can grasp. Finite individuals are incapable of recognizing themselves *as* individuals. It is from the standpoint of divine universality that individuality is conceived in Leibniz; the representational character of its infinite determinacy is conceived from the standpoint of the presence of an absolutely necessary being—the vanishing point where all the determinations of the individual gather together and where, in turn, the individual vanishes *as* an individual into the most universal thing of all. Thus conceived, individuality is fundamentally a theological concept the purpose of which is to redeem the finite individual of its contingency. If Christian Wolff's *Philosophia Prima sive Ontologia* determines the individual entity as *quod omnimode determinatum est* (that which is determined in every possible way),[2] it thus expresses in the simplest possible way the consequence of Leibniz's thoughts concerning individuality: the individual is thoroughly determined *by* the totality of its logical, historical, social, and psychic conditions; indeed, it is so completely destined *for* this totality that no genuine force of self-determination—no force by means of which it would have the ability to break out of its predetermined teleological movement—could ever be attributed to it. Individuality is not only a theological but also a teleological concept of a totality of determinations, each of which relates to all the others on the basis of a pre-established harmony, and this harmony protects them all from any fundamental destabilization. The *compossibilitas* of all individual determinations is the reassuring and totalizing ground for the individuality it determines, and it is also the basis for the cognition of individuality in general. The individual is a being held in place by its thoroughgoing determination—by its definition, its position, and its end.

2. The entire sentence runs as follows: "Cum entia singularia existant, evidens est, *Ens singulare,* sive *Individuum* esse illud, quod omnimode determinatum est." It can be found in Christian Wolff, *Gesammelte Werke,* ed. C. A. Corr, reprint edition (New York: Olms, 1983), Abt. II, 5: 188; *Philosophia prima sive Ontologia* (orig., Frankfurt, 1736), § 227. Wolff thus treats the concepts of "singularity" and "individuality" as synonymous.

Rejecting the fundamental ontological and epistemological assumptions of the Leibnizian and Wolffian schools, Kant made it clear in his reflection on *prototypon transcendentale* that thoroughgoing determination can be attributed only to an absolutely necessary being, thus to a highest being—an *ens entium* that, because it remains inaccessible to every finite understanding, can never be considered an objective thing but only a regulatory form of representation underlying our constitution of objects. Individuality thus figures here as an unknowable and nonpresentable prototype of objects that, as imitations of this thing, always fail to achieve its degree of positive determination. The individual, as something infinitely determined, is made finite by finite reason itself: the particular turns into an unspecified generality, the typical is ec-typified, and its being is reduced in every one of its representations. Since the archetype is no longer given but is merely assumed or assigned as a task, objects are on the verge of forfeiting their imitative character and thereby losing their form. After Kant, the thought of individuality lacks the secure ground of determination that could make it into an object of knowledge, and it thus lacks the unproblematic theo-teleological destination through which the demand for its internal totality could alone be fulfilled. The formula Goethe used in his letter to Lavater on September 20, 1780—*individuum est ineffabile*[3]—does not arise from a sensualist's animosity to conceptual rigor but from an insight that results from the collapse of the great rationalistic systems of the seventeenth and eighteenth centuries: the individual remains inaccessible to a finite faculty of presentation; its particularity cannot be captured by general linguistic conventions; and being finite, it does not even have at its disposal the means to express itself in its entirety *as* an individual. By expressing itself as an individual, it does not express itself in its entirety and does not entirely express itself: for cognition and for language, the whole has become something merely finite, an incomplete generality not only temporally but also structurally. Henceforth, individuality can stand for the capacity to project itself onto an indeterminate plurality of possible forms, each of which is open to further possibilities of determination, but none of which can conclude in a paradigmatic form. Singularity is no longer a representation of a prior or transcendentally guaranteed

3. Johann Wolfgang von Goethe, *Gedenkausgabe der Werke, Briefe und Gespräche,* ed. E. Beutler (Zurich: Artemis), 18: 533.

present, and it is no longer the prelude to a universality in whose realization it could find its final determination. Schlegel's thoughts on individuality, acquired in the course of his confrontation with Fichte, and Kierkegaard's remarks on "that single individual," which are extracted from his confrontation with Schlegel and Hegel, have to be read in this context.

For Nietzsche, the individual, considered in terms of its history, is first of all a form of past greatness, and this greatness is necessarily truncated whenever an attempt is made to secure its objectivity for the sake of knowledge or to carry out an historical repetition. In the second of the *Untimely Meditations,* "On the Use and Disadvantage of History for Life," he connects the conditions not only of writing history but of history itself, and thus the condition in which history is first made, with the efficacy of authentic individuality:

> How much variety must be overlooked if it [a comparison between the greatness of the past and the greatness of the present] is to have that strengthening effect, how violently must the individuality of the past be forced into a general form and all its sharp angles and lines broken to pieces for the sake of the comparison! At bottom, whatever was once possible can only present itself as possible a second time if the Pythagoreans were right in believing that given the same constellation of heavenly bodies, the same things would have to repeat themselves on earth down to the very last details.[4]

4. Friedrich Nietzsche, *Werke in drei Bänden,* ed. Karl Schlechta (Munich: Ullstein, 1966), 1: 222; cf. *Untimely Meditations,* trans. R. J. Hollingdale (Cambridge, England: Cambridge University Press, 1983), 68; hereafter, "UM." As in the previous essay, "The Promise of Interpretation," references to Nietzsche's writings indicate, whenever possible, the Schlechta edition (volume number, page number) and then a readily available English translation. Other abbreviations for the English translations used in the chapter are the following: "BGE" = *Beyond Good and Evil,* trans. Walter Kaufmann (New York: Vintage, 1966). "CW" = *The Case of Wagner* in *The Birth of Tragedy,* trans. Walter Kaufmann (New York: Vintage, 1967). "EH" = *Ecce Homo* in *The Genealogy of Morals,* trans. Walter Kaufmann and R. J. Hollingdale (New York: Vintage, 1969). "GS" = *The Gay Science,* trans. Walter Kaufmann (New York: Vintage, 1974). "HATH" = *Human, All Too Human,* trans. R. J. Hollingdale (Cambridge, England: Cambridge University Press, 1986). "Truth" = "On Truth and Lying in an Extra-Moral Sense," in *Friedrich Nietzsche on Rhetoric and Language,* ed. and trans. S. Gilman, C. Blair, and D. Parent (Oxford: Oxford University Press, 1989), 244–57. "TI" = *Twilight of the Idols* in *The Portable Nietzsche,* trans. and ed. Walter Kaufmann (Harmondsworth: Penguin, 1976).

As this passage suggests, the conditions in which the presence of an individual thing could be secured are the conditions of its generalization, and that means the conditions of its de-individualization, of the violation, rape, and destruction not only of the individual but of the very possibility of individuality—all of it carried out by a universal law. Whenever the individual is repeated, it is no longer the individual it once should have been. Individuality, whose image the past holds in store, is simply a mythical figure that can serve as a stereotype through changing times, lending them an aura of lasting greatness. The individuality of the historical ideal, whose destiny is to distribute impulses of life in the present, must—by virtue of its character as ideal type—dig the grave of the living. It is not the individual as such but its stiff, typical, and typifying form that is grasped in such individuality.[5] But the individual would be precisely that which cannot be absorbed into any type, form, figure, or codifiable meaning.

As long as it stands under the law of repetition, the present is incapable of offering what the form of re-presentation destroys:

> The individual has withdrawn into the interior: outside, one no longer notices anything individual at all; it is to the point where one may well wonder whether there can be causes without effects. Or is a race of eunuchs needed to watch over the great historical world-harem? As for them, of course, pure objectivity makes their faces beautiful. Yet it almost seems as if their task were to stand guard over history to make sure that nothing comes of it other than stories—but certainly not an event! (1: 239; UM, 84)

Under the pressure exerted by the representative types of individuality handed down from the past, the individual has forfeited its capacity to distinguish itself effectively from the historical world to which its actions and its knowledge nevertheless refer. It has assimilated to the types against whose background it was to have borne witness to its own historical, sexual, and semantic difference; it is an equal among equals, cut off from what made it individual and thus unequal, castrated, a eunuch among women. But in the realm of equality—whether historical

---

5. On the problem of type, typology, and "ontotypography" in the philosophical tradition between Plato, Nietzsche, and Heidegger, see the important studies of Philippe Lacoue-Labarthe, *Typography,* ed. Christopher Fynsk (Cambridge, Mass.: Harvard University Press, 1989).

equality between past and present, epistemological equality between the act of thinking and the object thought, juridical equality among citizens of bourgeois society, or physiological equality between different genders and generations—there is no history. For history, as Nietzsche conceives of it, is linked to the condition of inequality, indeed to a condition in which each of the moments partaking of history is incommensurable with every other. It is in the individual that this incommensurability steps forward and becomes a power that breaks down and transforms the uniformity of historical circumstances and the generality of cognitive forms; only in this way does it become a historical power proper, that is, a power capable of opening up history in the first place. Individuality is so completely determined as incommensurability that no individual could correspond to its concept if it were to be at one with—and equal to—itself, if it were to be a completely determined form. It corresponds to its concept, paradoxically, by being inadequate to it. *Human, All Too Human* recommends as a means to knowledge that one not "uniformize" oneself by striking a consistent pose and that one not treat oneself "as a rigid, constant, *single* individual" (1: 719; HATH, 196). Only the nonidentity of the individual with itself constitutes its individuality. Measured against itself as concept, bearing, and function, individuality proves to be other and more—or less—than itself: it is always only that which reaches beyond its empirical appearance, its social and psychic identity, and its logical form. Individuality is unaccountable excess.

If individuality is the irreducibly unequal, and if the individuality of past and present life is betrayed in the typological identifications of idealist, positivistic, archeological, and teleological historiographies, then the basis on which individuality is first made possible—and therefore the basis of every affirmative or critical discussion of it—can only lie in the difference between the uniformity of the hitherto historical and a future not yet invested with types, meanings, and values. The term "individuality" properly applies only to that which transgresses the series of forms and the form of the forms itself—knowledge according to types—and undertakes this transgression in the direction of a future that withdraws from typology, objectification, representation. This movement alone dissolves the rigor mortis of canonical forms of life and derails the characteristic compulsion of universal concepts to subsume everything under their forms. Individuality is always still to come; it is never already given, for it is what arises from the future as a possibility for the present, what is always still to arise, and what in this way—in its giving—withholds its own arrival. There can be no life unless individuality arises from and gives itself over to its futurity. And it is for precisely this reason that the concept of individuality achieves such an eminent position in Nietzsche's thought: "We ourselves are not convinced . . . that we truly have life within us," he writes in the second of the *Untimely Meditations*. As a "lifeless and yet uncannily mobile factory of concepts and words, I may still have the right to say of myself *cogito ergo sum* but not *vivo ergo cogito*. I am guaranteed empty 'being,' not full and verdant 'life'; my original feeling assures me only that I am a thinking being, not that I am a living one, not that I am an *animal* but, at best, a *cogital*. 'First give me life'—thus cries out every individual. . . . Who will give you this life?—Neither a divine nor a human being: only your own *youth*" (1: 280–81; UM, 119–20). No power that transcends the individual—neither another human being nor an authority that lies beyond the human, nor even the individual human being—is the source of historical life; rather, its source is only that which, in the individual itself, reaches out as "youth" beyond the limits of its own historical and epistemological determination and reaches toward a still open future. The proposition with which free individuality grants itself existence—but this does not mean it asserts or states its being, since substantiality is not given to it—no longer reads *cogito ergo sum*, nor even the simple performative *ego sum* but rather *ero sum*. With respect to my indeterminacy in relation to any totality, and in view of my constitutively inconclusive futurity, I grant myself being. Only my futurity gives me life. This life is never something present to hand that could be available for discursive description; it is never already there and is never expressed as something already in existence; rather, it is always what is still to come in all futures and what is only announced in language. The discourse of the individuum— and its own discourse—is not predication but pre-dication in the sense of pre-saying, pre-diction, and promising: it is the discourse of saying beforehand and, as stated in the *Genealogy of Morals*, vouching for the future.[6] By promising in this way, I grant myself being and grant it to myself each time in a singular manner. Being—singularity—is a promise.

---

6. "To breed an animal *with the right to make promises*—is this not the paradoxical task that nature posed with respect to man? Is not this the real, the proper problem *of* man?" . . . To be able to vouch for himself *as a future?*" (2: 799–80; GM, 57–58). If these

Being is never established in my speech but is announced there as a claim with a single reservation, that of futurity. It is, therefore, never sufficiently announced and never with such completeness that it could be generalized. If the life of historical generalities is subject to laws (the second of Nietzsche's *Untimely Meditations* attempts to describe some of these laws), then the futurity of this life and the form of an always insufficient promise—the only one that corresponds to such futurity— constitute the law of these laws. It singularizes even the most universal.

One objection to this thought of the futurity of life, which the language of free individuality opens up, is that there is no language that can do without conventional rules of meaning. Nietzsche not only never denied the conventionalism of linguistic forms and of forms of life in general; indeed, a large portion of his analytic labor was devoted to demonstrating that even the forms of logic which do not wear the signs of their historicity on their sleeves have a conventional character whose motivation is historical and economical, at least in the sense of wanting to economize on thinking. But meaning accrues to these forms because they all refer to a future whose shape cannot be thoroughly defined by any convention, a future that will decide on the survival or decay of such conventions. Thus even the phenomena of the past and the present can never be understood within the framework of conventional rules alone but only in view of that which, as the future, sanctions the legitimacy of any given rule or threatens to withdraw this sanction from every one. Nietzsche writes: "The judgment of the past is always an oracular judgment: only as an architect of the future, as one who knows the present will you understand it," and "Only he who builds the future [has] a right . . . to pass judgment on the past" (1: 251; UM, 94). Only a gaze coming from the future lets the individuality to which the images of great historical individuals and individual epochs refer come into view. Even

---

formulations and the ones that follow recall Heidegger's privileging of the future as the domain of authentic being-able-to and his interpretation of "understanding" as forerunning *(Vorlaufen)* in the possibilities of *Dasein,* it is because Heidegger's reflections look back, in part, to Nietzsche. Heidegger offers his thanks to Nietzsche in a brief, impressive analysis of the "Uses and Disadvantage of History for Life" *(Being and Time,* § 76); but this debt is poorly repaid when, in his lectures on Nietzsche, he no longer deems Nietzsche's contribution to the development of a new appraisal of the futurity of *Dasein* even worth mentioning.

if language and social life are subject to conventional rules, they nevertheless become persuasive and comprehensible only in the space open to the future as a realm in which the validity and comprehensibility of these rules are no longer secure. Understanding is possible only on the basis of the suspension of self-evident understanding; language is possible only on the basis of the exposure, interruption, and breakdown of both its traditional forms and the compulsion of its present state. And every foundation of a possibility arises only when foundations and possibilities are no longer seen as secure. Even the most universal entity can appear only at the site of whatever escapes its grasp: on the spot where it bears the signature of a coming—but always still coming and never already arrived—singularity.

Past and present thus owe their capacity for meaning to that which, as an individual, surpasses their totality, their semantic rules, and their constitutive forms. Life springs forth out of its own future, the whole out of a part severed from itself; the progressive distancing of this part constantly displaces the borders of the whole and thereby prevents it from closing in on itself and locking itself into a rigid stance. Individuality undoes the determination of every form of life determined by types and values, and so individuality is, for Nietzsche, the very in-determination of that which Leibniz and his school considered to be the *omnimode determinatum,* namely the *individuum.* As the open ground of anything determined in a thoroughgoing manner, the individual is the in-determination of this determination.

The emphatic formulations found in the introduction to the third part of *Untimely Meditations* on "Schopenhauer as Educator" can be properly understood only when one takes into account the excessive function, indeed the dysfunction that Nietzsche assigns to individuality and the idea of the sovereign individual:

> At bottom, every human being knows quite well that he is only in the world once, as a *unicum,* and that no accident, however strange, will shake together for a second time such a wonderfully motley multiplicity into the unity that he is. . . . Artists alone hate this negligent romping about in borrowed mannerisms and drapery of opinions, and they reveal the secret, the bad conscience of everyone, the sentence: every human being is a one-time miracle. . . . The man who does not want to become part of the masses needs only to stop being comfortable

with himself; let him follow his conscience, which calls out to him:
"Be yourself! What you're doing, thinking, desiring now—that's not
you at all." (1: 287–88; UM, 127)

And he writes later on: "Each one bears a productive uniqueness within
himself as the core of his being; and when he becomes conscious of this
uniqueness, a strange radiance appears around him—that of the un-
usual" (1: 306; UM, 143). It certainly appears as though the Nietzsche
of this text and of countless others subordinates "productive uniqueness"—the production and education of which, despite its debt to a
certain "chance," are the main concerns of "Schopenhauer as Educator"—to an altogether anti-individual aim: the "metaphysical purpose"
of helping nature to achieve enlightenment about itself and thereby
bringing itself to perfection. This purpose is served by the "production
of the philosopher, the artist, and the saint inside and outside us" (1: 326;
UM, 160). According to a roughly contemporaneous sketch entitled
"We Philologists," a human being remains "an individual only under
three forms of existence: as philosopher, as saint, and as artist" (3: 326).
The *summum* of individuality, which nature achieves in the philosopher,
the saint, and the artist touches only what is bereft of all individuality.
Indeed, the ultimate destiny and determination of individuality, its telos
and its meaning, is to lead the natural universe—which has been estranged from itself through spatial and temporal existence and therefore
has fallen under the influence of the *principium individuationis*—back to
itself, to reconcile itself with itself, and thus to become the organ of its
self-knowledge, its self-relation, its self. At its peak, individuality is destined to be extinguished in the altogether undifferentiated—at the point
"where the I is entirely dissolved and its life of suffering is no longer, or
almost no longer, felt individually but rather as the deepest feeling of
sameness, togetherness, and oneness in all that is alive" (1: 326; UM,
160–61). According to this conception of individuality—which is anything but "individual" since it hardly differs from that of Schopenhauer—the individual is essentially a function of the self-totalizing of
the totality, the systemization of the system. And yet, as Nietzsche
acknowledges in the *correctio* from "no longer" to "almost no longer,"
only *almost*. The articulating member that joins the system of nature
with the "feeling of oneness in all that is alive" cannot be sutured to
either side without the minimal additive of individuality, without an

individual that transgresses and transcends the forms of universal consciousness subjected to the *principium individuationis*. Since this individuality beyond individuality, this ultra-individuality, is still subjected to the principle of disarticulation, it can only *almost* sew up the gap between the oneness and the allness of the living. In terms of unity, individuality is the moment of difference from itself; in terms of difference, it is the moment of its possible but never conclusive unity. Individuality—and *a fortiori* the individuality of the philosopher, the artist, and the saint—is here the moment in which the totality of the living comes to itself, without ever arriving at itself. Its "productive uniqueness" is productive difference: the difference, in other words, that produces the illusory appearance of the unity among the living, a difference that could never be reduced to this illusion.

The thought of the mutual implication of the twin principles to which the *Birth of Tragedy* is devoted—the Apollinian and the Dionysian—had allowed Nietzsche to free himself in this early work from the Schopenhauerian hypostasis of an indestructible life-substance from which individuality would be only a regrettable and even sinful deviation.[7] Soon after his homage to Schopenhauer in *Untimely Meditations,* he could explicitly turn away from the philosophy of his teacher, a philosophy that vilifies all individuation as the original sin of the human race. And this turn occurs with increasing emphasis in *Human, All Too Human* and *The Gay Science.* A note from the posthumous papers of the 1880s returns once again to a critical appraisal of Schopenhauer's theory of individuation and, in particular, to the presentation of individuation as false step, error, and aberration:

The pessimistic condemnation of life in Schopenhauer is a *moral* translation of the herd's criteria into the language of metaphysics.—The "individuum" is meaningless, so let's give it an origin in the "in itself" (and give it a meaning of its existence as "aberration"). . . . Science's

7. "For," Schopenhauer writes in the chapter "On Death and Its Relation to the Indestructibility of Our Being" in the second volume of *The World as Will and Representation,* "at bottom every individuality is only a special error, a false step, something that would be better had it never existed; indeed, it is the actual purpose of life for us to recede from it" (*Die Welt als Wille und Vorstellung,* ed. A. Hübscher [Wiesbaden: Brockhaus, 1949], 2: 563; cf. Arthur Schopenhauer, *The World as Will and Representation,* trans. E. F. J. Payne [New York: Dover, 1958], 2: 491–92).

inability to comprehend the individual takes its revenge: *the individual is the entire life up until now* in *one line* and *not* its result.   (3: 545)

The individual is not merely a tangent flying off from the circle of totality nor an aberration from the way of the will into the nothingness of its being; likewise, the individual is not the result of a generic process, for as such it would not be independent but only an example of a genus or genre. Rather, the individual is the entire life process itself: "each individual being [is] just the *entire process* in a straight line . . . and so the individual being has *enormously great significance*" (3: 558). This Leibnizian thesis—that the individual is the entire process and that no foreign instance opposes its internal universality—must be supplemented and counterposed by a further determination: the individual can lay claim to "enormously great significance" only as a being capable of autonomy. Only when it "sets new goals for itself," only when it projects itself into its own future and proves itself free *from* conventions, customs, and morals and at the same time free *toward* its own futurial "self"—only then does the individual become an enormously significant singularity in which the entire process of its becoming is presented under the sign of its futurity. Only in relation to itself as to the still-outstanding, futurial "self" is the individual a united whole and, beyond that, singular: free from every pregiven totality and from every totality it gives.

Another closely related draft emphasizes both the tendentious character of the individual and the imperative of futurity that stretches beyond its immanent totality: "*The excessive force* in *spirituality,* setting new goals *for itself;* certainly not merely to command and lead the lower world or for the maintenance of the organism, of the 'individual.'—We are *more* than the individual; we are the entire chain as well, with the tasks of all the chain's futures" (3: 561). This accent on "new" goals is reinforced by the following note, which emphatically reclaims the category of the *novum* for the theory of interpretation:

The individual is something entirely *new* and *creator of newness,* something absolute, all actions being entirely *its* own.—The isolated one ultimately draws the values that guide his actions only out of himself, for he must *interpret* for himself *in an entirely individual manner* even the words he inherits. *The interpretation* of the formula is at least personal; even if he does not also *create* a formula, as *interpreter,* he is always still creating. (3: 913)

The innovative character of the individual is the result of a specific trait of the force that posits values and new interpretations of words—a trait that functions beyond the narrow sphere of literary hermeneutics and is in every sense decisive not only for the structure of inherited formulas and traditional types of action but for the structure of individuality as well. This force does not "preserve" the organism or the process that results in an organism, for in that case it would merely be a function of whatever preceded it. It is also not the force of *self*-preservation, for in that case it would only maintain what is already given. It is a force of particularization and individuation only as an "excessive" force: a force that wastes itself, a force through which the self and its capacity for self-preservation are squandered. Only the excess of force, only the "feeling of fullness, of power wanting to overflow . . . the consciousness of a richness wanting to give and send gifts" (2: 730–31; BGE, 205) transgresses the borders of a given context of traditions; only this transforms the formulas, types, and values of social actions, the grammatical rules, the "words" and codified meanings of a language, dissolving them in the act of interpretation by way of the new. The force of individuation—the self-surpassing force—surpasses the individual as determined by the historical totality of its moments. The excess of singularity—and singularity is nothing but this excess—de-termines the determined. This force ruptures the determinations and limits of a thoroughly determined thing, interrupts it, and leaves it—as a task—to the discretion of the temporal excess called "the future," an excessive share that no past and no present can ever completely ration.

The motor force of the transition from a conventional formula to its interpretation, from a general type to its singular alteration, is neither the individual as an organic unity or a unity of apperception, nor individuality as the essence of personal identity, but the force that individuates by its excessiveness and expenditure—an excessiveness thanks to which individual beings and their configurations are there in the first place. Excess alone individuates. The individual is therefore not a moment of the whole—whether conceived as *totum* or as *compositum*—and still less the autonomous form of a self-positing, substantial subject. What emerges as individuality from "excess" structurally outdoes totality and subjectivity, and since there could be neither totality nor subjectivity without this excess, the outdoing of both belongs, paradoxically, to the conditions of their possibility. Individuality—or, more exactly, singularity—is, as *transcendens,* the transcendental of subjectivity. If there is individual autonomy, it is only by virtue of that which exceeds this autonomy.

The fact that the life of the individual is due to what exceeds the sphere of its personal or objective givenness makes the concept of life and the concept of individuality and its Being problematic and also confounds the language in which these concepts are articulated. In aphorism 262 of *Beyond Good and Evil,* which concerns the question "What Is Noble?," Nietzsche pursues this problem. It never exhausts itself in individual forms of speech on individuality, for it is, beyond that, a problem of the linguistic articulation of transcendental forms in general and thus the very problem of a transcendental language. According to the fictional history of society developed in this section, which is at the same time a history of socialization and its collapse, "a kind" or a "type" with few but very strong traits is fixed "by a long struggle with essentially the same *unfavorable* conditions into hardness, monotony, simplicity of form." If the "enormous tension" to which the type is subjected slackens during some "fortunate situation," then "all of a sudden the fetters and pressures of ancient training" are torn apart: "The variation—whether as deviation (into the higher, finer, stranger), or as degeneration and monstrosity—suddenly comes on stage in the greatest fullness and splendor; the individual dares to be individual and to separate itself" (2: 735–36; BGE, 210–11). "Deviation" and "degeneration," atypicality and monstrosity—individuality, in short—arise not simply from a continual historical process but from the supplemental contingency of a "fortunate situation," a lucky break that allows the fetters and the traits of training to be broken and lets a suddenly old morality be transgressed, so that the "as it were, exploding egoisms, wildly turned against one another . . . no longer know how to curb themselves by means of this morality." Trait, training, and restraint are ripped apart in the fortunate situation in which the type seems to have blossomed into pure autonomy. From the immanent tension of trait, training, and restraint, from the very pressure of a sociality that has suddenly become excessive, the type is driven beyond itself: "It was this morality itself that had accumulated the enormous force that bent the bow in such a threat-ening manner—now it is, now it becomes 'outlived' [*überlebt*]." The morality of the type—of unity and generality, of sociality and form, of determining traits and training—has therefore "'outlived'" itself and is "'outlived.'" The type outlives itself, lives beyond its own life, yet it sur-vives its life not as itself, not as a type and not according to the measure of life established in a typology, but as "the greater, more multifarious, more extensive life." The type "outlives" itself as "the 'in-dividual'" (2: 736; BGE, 210). When the individual "outlives" itself, a structurally limitless multiplicity replaces unity; a disorganized anarchy of individuals replaces the generality of the polis and the State; the sumptuousness of a concept that no longer grasps itself replaces logical generality; infinite self-retreat replaces the "trait" that holds everything within fixed, objectifying contours; and "young, still undrained, still unexhausted decay" replaces the life that was coextensive with the sphere of form. For, insofar as it "outlives" itself, life becomes—in accordance with a nuance in the meaning of the German as well as the English word—obsolete, useless, extinct. Life itself is "outlived." It no longer lives. "Outlived" in this way, life goes on, altered, having become some-thing other than itself: it lives on out. Nietzsche writes, "Now it is, now it becomes 'outlived,'" and takes up one meaning of the "word" *out-lived*—the potential meanings of which he runs through during the course of this aphorism—in the very next sentence: "the dangerous and uncanny point [has been] reached where the greater, more multifarious, more extensive life *lives out away* from the old morality"—and from the forms of life contained within it. "The 'individual' stands there, forced into being his own lawgiver, into conceiving his own arts and stratagems for self-preservation, self-elevation, self-deliverance." For this reason, the individual is doubtless, as another phrase puts it, "the genius of the race," a genius that lives out away from itself; but the individual "out-lives" itself only as one "overflowing from all cornucopias of good and bad," as the excessive itself, not as one that preserves itself in the form of a "genius" and not as the genius of the ominous "race." It stays alive only in the monstrosity of the "individual" that no longer has the re-sources of race, type, and typisizing genius at its disposal. In the "indi-vidual," the life of society, its form and meaning, "outlives" itself. But far from sublating itself in the "individual," the life that is thereby formed "preserves" itself in the singular only in order to abandon itself to its "still undrained, still unexhausted decay." The "individual" is the sur-vivor and decomposer of itself and society.[8]

"Outlived"—this means, as in "to be outlived," to be exhausted, in-substantial, and powerless; it also means, as in "to become outlived," that something not used up, not quite exhausted, endures beyond life; and it means—according to a sense of the word that had become "out-lived" and outmoded but that Nietzsche revived with his metaphorics of luxuriance—to live too much, to overlive, to live to excess. In the sentence "the individual, outlived, outlives" to which Nietzsche's aphorism can be condensed, all these threads of meaning tie themselves into a knot: having become obsolete, the type—of life, of society—"lived on out" so far beyond itself in the "individual" that it decomposes into an "individual." "Individual" is no longer anything other than the unfet-tered and untrainable self-outliving, the dying out, and, if this word is allowed, the self-outdying of life: the passing away that "lives on out and beyond" all limits, the dying out of Being understood as the unity of a historical, social, or logical form. Individuality "is" out-life; living out away from every manageable life; life without life; "life" in quota-tion marks. And as it survives in its out-living, as it survives its "death," the "individual" "is" out-dying itself—dying beyond every conceivable

---

8. At this point one of the many traces that Nietzsche left behind in the work of Adorno makes itself apparent. In the section of *Negative Dialectics* devoted to "World-Spirit and Natural History—Excursion to Hegel," the relation between individuality and social history is presented in the following manner: *"The individual outlives itself.* But in its residue which history has condemned lies nothing but what does not sacrifice itself to false identity. The function of the individual is that of the functionless—of the spirit that does not agree with the universal and is therefore powerless to represent it. Only as exempt from the general practice is the individual capable of thoughts that would be required for a practice leading to change" (*Negative Dialektik* [Frankfurt am Main: Suhrkamp, 1965], 335; cf. *Negative Dialectics,* trans. E. B. Ashton [New York: Seabury Press, 1973], 343; italics added). Individuality, for Adorno as well as for Nietzsche, has "outlived" itself and is "outlived" in the process of a society that essentially produces itself according to the law of equivalence and, as a result, to the law of the most complete assimilation possible. But it is not, for this reason, erased. Individuality is residual, a remainder whose only function in the social process of universal functionalization is that of the functionless, the unwieldy point of resistance. The slightest transcendence mani-festing itself in the individual—in the "outlived" individual—(which Adorno calls "spirit") marks the distance from which it can first be thought and the form of socially sanctioned praxis can be altered.

death. Dying without dying, it is "itself" its out-death: "death" in quotation marks.

And in Nietzsche's text the "individual" stands in quotations marks as well: ". . . the 'individual' stands there. . . ." The "individual" does not live. It "outlives" (itself). Its being is being-out and being-left-over, insubstantial remainder, and excess beyond every determinable form of human life. Instead of being a social or psychic form of human existence, the individual—exceeding type and genus—is the announcement of the *Über-mensch.* Generally translated as the "overman" or "superman," in this context it ought to be understood as the "out-man," man the remainder and man the excess. But the individual is this announcement only in the mode of an "uncanny," "dangerous," "luxuriating" "monstrosity," only in the form of one who, having outlasted the death of its type, has returned to haunt the living: a living corpse, therefore, that respects neither the borders of life nor those of death, nor even the conventional semantic difference between them. Nietzsche diagnoses in the individual "a fateful simultaneity of spring and autumn," which recalls the "signs of ascent and descent" that he discovered in himself and announced in *Ecce Homo* by way of a riddle: "I have . . . already died as my father, as my mother I live on and become old" (2: 1070; EH, 222). Nietzsche thus sees the good fortune of his existence and its "singularity, perhaps" (2: 1070; EH, 222) in the fact that he, as his own mother, outlives himself as his own father—that he outlives himself, and by surviving in this way, doubled, he is his own *Doppelgänger* (2: 1073; EH, 225).[9] It is not the unifying but only the splitting and doubling of the trait forming the type that constitutes the uniqueness of its existence. Only in its duality does individuality carry itself out; only the *dividuum* is the *individuum*[10]—"perhaps." And this "perhaps" signals beyond all empirical uncertainty the impossibility of achieving unambiguous knowledge of a being whose singularity lies in its splitting.

---

9. On the movement of the *Doppelgänger* in Nietzsche, cf. my *pleroma—zu Genese und Struktur einer dialektischen Hermeneutik bei Hegel* in G. W. F. Hegel, *Der Geist des Christentums, Schriften 1796–1800,* ed. W. Hamacher (Berlin: Ullstein, 1978), 306–18. On the same problem, see Jacques Derrida, *The Ear of the Other: Otobiography, Transference, Translation,* ed. Christie V. McDonald, trans. Peggy Kamuf and Avital Ronell (New York: Schocken, 1985).

10. In *Human, All Too Human,* under the title "Morality as Self-dispersion of Man"— and before the aphorism "What One Can Promise"—Nietzsche writes in a different vein,

If the formula "something becomes outlived" may leave room for the hope that what outlives, in contrast to what has become outlived, is still useful and forceful, if it suggests that what outlives is opposed to what becomes outlived as life is to death, or that the line of demarcation between the two is as distinct as whatever stamps the type—if this is the case, then the phrase "fateful simultaneity of spring and autumn" in the epoch of individuality informs us that there can be an outliving only by virtue of the alliance, or mesalliance, between this outliving and decay. No primordial, positive power lives in the individual: the "still un-drained, still unexhausted decay" lives on. Individuality is not only spring and autumn at the same time; it is the spring of autumn. If power, life, and Being were supposed to manifest and preserve themselves within the typical form, then the "excessive force" and the "outliving" of the individual releases whatever ruptures the form of Being, the type of social life: this "excessive force" thus releases the finitude of Being. The Being that "outlives" itself in the individual—singular Being—is the passage into a finitude that knows no limits because it "is" the limit. Singularity, "outliving," does not live on. But it also does not die; rather, it "outlives"—and this improper, figural "outliving," this "outliving" only in quotations marks or in metaphor, is its opening onto a finitude that can no longer be thought from the perspective of death as the limit of life and can no longer be understood from the perspective of life as something with an externally and retroactively imposed limit. Just as the singular belongs to a future, so too does the finitude of this singular-ity—and neither a form of life nor death could ever correspond to this future. Since it arises from an irretrievable and indefinite futurity, from the hyperbola of a trans-formative project, "finitude" must be thought in quotation marks and thought as an "improper" concept—as out-fini-tude and in-finitude.[11]

"In morality the human being does not act as *individuum* but rather as *dividuum*" (1: 491; HATH, 42). In still another vein, Novalis writes, "The genuine dividual is also the genuine individual" ("Das allgemeine Brouillon," no. 952, *Die Werke Friedrich von Har-denbergs,* ed. Richard Samuel, Hans-Joachim Mähl, and Gerhard Schulz [Stuttgart: Kohlhammer, 1965], 2: 692).

11. It has been pointed out to me that Nietzsche's *"überleben,"* as it is read here, resembles the *survivre* that Jacques Derrida has read in certain texts of Blanchot and Shelley. Such may be the case. I assume, however, that this resemblance is broken by a

At the end of his aphorism, Nietzsche takes up the problem of "out-living" one more time and thereby emphasizes once again the impor-tance of this word for the thought of the individual. Concerning those who endure under the conditions of a society decomposing into indi-viduals, he writes: "Only the average ones have the prospect of continu-ing, of propagating themselves—they are the people of the future, the only ones to live on and out" (2: 737; BGE, 212). The criterion of the type, lost in the individual, is reinstated for the purposes of self-preser-vation in a quantitatively determined, mediocre standard. Yet the mo-rality of the standard and the average owes its existence to the excessive-ness of individuality that such a morality itself rejects. Mere survival is an apotropaic movement against the finitude of the "outliving" from which it arose. Because the norm it suggests has already become histori-cally obsolete, all talk of the survival of the mediocre is condemned to contradiction. The norm is—no less than the "individual" it seeks to discredit—structurally ironic:

> What will the moral philosophers emerging at this time have to preach now? These acute observers and loiterers discover that the end is fast approaching, that everything around them deteriorates and makes things deteriorate, that nothing will stand the day after tomorrow, except *one* kind of man, the incurably mediocre. . . . "Be like them! become mediocre!" bids the only morality left. . . . But it is difficult to preach, this morality of mediocrity!—. . . . It will have a hard time *concealing the irony!* (2: 736–37; BGE, 212)

All talk of the "outliving" of the individual that takes place only in the excess of passing away is as improper and ironic as this apologia of the normative. Nietzsche writes in one of his later notes under the title "Renaissance and Reformation": "What does the Renaissance *prove*? That the reign of the 'individual' can only be brief. The squandering is too great; it lacks the possibility of collecting, of capitalizing, and ex-haustion follows close at its heels. There are times when everything is *wasted,* when even the force with which one collects, capitalizes, piles riches upon riches is squandered" (3: 825). The realm of the *"indivi-*

---

series of individual differences; compare "Living On" in Harold Bloom et al., *Deconstruc-tion & Criticism* (New York: Seabury, 1979), 75–176.

duum"—Nietzsche again places this concept in quotation marks in order mark its inadequacy—is the realm of squandering, so much so that the force of "the individual," which alone could collect, bind together, preserve, and increase what has been spent is squandered. What wastes itself in the individual and its "outliving" cannot be converted into capital—not even, at the limit, under the rubric of the "individual." The individual is just this squandering, this inability to collect and grasp itself either in the temporal unity of the duration of its outliving, in the unity of social life, or even in the unity of a concept.

The meaning of the concept of "individuality" in Nietzsche is thus almost entirely opposed to the conventional one: it means that which is separated from itself and from every self susceptible of being made into a type; it means the "dividuum" that hyperbolically transcends itself; and, more exactly, it means the exorbitant process of this "dividuum," its hyperbole and "division." The word "outliving" proceeds along a similarly de-conventionalizing path. Instead of grasping in the unity of a concept what is in itself nonunitary, this word—and here it ceases to be simply a "word"—disperses in at least three different directions of meaning, each of which is determined according to its grammatical function and its place in the context: it means *longius vivere, supervivere, defungere,* and *excedere; darüber hinwegleben, überleben, über-leben,* and *"abgelebt"*—"living out away," "outliving," "living out," "living on," "surviving," "overliving," and "outlived." The word that is supposed to articulate the super-structure, the residual structure, and the ultra-structure of the individual is itself overdetermined and out-determined in such a way that its individual moments of meaning can no longer be brought together into a semantic continuum and thereby "capitalized." What Nietzsche writes about egoisms—that is, about individuals and their conflicting movements of individuation—applies equally well to the individual moments of meaning: "entangled and ensnared side by side and often in one another . . . an enormous ruination and self-ruin, thanks to the, as it were, exploding egoisms savagely turned against one another" (2: 736; BGE, 211). In "outliving," the individual moments of meaning outlive their own lexical significance and those of competing semantic tendencies, just as the social type, the principle of sociality, and the continuum of sense guaranteed by this principle outlive themselves in individuals. The word "individuality"—like every word in the epoch of "outliving"—takes on meaning only at the price of being incessantly irritated by some other meaning. Classical logic and ontology had excluded contradictory principles by defining the individual in terms of the immanence of its predicates in the subject; but these are the principles that flourish in the case of "outliving": "living on," "more than living," and "dying off" constitute a diffuse community of meanings. No instrument of semiological enforcement can bring this bundle of meanings under the control of a semantic or pragmatic type. The type is and becomes "outlived," the individual—"outlived"—does not live on: only an arbitrary reduction can bring the semantic excessiveness of these two or more sentences into the form of a noncontradictory assertion. Since, however, every semantic restriction and thus the production of an average continuum of meaning depend on the exorbitant character of "outliving," the hyposemantic exuberance of the "word" and the "thing" "outliving" is also the abyssal condition for every conventional employment of language and for every life that performs its functions according to the forms of consistent social codes. The overdetermination, the out-determination, and the indeterminacy of "outliving" determines every life. The individual—"outliving"—would thus be the transcendental of the universal. But to the same degree that the individual offers to generality—the generality of society and of conceptuality—the ground of its possibility, it lets it collapse. The individual, "outlived," grants neither the consistency promised by the "type" nor the duration that ironically announces the philosophy of the mediocre. The language that has become individual—the language of "outliving"—no longer speaks with the certainty of a general, communicable meaning or with the sureness of an ideal type that incessantly produces new variants of its generality. The sense of "outliving" is itself only that which "outlives" the "word" "outliving." It is a citation that always already speaks in the afterworld, never in its "original" context, always in another one, a context in which it leads a life with others, another life, and something other than life: a "life," an "outliving"—once again in quotation marks. If "outliving" is a transcendental, then it is a cited, ironic one: a "transcendental" of the exposition, interruption, and alteration of transcendental forms. All understanding—and, first of all, the understanding of the singular—plays itself out in the space of this cited, "outlived" transcendental.

Individuality's structure of dissociation, excess, and remainder also affects the central category of Nietzsche's late work—the category of the will. In a characteristically offhanded manner, Nietzsche indicates as much in the same aphorism 262 of *Beyond Good and Evil:* "The danger is again here, the mother of morality, the great danger, this time lodged in the individual, in the closest things, and in one's friend, in the street, in one's own child, in one's own heart, in all that is most properly and most secretly one's desire and will" (2: 736; BGE, 212). Like the individual, the will and indeed everything most proper to the will are in danger of squandering, exhausting, and ruining themselves. Because the will could only be a will to will itself, a will to unconditioned autonomy and a will to be the typic of willing, because the will was itself already excessive force, it must also outdo the organizational form of the type and its logical, aesthetic, and social formations; as a result, it must stop being a type and become singular. The will itself is and now becomes "outlived." It is no longer the origin of autonomous operations and is therefore no longer the operation of autonomization and self-formation; having collapsed into itself, it is, on the contrary, the citation of its own past, a remainder of its form, and its exorbitance is the movement in which it is exposed to its own singularity and to the singularity of another will and to something other than the will. This outliving of the will and the outlivedness of the will is, for Nietzsche, the signature of modernity. He described it in the positivism of modern science, in the rise of everything he understands under the rubric of "democratic ideals," and in the style of literary and musical "decadence"—above all, in the music of Wagner.

In a passage from *The Case of Wagner,* Nietzsche elaborates on certain formulations from the *Essais de psychologie contemporaine* (1883) written by the theoretician of "decadence," Paul Bourget:

I will dwell only on the question of *style.*—What characterizes every *literary décadence?* That life no longer is at home in the whole. The word becomes sovereign and leaps out of the sentence, the sentence invades and obscures the meaning of the page, the page gains its life at the cost of the whole—the whole is no longer a whole. But that is a parable for every style of *décadence:* every time, anarchy of atoms, disgregation of the will, "freedom of the individual," to put it in moral terms—and when expanded into political theory, "*equal* rights for all." Life, *equal* liveliness, the vibration and exuberance of life pushed back into the smallest formations; the remainder, *poor* in life.   (2: 917; CW, 170)[12]

Just as the word leaps out of the sentence and the moment out of the totality, so the whole leaps away from the whole and becomes its mere suggestion. The whole exists merely as a theatrical play: it "lives no longer; it is composed, calculated, artificial, an artifact." By contrast, the part is greater than the whole, more lively, more organic, and more authentic; and the whole is only a part of the part that has become sovereign over it. Stylistic decomposition does not simply make the whole collapse into a chaos of parts but makes it collapse, on the one hand, into a whole that is essentially illusion, theater, suggestion, rhetoric, hypnosis, and mass-persuasion and, on the other, into certain details in which alone life "outlives" and in which precisely this truth about the life of the whole can be said: that it is over and can now only be feigned. There are two sides of decadence, just as there are two Nietzsches and two Wagners: "Aside from Wagner the mesmerizer and painter of frescos, there is also a Wagner who leaves aside little treasures: our most grandly melancholic musician. . . . A lexicon of Wagner's most intimate words, pure little things of five to fifteen beats, sheer music, which *no one knows. . ."* (2: 918; CW, 171–72). Unconcealed decadence of style, dissimulated by no totalization, shows itself in the "overliveliness [*Überlebendigkeit*] of the smallest details" (2: 933; CW, 187), therefore, in those places where the individuated moments "outlive" both the style and the work and, through the exuberance of their life, give the lie to the illusion of life produced by technical devices and propagated by the "whole." The detail that has emancipated itself from the organism of the work does not lie: its mere existence tells the truth about the lie of the whole,

12. The section of Bourget's essay on Baudelaire to which Nietzsche refers runs as follows: "A style of decadence is a style in which the unity of the book dissolves in order to make room for the autonomy of the page; the page dissolves in order to make room for the autonomy of the sentence, and the sentence in order to make room for the autonomy of the word." In his commentary to his edition of the *Sämtliche Werke,* Mazzino Montinari points to this passage and to the discussion concerning it in the literature on Nietzsche since 1893; see *Kritische Studienausgabe,* eds. M. Montinari and G. Coli (Berlin: de Gruyter, 1980), 4: 405. Nietzsche repeatedly refers to this passage of Bourget, for example, in a sketch from the Winter of 1883–84: *"Style* of *decadence* in Wagner: the individual *phrases* are *sovereign,* the subordination and ordering is accidental. Bourget, p. 25" (*Kritische Studienausgabe,* 10: 646).

tells the truth that there is no truth that would not be artificially produced, and tells this truth in such a way that no one—no one, of course, besides Nietzsche—understands. Truth distances itself; it, too, is and becomes "outlived." The little things in which Wagner is great are such that—and Nietzsche underlines this—*"no one knows"* them. What no one knows can confront no one under the illusion of a whole. But where it is acknowledged, it stands under the sign of melancholy, of the loss of its own fulfilled presence. The "small treasures," the "smallest things," the nuances, without illusion and without even making an appearance, submerge into the sphere of absence. They are left "aside." With them left on the side, not only are the domains of technicity and positivity now deserted but so too are the domains of aesthetics and phenomenality.

The "disgregation of the will" corresponds in ontological terms to the "decadence" of style—and it goes without saying that Nietzsche does not simply repudiate this "decadence" and this "disgregation." Indeed, he uses them to diagnose a tendency of his own style. Just as the organic form collapses, so too does the will, for the will, as the will to will itself and its form, is nothing other than style. And just as style can only be feigned under the conditions of its decomposition, so the will itself is only theater, rhetoric, and mass-hypnosis. The will, "outlived," proves to be a technical installment. It degenerates into a play the movements of which it no longer dictates. It succumbs to "disgregation" in a passivity running exactly contrary to its concept. "Disgregation" does not simply mean disintegration, dissolution of a whole form closed in on itself; as a term in then-contemporary physics, with which Nietzsche was well acquainted, it also designates the separation of the molecules of a body upon increased heat. (It is difficult in this context not to think of Nietzsche's remark that Wagner's music "sweats.") But by virtue of its etymological connection with *grex,* disgregation—"dis-herding"—means more: it names the dissociation of the masses that Nietzsche again and again denounces, masses that follow a will that is not one of their members. The will itself, as this strange word "disgregation" implies, is the herd; its dull and hollow community is the form in which the will binds and increases its excess of force. Only at the point of a disgregation in which the herd, "will," disperses do its individual moments gain sovereignty and scatter, "outlived," in every direction. This emancipation of the moments of the will—which can only be called "a will" improperly, since they are no longer moments of a single will—

owes its existence to the dissolution of the will itself and the dissolution of its generative as well as regenerative force. Disgregation thus frees the will from its herd-form, from its form *tout court*. It does not, however, bring it thereby to the heights of unconstrained power but opens it up to whatever withdraws from its power: the heterogeneity of individuals who do not will, who do not will the will, and who cannot want the will, since to do so would still be a form of gathering, preservation, and capitalization. The "disgregation of the will" into the most particular and smallest things designates—as in the laying aside of the "little treasures" in Wagner's melancholy music—a possibility of the will to escape the compulsion of form and of every relation to itself imposed by its own formal characteristics; to work its way free of the technical-speculative style and its totalitarian self-presentation. The will does not experience this freedom through itself and does not therefore even experience it as a will; it is experienced only in the passivity of a disgregation that, itself without a subject, suspends the law of the will and the will as law and subject. That the will suffers this disgregation does not even mean that it can be sure of it or can secure it as the movement of negativity, for the will can no longer be considered a subject, and disgregation is the way to withdraw from every objectification. Disgregation is without subject, closure, determination, and destination.

In this sense, the dissociation of the will is, according to Nietzsche's own term, an "ascent," although everywhere he describes it as a descent. But, in this sense, it is not the beginning of a new unity, the foundation of a reign of freedom, license, and formless raving. By virtue of its specific inconclusiveness, incompleteness, and defenselessness—and the logic of disgregation is, like that of "outliving," a logic of ex-position, interruption, breakdown—disgregation remains open onto other ideologies of freedom, other moralities of undifferentiated equality, and a politics of authoritarian leveling that needs violence to establish a common measure where no measure is to be found. But the "interconnection" among those who have forfeited or are about to forfeit every organic or quasi-organic community is absolutely impossible to represent unless the *fiction* of such an interconnection is maintained: unless, for example, there is the fiction of the concept of "individuality," which asserts nothing more than that incomparably unique beings are all individuals in equal measure. The economy of this interconnection—which finds expression in the various juridical and political fictions of individual equality, freedom, and personality—cannot stop exerting a binding force even on the dissociated will as long as linguistic and other general determinations of communication are in play. The disgregation of the will is not a dissociation driven by the will itself; but as long as the will is exposed to this disgregation as a "will," the representation of objectivity, unity, and possible substantiality is still at work in it. Disgregation still takes part in the theater of the will, and since it is interminable, its participation in the play of representations has no end. But its taking part in the representations of this play *takes* from them an essential part of their stability, their consistency, and their power. And the participation of disgregation delivers this part over to a movement that cannot receive political or moral, linguistic or phenomenological determinations.

In the epoch of the "disgregation of the will"—and this epoch is the modern one, indeed the epoch of the modernity of all epochs—the individual speaks by leaving linguistic conventions behind and appears by withdrawing from the theater of generality, by retreating to an aside and drawing its own generality into this withdrawal. If this process of secession—and this secession from the very form of process—is undetermined, this is because it lacks a goal, a purpose, or an addressee that would be immune to this movement. Long before the *Case of Wagner*, already in *The Gay Science,* Nietzsche expressed such thoughts in loose connection with his objections to Wagner's music and, in particular, his rejection of the notion of total theater. In aphorism 367 of *The Gay Science,* he links his distinction between the art of the actor and the illusionless art of strict "individuation" with the declaration that God is dead:

Everything that is thought, made into poetry, painted, composed, even built and imagined belongs either to monological art or to witnessed art. The latter also includes the apparently monological art that involves belief in God, namely the lyric poetry of prayer. For there is as yet no solitude for the pious—this invention we alone, the godless, have made. I know of no deeper distinction in the entire optics of an artist than this: whether he looks out with the eyes of a witness toward his developing art-work (toward "himself") or whether he "has forgotten the world," the essential aspect of every monological art—it rests on *forgetting;* it is the music of forgetting.   (2: 241; GS, 324)

There could be no distinction in all artistic optics more profound than that between an art intended for a spectator—even if it be a transcendental spectator—and an art without regard for the gaze of another, even the gaze of one who is entirely other. For this distinction is the difference between an art of phenomenality—which always succumbs to the optical criteria of perceiving and being perceived, intuition and being intuited—and nonphenomenal art; it is therefore the distinction between an art of appearance and an illusionless, nonapparent art, between an aesthetic art and one that is no longer aesthetic, no longer a presentation or a representation at all. More precisely, since this distinction not only concerns sensual intuition but also, and more importantly, ideal intuition (explicitly included by the phrase "everything that is *thought* belongs. . . ."), it amounts to the distinction between an art *for others* and an art intended for no one—neither for a spectator, even a self-spectator, nor a thinker thinking of thought, neither an earthly public nor an unearthly God in whose eyes, according to the theory explicated in the *Genealogy of Morals,* the suffering of human beings could be determined as theater and, to this extent, appear justified as an aesthetic phenomenon. All art and all philosophy, every thought and every discourse that has an addressee, arise in the last instance out of a belief in God, and all unfold as conscious or involuntary theodicies. In contrast to the social and therefore also theological art of dialogue with another, monological art—including the art of thinking to the extent that it is intended neither for others nor for oneself—is theocidal. It knows no other and acknowledges no god who could authorize its destination. Dialogical thought, action, and life are forms of prayer. The only life capable of monologue would be a life without gods, life no longer in need of an addressee who would bestow meaning on it in order to make suffering bearable. Only such a life could accept its isolation without the illusion of a transcendental shelter and could assume its singularity without hoping for generalization. Only the life into whose solitude no god reaches would be singular; only the life that does not even address its one-timeness would stand on its own. As long as the addressee is not "forgotten"—which does not mean "repressed" or "unconscious"—there is no individuality. Whatever still shows itself or presents itself, whatever can still hear itself or even still think of itself, would still have a listener or a god, would still be prayer and would therefore still be an aesthetic—not a monological—art: not an art of singularity, not "our" art. Only the "music of forgetting," which, although still music, can no longer be heard and no longer be thought but only experienced in forgetting—by whom then?—only this music would be "monological." There is singularity only as *Aufgabe* in its double sense—a "task" given out and the "act" of giving up, only as forgetting and as promising, as a promising of forgetting and as the indefinite and intransitive forgetting of the very promise of any singularity that could be presented in terms of theory, intuition, or speculation.

The solitude of monologue Nietzsche describes is anything but the indigenous form of a discourse that would finally reflect on its truth and independence, having discarded all supporting illusions. This solitude, as Nietzsche explicitly writes, is an "invention," just as the death of God—no less than God himself—is an "invention." And indeed it is an invention that was not made by an individual in all solitude but by a community with regard to its solitude: "This invention we alone, the godless ones, have made"—thus a "we" that the solitude of its society invented and that it invented as a forgetting of society. Inventing this lonely society also means forgetting it, for society no longer looks "with the eyes of a witness toward [its] developing art-work (toward 'himself')." Inventing is the forgetting of what is invented. And yet it is always a "we" that speaks in Nietzsche's aphorism of its invention, of the invention of this "we": a "we" that exhibits its self-forgetting in the gesture of self-consciousness and recognition, that remembers and repeats its forgetting, letting it be known to itself—its addressee—that it is not an auditor, not a reader, not an addressee, and that there is no longer anything to be "known" or "understood" beyond non-knowing and non-understanding. Forgetting—and with it, the forgotten—can still be cited and must be cited if anything should still be said of "forgetting" and anything be said at all. Under the sign of "forgetting," however, nothing can be said *unless* it is in citation: in the form of that which has "outlived" itself. And a discourse that is determined by forgetting and its remainder, by its citation, its promise, and the promise of forgetting—this discourse no longer speaks as the predicative determination of intentions directed toward an object or an addressee but as their continual suspension.

Citation makes the intention of whatever has been cited indeterminate—and more exactly, it exposes the very in-determination through which it was citable in the first place. What loses its determination in this way, however, can never appear as a finished product of the power of imagination or formation *(Bildung)*. Indeterminate it remains despite the changing determinations it may undergo, open in all futures and withdrawn from the effort of propositional discourse to establish it in a statement. In aphorism 125 of *The Gay Science,* where Nietzsche lets a madman proclaim "God is dead," he writes: "This monstrous event is still on the way and wanders—it has not yet penetrated the ears of human beings" (2: 127; GS, 182). That it is still on the way and wandering, that it has not yet penetrated human ears remains a fact despite the madman's speech: it remains uncomprehended. But in his speech, this "monstrous event" is on its way, wandering, and that renders this speech, however much it may aim at dialogue, monological—without referent and addressee, withdrawn from propositional knowledge. The monologue, always still under way and coming nearer, never already present as such, is nothing but the progressive indetermination of the dialogical structure of language and understanding. This indetermination is the way in which the death of God is invented. In this indetermination God is forgotten and dies. With it, the "monstrous event" of isolation enters into the social space of linguistic and behavioral conventions, lets them forget every possible glimpse of another and of oneself, dissociates every "we," every possibile community, even one with a God or one with a language capable of reporting his death, his having been forgotten, or the forgetting of language. The "enormous event" in which everything—every other, everyone, and so every self—is forgotten is nothing but the event of disappropriation, *das Ereignis der Enteignung:* the event of alteration. The monologue of singularity never arrives, never comes home, never enters any "house of Being." It is enormous, uncanny, and monstrous—it is *ungeheuer* because it, without arriving, keeps coming. The invention of isolation is an ongoing event in all speaking insofar as language forgets, "outlives," and disgregates itself in this monstrosity, insofar as language therein outspeaks itself. The monologue of singularity is under way.

At once inside and outside discourse, the monologue is always not yet—already there. And since it is the discourse of the departure from the obligatory and communal forms of language, it is the "always still" of the "no longer" of this language; it is the "outliving" of individuality in a mask-like, posthumous figure: a figure foreign to individuality itself. The monologue is always the discourse of the death of God or his representatives—life, the will, the subject—and it is spoken as a posthumous discourse and as the discourse of posthumous beings. Such a discourse still goes on and on about human beings, but these goings-on are the visitations of ghosts. Of these "visitations"—or *Umgehen,* another of the many highly ambiguous words that Nietzsche favored—there is something said in aphorism 365 of *The Gay Science,* entitled "The Hermit Speaks Again":

> We, too, visit with "human beings"; we, too, modestly put on clothes in which (*as* which) one knows, respects, seeks us, and thus we take ourselves into society, that is, among the disguised ones who do not want to be called that; we, too, act like all prudent masks and politely show the door to each curiosity that does not concern our "clothes." But there are also other manners and tricks for "visiting" human beings, among human beings: for example, as a ghost—which is highly advisable if one wants to get rid of them soon, to frighten them away. Test: one reaches out for us but does not get a hold of us. That's frightening. . . . Or we come . . . after we have already died. The latter is the trick of the *posthumous* ones par excellence. (2: 238–39; GS, 321)

Dead during their lifetime because buried under the mask of conventional manners, alive only after their deaths—as writing, rumor, remembrance, delayed action—the posthumous ones announce their individuality only as the vivid dead, as ghosts, or as those who "outlive" themselves. The form in which they present themselves and therefore simulate presence is dissimulation. This form stands under the sign of withholding, retardation, posthumousness, *Nachträglichkeit;* but it does not put them in a position where they could, appearing at the right time, avoid dissimulating and thereby be able to express themselves in the *oratio directa* of their authentic and peculiar essence. Their language, like every language, is a mask, and whoever wears this mask, this schema of death, lives only as a departed one. The individual is the discretum, the departed being *par excellence,* and for this reason Nietzsche, instead of speaking in his own voice, speaks through the mask of the hermit. The individual is not only departed from life but is departed because it "outlives" death and whoever has died. The mask, mimicry of death, is a defense against death as well. In this between-realm of indeterminacy—between life and death, solitude and society, singularity and universality—the language of the individual is social synthesis only when it becomes an agent of disgregation; it is communication only when it becomes proliferated discretion. Language is essentially discrete: what it expresses can always also be an instrument of encryption, a means of dissembling, disfiguring, or lying. Since, however, it constitutes all oppositions in the first place, it can belong to none of them, neither to concealment nor disclosure, neither publicity nor privacy and its idiosyncrasies. As parting—as mask, as clothing, as "survivor," specter, ghost, or *Gespenst*—it precedes those who have departed and takes part as this parting in every departed one: it is a web, a *Gespinst,* that links outside and inside in their very separation.

Language is departure—from every deeper or hidden meaning, from the subject that intends to express itself in language but only draws the fiction of its substantiality from language, and from the addressee to whom it shows, as an instance of possible determination, only one thing: the "door." At the moment of departure, which language marks— and only at that moment, nowhere else—individuals contact one another and make a stab, in their division, at co-division, at communication, at *Mit-teilung*. The mobile site of society, like that of the individual, is this departure in which the two never stop separating from each other and from themselves. In this way, individuals are—with themselves and with others—in a society that precedes every shape, every totality, and every type: a society "outliving" every one of these. And only in this way is there society at all: as the "visitations"—which is to say, as simultaneous "distancing," "returning," and "being together"—of those who have taken leave from one another, from their common medium, from life, and from death. Socialization and individualization are not, therefore, carried out as processes of identification oriented toward a model or an idea; they carry themselves out as movements of their repeated, already cited division and, at the very least, dualization.

As is sufficiently well known but never sufficiently thought out, Nietzsche accords a special status to the emblem of the mask in his remarks on language and individuality. Although this emblem can be a point of interpretive contention because of its indeterminacy, it nevertheless allows for a very precise demonstration of the relation between language and individuality, on the one hand, and phenomenality, wholeness, and necessity, on the other. From as far back as "On Truth and Lying in the Extra-Moral Sense," Nietzsche's reflections on language proceed from the premise that language morphologizes a world that would otherwise be a chaos of infinitely differentiated impressions. Even the individual, which Nietzsche champions in this context against the power of the concept, proves in the course of his reflections to be a morphological and indeed anthropomorphic construction whose objective validity cannot be ascertained in judgment for the simple reason that the name "objectivity" is itself drawn from the process of morphologization:

> Overlooking [*Übersehen*] the individual and the real gives us the concept, as it likewise gives us the form, whereas nature knows no forms or concepts, hence no genera or species, but only an X that is for us inaccessible and undefinable. For even our distinction between individual and species is anthropomorphic and does not stem from the essence of things, although we also dare not say that it does not correspond to this essence: that would be a dogmatic assertion and, as such, just as unprovable as its opposite. (3: 313–14; Truth, 249–50)

If even the individual is anthropomorphically schematized and if, therefore, only an "overseeing of the individual" gives rise to an "individual," then only the inaccessible—as something different from whatever is grasped—is individual, whereas the object caught by the concept of individuality must bow to the reservation that it could be fictional. Nietzsche later expanded these reflections, acquired from readings of Kant and Schopenhauer, to the self-relation of human individuals, and he drew from them certain consequences for self-consciousness: "Consciousness does not actually belong to the individual existence of human beings . . . and so even with the best of wills, each of us, trying to *understand* ourselves as individually as possible, trying 'to know oneself,' will always bring only the nonindividual to consciousness, its 'averageness'" (2: 221; GS, 299). The consciousness of a self that is "incomparably personal, unique, unconditionally individual" can *as* consciousness—that is, as subject to the criterion of communicability—only conceive of this self as "a world of surfaces and signs," hence only in a way that draws a mask over the self. And this mask can have no point of correspondence with what it hides, for it withdraws in principle from every designation and every presentation. Designation phenomenalizes individual differences into something shown. It generalizes its communication in accordance with an economy of representability that is foreign to the unconditionally individual. The "phenomenalism and perspectivism" of "communicative signs"—of the "markings of the herd" (2: 221–22; GS, 299–300)—rest on the systematic restriction of difference and on a morphologizing of what has neither shape nor self, neither substance nor subject. Consciousness, even the most "individual," is a mask.

This "phenomenalism" of consciousness and language is irreducible, for whatever lies hidden "beneath" the mask of its forms can only appear masked yet again for consciousness and language. For us, there is nothing behind the mask but masks: ideas, essences, and meanings succumb to the anthropomorphizing schematism that generates systems of signs, gestures, and languages. Just as Kant had to insist that finite reason cannot step over the border to the individual and achieve a thoroughgoing determination of the *ens entium,* Nietzsche insists that the "unconditionally individual" must indeed be conceived by consciousness and its language as a determinate thing; but for this very reason it must also be distorted and disfigured beyond the possibility of correction. In the phenomenal and morphological determinations to which language and consciousness subject the indeterminable, an original difference—a difference before and from every origin, every idea and substance—is still at work, and continues to disfigure every form of consciousness. Only because of this is it possible and proper to speak of the indeterminate in terms of the individual and to determine it as something indeterminable. In the same aphorism of *The Gay Science* where Nietzsche analyzes the "phenomenalism" of the "communication-signs" of consciousness, he writes of an "excess of this force and art of communication," the excess of capacity and capital that finds an heir in the artists and philosophers who "lavishly squander" it (2: 220; GS, 298). But this excessive capacity to designate and to communicate, this hypertrophy of schematisms, their overdetermination, must always co-determine—and therefore undetermine—the determinations of linguistic and psychic forms, stir their stiffened distinction, and shake up the opposition between the "brand-mark of the herd" and the "individual-existence" incapable of designation, or that between the phenomenalism of consciousness and the aphanisis of its objects. If the determinations of linguistic signs cannot be verified for their adequacy or inadequacy according to the things they have determined; if, therefore, they lack a transcendent foundation on which their validity could rest; and if their immanent lawfulness is subject to unforeseeable alterations, then the general assertion that all general assertions are fictions denounces its own fictive character. And within the economy of general determinations this difference from itself—being the truth about itself as fiction—mobilizes an economy of another sort: an economy of lavish squandering, an economy whose project is to give up determinations themselves, an economy of affirming difference even within the domain of truth. Since no determination can become an object of determination in such a manner as to guarantee their strict correspondence, each determination, however general and capable of consensus it may seem, is an unrepeatable, singular event. Truth is singular. Its singularity—the singularity of the most universal—consists in its destining itself for over-determination and thus for indeterminacy. Since every singular event is still an event of determination and is exposed to further determinations, it is also exposed to its own repetition, to its return, and so every event can be thought of as unrepeatable in its repetition alone—as the repetition only of its unrepeatability. The over-singular alone is singular. The law of singularity is thus the law of excess *and* the law of repetition, always an aporetic double law, the law of a repetition that is excessive and the law of an excess even beyond the repetition of determination and thus, once again, the law of the "visitation," of *Umgehen*—where the goings-on of ghostly "visitations" are understood to take place in every semantic determination of the law: as a contouring definition, as avoidance, as social intercourse, and as the return of whatever escapes absorption into connections and determinations. Every discourse of the singular and every singular discourse go on "visiting" in this sense, and each one, repeating itself, "visits" something other than, something beyond, itself.

This goes, *a fortiori*, for art—for every art, including the art of thinking. Art is the squandering of the "art of communication." It is never simply this art itself. There is no form unless it abandons the domain of form by means of its own morphological excess, unless it disfigures the figure and revokes the claim of the image to render or produce reality. "Everything that is deep," Nietzsche writes, "loves masks; the deepest things of all even have a hatred for image and likeness" (2: 603; BGE, 50). Excessiveness, surplus, hyperbole deny the illusion of measure, correspondence, and transparency in the acts of presentation that constitute the "symbolic" intercourse among human beings (and not only human beings). And consequently, hyperbole disavows every hermeneutics that takes its point of departure from the correspondence between sign and signified, phenomenon and meaning.

> The hermit does not believe that a philosopher—supposing that a philosopher was always foremost a hermit—has expressed his genuine and final opinions in books: Does one not write books in order to conceal what one keeps to oneself?—The hermit will indeed doubt whether a philosopher *could* have "final and genuine" opinions in general, whether behind every cave there did not loom, must loom another, still deeper cave within him—. . . . An abyss behind every ground, beneath every "grounding." Every philosophy is a foreground philosophy—that is a hermit's judgment. (2: 751; BGE, 229)

And so one must add and is indeed *invited* to add that this hermit philosophy would also have to be a philosophy of the foreground and the mask; it, too, would not be the expression of a "more profound," "abyssal" truth but would itself succumb to the law that it sets in place: that no communication at first communicates a communicable content but every one communicates itself as a *withdrawal* from communication as such. Communication is therefore not the mediation between various already constituted positions but is the constitution of these very portions from the distribution of the difference that holds them apart. The commonality—the *Mit* of *Mitteilung,* the "co-" of "communication" and "correspondence"—is never the commonality of a code that defines individuals as elements of the whole; it is the "co-" of their difference, the co-difference in whose medium individuals, society, and societies of individuals stand apart in common, always in different ways. Society is the co-difference of individuals. Nothing precedes this difference and nothing goes beyond it, except this difference "itself" distinguishing itself from itself.

The "squandering" of the "art of communication" that, for Nietzsche, belongs to the very structure of this art is thus double: on the one hand, it is the distribution and proliferation not only of this art but of the integrative and assimilating power of society in the medium of presentation, performance, aestheticization, and socio-political theatricality; on the other hand, it is the splitting apart and disintegration of this "art of communication," the dissolution of its normative compulsion, the suspension of its mimetic suggestiveness as well as its phenomenalism. In this squandering, the phenomenalism of the sign opens onto the illusionless, the unseemly and unapparent, the discarded and discrete. If anything is still shown, presented, or brought to light, it is the extinguishing of phenomenality, the dying out of the *eidos* and of significance in general. And it is this extinguishing that, according to Nietzsche's formulation, Wagner had composed in the "secrecies of dying light" (2: 918; CW, 171). In this kind of art, communication denies both its claim to be able to operate in the space of appearances and forms and its claim to be able to belong, without any distance, to this sphere. It denies not only its claim of being mimesis but also the corresponding claim that it is an autonomous positing. Art is nothing but the squandering of its appearance, and the lavish expenditure of its communicative capital is also the wasting of the internal communication among its moments. It is not wholly itself but is the whole that distances itself from itself. Its form—and not the form of a particular genre or a particular region of communication but the form of communication insofar as communication imparts—is *aphoristic* in the most precise sense, for the aphorism is what is singled out, separated off, differentiated, and cut out. The movement of communication is separation—and indeed separation from the formalism of the concept of separation. It makes everything, including "the whole," into a *singulare tantum*. Nietzsche played out the possibilities of their association in his books of aphorisms. If there were such a word, one could designate them *metaphorisms:* aphorisms the commonality of which consists in being separated from one another, parting one from another, imparting each one to every other, communicating one to the other, and carrying everything imparted over and into one another. The art of socializing the individual—another act of solitude—shows itself here as an art of tangential touching: not a differential unfolding of a single thought that must constantly demonstrate its formal necessity but an art of contingency.

If communication denies its own claim to totality, then it also repudiates its claim to the necessity of its forms. As an example of this, Nietzsche again and again returns to the explanatory figure of causality. Against, for example, the teleological assumption that all appearances must be referred to a common end as their *causa finalis,* Nietzsche had already summoned the concept of the "coordinated possibility" of chance in his notes on "Teleology Since Kant" so as to defend the rights of the uncalculably individual.[13] In contrast to the necessity that every totality of representation demands, the individuality of the individual is contingent. Only contingency can do what is denied to every natural law and every autonomous act of consciousness: its groundlessness lets it "ground" the singularity of the individual without abandoning the individual to a more than contingent generality. Each time, contingency is the other and the other yet again. Each time, it is singular. Whatever owes its existence to contingency or to contingency "as well" is singular in relation to itself and to the other. Whatever is singular is not possible before it is there. In this sense, it is the impossible. Even its future is owed to chance.

Whatever is without ground "is" thus individual. It does not speak as the substance of an indivisible subjectivity but speaks from the undecidability between determination and indeterminacy, thus from the "pathos of distance" and from the interminable "widening of distance within the soul" and its "life-signs" (2: 727; BGE, 201). "The human being" is, for Nietzsche, the "not yet established animal . . . the scanty exception," and no stability, stabilization, or fixed presentation—hence, no positional or propositional assertion—can definitively delimit "the accidental, the law of nonsense" (2: 623; BGE, 74), a law to which human beings owe their ability to resist statements and stabilizations. The individual shows itself only in the slipping away or in the breach of its sign—at the place where its showing gives itself up.[14] If the individual can be asserted, then only in an assertion that deserts speech. It is—to use a formula for sublimity that Nietzsche applies to "free spirits"— "what remains concealed under the cloak of light," and, in less Biblical locution, at once "night owl" and "scarecrow" (2: 607; BGE, 55–56): the Hegelian bird of absolute spirit and what keeps this bird at a distance. It is thus auto-tropaic, a self out of the difference from the self, a self out of de-stancing, the undoing of stances and distances, the self out of *Ent-fernung*. Still to come, individuality is always only promised, a breachable promise. It "is" not—and is nothing that "is"—but it comes. Since, however, it remains without a destination or addressee, thus

---

13. Friedrich Nietzsche, *Gesammelte Werke* (Munich: Musarion, 1922), 1: 412–13.

14. In the style of the early romantics, one could note it thus: Individuum = Anak<olouth> d. Prosopop<oie>.

without any aim and direction, individuality never comes as something destined for me, addressed to me, coming for me, coming on its own, but remains ever futurial, coming without an end—the open distance out of which a substantial self could never emerge. As a promise, the monologue of my singularity deserts itself, and only as promised, as a contract with an*other* future and a future that remains other—only, therefore, as promised to that which deserts any promise does this monologue, this singularity, have existence. I do not speak the monologue of my futurity; rather, the speaker is whatever in this monologue—never having arrived, undetermined—withdraws from my will. Nietzsche calls it *fatum,* that which has been spoken, a law that does not owe its existence to a subjective act of positing but to a distance, a disgregation that could never be controlled by a subject—be it immanent or transcendent, conscious or unconscious—and that is never sufficiently spoken, never maintained as the whole and as the law itself, but is only spoken fragmentarily and perceived piecemeal. "The individual is a piece of *fatum* from the front and from the rear, one more law, one more necessity for all that is coming and will be. To say to him, 'Change yourself!' is to demand that everything be changed, even retroactively. . ." (2: 969; TI, 491). But if this law of the individual, the law of its uniqueness and one-timeness, is fate "from the front and from the rear"—fate not only from and for the past but also from and for the future—then the individual is more than *one,* more than *law,* more than *necessity*—"one more law, one more necessity for all that is coming and will be"—a surplus that cannot be resolved into time, history, or unity: an exorbitant law that latches onto all other laws of the past and the future, altering both past and future in a singular way. The singular—a broken piece and a surplus—is a law for the totality that alone could determine the pieces *as* pieces and thus determine the measure of excess. Thus, the singular *also* remains always more and always less than totality and universality, always more and always less than *fatum* and singularity, undeterminably other and always otherwise determinable. What remains for the individual—without further consolation—is its freedom: the freedom to assume that under the law of disgregation and the law of "outliving" and thus under the law of ex-position, it is indeterminate, unsent-for, undefined. Finite, without end.

"Lectio"

de Man's Imperative

It is not certain that there can be a science of literature.

If the goal of literary scholarship *(Literaturwissenschaft)* is understood to be the systematic clarification of all the specifically literary aspects of literature, then one is inclined to treat this specificity as a riddle that can be solved by the translation of literary figures into the generally comprehensible language of science. Literary language is then declared to be a systematic distortion of a normal language with literary scholarship operating as its orthopedic agent. Should the process of decoding—a process the epistemological presupposition of which is the general validity of linguistic rules of composition along with their usage—meet with failure, in terms of the positivistic ideal of knowledge this would be only a momentary hesitation within the course of clarification, a hesitation that technical refinement or further improvement of the decoding cutlery could ameliorate. Pursued in this way, literary scholarship is essentially in the business of rehabilitation: it strives to recuperate all deviations, whether historical or formal, within the rationality of the present or in view of a more enlightened future. The basic premises for the science of literature—the epistemological premise that there are general rules of comprehension and the corresponding historiographical premise that language must be used in accordance with these rules—exclude the possibility that literature will ever be known *as* literature. This kind of literary scholarship is not a science of literature; it is more or less clandestinely a science against literature.

The type of literary scholarship concerned with literature as a specifically aesthetic phenomenon shares at least one fundamental trait with the structural and historicizing philology that aims for clarification—namely, the conviction that literary texts are the sensible presentation of a meaning or a meaningful structure. Literary scholarship of this sort pays less attention to the meaning of a text and the possibility of its general mediation and more to the constitution of linguistic images and figures in which meaning is supposed to have attained concrete form. But if the meaning is visibly given in the works themselves, if it can be intuited, then nothing remains for this kind of scholarship but to revel in the works, to set up a hedonistic cult of images, or to offer itself as the *maître de plaisir* to a holiday public. Not only in the now suspect idealistic systems of aesthetics that center on the sensible appearances of the Idea but also in the semiologically cultivated aesthetics of more recent times does the pleasure of the text, guaranteed by the imaginary correspondence between the movement of meaning and its linguistic articulation, play a seductively dominant role. Indeed, the pleasure of the text plays an ever greater role the more the literary text, relieved of the burden of the Idea and the weight of referentiality, is declared in a extremely diffuse sense to be a "free play" of signs, the volatility of which, so goes the claim, eschews any rigorous determination. If it is seduced by an aestheticizing reduction of its objects, literary scholarship ceases to be scholarship and becomes impressionistic literature.

It is not certain that there can be literary scholarship or a science of literature. The ground of its possibility would have to lie this side of the norm-oriented and aestheticizing reduction of literature carried out by a concept of science modeled either on the natural sciences or on edifying discourses. This ground would have to lie in the texts of literature themselves. But in literary texts this ground cannot simply lie there as an abstract possibility of its objectification by means of knowledge, and it cannot lie there as mere passivity that, without resistance, yields to the will to knowledge or the will to aesthetic pleasure; rather, this ground must lie in the texts in such a way that a dimension of critical knowledge of their own constitution pertains to these texts themselves—and indeed pertains to them as texts. Only if literary texts are distinguished by the articulation of a knowledge of themselves can a science of literature have a foundation in the objects it studies. But only if the knowledge of itself articulated by literature has the propositional structure of an objective knowing can this self-knowledge serve as a legitimate foundation for a literary scholarship that lays claim to objective cognition of its objects. What knowledge, then, speaks in literary texts, and in what figures? Is this knowledge of such a kind that it speaks unequivocally and even speaks at all? Or is it a knowledge that negates its generality and its own internal coherence? And if that is the case, what should scholarship seek in the domain of literature? What must it avoid? What is the law of literature's relation to itself, and what law determines its relationship to reading?

Answers to these questions can be expected from only a very few literary theoreticians of modernity. One of these was Paul de Man. The answers he formulated or intimated will be discussed and pursued through some of his texts. The questions are not de Man's, to be sure, but they are questions that literary scholarship has to ask itself with regard to its own possibility, and they are questions that can be deciphered in the very texts to which de Man's studies are devoted. Otherwise, they would be idle questions and their authority would be exhausted by the personal authority of the one who tried to pose them. For only if it can be shown that these questions expose a dimension of the literary texts themselves and that these texts are themselves concerned with the possibility or impossibility of understanding and coming to an understanding, of knowledge and knowledgeable action—only then can one measure the proximity and distance between literature and its science, between literary texts and literary scholarship. Only then is it possible to determine whether, and in what sense, literary criticism can have its foundation within literature.

With admitted naïveté, de Man first localizes the problem of the comprehension and the pleasure of literature at the thematic level. The essay whose original title provided the name for de Man's second book, "Proust et l'allegorie de la lecture"—in *Allegories of Reading* the title dryly reads "Reading (Proust)"—seeks an answer to this question in the scene of reading found in the first volume of Proust's *Recherche:* "What does *A la recherche du temps perdu* tell us about reading?"[1] The same question—a question that seems to pave the way for a movement of reflection but will in fact reveal itself as a *mise en abyme*—reemerges in the Rousseau section of *Allegories of Reading,* above all, in the chapter that

---

1. Paul de Man, *Allegories of Reading* (New Haven: Yale University Press, 1979), 57; hereafter, "AR."

complements the Proust essay and bears the title "Allegory *(Julie)*": "What does the *Nouvelle Héloïse* have to tell us about the problematics of reading?" (AR, 193). The Proust essay, initiated by the question of reading as a theme of the *Recherche,* ends with the conclusion that a text, whether it is assigned a place in literature or in literary scholarship, can only thematize reading under the sign of the impossibility of thematization. Thematization presupposes the possibility of an unambiguous referential relation of literary language. Since, however, the theme "reading" can always be used in a text as a metaphor for something else that would not be "reading," it is impossible to ascertain whether or not reading is in fact thematized. Because no text can provide the criterion for a distinction between the literal and the figurative meaning of its elements that would not itself succumb to the same undecidability, every reading is exposed to the unsecurability of the referential relation, and this inability to secure and ensure is only intensified when reading itself becomes an element of a text, be it literary, exegetical, or theoretical. For referential ambiguity then becomes a distinguishing mark of reading itself, which can no longer be sure of the meaning that comes its way. However much reading may be thematized, it can never be certain of its own thematic content: it can never be certain of itself. Reading *must* be read, if only for the sake of literary scholarship's self-assurance; but reading *cannot* be read.

The specular structure of self-reflection in which the text strives to assure itself of its own understanding and in which reading seeks to guarantee its objective basis founders on the impossibility of determining without any doubt the referential status of the bond by which reflection and the object reflected could cohere. In "Allegory *(Julie),*" de Man draws the following consequence: "Reading is a praxis that thematizes its own thesis about the impossibility of thematization and this makes it unavoidable, though hardly legitimate, for allegories to be interpreted in thematic terms" (AR, 209). In every case, the referential intention of an assertion can be denied by indicating that its status could be merely figurative. If literary language differs from the language of science and the language of everyday life, this difference is most conspicuous when it exposes the tension between the two possibilities of language: to be referential or to be figurative. This exposition does not smooth over the antagonism between reference and figuration but intensifies it. The critical analysis of literary texts that de Man calls the praxis of "reading" in the sentence cited above cannot in every case—and never in the limiting cases—decide between two functions of language, the referential and the figurative. It is in principle exposed to the unde-cidability between meaning and sign, what is meant and what is said, thing and symbol. Wherever a text makes the reading of a text into a "theme" and thereby offers a paradigm of self-reference that could guar-antee the adequacy of literary scholarship with respect to its object, it is precisely there that this "theme"—reading, understanding—can be a metaphor for something else, and so in principle it exposes reading and hence the science of literature to something other than itself and indeed exposes it to its own impossibility. No text offers a ground for a positive knowledge that would not already be set to withdraw from all presen-tation—even from a negative presentation, the exposition of its with-drawal. But the unsecurability of its meaning is not an effect of the temporal succession in which texts unfold, as phenomenological and historico-hermeneutic approaches gladly assume, nor is it a consequence of the historical distance between the text and its understanding. On the contrary, time and history are first opened up by the semantic indeter-minacy of language. "Reading (Proust)" concludes with these words: "As a writer, Proust is the one who knows that the hour of truth, like the hour of death, never arrives on time, since what we call time is precisely truth's inability to coincide with itself. *A la recherche du temps perdu* narrates the flight of meaning, but this does not prevent its own meaning from being, incessantly, in flight" (AR, 78).

De Man does not speak of the meaning of meaning. He speaks of the flight of the meaning in which the flight of meaning is thematized. This flight of flight first opens up time and, with it, a world that, torn apart by the rifts between the various signifying functions of language, can at no moment coincide with the concept of the world that a thematizing consciousness forms for itself. This consciousness is a thematizing con-sciousness only because it itself takes flight from the tautologies of its own self-confirmation. As is clear from the formulation of an "unavoid-ably thematic interpretation," de Man again insists on the vocabulary of necessity: this consciousness *must* take flight. In the Proust essay, de Man writes in a paragraph devoted to the ambiguities of consciousness: "it seems that the language is unable to remain . . . ensconced and that . . . it *has to* turn itself out" (AR, 70; my emphasis). The epistemological meaning of this movement of consciousness into the external world lies in the fact that consciousness could find a guarantee for the truth of its experiences only outside itself. Language can verify its referential function and secure one of its constitutive functions—its capacity for meaning—only in something other than itself. "Like Albertine," de Man writes, "consciousness refuses to be captive and *has to* take flight and move abroad" (AR, 71; my emphasis). The flight of consciousness into a world not mastered by its projections and independent of the schemata of its language is subject to an imperative, an obligatory constraint that is not made less harmful by the assumption that only an entity that suffers anxiety and knows the need for self-assurance can fall prey to it. But this imperative of flight is not dictated by some vague need for security; on the contrary, consciousness is subject to the imperative as an imperative of its own linguisticity: language has to save itself by securing its capacity for meaning within a sphere posited as independent of itself—of language. The imperative of flight into referentiality is an imperative of language. It commands—and this makes for a confusing paradox—the abandonment of the uncertain basis of language in order to seek in a supposedly nonlinguistic domain the stable ground for its capacity for truth and the solid foundation for the knowledge that it really is language after all. But access to this domain outside of language can only be attained, problematically, by means of language, because this outside can be encountered in language only as a "theme," that is, only under an untenable premise and therefore no longer even as a criterion of verification. Nor can this domain, which is not language and cannot be indubitably represented in the phenomenalizing figures of discourse, be definitively excluded from language, unless language is supposed to be hypostatized into a self-sufficient play of internal references whose capacity for meaning extinguishes itself into stale functioning. That which is not language and is therefore not a mechanically self-reproducing code categorically announces itself in the command to abandon the "inter-textual closure" of rhetorical and grammatical figures and "to move abroad" (AR, 70). This command is neither a compulsion of nonlinguistic reality, nor is it conferred by the language of representation, which in any case owes its existence to this command; it speaks, rather, from the possibility of a rift that opens up between the two, and it speaks from the impossibility of maintaining with *a priori* certainty the homogeneity of these spheres and thus the referential content of language. The imperative articulates the difference between language and its meaning. It articulates this difference in view of its reduction, to be sure, but the necessity of this imperative "to move abroad" already signals the impossibility of completing the task it poses. Every science of literature and—since we cannot assume that one is possible— every effort at critical reading is subject to this imperative, for the structure of linguistic signs and their concatenation can never exclude the possibility that, as the mere effects of chance, they are without distinct meaning and all attempts to understand, to recognize, or to know are to be dismissed as mere pretense.

The imperative "to move abroad" is thus not simply an epistemological one but issues from the unreliability of linguistic knowledge. It is an imperative in the strict sense, a practical imperative that commands one to fill up the lacunae in the structure of knowledge by turning toward the world of action. In his essay on Proust, de Man points with unmistakable precision toward the ethical dimension that opens up in a brief passage on reading in the first volume of the *Recherche:* "Mais ma grand'mère . . . venait me supplier de sortir."[2] The first time he mentions the grandmother's request, de Man already intensifies its emphasis by writing that grandmother forced Marcel to go outside, *"forcé à sortir,"*[3] whereas the English version runs: "his grandmother *orders* him to go outside" (AR, 58; my emphasis). In the second, more detailed reference to this phrase, the grandmother's mode of speaking is "correctly" reproduced, although the first paraphrases are also "correct" with respect to the effect of the request, and the issue here is not "correctness" but what de Man perceived in this sentence. De Man's commentary lays great emphasis on the imperative gesture with which the sentence is concerned. In the first, French version of the essay, he writes: "Contre l'impératif moral de la bonne conscience, *représenté* ici par la grand'mère qui 'supplie Marcel de sortir,' Marcel doit justifier son refus de 'renoncer à la lecture' avec tout ce qu'elle comporte de joies secrètes."[4] Here, the moral imperative that, like the imperative of consciousness, issues the order "to go outside" appears *as represented* by the grandmother; by contrast, the representability of the imperative has become a problem in

2. Marcel Proust, *A la recherche du temps perdu,* ed. P. Clarac and A. Ferré (Paris: Bibliothèque de la Pléiade, 1954), 1: 83; cf. *A Remembrance of Things Past,* trans. C. K. Moncrieff and Terence Kilmartin (New York: Vintage, 1981), 1: 90.

3. De Man, *Movements Premier,* ed. George Poulet (Paris: José Corti, 1972), 232.

4. De Man, *Movements Premier,* 237; my emphasis.

the English version, which speaks only of a speaking of the imperative for which the grandmother has become the means: "Against the moral imperative *speaking through* the grandmother who 'begs Marcel to go outside,' Marcel must justify his refusal to give up his reading" (AR, 64; my emphasis). Thus, for de Man, it is not an empirical grandmother whom Proust may well have had in mind when he wrote this sentence; rather, it is the grandmother as a figure of the text, speaking as the agent of an imperative that the movement of the text itself brings forth. Contrary to the thematic suggestion of the narrative, this imperative is not the imperative of a morality Nietzsche characterized as the morality of conventional *mores* and Kant as mere observation of a rite; it is not an imperative of conventions and dominant values but a more compulsory imperative, independent of the intentions of an agent and the contingent pressure of its historical or social position—an imperative imparted as the commandment of language and indeed as the commandment of language to decide on its semantic status. No empirical or historical authority—whether the psychological authority of the Grand Mother, or the repressive authority of the grand institutions of state, church, and diffuse ideology—can adequately represent the force of this imperative. These empirical and thematic authorities, as figures of representation and normative instances, conceal the aspect of themselves that the imperative puts to work; but this aspect is precisely what withdraws from representation, inspection, and figuration. Its structure becomes apparent only at the point where all attempts to grasp it conceptually or figuratively, to localize it in institutions, and to bring it into consistency with a determinate type of language and its application break down. The imperative of language speaks only in the break of language.

De Man describes this breakdown through the particular turns in the passage on reading and its metafigurative self-commentary. Here, Marcel suggests that the act of reading, experienced in a specific ambiance and at a specific time, can synthesize the interiority of subjectivity with the external world into which his grandmother sends him—the world of imagination with the world of reality, the sphere of passivity with that of action. The synthetic totality would preserve the elements of these oppositions in a purer form than the separate domains would allow. Proust writes, according to the translation de Man offers in "Semiology and Rhetoric" where he again discusses the same passage: "'it gave my imagination the total spectacle of the summer, whereas my senses, if I had been on a walk, could only have enjoyed it by fragments'" (AR, 14). The synthesis of the imagination, which for Proust and for a long history of European aesthetics possesses a power of totalization greater than the synthesis of the senses, finds its figurative correspondence in the trope of metaphor: "'It was hardly light enough to read, and the sensation of the light's splendor was given me only . . . by the flies executing their little concert, the chamber music of summer'" (AR, 13). Synesthesia, grounded in the substitution of light by the chamber music of the flies—and thus in the language of metaphor—is the condition of reading: only in the light that the music of the flies sheds on the pages of his book is Marcel able to read, understand, and bring into harmony the divided realities of the world he experiences. Reading itself becomes for him the event of metaphor. In reading, the contingent spatial and temporal conditions within which this event takes place disappear and are replaced by a necessary and essential relationship, lasting and immediate, between the external world of sound and light, on the one hand, and the inner world of fantasy, on the other. Through the metaphor of the chamber music, reading is thus "'connected to summer by a more necessary link: born from beautiful days . . . containing some of their essence . . . it guarantees their return, their actual, persistent, unmediated presence'" (AR, 13). This necessary bond that links metaphor—and thus synesthetic imagination—with the external world makes reading into an act of subjective synthesis through which the whole world of appearance and activity is supposed to comprise into a single moment of sound, and it likewise makes reading into the experience through which the world's duration, its reality, and the immediate presence of its meaning, beyond its aesthetic character, is supposed to be secured. Reading—this inconspicuous, unseemly activity—becomes for Marcel a fundamental ontological operation. Literary scholarship has contributed to the hypostasis of this operation, a hypostasis prepared long ago by an aesthetic and literary tradition, and never more so than when it sees in texts like Proust's the self-objectification of subjectivity in the process of its presentation and then takes over the task of delivering a corresponding suggestion of self-assurance to the public through paraphrase. De Man, whose critical stance is closer to the French and Anglo-Saxon tradition of skeptical literary *criticism* than to the German tradition of "literary *science*" infatuated with synthesis, remains aware of the difference between the theoretical statements of the text and its rhetorical praxis. His diagnosis runs: the text—this one, like every other—does not do what it claims to do: "the figural praxis and the metafigural theory do not converge" (AR, 15).

Metaphor in Proust's text can thus succeed in suggesting a phenomenal presence, the immediate meaningfulness, and the immediate necessity of the totality it engenders; but it can do so only at the cost of severing itself from the determinations of its context, by forgetting the contingency of the specific situation that gives rise to it. De Man can show that it is precisely at the point where the metaphorical structure—and with it, reading as an operation of metaphor—seems to reconcile the opposition between meditation and action that linguistic forms of contingency infiltrate this structure and obstruct the work of totalization. De Man cites the following as such a point in Proust's text: "'The dark coolness of my room . . . matched my repose which . . . supported, like the quiet of a motionless hand in the middle of a running brook, the shock and the motion of a torrent of activity'" (AR, 13–14). The metaphorical intention of this sentence not only breaks down because the coolness of the brook stands opposed to the heated activity with which it is supposed to coincide; it also fails because the *torrent d'activité* that the motionless hand of the reader is supposed to support is an image of contradiction, not of reconciliation. For, whereas the literal sense of this expression connotes coolness, the figurative meaning of intensive activity—which adheres to it not as a metaphor but as a cliché—connotes the quality opposed to coolness, and this connotation is only intensified by its association with *torride,* "hot" (AR, 66). Grammatical contiguity, figurative ambivalence, and the merely conventional and utterly inessential character of the cliché dissolve the unity of the metaphor, undermining its supremacy over the merely external, accidental nexus produced by metonymy. The connections that Marcel's text establishes between the competing forces of his world are not necessary but only contingent, not essential but accidental, not paradigmatic but syntagmic and indeed atagmatic—if not simply asthmatic. Along with the failure of reconciliation comes the failure of the attempt to appease the imperative to go into reality and to solve the ethical conflict between reading and action.

Reading, as a process of knowledge, aesthetic experience, and their synthesis under the sign of metaphor, breaks down. Reading fails because the disparate elements it tries to bring together into a closed figure, structure, or form belong to a system of articulation different from the one in which figures of totalization are possible. De Man's rhetorical analysis remains largely determined by Jakobson's distinction between paradigmatic and syntagmatic levels of linguistic utterances, despite important extensions, radicalizations, and hints of a fundamental critique. But in contrast to Jakobson, whose definition of the poetic function of language is consistent in privileging metaphor, de Man shows that metonymic relations of contiguity and contingency continually disturb the field of language and countermand every figure that promises constancy, necessity, and the immediacy of meaning. The element of contingency in the concatenation of signs is the unreliable and uncontrollable ground of the metaphor that denies it. Even in terms of the linguistic structures claiming to be paradigmatic, like *torrent d'activité,* one can distinguish a figurative and a literal meaning, which are related to each other not paradigmatically but syntagmatically. Even in the name and in the atom of the word, the sentence is at work, shattering their unity. If reading is only possible under the assumption that it can successfully grasp the meaning inherent in the sign, then the fundamental contingency of the relation between sign and meaning condemns its effort to failure and deprives readers of the illusion that they, too, could experience the world of reality and action in the synthesizing act of reading. That is why the sentence in Proust's text, "mais ma grand'mère . . . venait me supplier de sortir," immediately follows the failed metaphor of the *torrent d'activité.* The imperative to go outside and discover truth in action is governed by the law of metonymy and thus subject to the law of an external and contingent bond—inconstant and momentary, sanctioned by no higher law—between language and its meaning. Even if it speaks through the figure of the grandmother and this figure, by giving it form and direction, already indicates the illusory promise of a possible reconciliation, the law to which both this imperative and the figure of its agent subordinate themselves is still the law of the irreconcilable disparity between the figurative and literal meaning of linguistic signs: the law of the impossibility of identifying any epistemological instance that could secure not only the meaning of language but even its capacity for meaning and reference. It is the imperative of nonagreement, disharmony, effective only as the dumb and unseemly defacement of linguistic figures. It is not dictated by a transcendental subject; it cannot be exhausted by figures or conventional rules, nor can it be accomplished by acts of consciousness. The law to which the imperative is subject—the law of the law—makes this imperative into a linguistic event that can appear in the world of figures disposed towards synthetic totality and rational necessity only as a contingent force: as accident and incident, as meaningless mechanical repetition, as groundless positing, as failure and disruption of the intentions of a self-willing will. Only in this sense does necessity accrue to the imperative: not the internal necessity claimed by a consciousness, a will, a subject, or any other transcendental agent, but the necessity of an accident that dashes every hope of securing a transcendental ground. Insofar as it shows that the coalescence of intuition and meaning in texts is illusory, the imperative is an imperative of de-aestheticization. Insofar as the unensurability of meaning speaks through this imperative, it is the imperative of undoing meaning, of de-meaning. If reading is still possible, then it can take place only in the aporia of unreadability articulated by literary texts themselves. In all writing and in all meaning this imperative is read: *Sort de la lecture. Sort.*

If literary texts are characterized by the dissolution of their figurative and, more precisely, metaphorical structure—and it can be shown that this is a thoroughgoing characteristic of all literary texts of any rank—then they are also characterized by their attempt to posit the pathos of their negativity in place of the indubitable existence of a referent. In "Allegory *(Julie),*" de Man describes this movement of the restitution of meaning through the power of its negation:

> The very pathos of the desire (regardless of whether it is valorized positively or negatively) indicates that the presence of desire replaces the absence of identity and that, the more the text denies the actual existence of a referent, real or ideal, and the more fantastically fictional it becomes, the more it becomes the representation of its own pathos . . . pathos is itself no longer a figure but a substance. (AR, 198–99)

In the passage from the "Second Preface" to the *Nouvelle Héloïse* toward which de Man turns his attention during his discussion of the interconnection between pathos and language, Rousseau writes: "Love is only an illusion . . . it surrounds itself with objects that do not exist or to which it alone gives being; and as it renders all its feelings into images, its language is always figurative."[5] The language of love does not correspond to any object that it itself has not already projected through its tropes. Its images and turns of phrases, its sentences and words, refer to something that does not exist and that they cannot wholly produce because they lack the ability to say it completely and effectively. A letter dictated by love, Rousseau writes, "always says the same thing over again, and has never been able to speak." The language of pathos does not speak but, almost in a stammer, only repeats its own incapacity to speak. Its figures are not figures of an objective reality located somewhere beyond language but are figures of the incompleteness of all objective worlds that could occupy the position of a referent, and indeed they are figures of the impotence of their claims to referentiality. However much its essence lies in illusion, the language of pathos—of love, longing, desire, or of anxiety and suspicion—is a language of disillusionment about the referential capacity of language. It obeys the imperative of metonymy that dissolves the metaphoric pretension of the unification of reality and knowledge, of language and action. In de Man's formulation, this negative activity renders pathos a "figure that disfigures, a metaphor that confers the illusion of proper meaning to a suspended, open semantic structure" (AR, 198). His language—no longer referential but self-referential in a negative manner and therefore a language of the interminable project of language—demonstrates its own illusory character; it is "the monster of its own aberration, always oriented toward the future of its repetition" (AR, 198). The language of affects has the power of disillusionment at its disposal only because it does not articulate something but only articulates its own speaking, because it no longer articulates representations but only the form of representation itself. To this extent, the figure of pathos is no longer a figure *of* pathos but pathos itself; the figure is the substance and subject of language: substance and subject are nothing but figures. Because every referent must appear illusory to this language, as the pure speaking of gliding metonymy, because every referent constitutes an always transgressed limitation, and because, for the language of pathos, the infallible ground

5. Jean-Jacques Rousseau, *Oeuvres complètes,* ed. B. Gagnebin and M. Raymond (Paris: Pléiade, 1959), 2: 15. De Man does not, to be sure, quote from this passage; but it strikes me as central to his argument.

and abiding meaning of its speaking appear only in this very language, it is not merely the referent and figure of its discourse but is also the form of the referentiality and figurality of speaking itself.

Pathos, denuded of all empirical, individual affectivity and positive meaning, is sheer intentionality. In the texts of both Rousseau and Proust, pathos claims a transcendental function. The energy of intentionality is hypostatized not only as the organizing principle of its texts but, beyond that, as the only reliable ground of their comprehensibility—not only as the form of its speaking but also of its being heard and perceived independently of any acts of consciousness. In the "Second Preface," Rousseau writes: "If the force of feeling does not strike us, its truth touches us, and it is therefore what the heart knows how to say to the heart."[6] Not the power but the impotence of feeling—its truth, that it is not the master of language and that no language could ever correspond to it—links the subject of the discourse and the subject of understanding. The substantial figure of pathos, the figure of subjectivity itself, is also the figure of immediate communication—immediate because it excludes all figurative mediation. The language of pathos would thus be the language of pure understanding in the medium of negativity. In this language, no longer would a determinate intention be spoken but rather intentionality itself; no longer would a determinate content be communicated but rather pure communicability; no longer would an empirical subject articulate itself but rather its subjectivity. Pathos does not restore the transparency of language with respect to representations or things; it speaks as the language of referentiality itself. Its imperative, as the imperative of pure subjectivity, is at the same time that of universal communicability in the medium of negativity. But precisely to the same degree, it is no longer an imperative. Its negativity has already resolved the tension between what the imperative demands and what the demand of this imperative fulfills; by resolving the tension between what it asserts and the form of its assertion, it generates a more potent homogeneity than even the synthesis of metaphor.

De Man does not succumb to the seduction of negativity, a seduction that presents itself as the substratum of the subjectivity belonging to the subject of language. In this negativity he recognized one of the generative functions of texts destined to deny their own contingency. He

6. Rousseau, *Oeuvres complètes*, 2: 15.

writes: "Contrary to received opinion, deconstructive discourses are suspiciously text-productive" (AR, 200). This productivity of negative pathos is not, to be sure, the productivity of organic extension and fulfillment but that of the mechanical repetition of one and the same, as it were, grammatical pattern. If literary texts unfold themselves both thematically and according to their rhetorical structure as forms of dis-illusionment and unveiling, of critique and self-critique, it is because they can promise themselves and their readers a greater certainty in these forms than in affirmative statements and reassurances; more precisely, they offer the certainty of the unreliability of the world and of all asser-tions that can be made about it. In this negative certainty, critical schol-arship concerning literature also communicates with its objects. The pathos of infinite self-denial is just as suspiciously productive for literary texts as for the texts of literary scholarship; traces of this pathos are particularly noticeable in the Anglo-Saxon concept of literary criticism and even more so in its practice. As de Man writes, scholarly texts are also characterized by that "negative assurance that is highly productive of critical discourse" (AR, 16). No matter how sober, pragmatic, and free of illusions it pretends to be, every mode of literary scholarship that ascribes to itself such a *docta ignorantia* and erects upon its basis a system of negative epistemology, negative hermeneutics, or negative dialectics of literary works and their understanding will cultivate a logology of pathos—a pathology that, uncritical toward its own concept of critique, mechanically repeats the movement of intentionality rather than analyz-ing and reading it as it is already analyzed in the texts to be read. If the pathos of defiguration were actually the determining trait in the struc-ture of literary texts, then, paradoxically, the one reading that would correspond to its metonymic movement would be its metaphor. The text and its scholarship would converge in a figure—the figure of permanent defiguration—whose universality would erase its figurative character and, in pure mediation, sublate both the text and its scholarship: both "a text of desire as well as a desire for text" (AR, 289).

But the will to the text, the text that wills itself—another version of the will to power—when it articulates itself in the text, is no longer sheer referentiality, no longer the mere figurativity that it thematizes itself as ("Love is only an illusion"); rather, it is a figure that must be subjected to a decision concerning its referential status in order for it to be under-stood. The assertion is that love is merely an illusion and can exclusively be spoken in figures, because its object possesses only a reality it itself generates. This assertion, however radical the theory it enunciates about literature as the language of love, is above all a flat statement in a literary text, a statement that could just as well be a strategic fiction in service to the argumentative consistency of this text as a serious statement intended to designate the real character of love. Just as there is no definite criterion for the decision concerning these alternatives, there is no possibility of naming an ultimate ground for the determination of the intentions of the author, who may have meant these statements quite seriously but may just as well have limited this seriousness to the field of a particular text or particular cases of its application. There is no word, no sign—from whatever conventions of language or action it may originate—that would not forfeit its strict semantic intention at the instant it is posited and exposed to the possibility of being understood. But neither word nor sign is thereby disburdened of its semantic gravitation, as de Man emphasized with singular clarity. For, if the referential content of an utterance is also unreliable and cannot be secured by any device, the contention that the utterance, once liberated from all referential relations, is a free play of signifiers, would itself necessarily be referential. No text has the power to exclude the possibility that it says the truth, or at least something true; but no text can guarantee this truth because every attempt to secure it must proliferate the indeterminacy of its meaning. And this goes for the negativity of the language of pathos as well. Precisely those things that want to nominate themselves as the *ultima ratio* of literary discourse—the defiguration of figures, the infinite suspension of reference toward pure referentiality, the sublation of subjective intentions in the general structure of intentionality, negative totalization, and whatever also claims universal comprehensibility on the basis of this generality—are exposed to a semantic indeterminacy for this reason: they, too, are at first nothing but elements of a literary operation, and this indeterminacy can no longer be called a *ratio,* a reason, a ground, or an essence of understanding and language. The structure of pure subjectivity is shattered, the transcendental function of the negative figure founders, the text as the will to itself and to its unrestricted communication is splintered. Pathos—including the pathos of an imperative whose mere perception would already be its pure fulfillment because it would therein express itself as the imperative *itself* and the imperative of the self—this pathos can at no time escape the risk of being read as an affected affect, as that *pathos affecté* about which Rousseau also speaks in the context of his determination of the language of love.[7]

However seriously it may be meant and however painfully it may be experienced, pathos is always also and always at first an effect of language and of *another* language than that of pathos itself. Even the imperative of negativity cannot therefore be read. No more than the figures of totalization does the command of their subversion, which establishes a powerful totality beyond figures and language in the mode of demand itself, offer a support for the work of understanding. Even this totality of the imperative of subjectivity is not the entire, absolute one; it, too, is partial and must collapse under the pressure of another language, of a language of otherness and, perhaps, of something other than language.

Literary texts devoted to the tension between language and what it is about are not exhausted by figurative—and in the final analysis, meta-phorical—discourse and by the suspension of this discourse in the process of infinite negation. By repeating the aporias of defiguration, they also expose another way of reading them: they present themselves as allegories, as a discourse of another.[8] In "Allegory *(Julie)*," de Man writes:

7. Rousseau, *Oeuvres complètes*, 2: 18.

8. One of the connecting points for de Man's concept of allegory may well be the one developed by Walter Benjamin in his *Origin of the German Mourning-Play*. Of particular importance are the ethical implications Benjamin touched upon in connection with a line by Sigismund von Birken: "'Mit Weinen streuten wir den Samen in die Brachen und gingen traurig aus' [In tears we scattered the seeds onto the fallow ground and sadly went away]. Allegory departs empty handed. Absolute evil, which it cherished as abiding profundity, exists only in allegory, is only and alone allegory; it means something other than it is. And indeed it means precisely the non-being of what it represents" (*Gesammelte Schriften*, 1: 406; cf. *The Origin of German Tragic Drama*, 233, trans. J. Osborne [New York: Verso, 1977]). In the essay "New Criticism et nouvelle critique" first published in 1966, de Man already cites a part of this passage (see the English version, "Form and Intent in the American New Criticism," in *Blindness and Insight,* 2nd ed. (Minneapolis: University of Minnesota Press, 1983), 35; hereafter, "BI." For a more detailed discussion of this and other points, see my introduction to the German translation of sections from *Blindness and Insight* entitled "Unlesbarkeit," in Paul de Man, *Allegorien des Lesens* (Frankfurt am Main: Suhrkamp, 1988), 7–26. Heidegger's formal characterization of the artwork as allegory, in accordance with the etymology of the word, also stresses that it says some-thing *other* than the mere being-at-hand of its representational, thing-like substance: "The artwork is, to be sure, a thing that is made, but it says something other than the mere thing itself, *allo agoreuei*. The work makes public something other than itself; it manifests

The paradigm of all texts consists in a figure (or a system of figures) and its deconstruction. But since this model cannot be closed off by a final reading, it engenders, in its turn, a supplementary figural supposition which narrates the unreadability of the prior narration. As distinguished from primary deconstructive narratives centered on figures and ultimately always on metaphor, we can call such narratives to the second (or third) degree *allegories.* Allegorical narratives tell the story of the failure to read. . . . [They undo] both the intelligibility and the seductiveness that the fiction owed to its negative rigor. (AR, 205)

With the "supplementary figural superposition" presented by allegory, the literary text does not attain a genuinely new dimension of language, structurally superior to the prior ones; rather, it expounds and repeats the aporias of the previous level: "the allegory does not erase the figure. Allegories are always allegories of metaphor and, as such, they are always allegories of the impossibility of reading—a sentence in which the genitive 'of' *has* itself *to be* 'read' as a metaphor" (AR, 205; my italics). This "unreadable" genitive can be read in the following way: allegories are always allegories of the metaphor "metaphor" and thus allegories of the translation of precisely that which must resist all attempts at translation, because there is no certain criterion for its translatability into a proper or literal meaning. Allegories are always allegories of the untranslatability and therefore of the unreadability of that which, as a translation, asserts its absolute readability, and yet they repeat the very same hermeneutic failure they denounce by remaining allegories *of* unreadability and thus clinging to their genealogical or epistemological relation to the altogether nonrelational. Repetition is the repetition of an error: it does not justify this error and does not raise it to the ranks of truth but is itself an aberrant repetition and an error about the status of repetition itself. For the repetition does not repeat; it "repeats" the unrepeatable, untranslatable, ametaphoric only by adding another such to it (de Man uses the term *superposition*), by altering it, by referring to it as to another,

---

something other; it is an allegory" ("Der Ursprung des Kunstwerks," in Martin Heidegger, *Holzwege* [Frankfurt am Main: Klostermann, 1950], 9; cf. "The Origin of the Work of Art," in *Poetry, Language, Thought,* trans. Albert Hofstadter [New York: Harper & Row, 1971], 19–20). It is remarkable that Heidegger does not return to the motif of allegory in his essay on the artwork; evidently, his entire effort must amount to the exclusion of rhetorical concepts, which for him promulgate certain metaphysical naïveties.

and by referring to it in another mode than that of translation, substitution, or even the mode of reading modeled on the pattern of mimesis. Reading now proceeds allegorically: not as allegoresis, which interprets the figures of a text as something other than they literally mean, but as an allegoresis of precisely that allegoresis as that which reading thematically becomes in its texts—hence as a sheer process of its "own" alteration. Reading does not therefore *read;* rather, it "reads," as de Man writes, putting the word in quotation marks. It is the reading "of" unreadability, suspended between what it is and *has to be,* on the one hand, and its incapacity to be itself, on the other. The language of reading is therefore another language, perhaps something other than language, in any case a "language" that does not manage without a distancing through quotation marks: a "language" "of" "language."

As de Man shows, the negative synthesis attempted by allegory—a synthesis through which allegory distinguishes itself from the merely mechanical execution of the metonymic model—goes along with an alteration of both the thematic subject-matter and the tonality of the text. The work of negation, carried out on the figures by pathos and on pathos by its figures, is always already subject to a linguistic imperative demanding the proof of its own truth-value in *another* sphere and, preferably, in the sphere of practical action. *Although* the decision about this truth-value must remain suspended, it is "the way abroad"—for both Rousseau and Proust—which makes this epistemological imperative into a practical one as well. But *because* the epistemological decision must remain suspended, the practical intention is released from the intention toward truth and establishes its independence in allegory: it becomes edifying, instructing, demanding, ethical discourse. Allegorical texts are imperative.

In one of the central passages of *Allegories of Reading,* in "Allegory *(Julie),"* de Man writes:

> The concatenation of the categories of truth and falsehood with the values of right and wrong is disrupted. . . . We call this shift in economy *ethical,* since it indeed involves a displacement from *pathos* to *ethos.* Allegories are always ethical, the term ethical designating the structural interference of two distinct value systems. . . . The ethical category is imperative (i.e., category rather than value) to the extent that it is linguistic and not subjective. . . . The passage to an ethical tonality does

not result from a transcendental imperative but is the referential (and therefore unreliable) version of a linguistic confusion. Ethics (or one should say, ethicity) is a discursive mode among others. (AR, 206)

Allegories do not merely thematize the incapacity of language to verify its assertions by its own means; with the characteristic gesture of the "nevertheless," they suspend all epistemological uncertainties and become demands—demands that do not themselves correspond to any as yet existing reality but whose fulfillment is supposed to confirm their truth-value and grant them legitimacy. Allegories are not actually epistemological figures, for they yield no knowledge and in fact originate in an epistemological obstacle inherent to the structure of language; but they are figures disposed toward possible knowledge and future verification. Nor are allegories moral figures, for they do not necessarily preach determinate conventions of behavior and values that would be thematically preformed within them; but they are figures constructed within the perspective of the formal possibility of a universality of action. And above all, what first determines the gesture of allegory is this: they *must* be constructed; they are not random positings of an empirical or fictive subject but are *necessary* expositions of a determining trait of language itself. This trait is the referential function. No statement can exclude the possibility that, with it, something is meant. Where the unensurability of the semantic content of language itself becomes the theme of statements—and this happens in allegorical texts—its referential function is not extinguished but is, rather, related to the possibility that what is said is not simply without meaning but has a meaning that remains still unredeemable: the possibility, therefore, that what is said is not *not* meant as such, but only not *yet* and not sufficiently meant. In this relation to its possible being, the referential function of language, emptied of all thematic content, steps forth as a barren, formal constraint. It is this referential constraint without referent that presents itself in allegory and in its imperative gesture.

It is not because allegory makes demands that it is an ethical figure. On the contrary: the language of allegory is a language of ethical demands because it itself is requisite and indispensable; it is a language of constraint because it is itself necessary; it is a language of compulsion because it is itself subject to the structural compulsion of language. "The ethical category," de Man writes, "is imperative . . . to the extent that it is linguistic." The ethical character of language, its allegorical quality, is not due to a speaking subject prior to language, nor to historically determined conventions of speaking: its ethical character is not something that could just as well not be at all, that could be restricted to a merely conditioned, empirical validity. This ethical character of language is not only unconditional—and for this reason de Man is right in calling it categorical—but is also a character of language itself, that is, a necessary trait that makes language into language in the first place. Language is imperative. It is imperative because its referential function gives the directions for possible reference, even if no referential meaning answers to it and even though it corresponds to no referent. And only because language itself is imperative can there be and must there be imperatives in language, in its figurative structures and in its thematic content. And only because language itself is imperative can there be and must there be the categorical imperative. The law of action formulated in the imperative is itself subject to the law of language.

It is subject to *one* of the laws of language. Language is imperative, and only under its constraint can there be categorically imperative utterances. Nevertheless, language is not a thoroughly ethical formation able to fulfill its own demands, including the unconditional demand to make demands. Thus we can understand de Man's assertion, lapidary but uncommonly rich in consequences: "The passage to an ethical tonality does not result from a transcendental imperative but is the referential (and therefore unreliable) version of a linguistic confusion" (AR, 206)—transcendental, therefore, not as a consequence of a transcendent power but as a result of a structural compulsion within language, a compulsion upon which every will, every subject, and every merely transcendent instance depends. But the imperative in language, in allegory, is still very much transcendental, and for precisely this reason the validity of de Man's concluding consideration remains only problematic for now: "Ethics (or, one should say, ethicity) is a discursive mode *among others*" (AR, 206; my emphasis). The ethical character of language—and *a fortiori* of the language of literature—is not an arbitrary mode of language, its function interchangeable with others, for it is indissolubly bound up with the function of language—the referential one—that alone contains a directive for meaning and can thus first make language into language. Attention is drawn to this function about a page later in *Allegories of Reading,* and this page contains a remarkably parallel formulation, but one with an opposite sense. The sentence refers to Rousseau, although its similarity to a whole series of de Man's statements suggests that it also expresses an insight of his:

> His radical critique of referential meaning never implied that the referential function of language could in any way be avoided, bracketed, or reduced to being just one contingent linguistic property *among others,* as is postulated, for example, in contemporary semiology which, like all post-Kantian formalisms, could not exist without this postulate. (AR, 207; my emphasis)

But if the referential function of language does not fall among its contingent properties and is indeed a constitutive structural element of all language; if it is not therefore simply a function "among others," then its ethical function, characterized by de Man as a "referential version of a linguistic confusion," cannot, as he maintains, issue into a "discursive mode among others" (AR, 206). Ethical propositions and, even more, imperatives are not incidental contents of language that are "also" possible within it "among others," for they belong indissolubly to the occurrence of language itself.

But the law of language out of which ethical imperatives arise, its ineluctable referential function, is not the only law; its validity is continuously contested by another law: that of language's figurality. As little as the referential meaning of statements can be secured, no more can the directives for reference contained in the referential function ever be converted into an imperative that would correspond to these instructions without residue. Only because the referential function that drives the imperative in language, in allegory, finds no correspondence in this imperative can there be imperatives at all, for the imperative means precisely this: it must, but it cannot be. Because the referential and, furthermore, the ethical function of language is traversed by its figurative function, it cannot be determined with certainty whether this imperative—and even the categorical imperative—is an unconditioned one, and so it cannot be determined with certainty if it is an imperative at all. For this reason, every imperative must remain exposed to the question of whether it is not merely in the service of contingent authorities and ephemeral experiences. The problem of the imperative, which de Man places at the center of one of the central concepts of his work, at the center of allegory, must therefore remain exposed to the suspicion that the *demand* enunciated within it could be, for example, merely onomastic: a nonobligatory, disconnected effect of his name—*de Man*. De Man does in fact touch on the problem of the proper name and of the connection between name and proper name in one of the sentences from "Promises *(Social Contract)*," where he writes: "There can be no more seductive form of onomastic identification . . . [insofar as] it satisfies semiological fantasies about the adequation of sign to meaning" (AR, 262). And in a passage on the imperative character of allegorical language, one finds: "Morality is a version of the same language aporia that gives rise to such concepts as 'man'" (AR, 206). Insofar as the figurative function of language excludes all certainty about whether an imperative is an imperative, de Man is therefore justified in saying that "ethics (or, one should say, ethicity) is a discursive mode among others" (AR, 206) after all. The reliability of the one linguistic law is rescinded by the other, although the latter is itself no more reliable.

Since allegory is always an allegory of the unsecurability of meaning— and of the unsecurability of the imperative to secure meaning—it does not offer itself as the object of theoretical consideration but in every case as a prop in the hands of the ponderer. But because its functions still remain in effect, allegory speaks and works as praxis (AR, 208–9). Not in reflection but as an epistemologically insecure praxis—as demand, prohibition, instruction, critique, or promise—the language of allegory relates and refers to the linguistic world. And as a praxis of demands on the meaningfulness of "symbolic systems," as a critique of their inconsistency, and as a promise of a future meaning, the language of allegory offers to the science of literature the model of *its* praxis. Allegories, as de Man describes them, are the texts of that quasi-literary-scientific action that literature itself contains. If there is to be a "literary science" in a genuine sense, it must have its actual ground in the praxis that literature itself exercises as allegory. Since this praxis nonetheless stands under the sign of the insufficiency of theoretical statements, literary-scientific praxis, including that of literary criticism and literary scholarship, finds in allegory a ground only at the cost of diminished scientificity. However much it must obey the imperative of referentiality, which offers it the chance of relating every element of the text and every text in its entirety to a possible meaning, the meaning nevertheless cannot serve as a norm of its action, for this meaning is not yet given. Beyond that, the science of literature has to place one reservation on the imperative of referentiality, which alone contains the promise of a commonality between it and its texts and the promise that its knowledge is grounded in the matter itself: it could be figural; the imperative of allegory could still be the mere allegory of an imperative. The science of literature must, for the sake of its scientificity, give up its claim of being immediately scientific, and yet it cannot replace this claim with another one: with that of being immediately practical. If it, as it must, obeys the aporetic logic of literary language—and of language in general—it can never be other than the allegory of the inconclusiveness of its own project. And it can never be founded on anything other than an allegorical ground.

Whatever obeys the imperative of allegory not only says something other than it means but also says something other than it can say. It speaks beyond the limits of its own possibility. Language speaks only in exposing itself to the possibility of its own impossibility. Language itself has no ground, and the ground that it lays down—by, for example, positing imperatives—bears the mark of possible contingency, possible groundlessness, possible impossibility.

It is not certain that there can be a science of literature, for it cannot be ascertained that this science can obey the imperative of language and can produce secure meanings, nor can it be certain that this imperative is even an imperative and therefore a ground that ever makes secure meanings and thereby language possible.

A series of consequences arises from the allegorical constitution of the imperative to which the literary scholarship is subject. Four of these will be briefly outlined below.

Because the imperative of assigning meaning arises from a law of language—namely, its referential function—but is yet traversed and suspended in each of its moments by another law of language, the law of its figurality, there is no reliable criterion for the distinction between referentiality and figurality. The imperative, however well it may be set up to establish the legitimacy of certain interpretations and the illegitimacy of others, can never completely legitimate itself, since its rightful basis, the referential function of language, does not express itself in this imperative without a stroke of figurality. Contrary to its totalizing tendency, it is *also* an imperative of collapse, of defection from every principle, an imperative of hermeneutic apostasy. Since the figurality of language holds the arena of its meaning open to the power of sheer contingency, every hermeneutic imperative[9] that is subject to its law must be contingent, an accidental imperative. Not only the connection between the literal and the figurative sense of an utterance and not only the connection between a text and each of its reading but even the internal structure of every reading falls under the law of contingency, a law that never allows its elements to converge in a systematic unity. No history of interpretation, of hermeneutic principles or exegetical "methods" can constitute a reliable basis of unity or a teleological orientation in the interpretations of literature that would be able to emancipate them from their erratic character. Every history of literature that attempts to accomplish this emancipation still acts as the agent of law and order. But if such a history is to be scientific, its task is to articulate precisely this erratic character, which is just as much its own character as that of literature. The imperative is an imp of the erratic. The entanglement of the imperative in the figures of contingency has this consequence above all: as an imperative, it puts forth a command that, as a mere figure, it revokes. There is no possibility of strictly distinguishing between the demand and the countermand, no possibility of deciding between them. De Man has expressed this consequence with a sobriety free of illusion: "the intolerable semantic irresolution" that properly inheres in allegory and its imperative is "worse than madness" (AR, 202) — worse than madness because it is no longer distinguishable from sense. Like the categorical imperative, the imperative of literary scholarship — and once again, without this imperative such scholarship has no chance of becoming a science of literature — is, monstrously enough, to bring a paronomasia of de Man's own name once more into play, *a demented demand.* It is an excessive demand, because it is perhaps no demand at all. We must speak under the rule of this imperative, and every gesture that literary scholarship can make is subject to it.

A second consequence of the aporetic structure of the imperative concerns what we may provisionally call the communicative structure of reading. If the referential movement of language is traversed in each of its moments by its contingency, then the imperative can be universal

---

9. "Es giebt einen hermeneutischen Imperativ" (There is a hermeneutic imperative), Friedrich Schlegel laconically noted. Schlegel was one of the literary theorists whom de Man esteemed very highly; see *Zur Philologie II,* § 95; *Kritische Friedrich Schlegel-Ausgabe,* ed. Hans Eichner (Paderborn: Schöningh, 1981), 16: 69.

only insofar as it is the imperative of the universality of its singularization. This not only means that the imperative has a unique tone in any
particular case and can make valid demands only for this case at best;
foremost, it means that the imperative, torn within and from itself, is an
imperative of parting and departing from itself. Despite its intention
toward unity and universality, in accordance with its own structure, it
can command only an infinite diversification. It is a truism of literary
scholarship that every text makes possible an illimitable abundance of
interpretations, applications, and reactions, but this multiplicity of interpretative possibilities does not indicate the interpreters' lamentable
insufficiency, which might be healed in a messianic moment; rather, it
is a structural effect of the constitution of language itself, an effect that
every project of literary scholarship must take into account. The structure of language does not simply make different interpretations of texts
possible; it does so with necessity. Polysemy is a necessary possibility of
linguistic utterances. And this possibility is indeed necessary because the
figurative connotations of utterances are not reducible to a single meaning, and moreover because they—perhaps—have no meaning at all.
Only the guaranteed unity (even of a manifold) of meaning could
ground the universality of the imperative of understanding. As a result
of the circumstance that no such unity is given, or if it is, it cannot be
perceived, the imperative of interpretation is the imperative of the unlimited alteration of meaning bereft of beginning and end. And a text
can impart itself only by virtue of its internal partition and as parti-
tioned. In the *cum-* of any communication this partaking partition must
already be at work, and only in the partitioning of communication can
the meaning and the interpretation of a text communicate. They communicate, then, not at the locus of their convergence but at the place of
their contingency, which can be localized within no order and which
can therefore never be ascertained or secured. Because self and other are
first constituted by language—and indeed by im-parting language and
by the partitioning of language—reading is never an intersubjective
process in which two or more already constituted subjects could come
to an understanding on the basis of a common and, for its part, already
constituted language. On the contrary: reading is the uncontrollable
process of imparting the partition that pervades every language along
with everyone who uses it. Reader and text meet in the pause of mean-

ing—where every possible imparting of communication is interrupted. When de Man speaks of the text as an allegory of unreadability, perhaps it should be read thus: it is first and foremost this unreadability, namely, the impossibility of verifying and universalizing the text's meaning that compels it to be read in always differing ways, always in irreducibly different ways and, at the limit, always as unreadable. The imperative governing literary scholarship is not the imperative of communication but of im-parting. The imperative is impartive. Only under its command can scholarship take part in literature without falling into the illusion that it could ever grasp literature as a whole or conceive of it as it is.

A third consequence of the imperative character of allegory concerns its relation to what de Man calls aesthetic ideology. Because allegory thematizes the unreliability of its own statements and the impossibility of the distinct thematization of its own structure, an ideological moment will always latch onto it. In "Allegory *(Julie),*" de Man writes: "The question is not the intrinsic merit or absurdity of these pieces of good advice but rather the fact they *have to be* uttered" (AR, 207; de Man's italics). Independently of the intentions of its author, allegory *has to* repeat its claim that it refers to an extralinguistic world, although it itself rejects this claim as untenable. But the compelling repetition of allegory is a constraint of language. In the same context, de Man writes: "The reintroduction of the intentional language . . . into the allegory is not itself intentional but the result of a linguistic structure. The entire assumption of a nonverbal realm . . . may well be a speculative hypothesis that exists only, to put in all too intentional terms, *for the sake of* language" (AR, 210; de Man's italics). De Man answers the question of why the language of intentionality must be repeated in allegory, itself essentially a critique of intentionality, in this way: it is in this repetition that language possibly seeks to preserve or prove itself as language. And it is, once more, the referential function of language that hypostasizes itself in the privileging of intention and in the assumption that it would find fulfillment in a referent. Every science of literature that confounds a linguistic possibility with its unrestricted realization corroborates this hypostasis, that is, the illegitimate inference from a function to its successful functioning. In this way, literary scholarship serves as the agent of an ideological moment within the structure of language itself. In "Resistance to Theory," de Man writes: "What we call ideology is precisely the confusion of linguistic with natural reality, of reference with phenomenalism."[10] Just as the referential function is not already reference, reference, as linguistic referral, does not already correspond to a reality that is not linguistically determined at every point. Instead of accepting the ideologies of referentiality and mimesis, literary scholarship has to learn from the allegorical structure of literature that language does not function "according to principles which are those, or which are *like* those, of the phenomenal world" (RT, 11; de Man's italics). The science of literature must learn from allegory that neither literature nor its science operates according to the laws of the phenomenal world, for example, those of cause and effect (which puts the legitimacy of every literary sociology and every reception-aesthetic into question); it has to learn from allegory that literary texts, conceived under the pressure of a long philosophical tradition as aesthetics—that is, as the phenomenalization of a substantial reality—cannot be grasped under the category of the aesthetic. But literary scholarship also has to learn—and what is of concern here is not to be *sondern/ Zu lernen* (but to learn)—that so long as it proceeds in accordance with the prescription of allegory, a residue of the phenomenalistic misunderstanding of literature will also survive within it. It has to consider the emancipation of the imperative from its phenomenological implications: for example, no longer to consider it a commandment that could fulfill itself successively in a stretch of "natural" time, even if only approximately; no longer to see it as a demand that makes itself generally and clearly perceptible and comprehensible, as if with a truly penetrating perlocutionary force; it has to cease to consider the imperative as the cause of an effect that can persist in the normative apparatus of a systematic science of literature, provided the cause is sufficient. The imperative of literary scholarship can no more be the object of knowledge than the movement of literature it demands to read, for all knowledge depends on the unrestricted functioning of linguistic phenomenalization. But it is still imperative—not because it could be secured, understood, and presented as universally operative, but because the imperative remains the mode in which language relates itself to its possibility and the possibility of its interruption. Since this possibility can never come up in language except as a possible reality,

10. Paul de Man, *The Resistance to Theory*, foreword by Wlad Godzich (Minneapolis: University of Minnesota Press, 1986), 11; hereafter, "RT."

there are no means for staving off the delusive effects of the imperative. Even the language of denomination, still in use when one says "demand," "law," "imperative," ideologically suggests the existence of an essence that is disavowed by this demand, this law, and this imperative. Reading is never in the stance of truth, not even when it is certain of its own imposture. However great the demystifying power of analytic reading may be, it is never sufficient to prevent itself from making ideological suggestions. But reading does have the power to analyze the constraints of language to which it succumbs; it does not, to be sure, have the power to distance itself, by analysis, ever farther from them—for what would be the immobile measure?—but it can distance itself over and over again, in always new ways, from such constraints. Only in this distancing and de-stancing, only in this *Ent-fernung,* does reading become the experience of language.

The fourth and perhaps most important consideration, no longer really a consequence, concerns the relation between the imperative gesture of allegory and its performative character. The imperative announces itself in the failure of reference. It is valid as an imperative of interpretation because meaning can no longer be considered given but only as given up—as a task. Referentiality persists in the imperative, therefore, but no longer as a natural or technically installed relation of language to an object but as the mere possibility of such a relation, and indeed—this is decisive—as a possibility first *posited* in the imperative. But the act of positing—an act that cannot be the action of the transcendental "I" of German idealism since Fichte or, more precisely, the linguistic event of the imperative—is without internal relation to its referential use, for this linguistic event cannot be the expression of an already constituted subject, nor can it ever be the instrument of its self-constitution. On the level of sheer performance, language is prepredicative, with no subject or determination, destination or definition; it is language without language, the bare possibility of its determination as language, without being already destined in a teleological manner to become language. By connecting the errant performative force of language with the possibility of a direction, an intention, and a telos, the imperative, itself still this side of a constituted language, projects the possibility of its constitution; it itself is, if one can speak in this manner, pre-possible. Every question concerning the ground of this determination, as a question concerning a *causa finalis,* already moves in the space that the imperative first opens up. The question concerning the ground closes down this ground and excludes the insight into the structure of the imperative, for not only does this question operate with the presupposition of an already constituted language but, beyond this, it obeys an epistemological principle according to which the performative event—the very concern of the question—does not itself exist. The power of the performative function of language is always greater than its referential function. But just as there is no referential function without a performative one, without the performative function as such, there can be no manifestation of this latter function without its diminution, distortion, and denial through the language of reference. The imperative of interpretation is the site where the tension between these two functions of language—which need each other just as much as they are incompatible with one another—takes place: the functions, that is, of unverifiable and nonreferential positing, on the one hand, and of a referentiality that knows no more secure ground than the very positing it contests, on the other.

In every allegory—and all are, according to de Man's presentation, allegories of the indeterminability of language—a negative insight breaks through: there is no constituted language (yet). De Man writes: "The assumption of readability, which is itself constitutive of language, cannot only no longer be taken for granted but is found to be aberrant" (AR, 202). If the assumption of readability and, with it, of an already constituted language is aberrant, then there is no language yet and there can never be language in any other mode than that of its aberrant assumption. The imperative of interpretation and of meaningfulness is first and foremost an imperative that can never be epistemologically grounded in the strict sense, an imperative that there ought to be language. It commands not only "read" or "write" or "understand" or "speak," but first of all, in all these demands: "There shall be language, a language, one language." This Babylonian imperative, the only one that does not proceed from a previously given language or other already constituted essences, is the only one with which literary scholarship—or more precisely, analytic reading—can project a common foundation to share with literature and with language at large. To be sure, as a science it can never grasp this ground nor, as knowledge, contain it, for no knowledge is possible without a closed and completed language, whereas this imperative first demands the constitution of a language. In

always different ways, de Man has indicated the efficacy of this imperative and its consequence for interpretation. "In Reading (Proust)," he
writes: "no one can decide whether Proust invented metaphors because
he felt guilty or whether he had to declare himself guilty in order to find
a use for his metaphors. Since the only irreducible 'intention' [note here
the quotation marks around "intention"] of a text is that of its constitution, the second hypothesis is in fact less unlikely than the first" (AR,
65). Despite all the reservations about the decidability of this problem,
we read here that a text is not to be understood as an available linguistic
tool destined to help this or that feeling come to expression. Rather, the
text is only to be understood *as text* in this way: it is disposed toward its
own constitution, and everything that touches upon it—experiences,
feelings, cognitions—is drawn into the movement of its constitution. A
text is not to be read as a *fait accompli* but as a project of its constitution.

"Language" is not to be understood as a given structure or as a
teleological process but as the imperative that there ought to be (one)
language. We do not make use of language without first being in need
of it and therefore demanding it—and with it, ourselves. The apparent
fact that we speak—but do we *speak,* and is it *we* who speak?—does not
contradict this assertion, for there is no way of ascertaining that we, as
subjects independent of language, use language instead of being claimed
by a linguistic function.[11] Referentiality is a function rather than a contingent possibility that we could simply neglect, because the very possibility of language depends on the imperative demand to engage in its
referential project. Since, however, referentiality does not imply an as-
certainable reference, and figurality does not imply the reality of the
figure, *linguisticity* does not imply an already constituted language or
even the unrestricted possibility of its constitution. Language is not just
possible but *has to be.* This imperative structure of linguisticity would be
the principle and the project of language itself; it would be its essence
and its substantial form. It *would be* so—if the referential function were

---

11. Some sentences in the first paragraph of "Self *(Pygmalion)*" should be read in this
context; they contain, among other things, a confrontation with Heidegger's understanding of man as a property of language: "But we do not 'possess' language in the same
way that we can be said to possess natural properties. It would be just as proper or
improper to say 'we' are a property of language as the reverse. The possibility of this
reversal is equivalent to the statement that all discourse *has to be* referential but can never
signify its actual referent" (AR, 160; de Man's italics).

not from its very inception traversed, thwarted, and fragmented by a referential function that does not allow for a strict determination of a referent and, before anything else, of language "itself." The collusion rather than the collision between the positing, the referential, and the figurative functions corrodes the possibility of language, its substance, and its project. Language *must* be, but its "must" already means that it cannot be. Speaking—and therefore speaking of language—we are still speaking *before* language, *before* its arrival, and do not stop speaking it away from us.

A passage from "Excuses *(Confessions)*" again takes up the line of thought from the Proust essay:

> It is no longer certain that language, as excuse, exists because of a prior guilt but just as possible that since language, as a machine, performs anyway, *we have to* produce guilt (and all its train of psychic consequences) in order to make the excuse meaningful. Excuses generate the very guilt they exonerate, though always in excess or by default. (AR, 299; my italics).[12]

We have to: this necessity, this compulsion—regardless of the "we" subjected to the compulsion—is a law of language and therefore a law for all those who are exposed to the capacity of language to become effective without regard to meaning. Under this law of language they have to generate the possibility of its meaning, because otherwise there would be no language at all, only a heterogeneous chaos of positing acts. But the meanings that must be assigned to the blind arbitrariness of these positings, no matter how consistent they may be, are erroneous, for they cannot have been "meant" by this never entirely subdued arbitrariness. De Man, with a decidedness that could hardly correspond more exactly

12. This passage does not contain a plea to dissolve moral categories like "guilt," "conscience," and "responsibility." Rather, it is an attempt to *clarify* in terms of linguistic theory these categories (and experiences), their "genesis," and *their indissolubility.* The passage thereby opens up a possibility of thinking—and practicing—a responsibility that is not limited to the domain of conventions but, instead, concerns another domain altogether, a domain that cannot be subjected to this or that supposed instance of security and the secure tyranny of conventions. Language, for de Man, stands for this otherness. I have tried to indicate how distant these considerations are from the deplorable productions of the young journalist de Man in a contribution to *Responses,* ed. W. Hamacher, N. Hertz, and T. Keenan (Lincoln, Neb.: Nebraska University Press, 1989), 438–76.

to its subject, writes in one of his most radical texts, "Shelley Disfigured": "language posits and language means (since it articulates) but language cannot posit meaning; it can only reiterate (or reflect) it in its reconfirmed falsehood."[13] If, however, the first meaning we connect with the arbitrary acts of an absolutely positing language is the constitution of meaningful language itself, then not only any single meaning but the entire system of meaningful language is deceptive. For it is grounded on nothing but an incident, on what simply happens to come to mind, the eruption of a random event that follows no intention, not even that of its own preservation. And if in the first instance the imperative, indeed any imperative, is the imperative of the constitution of language, which, for its part, can only be established in the trait of a positing that doubtless allows for the generation of meaning but does not itself mean anything and thus indicates in language the locus of speechlessness, then this imperative of linguistic constitution and thus of its own ground can only be a speechless, a mute imperative. It is constitutive for the imperative—of language, of interpretation—that it be traversed and thwarted by the deconstituting trait of the incapacity for meaning.

There is thus no foundation of, and no program for, the imperative that is not undermined by the performative force at work in the imperative itself. For this reason, the intention toward language, which the imperative links with the uncodifiable act of positing, is interrupted and ex-posed in each of its utterances, able to alter itself only in always singular ways and capable of "repeating" itself in every other way. There is no imperative—of interpretation, of language—that is not suspended by its intentionless force. Only where the course of its meaning is exposed is it posited as an imperative. Where the "is" of meaning fails, a "must" steps in. Where there is no sense as yet, an imperative demand sets out. As regards the relation of understanding to language and especially to literature this means that the referential indeterminability of its assertions does not hinder comprehension; on the contrary, only where a logical aporia, a radical inconsistency, or a lacuna in meaning opens up does the work of understanding set in, and only there does something of what is true of language communicate itself to this labor. Inde-

13. Paul de Man, *Rhetoric of Romanticism* (New York: Columbia University Press, 1984), 118–19.

pendently of subjective motives and conventional rules, language's force
of positing makes its first appearance in the foundering of the cognitive
intention toward language, and it does so with necessity, imperatively.
And along with this force, piercing through all ideological distortions,
a necessary, imperative understanding arises. In the foreword to Carol
Jacob's book *The Dissimulating Harmony,* after showing that all ethical
and aesthetic premises of understanding must be epistemologically legitimated, whereas all understanding that reflects on the critical conditions of knowledge is "productive of its own ethical imperative," de Man
writes:

> What makes a reading more or less true is simply the . . . necessity of
> its occurrence, regardless of the reader or of the author's wishes. "Es
> ereignet sich aber Das Wahre" (not *die Wahrheit*), says Hölderlin,
> which can be freely translated, "What is true is what is *bound* to take
> place." And, in the case of the reading of a text, what takes place is a
> *necessary* understanding. What marks the truth of such an under-
> standing is not some abstract universal but the fact that it *has to* occur,
> regardless of other considerations. . . . Reading is an argument . . .
> because it *has to* go against the grain of what one would want to happen
> in the name of what *has to* happen.[14]

The "freedom" of de Man's translation lies in his decision to translate
the impact of Hölderlin's gnome into an imperative, into "is about to"
and "has to"—into the formulas for an internal necessity of language.
This necessity is problematic because it absolutely precedes every
verification and is itself unverifiable. And the imperative of interpretation has a *problematic* necessity, in the etymological sense of the word,
insofar as what it imposes does not necessarily imply the possibility of
its realization. The necessity of the imperative—of interpretation, of
language—is the necessity of a demand for language, for interpretation,
the reality of which has no other guarantee than the incomplete facticity
of this very demand. The imperative commands, before all "real" language, that there ought to be (one) language—(one) meaning, (one)

14. See Carol Jacobs, *The Dissimulating Harmony: The Image of Interpretation in
Nietzsche, Rilke, Artaud, and Benjamin,* foreword by Paul de Man (Baltimore: Johns
Hopkins University Press, 1978), xi.

interpretation. It does not speak properly. It is, in every sense, in advance of language. It is—and its being is—a *problem*.

The proleptic trait of the imperative turns it into a law—a law of language, no longer simply the law of its referentiality or its figurality but of a specific performative mode. In "Promises *(Social Contract)*," de Man writes: "All laws are future oriented and prospective; their illocutionary mode is that of the *promise*" (AR, 273).[15] Language itself is promised in this law of language. In the imperative, language is "foresworn," "forespoken," spoken in advance of itself, spoken before it, as constituted, can speak. De Man did not always accurately assess this fore-structure of language, which was perhaps first worked out in the romantic theory of irony. In his 1969 essay, "The Rhetoric of Temporality," he writes of Starobinski's and Szondi's presentation of irony: "In temporal terms it makes irony into the prefiguration of a future recovery, fiction into the promise of a future happiness that, for the time being, exists only ideally" (BI, 219). While de Man aptly criticizes the assumption that romantic irony is a disguised form of messianism, the global nature of his critique does not do justice to Szondi's characterization of the temporal mode of irony, although the latter partly misses its mark as well. In "Friedrich Schlegel und die romantische Ironie," Szondi writes: "durch Vorwegnahme der künftigen Einheit, an die er [the one who has succumbed to self-division] glaubt, wird das Negative für vorläufig erklärt, damit zugleich festgehalten und umgewertet."[16] De Man translates: "the negative is described as temporary *(vorläufig)*," and he adds the following commentary: "Contrary to Szondi's assertion, irony is not temporary *(vorläufig)* but repetitive, the recurrence of a self-escalating act of consciousness" (BI, 219–20). "Temporary" is doubtless one of the possible translations of *vorläufig* and corresponds exactly to the meaning that the word assumes in the context of the sentence cited; but Szondi takes up this word again on the same page of his text, in the appendix "Über Tiecks Komödien," and there he does indeed grasp this word

15. In a remark appended to this sentence de Man writes, "In the *Genealogy of Morals,* Nietzsche also derives the notion of a transcendental referent (and the specificity of 'man') from the possibility of making promises." See "The Promise of Interpretation" in this volume. Jacques Derrida has discussed in detail the motif of promising in his *Mémoires— for Paul de Man* (New York: Columbia University Press, 1986); see, in particular, the third section, "Acts—The Meaning of a Given Word," 91–173.

16. Peter Szondi, *Schriften* (Frankfurt am Main: Suhrkamp, 1978), 2: 25.

according to a meaning that, although it remains out of consideration in de Man's translation and commentary, all the more legitimates the precaution with which he lets this word, decisive for his critique, persist in the original German even after he has translated it into English. Szondi writes:

> Romantic irony grasps reality as a something provisional [*ein Vor-läufiges*] and for its part brings forth only the provisional [*Vorläufiges*]. In the dramatic world of forms, it is the prologue whose meaning is provisionality [*Vorläufigkeit*]. . . . Life is to be shown in its provisionality; the prologue is shown in its finality. The question of whether its meaning is immanent in reality, if it is already serious or only fore-play [*Vor-spiel*], something provisional that is to be endured playfully, is not discussed in a concrete situation; rather, the point of departure is already a prologue.[17]

But if the fore-play offered by the prologue as the dramatic form of provisionality is "final," then the "future unity" of reality and fiction, the "future unity" of the subject and object of the divided I's self-reflection, is possible only in the mode of its ironic "anticipation." The site of the future is its prologue, the site of unity is division. The "fore" has taken leave from the "after," provisionality is absolute, the future of happiness is nowhere given but in its promise.

By uncovering the fore-structure of language, de Man in *Allegories of Reading* also discovers the complicated rift between two functional traits of language: it is the sheer, nonreferential speaking of language that in its positional violence rips apart the web of its meanings and even breaks open the system of negative semantics first crystallized in allegory. Yet these meanings, however negative they may be, owe their existence to the nonintentional positings that disrupt them. If meanings could be posited and positing acts as such could be meaningful, there would be a transparent, communicative, and universal language; there would no longer be *language,* only a code without the open arena of indeterminacy in which tropes move, only the terror in which everything said is one with meaning and everything meant is one with its effects. A momentary positing act is doubtless to be thanked for meaning, but such an act is to be thought without an intentional relation to this meaning.

17. Peter Szondi, *Schriften,* 2: 25.

A meaning can be tied to a positing only afterwards, *post positionem,* and so it can never be epistemologically legitimated before the authority of the sheer speech act. The connection of a meaning to an act has no ground in this act itself. The synthesis between positing and meaning has the character of an arbitrary position—an "imposition," as de Man says, taking this word from Shelley—and this synthetic accomplishment must fall apart in the face of every claim to universality, for it can always be irrelevant for another, no less arbitrary or aleatory, synthesis of act and meaning.

All imperatives are at once positings and demands. As demands, they are oriented toward the future, intentional actions that contain the measure of their consequences and thus present themselves as paradigms of an historical sequence of actions. As positings, imperatives are nonintentional linguistic events that escape temporal or historical sequences, for they occur this side of the polarity between accident and determination. As positings, imperatives therefore cancel the claim to correspondence that they raise as demands. Since, however, the claim cannot waive its status as a positing, every imperative and furthermore everything that may stand under it and follow from it must carry the index of its inadequacy and unrealizability, the index of its impossibility.

It is this impossibility that "Promises *(Social Contract)*" elaborates in the figure of the law and its positing, thus in the imperative and in the illocutionary mode of promise implicit in every imperative. The imperative of language, of reading, considered as an act directed toward the future, contains the promise of a future language, a future understanding, in such a way that the formal conditions of all individual acts of understanding are outlined in this project. It announces for the future what cannot be performed in the present. Now, however, a consequential complication emerges as a result of the transcendental status of such a project: the performative act of promising a possible understanding must be structured as an epistemologically illegitimate rhetorical figure, as metalepsis, in order for it to be carried out at all. For what is announced by the promise only for the future—a possible understanding—is asserted to be already effective in the present. The rhetorical figure of confounding a future with a present, which is at work in every logic or dialectic of presupposition and, in another manner, also in the hermeneutic circle, is unavoidably a figure of deceit insofar as that which it implicitly states to be present can be disclosed only by the illocutionary act as futurial. So the constative moment of disclosing a possible under-standing is not only in constant conflict with its performative func-tion—and thus makes the establishment of the law itself into an illegiti-mate act—but this unavoidable and irreconcilable conflict within the original constitution of understanding becomes valid as an endless sus-pension of this very constitution. The interlacing of constative with performative brackets both: the presupposition of a possible under-standing could be formulated only under the condition that it is given, and its givenness only under the condition of its presupposition. Since neither of these conditions can be without the other and since, in turn, neither can already be fulfilled when the presupposition is asserted, every project of a possible understanding remains a fiction that can neither be probed nor verified. The project remains suspended in the projection— and the fundamental operation of hermeneutics will never have offered a secure ground for individual acts of understanding, since it cannot verify its own performance. The promise, as primordial project of un-derstanding, can always only promise its possibility but never carry itself out as a genuine promise. The performative act of the imperative—of language—and the forms of speaking and understanding that depend on it remain suspended.[18]

The promise promises itself—this always means that the promise, in an as yet unconstituted language, does not yet speak; it only promises its own future. The promise does not therefore promise. Language, for de Man, is just such a promise. Heidegger's apothegm *"Die Sprache spricht"*—"language speaks"—still courts the misunderstanding that there is an already constituted language and that this language could correspond to its own Being. In an, as it were, objectively ironic com-bination of Heidegger's sentence with the vocabulary of Freud, de Man writes at the end of his essay on promises: *"Die Sprache verspricht (sich)"*

18. If the basic linguistic operation of understanding language, if the very constitution of language is not only one speech act among others but is the performative, the forma-tive *par excellence,* and if this "operation" remains suspended and thus keeps all its de-pendent performatives suspended as a result of its fore-structure, its foreignness to meaning, and its possible figurality, then the "operation" cannot be thought simply under the rubric of *performative* alone; rather, it must be thought as its condition of formation *and* as de-formation, as a pure positing *and* as deposing, ex-position—as *afformative* in every possible sense of this neologism. I have tried to show the necessity of thinking this play of the afformative in language—and in politics—in an essay on Walter Benjamin's "Critique of Violence." See "Afformative, Strike," trans. D. Hollander, *Walter Benjamin's Philosophy,* ed. A. Benjamin and P. Osborne (London: Routledge, 1994), 110–138.

(AR, 277). As finite, language is never already constituted but is always in the process of its constitution; it is language always only as promised. But since its promise can never be fulfilled by itself as promised, this promise, which is also the suspension of language, brackets *itself*—language—and confesses, since it is "effective" despite its endless suspension, despite its impossibility, that it is a failed linguistic performance, a parapraxis, *lapsus linguae.* Language, since it can relate to its own operation only in the epistemologically untenable figures of prolepsis and metalepsis, is a *lapsus.* And since no imperative, least of all the categorical imperative that (one) language has to be, can come out without the metaleptical suggestion that there is an already constituted language, every imperative is an epistemological parapraxis. The "ground" of language, of understanding, of literary scholarship is—a *lapsus.*

Every allegory, even that of unreadability, is still a figure of knowledge. Every imperative—and first of all: "understand!"—is still a figure of incomprehensibility that, as a figure, remains inscribed in a system of negative certainty. But this tropological system falls apart whenever the known negativity encounters in the impossibility of its self-legitimation its barren, groundless positedness. Imperatives—and first of all: "understand!" and "understand understanding!"—can be meant and understood as demands only if they are already encountered as nonintentional positings. That they are posited, *hypothesin,* before all thematization, formalization, allegorization—such is their truth, their only unverifiable truth: "as violent—not as a dark—light, a deadly Apollo" (RR, 118). Thus: *Es ereignet sich aber Das Wahre.* The imperative, the promise—no longer as the promise of a future truth but rather, here and now, as the true, the unavoidability of its promise: "to the extent that it is necessarily misleading, language just as necessarily conveys the promise of its own truth" (AR, 277). One cannot turn away from the force and violence of this truth, for every turn is already under its spell.

De Man has called this truth of language, the truth of its promise, irony. At the end of "Excuses *(Confessions),*" the concluding essay in *Allegories of Reading,* he describes the grammatical figure of anacoluthon, which designates the gap between two different linguistic systems, as irony and, borrowing Friedrich Schlegel's definition, as "permanent parabasis": "the permanent parabasis of an allegory (of figure), that is to say, irony. Irony is no longer a trope but the undoing of the deconstructive allegory of all tropological cognitions, the systematic undoing, in other words, of understanding" (AR, 301). No allegory can grasp the incidences of irony by which it is disrupted; none can catch up with the positing violence of the imperative; but each one—for each one remains exposed to its positing—must undertake the attempt to translate it into a cognitive content. The allegory of the imperative is the endless labor of mourning the traumas inflicted by irony. But the imperative is, as positing, as ex-position and interruption, itself the irony in whose light its allegory breaks down.

The science of literature, if it is to have its justification in the structure of the literary text and in the structure of language in general, obeys this duplicitous imperative in every one of its operations. It obeys the imperative of allegory, to which it compels the confession of its foundering in always new figures and arguments, and it obeys the ironical imperative that withdraws from allegory every epistemic and legitimating ground under which there is no foundering and every word, however erring it seems, fits. Ironically, the imperative—of language, of understanding—allows no decision whether it is to be allegorical or ironic.

It is not certain that there can be *no* science of literature. But if there were one, literary scholarship and literary criticism would be the last ones to know it. That it is and has to be—this experience could be imparted to it always only on this side of the figure of understanding and its foundering. But no experience other than this one and thus only the disfiguration of literary scholarship itself could become the foundation of literary scholarship and the basis of a scientific study of literature. If there were one, then only as the permanent irony toward itself, which de Man associated just as often with Nietzsche's *gaya scienza* as with madness and with death.

"Envie" and "Charité" are the two allegorical figures by Giotto, from the arena in Padua, to which Proust's Marcel compares the pregnant maid in his parents' house. Like Giotto's figures, so heavily weighed down by the burden of their emblems that they can no longer express the idea represented in them, the maid is so burdened by what Proust calls, oddly, "the additional symbol she carried before her belly" that she can no longer grasp its meaning: "without appearing to understand its meaning, without anything in her face to translate the beauty and spirit."[19] Like the reader in the "Seconde Préface" to Rousseau's *Julie,* they are all dyslexic (AR, 74, 202). Through the material force of their meaning, these figures lose all relation to precisely those things to which

19. Proust, *Recherche,* 1: 81; *Remembrance,* 1: 87.

they have been determined to refer in the most intense way: their allegorical meaning. They remain readable only because their "proper"
meaning—KARITAS, for example—is attributed to them by an author-
ial act. These allegories become unreadable because their material appearance always indicates some meaning other than the intended one,
finally robbing them of all determinable meaning. "Proust may well spell
out all the letters of LECTIO on the frames of his stories . . . but the
word itself will never become clear, for . . . it is forever impossible to
read Reading" (AR, 74). The violence of that which deflects from the
understanding of the figure of understanding, from the reading of the
allegory of reading and, still more, from the reading of the allegory of
unreadability—the violence "that sidetracks our attention" (AR, 74) is
not a cognitive force and not a force of meaning, not even a force of
language but, rather, a force of their failure: "in the case of Envy, the
mind is distracted towards something even more threatening than vice,
namely death" (AR, 75). The sentence in Proust to which de Man's
paraphrase refers, without quotation, reads: ". . . that Charity devoid of
charity, that Envy who looked like nothing so much as a plate in some
medical book, illustrating the compression of the glottis or the uvula by
a tumor of the tongue [*tumeur de la langue*]. . . ."[20] The cancer of the
tongue, the language tumor, deflects meaning into a region where there
is no more meaning. Language—of literature and its science—"sans
beauté et sans esprit" speaks only in this deflection of its themes, its
figures, its passions, and errors. It is this deflection, this distraction that
brings about muteness: *tumeur de la langue*.[21] But it is also what attracts
all speaking. It is what makes understanding necessary—and impossible.
One could read the deflection as an imperative of reading and as an
ironic suspension of the imperative: *tu meurs*. Or as a provisional end of
reading: *tu meurs de la langue*.

20. Proust, *Recherche,* 1: 81–82; *Remembrance,* 1: 88.
21. As I was writing this essay in April 1985, I knew that de Man had died of a
tumor—of course, not of a *tumeur de la langue*—but I did not know the fragment of the
last letter de Man had written to Derrida before his death and which Derrida communicated in *Mémoires—for Paul de Man.* After citing a line from Mallarmés' "Tombeau de
Verlaine"—"ce profond ruisseau calomnié la mort"—de Man added, "J'aime quand même
mieux cela que la brutalité du mot 'tumeur'" (*Mémoires,* 87). Derrida analyzes this word
into *tu meurs* and comments, as I do here: you die, you must die, you will die and I
condemn you to death, I say to you, you will die.

POSITION EXPOSED

Friedrich Schlegel's Poetological
Transposition of Fichte's Absolute Proposition

"Nothing is yet said."

This proposition can be found among Friedrich Schlegel's unedited fragments. Schlegel himself placed it in quotation marks. This can mean that he cites it from some text—perhaps one that he himself has written—or that the citation can be traced to another or perhaps many other texts. It can mean that this proposition was set down as a statement by a fictional figure for a projected writing, or that it should be qualified by quotation marks and placed in question for the final draft. . . . "Nothing is yet said"—this may simply mean that nothing, or nothing decisive, has yet been said, for example, about the theme of "genre," and that an expectation can arise that something in the near or distant future would still be said. It can also mean: nothingness is still said. This nothingness is still spoken; it is an asserted nothingness and therefore not nothingness "itself." It can also mean that a spoken or asserted nothingness is not absolute nothingness, not *nihil negativum,* but a linguistic nothingness, and that whatever is sayable about this nothingness is stored up in what is said. That nothing is yet said means, then, that this nothingness of language is not foreign to language but is at work in language itself, indeed at work in such a way that the nothingness of language is still a linguistic nothingness or, one could say, a *nihil dictatum.* And this proposition can mean further still: nothing is yet said; soon this nothing will no longer be said. Or nothing is yet *said;* soon it will be done. Or even when it is done, nothing is yet said. The proposition Schlegel sets down or cites does not become any less equivocal when a second, marginal remark is added to it. Schlegel's addition reads—this time without quotation marks but in a language that suggests it still has a citational character: *Tout est dit*. The first proposition does not become less equivocal, for it is not related under all circumstances to the intention of the other proposition. Schlegel could have forgotten the intention, or he could have oriented his second proposition toward a meaning of the first that escaped him as he wrote the second one down. But the second proposition does not conclusively clarify the first for another reason: it can be related to at least two of the first proposition's meanings. On the one hand, the second proposition can function as a formula for, and the assertion of, a sheer antithesis to the first: everything—or everything important—is already said, and so there is nothing more to add. On the other hand, the second proposition can mean that precisely because nothing is yet *said,* everything is already said. In this case nothing and everything (or *tout*) would be synonyms, and the addition of the second proposition would not constitute an antithesis to the first but its affirmation. *Tout est dit* would be read as another type of affirmation if it is supposed to mean that the nothing that is only said but soon will be done will still be done in a linguistic manner. Everything, including nothingness—everything, including action, omission or letting-be—is the action or omission of language. And furthermore, this additional proposition could also mean that with the proposition "nothing is yet said"—whatever this means—everything is already said and there is nothing more to say than this, that nothing is yet said.

"Nothing is yet said."— < Tout est dit. > [1]

With the proposition "nothing is yet said," everything is already said, because everything rests in a mere saying, even and especially when this saying is supposed to be a not—or not yet—saying.

None of these meanings of Schlegel's notes will be foreclosed, nor any

1. Friedrich Schlegel, *Literary Notebooks 1797–1801,* ed. H. Eichner (London: Athlone, 1957), cited according to the fragment number, in this case fragment 180; hereafter, "LN." The abbreviation "KA" refers to the *Kritische Friedrich Schlegel-Ausgabe,* ed. Ernst Behler, Jean-Jacques Anstett, and Hans Eichner (Munich: Schöningh, 1958–). The fragments from the *Athenäum* are cited from this edition (KA, 2: 166–255), but in the text they are designated by the abbreviation "Ath" with the number of the fragment. An English translation of the fragments can be found in Friedrich Schlegel, *"Lucinde" and the Fragments,* trans. and intro. Peter Firchow (Minneapolis: University of Minnesota Press, 1971).

of them qualified, by the passage in his essay "On Lessing" where he develops them in a definite direction. He writes:

> In response to the usual assertion "everything's already been said"—an assertion that is so apparent it goes without saying (for even a Voltaire expressed it, and it is already found in Terence)—one must counter with the exact opposite assertion with regard to objects of this kind [that is, "inexhaustible" objects like Lessing's "mind"], perhaps even regardless of the object under discussion: nothing really is yet said; that is, nothing such that it would not be necessary to say something more and not possible to say something better. (KA, 2: 101).[2]

Everything has therefore already been said—even this, that everything has been said. Schlegel calls this assertion "apparent" because it says something that has already been said, because it does not say it itself and does not therefore really say it; it does not say everything but, instead, merely cites and, by citing in this manner, admits that in the very assertion "everything is already said," neither *everything* is said, nor is this "everything" really *said*. The citational character of universal assertions runs counter to their claim to universality and truth. The fact that they are repetitions or that they can only be repeated immediately denies their semantic content and the intention of those who use them: it indicates that they are not universal assertions, that, for example, everything is not already said. The citation opens up a hole—a nothingness—in the cited "everything," it sets out the demand that it be filled. *Tout est dit* means, therefore, nothing is yet said and demands that more and better be said. Since, however, this inversion, as Schlegel remarks, is valid "regardless of the object under discussion," this nothingness—or hole—of the not-yet-said can never be completely closed: more than nothing or less than everything will always be said, and since everything and nothing are fundamental categories for the knowledge of both the self and the world, something other than what can be known or can be

2. In addition to Terence and Voltaire, whom Schlegel names, authors—or citers—of the statement *Tout est dit* ("everything is said") include La Bruyère. The first sentence of his "Caractères," which was surely not unknown to Schlegel, reads: "Tout est dit, et l'on vient trop tard depuis plus de sept mille ans qu'il y a des hommes et qui pensent" (Everything is said, and one comes too late, more than seven thousand years after men have been alive and thought) (Jean de la Bruyère, *Caractères* [Paris: Flammarion, 1965], 82).

knowingly asserted will always be said. Universal assertions, according to Schlegel's remark, are "apparent"—and indeed so apparent that they go without saying. Yet they not only do not correspond to the intentions of their authors or those who cite them; they do not correspond to themselves and thus do not really speak or respond: they are not said; rather, nothingness is still said in them. But there is more still: since no assertion, however modest it may be, can renounce the claim to be completely and altogether itself—for only in this way is it an assertion or proposition—and since every assertion must *cite* this still unfulfilled claim, there is no proposition that would already be everything; there is no language in which nothingness did not speak as well, and there is none that would not be other than language—would not be something other than language and would not be in another mode than language. If one could rightly view Schlegel's note as what he himself calls a fragment, and if one could, in addition, regard it as a fragment about the minimal structure of the fragment, then a fragment would each time be precisely the language that is not entirely language, not entirely itself but something other than, and different from, language itself: a fragment would be that which in the face of language passed behind or beyond it; a fragment would be the language in which something other than itself—nothing, for example—also spoke and, therefore, a language in which at least two languages always spoke—a broken language, the break of language.[3]

Nothing more need be said. But in order to clarify the proposition about nothing, it was necessary to add the proposition *Tout est dit.* In order for the relation between these propositions to be elucidated and the question posed whether and in what sense they are to be treated as propositions at all, it was necessary to say that no proposition is com-

---

3. In August Wilhelm Schlegel's polylogue "Languages: A Dialogue about Klopstock's Grammatical Dialogues," which was published in the *Athenäum,* a journal he edited with his brother, he said about the German world *Sprach:* "If the sound is also expressive, your word *Sprach*—and it is still called this in some dialects—is strangely enough characterized by this denomination: *St* is the designation for constancy, for firmness, for resting force. . . . *Spr* designates what suddenly breaks in, as in *Springen* [to spring], *Sprützen* [to spray], *Spreizen* [to spread out]. Then comes the extended, accented vowel, and finally a rough breathing. Indeed, Klopstock derives the word from *brechen* [to break] by an intensification of the *S*. . . . It would therefore be a true breaking out." See *Athenäum,* ed. Curt Grützmacher (Reinbek: Rowohlt, 1969), 24–25.

plete, none is itself, and it was also necessary to indicate that every sentence is a fragment of something that can no longer claim to be a totality—everything or nothing. The "more" has lost every measure when it is more than everything. The part is no longer a part of a whole if it is more than the whole. It is *a* part no more—no more an *entire* part—but is, rather, a mani-folding of the parts that exceeds the unity of consciousness and its objects. And now to make clear what links these propositions and the propositions about these propositions to the problem of genre, genus, classes, types and their multiplicity, and to pose the question whether and in what sense there can be propositions about genre, genus, classes, types, and thus in what sense there can be propositions at all—to do all this, more has yet to be said: more than everything or nothing.

The following pages will therefore concern themselves with genre, genus, classes, types and with the genre of genres, genera, classes, and types—with the process of generation in the poetological conception of Friedrich Schlegel and, consequently, with the transcendental conditions of the possibility of speaking about genre, genus, classes and types. Under discussion will be the possibility of speaking about the "about." About "about." About the duplication, the potentializing and depotentializing, the generation and annihilation of poetry. About the poetry and prose of thought, the possibility of a theory of poetry, and about the linguistic conditions of this possibility. Furthermore, therefore, about how the additional proposition *Tout est dit* relates to the first one, "Nothing is yet said," and about the fact that with these two propositions about genre everything is not yet said and that, in addition, not everything can be said.

The problem to which these thoughts return can only be outlined and paraphrased, for the description is inexhaustible and so always fragmentary. But only by way of this limitation is it possible to correspond to what Schlegel demands in one of the programmatic *Athenäum* fragments—a fragment that sets out the program for "romantic poetry" as "progressive universal poetry." This poetry cannot be "exhausted by any theory, and only a divinatory critique"—that is, a critique that guesses within the framework of an ever approaching objective result—"would dare to characterize its ideal" (Ath, 116). But romantic poetry—and "in a certain sense all poetry is, or ought to be, romantic" (Ath, 116)—cannot be exhausted by its theory, which is to say, by a discourse that speaks about it. Something is always left over, and this remainder cannot be grasped by theoretical reflection, for every theoretical articulation has to be, for its part, a moment of that poetry itself. It can never become a mere object in which it participates. Every reflective or self-reflective exertion is outdone by a further one. To every "about" there can be added a further "about" that is not absorbed into the first one. Theoretical formulations and classifications constitute only a specific form—if not an independent genus—of linguistic articulation that, as a specific form, can under no condition raise a claim to universality. Whether the particular is already the whole, or the part already the totality—this could only be decided by a further reflection whose appurtenance to, or participation in, the whole would have to be decided by a higher power of reflection, and so on *ad infinitum*. There are, to be sure, universals and particulars, poetry and its individual genres, and yet there is no last instance, a highest power that could decide which text should be charged to which genre or class. For such a decision could be made only under the aegis of a last instance, and to this last instance not only would every object in its entirety have to be given in a consistent and transparent manner but so, too, would the last instance itself. It is precisely this reflective, theoretical self-certainty of poetry and its theory that is, according to Schlegel's demonstrations, doubtless necessary—and for this reason imperative—but nevertheless impossible.

Self-certainty, self-transparency, self-presence become imperative in the program for a progressive universal poetry when Schlegel writes: "Its destination"—that is, its telos and definition—"is not merely to reunite all separated genres of poetry and to place poetry in contact with philosophy and rhetoric. It also wants to and ought to mix at times, unite at times, fuse at times poetry and prose, geniality and critique, art-poetry and nature-poetry, making poetry lively and sociable as well as making life and society poetic. . ." (Ath, 116). It should, in short, reunite the pairs whose isolated forms of life and language are separated from one another (separated, however, in such a way that they still remain related to one other); it should unite once again these pairs—the romantic imperative of genre demands it. According to this imperative, every genre should come back toward itself from something else and thereby convene with every other one. Critique and poetry should transcend themselves toward each other in the course of history. Their returning to themselves and going beyond themselves into the other—the process of their pairing—is the process of genre, of generation, of *Gattung:* it is the mating process. Genre would thus be the permanent historical transcendence of separated forms of life and thought. Their point of unification would be an instance in which there would no longer be an "about" of "about," in which no "about," no "on top of that," no possible transcendence and no transcendental remainder, no condition of possibility would be left over. At this point of generic unification, critique would itself be the poetry that it sought to analyze; poetry would be the prose of thought, a prose that succeeds poetry and leads it into its insubstantiality. This would be an instance or a process about which nothing is yet said as long as either one were still discussed in concepts drawn from the logic of position or opposition. It would be the instance of pure speaking about which nothing could be said because it alone is always speaking. And it would never have said anything because it fulfills itself in a saying that is limitlessly present but is, for this reason, never itself presentable. It would say nothing precisely because it would be mere saying. "Nothing is yet said."

Such a speaking of poetry in prose, of life in philosophy, of one genus in another—the mating, the pairing, and the pair—is, however, impossible. For this reason: "The romantic kind of poetry"—which means the kind of poetry that is "more than a kind and, as it were, the art of poetry itself"—"is still coming into being; indeed, that is its authentic essence, that it is always only coming into being and can never be completed" (Ath, 116). The mating of genres, the generation of the genus, the engendering of poetry, the "romantic kind of poetry" and thus the art of poetry itself can never be completed; it will never be actualized in its fullness. The de-actualization to which genre is subject by virtue of its processionality also strikes its individual members: neither tragedy, comedy, nor the lyric, neither philosophy, critique, nor prose are ever completed; neither poetry nor life is real as long as the pair remains unpaired and the generative mating has not completely come to pass. But the mating is under way—and the mating of genres is itself the way of its completion. The mating is under way, but it *is* not. The romantic kind of poetry, the very ideal of poetry, is still coming into being, so there is not yet an art of poetry—and nothing in poetry and in prose, in art and in its theory is yet said. Were it said—this goes without saying—there would be no genres, only their unity: everything would be said in it, nothing could still be said about it, and nothing would be said. If it were to take place, if it could be assigned a determinate location, it would be made into a thing, an object, the content of consciousness and, as a result, it would no longer be one with its critique; therefore, it would not be generative mating. There is the mating of genre only under the condition that it does not take place, that it never is *what* it is. There is mating, there is genre, only under the absolute condition *that* it is and that it is *under way*.

There is no mating of genres, and only because—which is to say, only as long as—there is no such mating, is there the process of mating, the generation of genre. And because there is only its process, there are different genres. "One can just as well say that there are infinitely many kinds of poetry as there is only a single progressive one. Thus, there is in fact none, for a kind cannot be thought without another kind, a co-kind" (LN, 583). Genre cannot be thought, because this thought would itself be a second genre, a genre that would disavow the uniqueness of what is thought. Thinking in numbers, whether one or infinite, does not think genre, and since "a kind without another kind, a co-kind," cannot be thought, genre can only be thought as a divided one—divided with thought itself—and thus as unthinkable or "in fact none." In the thinking of genre, both thought and genre ex-pose themselves, and precisely this ex-position, as interruption and beginning, is the always discontinuous generation of genre, the process of literature and of language in general. The nothing that traverses theory, art, and language is not absolute nothing but the transitive nothing, the nihilation of language. Nothing is still said, and so there is more than nothing, namely this: it can be said that it exceeds itself in speaking of itself, at once perseveres and remains still to be said. And so there are also more genres than none, namely more than infinitely many and more than a single one: the one in which the relation of one genre to its nothing is articulated.

"Nothing and everything," Schlegel notes, "are also romantic categories" (LN, 1503). They are categories that designate a tendency that cannot come to an end, whether in completion or in annihilation, because they not only must posit this end but must also present the process of this positing together with what they have posited; they must present the process of producing together with the product. This immanent doubling of genre into process and result leads to a splitting of their borders. Every borderline, once posited, must be doubled by the exponent that indicates the conditions of its production. Since, however, the seal of its productive character modifies the product, this alteration must be expressly marked as an alteration. The process of genre is an infinite commentary on an infinite project. Like everything and nothing, the "one and all" about which Schlegel writes in fragment 238 of the *Athenäum* is the genre that is at the same time poetry and poetry of poetry, the romantic category of a tendency that never comes to its end because it infinitely defers this end, precisely when it refers to it.

By positing itself, genre poses for itself a limit and posits itself, as self-positing, beyond this limit. It does not therefore take place: it must always designate its completion as completion, but with this designation it deposes itself from its own activity and is thus always at once before its end and beyond its end. Genre is an irreducible duality: more and less than itself.

With this concept of genre, transcendental poetry, and poetry in general Schlegel latches onto certain considerations developed by Fichte in order to give a new foundation for Cartesianism and for critical philosophy. The problems of self-foundation and self-reflection that Fichte's philosophy projects as tasks were understood very early by Schlegel and Hardenberg as those of linguistic philosophy, and they were brought into relation to the fundamental problems of aesthetics. In order to justify the autonomy of the beautiful as distinct from that of the true and the ethical, Schlegel refers in a lapidary manner to the connection between beauty and the unconditioned principle Fichte formulates—the proposition "I = I": "A philosophy of poetry in general would, however, begin with the independence of the beautiful, with the proposition that it is and should be separated from the true and the ethical, and that it has the same rights as they do, which for those who can understand it, already follows from the proposition I = I" (Ath, 252). *Athenäum* fragment 256 points to the same connection with the assertion that beauty is "the thing itself," and as such it is "one of human spirit's original modes of action," both a "necessary fiction" and an "eternally transcendental fact." No attempt will be made here to pursue in detail this gesture toward an aesthetic ontology; it can only be emphasized that by virtue of this determination of beauty as the thing itself, as one of human spirit's original modes of action, as a transcendental fact and fiction— and therefore as freedom, the Kantian "fact of reason"—beauty and the aesthetic in general are assigned a radically new place: it is autonomy.

Beauty is its own ground and no longer the mimesis of the Idea or an *imitatio naturae;* it is a form of action in general and no longer a reproduction or representation of an action of nature or consciousness. Such a gloss on the aesthetic cannot be thought independently of a specific interpretation of Kant's productive imagination and least of all independently of Fichte's absolute principle: the proposition "I = I."

According to Fichte's exposition, the sentence "I = I" leaps out of the logical continuum of interrelated and confirmable sentences to the extent that it performs the unconditioned, pre-logical positing that is not itself posited because it is pure positing, sheer thesis with no other actor and no other content than itself. The Fichtean proposition is fundamental in this sense: it is a proposition in which the ground *is posited* for all thinkable propositions as long as it *posits* itself as this ground. And furthermore, beyond the mere establishment of the identity principle of consciousness and subjectivity (to which it is still today gladly reduced), it is the very proposition in which Being accomplishes itself as positing. The fundamental proposition "I = I" is the site of Being. Selfhood is Being, and Being is, for Fichte as well as for Kant, absolute position.[4] Yet in contrast to Kant, the positing that constitutes Being is no longer a position with respect to the original synthetic unity of transcendental self-consciousness but is itself the position of the self. Fichte's principle is fundamentally tautological in the sense that auto-onto-logically, in this very proposition, the self as Being, the latter as language, and language as positing are installed: Fichte's proposition is the thesis of ontotheseology. For this reason, the proposition of the absolute Being of the I in unity with itself cannot be posed from somewhere outside this very proposition. It is not what is spoken by a subject but is this subject

4. "Existence *[Dasein]* is the absolute position of a thing and thereby distinguishes itself from every sort of predicate which as such is always posited merely in relation to another thing," writes Kant in the second section of his treatise of 1763 *The One Possible Basis of Proof for a Demonstration of the Existence of God (Kants Gesammelte Schriften,* ed. Königliche Preussische [later, Deutsche] Akademie der Wissenschaften [Berlin and Leipzig: Georg Reimer, later, Walter de Gruyter, 1900–]; 2: 73; hereafter, "Ak"). In a later place he makes clear that "Being *[das Sein]* or being absolutely posited . . . has exactly the same meaning as existence *[Dasein]*" (Ak, 2: 78). It is, above all, Martin Heidegger who has pointed out the central place of Kant's doctrine of position in transcendental and indeed in speculative idealism; see, in particular, "Kants These über das Sein" in *Wegmarken* (Frankfurt am Main: Klostermann, 1967), 273–307; "Kant's Thesis on Being," trans. Ted Klein, Jr. and William Pohl, in *The Southwestern Journal of Philosophy,* 4 (1973): 7–33.

itself as mere speaking. Before any effort to posit or presuppose it, it must have already posited itself in pure auto-thesis. In the interpretation of his fundamental proposition, Fichte must therefore restore by reduction Decartes's fundamental proposition: "The addition of *cogitans* is completely superfluous; one does not necessarily think if one is, but one is necessarily if one thinks."[5] *Sum*—the complete proposition of Being.

But in this proposition, which is at once the positing of Being and of the I, a proposition in which both Being posits itself as the I and the I posits itself as Being, on the one hand, and both Being and the I, auto-ontothetically, carry out each other, on the other—in this very proposition the proposition itself is posited *as posited*. The positing of the I is not simply, as Fichte expressly maintained, "a self-position as positing,"[6] nor is it simply immediate knowledge of itself as one that knows itself. Furthermore, it is not simply, as a result of this knowledge, an immediate unity of subject and object; this positing is also, as Fichte expressly postulates, a unity of active positing and of the resulting fact of the I. In the "Foundations for the Entire *Wissenschaftslehre*" Fichte says of the I: "It is at the same time the actor and the product of the action; the acting one and that which was effected through the activity; action and deed are one and the same, and therefore the 'I am' is an expression of both an enactment and a deed done [*Thathandlung*]" (SW, 1: 96). The unconditioned proposition of the I, its fundamental principle, is pure positing and as such performance and event, action and process of the proposition; yet it is also a positivity, and as such already the product, the outcome, the fact of the proposition. As pure positing,

5. Johann Gottlieb Fichte, *Werke,* ed. I. H. Fichte (rpt. Berlin: de Gruyter, 1971), 1: 100; cf. Fichte, *The Science of Knowledge,* trans. and ed. Peter Heath and John Lachs (Cambridge, England: Cambridge University Press, 1982), 100; since this translation of the "Foundations of the Entire *Wissenschaftslehre*" includes the pagination of the German edition, only the latter will henceforth be cited. Leibniz had arrived at a similar formulation: "To say *I think therefore I am* is not really to prove existence from thought, since *to think* and *to be thinking* are one and the same, and to say *I am thinking* is already to say *I am*. . . . Only God can see how these two terms, *I* and *existence,* are connected—that is, why I exist" (Gottfried Wilhelm Leibniz, *New Essays on Human Understanding,* trans. and ed. P. Remnant and J. Bennet [Cambridge, England: Cambridge University Press, 1982], 411; Book 4, chapter 7, § 7).

6. Fichte, "Attempt at a New Presentation of the *Wissenschaftslehre*" (1: 528); *Introductions to the Wissenschaftslehre and Other Writings,* ed. and trans. Daniel Breazeale (Indianapolis: Hackett, 1994), 113.

it is open, irreferential, without context and significance; as positivity, it is closed, a fact, both the determined—and no longer determining—subject and the possible object of an assertion. Because this proposition is both action *(Handlung)* and deed *(Tat)*, because it ought to be both *(Tathandlung)* and because—which is to say, as long as—it posits itself, transposing and translating itself into an "itself," it must always re-orient and once again limit the relationless enactment of mere positing by means of its product, a product in which alone it can find an object of reference and the fixed point of its provenance, namely the reflective subject. And it must always set in motion once again its hypothetical positivity by means of the act of its positing.

In the original principle of the I, as Fichte formulates it, two completely different and even incompatible propositions are accordingly at work: one is the absolute, subjectless, and objectless performance, and another which grasps this performance as a form of free subjectivity and knows it in a reflective manner. The relation between these types of propositions can be thought only as a unity, as Fichte requires, if between them mediates a third moment, a moment that guides the first two, action and fact, positing and posited, from the very beginning. The mediation in the sentence "I = I" is performed by the copula "is." Fichte writes in this context: "'is' expresses the transition of the I from positing to reflection on the posited" (SW, 1: 96). But this transition—or this translation—is at the same time the indication that the positing has not always already undergone transition, and in this positing it has not always already found the fixed point for its reflection. It thus gives an indication of what Fichte systematically denies in the theoretical part of his construction of the I and of Being: the possibility of a diremption between positing and posited in the unconditioned principle, a leap—or a *metabasis eis allo genos*—which impedes every immediate unity of the I with its reflection and which makes it possible for this unity to appear at best as an infinite project. Schlegel rested his conception of a progressive universal poetry on this leap and on this infinite project of making possible the unity of the I under the conditions of its impossibility.

As the description of the original "act" of the I that includes "knowledge" of itself suggests, the relation between the two types of proposition that are supposed to translate into one another in Fichte's absolute principle can be described with the help of concepts drawn from speech-act theory—the concepts, more specifically, of the performative and the constative. The performative, of course, can no longer be understood as a speech act within the context of already presupposed conventions and rules, for the act Fichte discusses is a positing without presuppositions and thus a positing of the minimal conditions for the conventions, rules, or norms of linguistic and social intercourse. The concept of the constative has to be redefined in a similar way: applied to whatever precedes the unconditioned proposition, it cannot refer to a pregiven empirical state of affairs but only to the imposing act of the transcendental I itself. What occurs in Fichte's proposition can be characterized in this way: in order for the proposition to be able to realize its constative character through which the identity of the I with itself is designated as Being, it needs an absolutely nonrelational, performative positing, a sheer act that can be neither the action of an I nor an action in relation to an I, hence no action of consciousness and no intentional correlate of consciousness. For if it were a conscious action directed toward itself—and Fichte leaves no doubt that it is supposed to be precisely this, a subjective action directed by and toward a subject—then the entire principle of the I would be a *petitio principii* that would contain nothing but an affirmation unable to clarify its own structure, let alone the ground of this structure. Fichte's analytic distinctions, particularly the distinction between production and product, action and deed, allow him, however, to distinguish tendencies in the unity he postulated, tendencies that are not immediately compatible with each another and indeed counteract the very unity he constructs. If Fichte characterizes mere positing, pure performance, as an action of the I, he hastens to anticipate the result of this positing, refers it to something already posited—namely, the I—and interprets it, *ex post facto,* as its production. But this simply indicates that he understands the pure performance already as a performing of precisely the constative that depends on it; he stabilizes this action into a fact and thereby subordinates it to a calculus of a constative statement that, for its part, would be objectless and powerless if it did not find its ground in that action and were referred to that imposing act alone. The mere position "I" is in itself just as meaningless and arbitrary as the letter "A." Nothing is stated in it, nothing asserted, nothing meant; it is a mere positing, and only as a nonreferential, irreflective, unconditioned positing does it correspond to the principle of freedom that, according to Fichte, holds valid for any absolute action. As a free position, the I, like the A, must be independent of any relation to a predecessor; that is, under no conditions can it be a constative that refers to a preceding action or a former state of affairs without having thereby interrupted its action and forfeited its original performative character.

The double proposition inscribed in the Fichtean principle thus tears this principle apart: the sheer performative, the positing called "I," is incapable of being stated; it is absolute excess beyond every possible objectification and every self-reflective subjectivity. If this performative nevertheless becomes the object of a constative statement, its positing must break down what it posits: it must be brought to, and broken off at, an end it never posited, and so it can no longer be stated as a performative or be reflected as a performance. A performative can be stated only if it is interrupted; a statement can be performed only if its constative and therefore epistemic character is disrupted.[7]

"I" is an action that exceeds every transcendental ego and every empirical self—everything, in short, that could be meant by the word "I." It can "translate" itself into the proposition of identity, "I = I," only if it is broken; it can become the proposition of self-reflection only if it is inflected. The pure action of the "I," which could also be "A," the meaningless and objectless action—this escapes Fichte's attention. It would not even be an action, not a positing, but an ex-posing, an interruption, a breaking down: not a *Setzung* but an *Aussetzung*. Fichte takes the position into consideration only as inflected and reflected, therefore, as a position that states itself from the beginning, turning itself into its own *fait accompli*. Because he nevertheless maintains that the structure of the I-thesis is that of an action, he is compelled to draw the conclusion that reflection must be thought as an action, and action as a reflection in itself. But it is clear that reflection without conditions and without presuppositions can only be reflection of reflection, that it must refer only to itself and must run the course of an infinite series of reflections about reflections without ever finding *itself* in a single reflection. Reflection turns into an empty project of reflection, into an infinite occurrence of flexing backwards, a bending-back that could never reach its initial

7. Despite his careful attention to every other peculiarity of Fichte's principle, Dieter Henrich, who is the first one to reconstruct this principle in a methodical way, nevertheless misses this invisible but decisive asymmetry between action and result, between performative and constative, and thus the irreparable inconsistency that is at work in Fichte's fundamental proposition. See Dieter Henrich, *Fichtes ursprüngliche Einsicht* (Frankfurt am Main: Klostermann, 1967).

point of departure—itself—and could therefore never reach itself *as* reflection. The endless mirroring that the early romantics consequently and consistently came to stage is also a flight of the mirror. Accordingly, even in the thesis of reflection, the hyperbole of a sheer, nonreferential, nonreflective performance—a hyperbole whose unconditionedness was supposed to have been bound by the interpretation of mere positing as the thesis of the I and the self-foundation of the subject—breaks through. For it is not enough to see the condition of reflection in a mere postponing or in a delay between the positing and posited I: reflection cannot arise from this difference between two poles, because neither the reflecting nor the reflected pole is ever reached. If these poles were ever established as firm facts, the reflection of one into the other could no longer be an original self-positing reflection but only a conditioned one. The solution to the infinite dilemma of Fichte's autotheseology can be put in these terms: if there is reflection, it is, paradoxically enough, only as the event of a project of reflection—a project that cannot in principle be limited by the horizon of a positing subject and cannot in principle reach a conclusion in the *fait accompli* of a consciousness that knows itself as its object. And furthermore, if there is subjectivity, it is neither as instantaneous knowledge of itself as knowledge, nor as a "self-position as positing" (SW, 1: 528), but only in the experience of a positing that overshoots the schema of reflective representation and, therefore, in the experience of the irreducibility of positing to itself *as* positing, in the experience of the leap that releases positing of *itself,* in the experience of positing as inconsistency and ex-positing.[8]

This leap in the proposition—the hiatus in the transcendental—trans-

8. The earliest attempt to clarify a fundamental problem of modern ontology by means of the analytic instruments of speech act theory is that of Jaakko Hintikka's "'Cogito, Ergo Sum': Inference or Performance," reprinted in *Knowledge and the Known* (Dordrecht: Reidel, 1974), 98–125. Hintikka proceeds from a conventionalist notion of the performative when analyzing the function of the Cartesian cogito despite the fact that it has a foundational character. Indeed, he never takes into account the possibility of an absolutely performative ego. In line with the best mathematical tradition, Hintikka finds the validity of the existence proposition *sum* only *e contrario,* from what he calls the "existential inconsistency . . . of performatory (performative) character" (105), that is, from the absurdity of the proposition "I am not." However, this would not have been an inconsistency for Descartes, because his *cogitatio* could very well have "I am not" *as a content* without thereby disturbing the *form* of representation and its performative existence in the least. Cartesian evidence is not diminished by "Cogito 'non sum,' ergo sum,"

poses and translates an absolute and absolutely free, prepredicative positing into a conditioned positivity, the being-posited of a self-predicative assertion that first results from this positing. Since this proposition is never purely itself, since it can be real and effective only in the leap between its first and second style, it does not posit itself, is not posited, is not and is not I. By wanting to say *itself*, the saying of this proposition—the principle of modern ontology—says itself always already as an objectified subject and thus says neither itself nor Being. By saying something, measured against the Being it is, it says nothing. Nothing is yet said in precisely this proposition in which everything is said as something. Because, however, this pure saying says nothing yet, it must ceaselessly go beyond and exceed itself. Because it has already become something said in its saying, it must transcend itself, its own limit, toward its future. "I = I"—proposition of positing, proposition of Being, and proposition of the I—asserts itself as this proposition only from the position of its being-posited and thus as something that it is not, and this means: it does not assert itself. The autothesis is autoprothetic. Posited by itself, the I is the "already" of its Being; since, however, it has to overtake itself as this *a priori* perfect, it is the "not yet" of its "already." "I = I" is the cover formula for the *a priori futurum exactum* of my Being: I will have become.

Being is in its proposition, its singular site, *deposed*. It is posited *as* Being—and therefore as its parasite. The foundation in its proposition *as* foundation—its own parabasis.

---

since it is an evidence of cognition, not of cognitive contents. If, however, this pure performance is existence, it is not, as Descartes wanted it, simply subjective existence and not simply the existence of the I, for this I is not mere action but is at the same time affirmed to be its content or subject. Another kind of inconsistency than the one Hintikka censures in "non sum" is implied in the *sum*, an absolutely irreducible inconsistency between the performative and its subjectivization, between the mere act—of existence— and its representation in the constative "I am the one that is." And since this absolute *cogitatio* for its part appears bound to the form of the subject, which in an uncontrollable manner it transcends as performance, there arises the inconsistency of this form as the structure—or destructuring—of performance as well as existence. There is performance and Being only as inconsistency—and therefore as always already more (or less) than performance and always already as other than Being. Hintikka's subtle concept of "existential" or "performative inconsistency" should be understood quite differently from the way it was meant, not as a denunciation (as such it fails) but as an affirmative concept.

I knows itself by knowing itself absolutely *as* I, no longer as unconditionally certain Being. I is only the fiction of its existence. Principle,
founding proposition, over an abyss, and this abyss in it, ex-posed. . . .

Fichte's interpretation of the unconditioned principle—a principle of
which we have not given a full account but only interpreted in its barest
outlines—seeks to articulate the elements of a transcendental theory of
language as action and fact. This interpretation understands itself as an
ontological foundation of a theory of knowledge, a *Wissenschaftslehre,*
which is to say, a science of the conditions for the possibility of epistemic
statements in general. In this science of science the romantics—and
among them, Friedrich Schlegel and Hardenberg most especially—were
able to decipher the program for a poetry of poetry, a transcendental
poetry. For the first time in a very long time they understood the concept
of *poiesis* in a literal manner—as making, producing, bringing forth—
and they recognized in this concept a cord that linked it with the basic
concept of Fichte's science of knowledge, the concept of action as the
positing of a fundamental proposition. Now, one may very well doubt
that, for example, Schlegel understood Fichte's *Wissenschaftslehre* as it
would be understood today, after and also through the mediation of
Schlegel. And yet, it is precisely because of Schlegel's "misunderstand-
ings" that the programmatic thrust and acute tensions of Fichte's theses
make themselves known. Thus Schlegel writes of the "inconsistency"
that Fichte developed in the thought of the I as its dialectic, simplifying
the Fichtean thought in this way: "The greatest inconsistency in Fichte
is that pure Being should be lively and yet without manifold." The
discovery of this "inconsistency" does not lead him to reject the Fichtean
principle and to preach the virtues of logical consistency; rather, in his
own way, he transforms this "inconsistency" into the calculus of transcendental poetry and thereby opens up a path that goes beyond
Fichtean philosophy. Schlegel thus comports himself in the way described in one of his fragments: "It can do little harm to a philosophy
if one annihilates it—and occasionally the careless one thereby annihilates himself—or if one shows a philosophy that it annihilates itself. If
it is really philosophy, it will, like a phoenix, rise again from its own
ashes" (Ath, 103).

The "manifold" Schlegel is unable to find in Fichte's "pure Being" is,
contrary to Schlegel's assumption, posited as non-Being by this Being
itself. By positing non-Being, pure Being limits itself and finds itself

limited by non-Being as an other. This non-Being, which takes up residence in Being, doubtless limits the positional power of the absolute I,
but since it is the absolute I itself that posits this limitation, only "pure
Being" determines the manifold of representations. Mediated by the
positing of a non-Being, the manifold of representations, reflections,
and self-predications is implicitly co-posited in the unconditioned
proposition of Being.

This "co-" of positing—infinitude and finitude, Being and non-Being,
I and non-I posited together and at the same time—is realized in the
reciprocal positing and reciprocal determination of unity and manifold.
This togetherness and simultaneity do not, however, owe their origin to
the pure activity performed in the positing of the unconditioned proposition but, as Fichte puts it, to a "particular law of our spirit": the law
of the divisibility of the I and the non-I (SW, 1: 108). More exactly, Being
and non-Being come together and take place simultaneously thanks to
a force that articulates itself in this law and the self-positional proposition of the absolute I: the togetherness and simultaneity of Being and
non-Being owe their origin to the power of the imagination. This power
may have only a particular, isolated, and supplemental position in
Fichte's *Wissenschaftslehre,* and yet it drives the unconditioned activity of
the self-positing of Being. The supplement of this force makes possible
the absolute activity of the fundamental proposition in the first place. It
is the condition of the unconditioned. But the power of imagination
does not therefore have to obey the law of self-determination that
Fichte's fundamental proposition sets up; rather, it responds to the mere
determinability of the undetermined or, even more paradoxically, the
mere determinability of the undeterminable:

> The power of imagination as such posits no fixed limits, for it itself has
> no fixed standpoint; only reason posits something fixed by first fixing
> the power of imagination. The power of imagination is a faculty that
> hovers in the middle between determination and non-determination,
> between finite and infinite. . . . This hovering characterizes the power
> of imagination even in its product; in the course of its hovering, as it
> were, and by means of its hovering, it brings this product about. This
> hovering of the power of imagination between irreconcilables, this
> conflict of imagination with itself is what extends the state of the I
> therein to a moment of *time.* . . . (For pure reason, for reason alone,

everything is at the same time; only for the power of the imagination is there a time.) (SW, 1: 216–17)

At work in the absolute proposition, at work in its self-positing, the power of imagination arrests the production of the I and arrests the I in a "moment of time." Time suspends the position of the I, the self-foundation. The fundamental proposition in which everything is supposed to be simultaneous stretches out its absolute punctuality, stretches into time, and pauses, for a moment, between itself and the self—or before the self.

The unlimited self-positing faculty of the I—a faculty that feeds on the faculty of the imagination—preserves itself only in suspending the positing of the I: only, therefore, in making this positing possible and "holding" it out as a mere possibility. The power of the imagination thus plays a double game with the absolute proposition: it makes it possible and threatens it with impossibility; the faculty of positing holds open the possibility of positing, and by maintaining a hold on itself, holds any actual positing back. Only the weakness of the power of the imagination is responsible for the transition from the sheer possibility of positing to its actualization. The faculty lacks the force to maintain itself as a faculty: "The power of the imagination does not hold it out any longer, that is, longer than a moment. . . . Reason enters the scene . . . and determines that the imagination make a transition to the *reflection of the I in itself*" (SW, 1: 217). The power of the imagination is not powerful enough to keep the determination of the fundamental proposition and, with it, the entire system of science in suspension; but the one praxis that is at every point guided by the imagination does indeed have the power to keep up, hold out, potentialize, and extend time: art as an operation evoking the feeling of sublimity. Schlegel, who, as was noted above, draws on Fichte's proposition to confirm the autonomy of the beautiful as separate from the true and the moral, also notes that "beauty is what is at once stimulating and sublime" (Ath, 108). And he characterizes transcendental poetry as the poetry that can only "hover between unifying and separating philosophy and poetry" (Ath, 252). The proposition just cited from Fichte's "Foundations for the Entire *Wissenschaftslehre*" reads in full: "The power of the imagination does not hold it [indeterminability] out any longer, that is, longer than a moment (except in the feeling of the sublime, where an astonishment, a checking of temporal change emerges)."

In the feeling of the sublime, in this astonishment, time is blocked: it holds out longer than a moment and indeed for so long that the power of the imagination does not make a transition to the determination of the I in its reflection but, instead, lingers at the mere determinability of the I. In the experience of the sublime, in astonishment, the power of the imagination works as a force of unlimited potentialization of reflective relations and thus of unlimited potentialization of the integral positing of the I. It holds out the possibility of determining the I and thus the possibility of a concrete positing of the unconditioned proposition; but it holds onto this possibility beyond the limits of its actualization at any definite point of time. In astonishment, in the philosophical affect *par excellence,* the determined Being of the I is suspended along with the change of time. In the feeling of the sublime—in the feeling therefore that arises from the moral law and that, according to Schlegel, should also be awakened by art—the fundamental proposition of the I is displaced into the hovering of infinite determinability and thus of permanent indeterminacy. In a highly paradoxical way, the I reaches the open field of its indeterminability when it undergoes the transition from its instantaneous self-positing to its practical determination in the sphere of moral action and in the experience of art. Art, philosophy, and the moral law hold up time and hold off the proposition of the I: each prevents the I from determining and fulfilling itself as a determinate proposition. The possibility of the I that they grant is the impossibility of actualizing this I. "In the practical field," Fichte writes and argues in rigorously Kantian fashion, "the power of the imagination goes on to infinity, until it reaches the absolutely indeterminable Idea of the highest unity, a unity that would be possible only after a completed infinity, which is itself impossible" (SW, 1: 217).

Schlegel's concept of poetry proceeds from the power of the imagination as a faculty that sets up the action of the fundamental proposition and keeps it suspended; it thus proceeds from the infinitization of the process in which the "practical field" no longer constitutes itself by virtue of an intellectual intuition but with respect to an I that can neither be thought in a determinate manner nor ever "really be" (SW, 1: 516). As a praxis, as self-directed intentional action, as *poiesis,* romantic transcendental poetry is a relational schema between the ideal and the real and the process of their generation: *genus generationis.* Like Fichte's principle, it is bound up with the suspending and virtualizing figure of the wavering power of the imagination, for transcendental poetry can only "hover," as Schlegel says, using Fichte's word, between unifying and separating philosophy and poetry, praxis and poetry, poetry in general and its genres and kinds. And transcendental poetry must even keep its "keystone"—which would be a "philosophy of the novel"—up in the air (Ath, 252). Yet by insisting, however implicitly, on the primacy of the imagination in the project of a transcendental poetry and likewise insisting on its connection with the problems of ethics, Schlegel inverts the *Wissenschaftslehre*'s hierarchy of theory and practice; more concretely, he inverts the hierarchy of the unconditioned enactment *(Tathandlung)* and the domain of practical imagination in which this enactment appears infinitely suspended. Since, for Schlegel, the transcendental enactment of the proposition can be an accomplishment only of literary-philosophical praxis and can be realized only in the unreachable distance of a messianic future—under the conditions, therefore, as Fichte writes, "of a completed infinite, which is itself impossible" (SW, 1: 217)—this transcendental proposition must stand under the pause of the imagination and, interminably, irreflectively, remain hovering. The transcendental of the poetic proposition is not given as the foundation of poetic texts but given up as a task: as their telos. What Schlegel says of life goes for this telos as well: "The transcendental point of view for this life awaits us. Then will it first be of genuine significance to us" (Ath, 285). The word "significance" is to be understood here in the strict sense: whether it be the significance of life or a text, it can only be given at the instant that the transcendental condition for the possibility of meaningful propositions toward which Fichte's principle aims is altogether fulfilled. But, as in the preceding fragment, "Spirit conducts an infinite self-proof" (Ath, 284)—a self-proof, in other words, that can never be concluded. The transcendental point of view is, for Schlegel, never more than the vanishing point of a perspective that is itself hypothetical and excludes a guarantee of its existence: interminable *fiction* of the possibility of an immemorial fact. Only insofar as transcendental poetry carries out the fictioning of this fact can it simultaneously raise the claim to be this fact itself; only insofar as it is the deed in the sense of a *fait accompli* can it be the form of transcendental action itself, "one of human spirit's original modes of action" (Ath, 256). It is both at the same time, and with every one of their movements it maintains the other in suspension.

With this immanent suspension of the poetic-transcendental proposition, as it appears in the program for a transcendental poetry, the onto-logical sense that language can claim on the basis of Fichte's un-conditioned principle alters in turn. In Fichte, poetry was interpreted as an action that, because of its roots in the original act, should be a form of self-production and existence-granting. In accordance with his inver-sion of the Fichtean perspective, Schlegel turns poetry into an organon of *projects* of possible existence, and indeed these projects cannot be understood as projections into the future, for the present would then be in possession of a faculty of action that could arrive at the unreachable ideal. Rather, these projects must be understood as projections *from* the future and, since this future is to be thought as an infinite withdrawal and thus analogous with the past, they can be characterized only as relics of the future. Schlegel calls them "fragments from the future" (Ath, 22) and thereby characterizes transcendental poetry as a torso of something it will never have been.

The concept of poetry as a project deposes all the crowning magni-tudes of transcendental as well as dialectical thought. Determined as a "subjective germ of an object coming into being" (Ath, 22), therefore as a seminal fragment and the fragmentary "sem," poetry is a projection of sense that can fulfill itself neither in the totality of a subject nor in that of an object. Subject and object become projects in the overall poetic project in which they combine with each other according to their respec-tive tendencies—and indeed they become projects not only of their selfhood, not only projects in which they become themselves, but pro-jects of their very Being. From the transformation of the proposition "I am I" into the practical imperative "I must become I," it ineluctably follows that the I is not yet I and, furthermore, that there *is* no I yet. The unconditioned proposition succumbs to a condition, and the tran-scendental is exposed to the attranscendental no longer of a proposition but of a pro-pelling, a leap, a project. Because the condition of possibility for the unique proposition that could guarantee existence can never acquire the form of a firm ground so long as it remains a fragment, a germ, a project, and because this condition thus always refers to the open horizon of the future, Schlegel ironically concludes that "nothing can be more presumptuous than existing" (Ath, 20). Just as subject and object remain, in Schlegel's poetological reinterpretation of Fichtean philoso-phy, only so many projects, nothing remains of the absolute subject's positing of Being but the hybrid fiction of existence. I am—a project. The sem-ontology of the absolute proposition transforms into the semi-

and simili-ontology of absolute poetry. Its works are only "claimants to existence" (Ath, 27)[9] and projects of (im)possible sense. But as claimants to sense and *only* as such, as hybrid fictions of Being and as these *alone*, they present the condition of possible meaning and possible Being.

Poetry is itself only when it fictions itself or makes itself into its own surrogate: "Transcendental poetry should be infinitely potentialized and analyzed; this can only be carried out by a fiction or a surrogate" (LN, 798). Transcendental poetry has to become the surrogate of itself because the ideal that would have prescribed its goal to the movement of poetry falls apart. This is what Schlegel's *Literary Notebooks* has to say about this ideal—the novel, which is the transcendental-poetic genre *par excellence:* "An individual novel can never be completed, since the very concept of genre, its ideal, can never be completed" (LN, 842). The theory of the novel—which, according to Schlegel, is the "keystone" of a philosophy of poetry (Ath, 252)—can refer to its object only if the theory itself, having been subjected to the imperative of poeticization, assumes the form of the novel. If, however, the concept of genre, which is to say, the concept of the novel destined to fulfill the postulate of genre, can never be completed, this also holds true for a theory that assumes a novelistic form: it cannot be completed either. The theory of the novel would be

9. Schlegel's *Athenäum* fragment 27 refers not to works but to human beings; it does not make a universal assertion but, as is often the case, only a quantitative one: "Most people are, like Leibniz's possible worlds, only equally justified claimants to existence. There are few existences *[Existenten]*." This reflection clearly refers to the passage in Leibniz's "Principles of Nature and Grace, Based on Reason" (§ 10) in which he writes, "For as all possible things have a claim to existence in God's understanding in proportion to their perfection, the result of all these claims must be the most perfect actual world which is possible. Without this it would be impossible to give a reason why things have gone this way rather than otherwise" (Gottfried Wilhelm Leibniz, *Philosophical Papers and Letters,* ed. and trans. Leroy Loemker [Dordrecht: Reidel, 1969], 639). The Leibnizian "strivings" *(prétensions)* that Schlegel had already ironically translated in the earlier fragment 23 as "hybrid pretensions" *(Anmaßungen)* are anthropomorphized in fragment 27 and become "claimants" *(Prätendenten)*. Whereas, for Leibniz, the totality of strivings— that is, dynamic possibilities or faculties—forms the universe of actual existence according to the proposition *existentia essentiae exigentia* (see, for example, "De veritatibus primis," *Philosophical Papers,* 267–70), for Schlegel—who takes his point of departure from an entirely different concept of possibility—there is no totality, no universe, and therefore not even existence but only "few existences." For corresponding reasons, the fundamental Leibnizian proposition—the principle of reason, according to which there must not be nothing but rather something—no longer holds.

a novel of the novel in which, as its potentializing and reflective form, the interminability of the novel were to grow exponentially. The farther the novel goes in its theoretical construction toward the ideal of the romantic genre, the closer the *Roman* approaches the romantic, the greater the distance it leaves between itself and this ideal. The romantic approximation of absolute poetry is the distancing and de-stancing of poetry: its *Ent-fernung.* As long as it is set into place with a "theory of the novel," the "keystone" in the vaulted architecture of transcendental poetry must break down and make room for another "keystone"— enough room for the collapse of whatever it seeks to hold up. The project of a philosophy of art and thus the project of transcendental poetry are their infinite ruin. The form in which the movement of poetry, the movement of philosophy, and most especially, the movement of the novel-like philosophy of the novel are built up and broken down is not the form of the ruin in whose image transcendental poetry's efforts have been allegorized: it is, rather, the process of ruining. As theory, according to Schlegel's dictum, the novel stands under the "categorical imperative" of "intellectual intuition" (Ath, 76). Fichte's translation of this Kantian concept—which Kant always disavows—was his fundamental proposition: "I = I." Since the theory of the novel and the philosophy of art in general heed this imperative and thus respect a demand that is in principle impossible to fulfill, they pursue the infinite blinding of intellectual intuition. Schlegel's transcendental poetry a-scribes the proposition of Fichte's transcendental philosophy, "I = I," to an impossible novel, and written in this way, they both fall asunder.

However problematic and hybrid all these concepts have become as a result of the interminability and insecurity of every self-reference and self-grounding, the reflection of the novel in itself makes the romantic form of art, from an epistemological point of view, into a person. The example Schlegel found for the reflective form of literary self-reference was Cervantes' *Don Quixote:* "The central character in the second part of *Don Quixote* is the first part. Thus it is the thoroughgoing reflection of the work on itself. . . . That the novel desires two centers points to the fact that every novel wants to be an *absolute* book; it points to the mystical character of the novel. This gives it a mythological character; it thereby becomes a person" (LN, 1727–28). The reflection of the novel in itself is a process wherein its two centers are supposed to refer to each other and to be recognized by each other as centers of the very same text.

Reflection personifies: one point bends back toward another as toward itself and, by referring to itself in this way, constitutes itself as a self; it gives itself a form, an intuitive as well as conceptual identity. Reflection is thus a prosopopeia. By way of prosopopeia the novel provides itself with the character of a person who makes its acts transparent by commentary or critique. The self-anthropomorphizing of the novel by means of its reflective activity is another formula for the theorization of the novel demanded by the program of transcendental poetry—a theorization in which poetry combines and mixes with science: "The novel is poetry in connection with science, thus, with art; thus, prose and the poetry of poetry" (LN, 1566). The poeticization of science presents itself as the complement to the theorization of poetry undertaken by novelistic self-reflection. The imperative of this poeticization is first directed at the prosaic language of philosophy, which is, according to Schlegel, essentially defined as a transcendental—or, in other words, as a language, that is, as a language of thesis, reflection, and personification. "Transcendental [prose] is logically or factually (thetic)" (LN, 811). As "thetic," as positing, transcendental style is, Schlegel keeps emphasizing, at the same time "legislative," law-giving (LN, 872, 874, 875). Whereas the transcendental prose obeys the logic of positing and cannot, therefore, "hover," the romantic and, in particular, the absolutely romantic prose must be "at the same time fixed and hovering" (LN, 879). But that means transcendental prose must displace and set into a hovering motion its own positing and self-positing, and it must likewise break open the reflection of the self that takes place between thesis and antithesis as between two centers of an ellipse. For it is not the task of the romantic form of art to bring thesis and antithesis into a synthesis and thereby to bring about a new form of thesis, figuration, and mythological personification; rather, its task is literally to analyze both, thesis and antithesis—to dissolve them, to set them apart, to distance them from themselves and from each other. About irony, the decisive gesture of the absolute romantic style, Schlegel therefore says this: "Irony is analysis of thesis and antithesis" (LN, 802). And in the next note, he continues: "Romantic comedy always evaporates, it's so light" (LN, 803). Romantic art—art *par excellence* and art in general—analyzes, sets into a hovering motion, and almost evaporates unconditioned positing and self-referential positing, thesis, reflection and, with them, the fixed figuration of the mythological person of the novel or the book. Transcendental style must be exposed to an ultra-transcendental, analytic, attranscendental one. Positing—and with it, the self and the Being it represents—must be suspended in a non-positing gesture. Only then does the prose of the novel correspond to the demand that it be absolute: disconnected from the position of subjectivity and set loose from the Being of the self that offers itself only as reflected form, as person, and thus in a mythological manner. The novel is absolute when it permanently de-mythologizes and de-morphologizes itself.

Because the analytic, hovering, and almost evaporating prose in the novel suspends the transcendental, thetic, and legislative prose, it can never arrive at the structure of reflection to which it nevertheless remains bound: "the true prosaic period should be dramatically constructed" (LN, 2045). The poetization of prosaic language breaks open the double-centered figure of reflection that, according to Schlegel's characterization of *Don Quixote,* connects the novel with the geometric path of an ellipse, and it opens this figure up into a parabola or a hyperbole—in either case, a figure one of whose foci remains visible while the other disappears into infinity. For reasons that have yet to be discussed, Schlegel described this figure in terms of drama: "The natural form of drama is that of death, or better yet, of natural spirit; thus, drama = tragedy. The other form = $\subset$ not merely the visible action but also the invisible pole that in Sophocles is given by fate, in Shakespeare by absolute psychology and irony" (LN, 2060). When the second pole of reflection is eclipsed, the path of the ellipse, which is the geometric analogue to the dual-poled figure of reflection, is stretched into the open figure of the parabola or hyperbola. This is done in the natural form of tragedy by death, in the artificial form of romantic drama by irony, in religion and sexuality by orgiastic voluptuousness (LN, 2063). Insofar as the novel is a "feminine mode of art, if one considers poetry as an animalistic universe" (LN, 1387), insofar as "the genius of voluptuousness belongs" to women (LN, 1442), and insofar as "the theory of dying belongs to the novel like the theory of voluptuousness and of femininity" (LN, 1434), the form not only of romantic drama but also of the novel and its theory—the form of art, language, and experience in general—must be essentially feminine, parabolic or hyperbolic, and can be presented only problematically as reflection and self-reference. Once the ellipse of reflection opens into a hyperbole, the novel tends toward the dissolution of every form of self-reference and self-relation. Its hyperbolic movement no longer allows it to refer to a finite correlate of its focus—whether this correlate be itself or an object in the outside world. It can no longer be a form of a repetition, whether this be articulated as a repetition of itself in the reflection or the imitation of a visible object or an imagined one. Schlegel insists on this point, but not by employing the geometric and rhetorical figure of the hyperbole; instead, he repeatedly draws on a dramaturgical "figure" well known in Attic comedy, parekbasis: "The *parekbasis* has, as it were, the form of voluptuousness. The repetition of the theme is set over against it" (LN, 2173); "Parekbasis and chorus necessary (as potency) for every novel" (LN, 1682). If Schlegel characterizes the repetition of the theme and the return to it—which is the poetological form of reflection in itself—as the opposite to parekbasis, and if he calls parekbasis the "potency" of the novel, then that figure cannot in turn be understood either as reflection pure and simple or as its condition of possibility. There would be no parekbasis if something did not interrupt the work, its immediate self-reference, and its implicit reflection—interrupt it not only in a thematic way but "completely," down to its very form. In his lectures on the history of European literature of 1802–1803, Schlegel still used these terms to characterize this dramatic—and paradramatic—figure:

> In its form Attic Old comedy is very much like tragedy. It takes from the latter a choral and dramatic-dialogic constituent, also monodies. The only difference consists in parekbasis, a speech that was given in the middle of the play by the chorus in the name of the poet to the people. In fact, it was *a complete interruption and cancellation of the play* in which, as in the play itself, the greatest licentiousness reigned, and as the chorus stepped out onto the edges of the proscenium, the crudest things were said to the people. The name comes from this stepping out *(ekbasis)*. (KA, 11: 88; italics added)

With parekbasis prose falls out of the role of reflection. It no longer obeys the imperative of self-referentiality in the thesis of the I; it passes sentence on the posited proposition of representational identity and abandons this proposition and everything posited along with it to another form of death—to infinite irony about its Being. If the reflection of poetry in itself is, as Schlegel demonstrates with *Don Quixote,* a prosaic form of representing the very character of representation, if it is an epistemological figure that sets the subject into a dominant position over everything given with it, and if it thereby lays the ground for every system of anthropocentric science, then parekbasis, emerging from the poetry of the novel, is the condition of possibility for, and at the same time the uncontrollable deposing of, every epistemological figure of self-reference. For, on the one hand, the reflection must step back from what is reflected—and indeed necessarily step back by means of the eccentric step of parekbasis—in order to be able to move in the medium of intuition, representation, or thought toward what is reflected. On the other hand, parekbasis brings to naught every representation and un-does the self-securing of the subject by "completely interrupting and cancelling" every relation in the act of positing. Poetic parekbasis con-stitutes an uncontrollable, dramatic-grammatical trope whose exorbitant movement displaces the framework for every epistemological paradigm of reflective representation. Only as a performative act does it step out of and overstep the strictly circumscribed scene of representational unity—only, therefore, as an act to which no cognition and no propo-sition correspond and which is impossible to identify *as* an act and *as* a performative. The movement of parekbasis oversteps the horizon of every possible cognitively circumscribed performance. In order for parekbasis to open up a space for reflection of any sort, including infinite reflection, it must be pre-reflective and trans-reflective, indeed ex-flec-tive, bending out absolutely and absolutely preceding every possibility of bending back. And it must also be trans-performative, trans-forma-tive, exformative before it can be restricted to a limited, epistemologi-cally controlled performative. Schlegel, who is never more consistent than when he touches on the monstrous inconsistency beyond the sphere of form, brings the movement of parekbasis into relation with the concept of "anti-form." In the *Literary Notebooks* he writes: "Parek-basis can just as well be *absolutely* mimetic or *absolutely* fantastic; actually both, however, entirely and purely together, thus the highest *anti-form* and *nature poetry*" (LN, 395). As "anti-form and nature poetry," as a linguistic form of death and voluptuousness, the principle of femininity as well as of irony, permanent parekbasis is the medium of pure positing even beyond the limits drawn by the unconditioned self-positing of transcendental subjectivity. The absolute proposition of positing beyond the limits registered by the formulas of reflection asserts itself in the novel as unlimitable, indefinable, and in the strictest sense unpresentable to the extent that it proceeds by way of, and is directed by, permanent parekbasis: it asserts itself as unascertainable and ek-thetic, parekthetic. "Parekbasis must be permanent in the fantastical novel" (LN, 461). The parekbasis of the novel could thus be characterized as the form in which the interminable presentation of the absolute, as a generation of the unconditioned proposition, is under way before and beyond every reflection. Parekbasis is the act that is no longer merely performative but trans-formative and ex-formative; it is no longer even an act, if every act is bound up with an already constituted subject. On the contrary, it is the event in which the project of an unconditioned, infinite proposition of positing propels itself forward. The work it permanently interrupts and suspends is "a great . . . anacoluthon" (LN, 989), that is, not only a break in the proposition, a leap in the principle of Being and of the I, but this very pro-position as break and leap in which its positing is made possible and at the same time exposed to the condition of its impossibility. Parekbasis or anacoluthon is the romantic "anti-form": the limit-figure, or the figure at the limit of figurality, a figure in which the "theory of dying" Schlegel demands is exposed to nothing less than the death of theory. If the Fichtean ontology of unconditioned self-positing can be characterized as ontotheseology, then its transformation in Schlegel can be called ektheseology. The latter opens up the possibility of Being as the positing of subjectivity only on the condition that, in the excess of its opening, it withdraws from Being any possibility of establishing itself as solid ground. It is the pro-position of Being—propelled.

As the modern form of art *par excellence,* writes Schlegel, the novel must be both sentimental and naive—a reference to Schiller's categorization of two historical genres (cf. NL 324, 327). Not only does the lyrical-centrifugal pull toward the absolute and, at the limit, toward the altogether unpresentable characteristic of the novel, so too do its rigorous plasticity and solidity. According to Schlegel, naive means "self-limited" (LN, 229), whereas the sentimental goes toward the unlimited, toward whatever cannot bear closed totalities: "In the novel there is unlimited totality, that is, limited non-totality, a striving toward the former" (LN, 213). The prose in the novel sets up the limit that parekbasis permanently oversteps. But the poeticization of scientific prose here confronts the prosafication of poetry: "Over against the poeticization of every still unpoetic object and sphere stands the universalization or permeation with the spirit of the other sciences and arts.—<Techni-

zation and naturalization. Idealization and Realization.>" (LN, 312). The forms of "mixing" metrical and prosaic diction that Schlegel observed in Shakespeare, Goethe, and Tieck "point," as he noted, "toward the absolutely romantic" (LN, 688, 827, 1233); but they do not yet realize the imperative of poeticization. The outcome of this imperative would be an "amalgamation." Where poetry and prose are only mixed together, "the whole thing must obviously be prosaic" (LN, 1024). If, by contrast, they are "amalgamated," the event occurs "in ennobled natural forms <like the five-footed iamb>" (LN, 823). Amalgamation occurs, in other words, in poetic forms that remain forever inadequate to the novel, regardless of whether the latter is conceived as a particular genre or the genus of modern literature in general. The manifest lack of determination in Schlegel's ideas about the relation between poetry and prose in the romantic genre points toward a certain resistance in the conception of transcendental poetry and in its imperative of universal poetization. Only relatively late, in his Paris and Cologne lectures of 1807, does Schlegel try to clarify this resistance and thereby solve a central problem in his theory of art. But even this solution can claim only problematic success.

In the notes he drew up for his Cologne lectures, Schlegel writes:

> The novel in general can be seen as the poetry of prose, as a struggle against the prosaic element that confronts it—as a striving to overcome everything prosaic, to conquer and form in a poetic fashion. This is, of course, a very great Idea as a universal perfection of prose. The universal postulate lying, so to speak, at the basis of the novel is that everything ought to be poeticized more and more, but this is [a] very dangerous undertaking, as we have learned from experience, since the earliest novels [are] very romantic and poetic, but later ones are all pulled down by the prose, as we have already seen, beginning with Boccaccio.[10]

Prose is a danger to the novel and to the generation of the absolute genre. With the rise of prose begins the descent of poetry into the sphere of practical communication. "The earliest novels" are thus the ones that most closely correspond to the postulate of poeticization, whereas all

---

10. Cited according to Karl Konrad Polheim, *Die Arabeske. Ansichten und Ideen aus Friedrich Schlegels Poetik* (Munich: Schöningh, 1966), 202.

later ones are "pulled down" by the burden of prose. The poeticization of the novel, its romanticization, would be the return to its origin in poetry. But the origin of poetry is, in turn, prose, for the latter—and on this point Schlegel leaves no doubt—is the condition for the ascent of poetry to the presentation of the absolute. In his lectures on the history of European literature of 1803–1804, Schlegel, following the tradition of Rousseau and Hamann, determines poetry as the "most original, the most natural form" of language and assigns to it the task of "designating and pointing toward the infinite" (KA, II: 113); but he also sees it closely bound up with "writing," for writing alone can prevent poetry from an unrestrained dissolution into the infinite. Language must be "held in place"; otherwise it loses itself to what it is supposed to present. Writing is, for Schlegel, the most solid figure of language's bond with finitude. He characterizes every other means for the retardation of its vanishing movement into the absolute, including the laws of rhythm and meter, as functional analogues and derivations of writing: "It is, therefore, completely natural that all language *held in place* by writing should be metrical, rhythmical, hence worthy of general participation" (KA, II: 113). If writing and its material hold on the finite are lost, as Schlegel supposed had actually happened in the earliest Greek times, something of it nevertheless remains—writing-like rhythm—and this alone secures the tradition and transference of remarkable facts. Like writing, rhythm imprints memory. If, however, rhythm and writing are compatible on the basis of their conserving and retarding function—and these functions alone determine, for Schlegel, the structure and performance of language—writing nevertheless precedes meter and rhythm. "Already in writing itself," Schlegel insists, "lies the origin of prose" (KA, II: 113), for writing stamps everything it touches with the character of determinacy and unalterability. In the Paris notebooks of 1803 he thus writes: "The origin of prose is to be sought in the *law;* this is writing, determined and particular, hence prose" (KA, 18: 499). Prose is, so to speak, writing in language. The origin of poetry does not lie in writing but in its loss. Characterized in contrast to prose by its indeterminacy, its arbitrariness, and its permanent excess beyond the limits of the real, poetry is only a rhythmical relic of writing. It is the ruin for the "memorial" that language seeks to set up in prose, and it is the constant transgression of the "law" that prosaically fixes the conditions of a life in the finite (KA, II: 114). If poetry is a danger to life in society, if it is a danger to the continuity of life in history and its reflection in philosophy, then prose—and, above all, the prose of philosophy—is a danger to nature and the life of the infinite.

Moreover, not only is prose a deadly danger to poetry and poetry to prose; prose as linguistic petrifaction of the infinitely moving life and poetry as infinite liquidation of the finite are mortal dangers to the expository function of language in general. Prose and poetry, each in its own way, break the law of language: the law of limiting, preserving, and meaning. Thus they break their own law. But the indetermination that they bring into language—prose, however fantastic, by the tendentious erasure of the infinitude of linguistic meaning, and poetry, however polished, by the infinite multiplication of its meaning—arises from the duplicity of writing to which they both owe their origin. Writing is, for Schlegel, the figure of an economized loss of the finite in the infinite, a figure that communicates to every form of language it has stamped— however diverse they may appear—its own unstable combination of contour and indeterminacy. Prose or poetry alone would be the end of language. Each one must realize the tendency of the other in order for language to remain. Thus does prose, before all determinate meaning, in its very structure, point toward the fleetingness of poetry as its own implicit tendency; thus does poetry point toward the constancy of prose. The fact that prose marks the poetic suspension of that which, descriptively or prescriptively, has been posited in it is indicated in Schlegel's note: "All prose is really poetic" (LN, 608). But the fact that it is really poetic says nothing about what prose really is: "What prose really is— this no one has yet said" (LN, 584). Prose and poetry are not *really*. Both are—in contrast not only to every positive determination but also to the infinite transcendence beyond all positions—always only that which "really" comes to the other: they are the event of their own alteration.

The relation between prose and poetry is, as the Cologne lectures maintain, a "struggle," a duel and indeed one in which they both collapse. The stage for this duel between prose and poetry is the romantic genre *par excellence,* the genre of genres, the novel. The novel no less than its theory tells the "tragic story of the decline of poetry in the present time" (LN, 1560). In the "Literary Notebooks" Schlegel says this about Tieck's *William Lovell,* one of the exemplary texts of the modern genre to which he repeatedly turns his critical attention: "Spirit of the book unconditional contempt for prose and self-annihilation of poetry" (LN,

525). And in the *Athenäum:* "The entire book is a struggle of poetry and prose, where the prose is trodden underfoot and the poetry breaks its neck" (Ath, 418). Prose is kicked by the metrical feet of poetry, and in the process poetry breaks its neck, tripped by its own feet. This is what the struggle between prose and poetry looks like—a struggle playing itself out as romantic universal poetry and as the art and theory of modernity. Moreover, this polemic is the linguistic polemic between thesis and parekbasis, the polemic in language between its stability and its erasure, the polemic of language with its own disappearance. The formal determinacy of poetry to which its semantic openness corresponds, and the semantic determinacy of formally unbounded prose reciprocally check each other to the same degree that they reciprocally potentialize each other. It is not everything or nothing, not the result of this struggle but the interminable "movement" of self-annihilation and self-totalization of prose and poetry that constitutes the subject and the subject-matter of literature and its philosophy: the struggle for language and language *as* this very struggle. But the presentation of literature—as Benjamin's statement that "The Idea of poetry is prose" indicates[11]—is bound up with the distorted and broken position of the prosaic. Torso of a lost writing, remnant of a memorial for a dead one, fragment of a law for future generations—this, the dumb remainder of prose, is all that survives the agon of language with itself, its excess and its salvation, its idea as "transcendental bagatelle" (KA, 16: 197).

The progressive and, more exactly, digressive transcendental poetry posits itself beyond the limits of all genres and forms, all classifications and codifications; indeed, it posits itself beyond the opposition between literature and its theory, between art and life, and as this overstepping, it is the very movement of self-transcendence: the auto-parekbasis of language as such. It is the movement that leaps out of the uncontainable excess of speaking over the spoken, of positing over every positivity, of the act of positing over its fixation in the position of subjectivity. In transcendental poetry language speaks as absolute ex-position: as *ekbasis,* as excess, interruption, and opening up. If this movement time and again turns into something posited, it never solidifies into an unshakable ground. The ex-position still survives in the positivity of the thesis; it

---

11. Walter Benjamin, *Der Begriff der Kunstkritik in der deutschen Romantik,* in *Gesammelte Schriften,* ed. R. Tiedemann and H. Schweppenhäuser (Frankfurt am Main: Suhrkamp, 1977–1985), 1: 100–01.

resumes in and from this positivity. Transcendental poetry—and with it, language, as Schlegel conceives it—distances, sets forth, and carries on: its *Aus-setzung* is *Fort-setzung*. Once a subject, it makes itself into a project: it re-sumes, taking itself up again and taking its distance from every mere position and, above all, from the positing of a ground; it goes on, generating itself—the genre of genres—as another.

Since language relates to its own Being as distancing, ex-position, parabasis—as *Fort-setzung, Aus-setzung, parekbasis*—and since this Being, as an original being-outside-itself, is not even Being if the meaning of Being is determined by the position of the I, the Being of language could easily be misunderstood as the equivalent of what Fichte calls the not-I or nothingness: as null and empty positing or as the mere negation of a previous I-position. But Schlegel frees nothingness from its merely relative and derivative position with respect to the objects of the I. The self-creation to which he regularly refers when he speaks about self-annihilation can be nothing other than a creation from nothingness: it must take place without presuppositions, and it must therefore be a creation in unconditioned freedom. "Illusion of self-annihilation," Schlegel notes, "is an appearance of unconditioned freedom, of self-creation" (LN, 204). Self-creation must be creation out of nothingness if it is to remain free creation and thus absolute positing. And yet, if unconditioned positing, positing from itself, and self-positing are all defined as positing from nothingness, then positing, self, and nothingness cannot be other than synonyms: then self-positing can no longer be understood as the positing of a self in the sense of the I; then the absolute position departs from the horizon of transcendental egoicity and becomes the effect of an original movement of nothingness, the effect of a vanishing and a vanishing of vanishing that thereby opens up the possibility of an egological Being to posit itself.[12] For Schlegel, who was presumably following Schelling, this original and pre-original sepa-

---

12. In a notebook entry from 1796, Schlegel's thoughts go in precisely this direction: "According to Fichte's reasoning, couldn't this just as well follow from 'A = A': 'The non-I posits itself'?—That would then favor Schelling" (KA, 18: 510). As other notes in the same context suggest, Schlegel is referring to Schelling's *Vom Ich als Prinzip der Philosophie* (On the I as the Principle of Philosophy), a treatise of 1795 in which Schelling tries to think, however tentatively, the independence of the not-I and therefore the independence of the nothingness from any I-positing. In his treatise of 1804, *Philosophie und Religion* (Philosophy and Religion), Schelling goes even further: "Freedom in its renunciation of necessity is the true nothingness. . . ." (Friedrich Schelling, *Werke,* ed. M. Schröter [Munich: Beck

ration of nothingness from "itself," this primal scene of a pre-subjective ex-posing constitutes the decisive fact toward which philosophy and poetology are to orient themselves. In a notebook from the end of the 1790s, he makes the following remark about the structure of nothingness: "Chaos relates to nothingness like world to chaos. Chaos the only real concept of nothingness. Nothingness itself the merely analytic concept . . .—infinite agility appears as nothingness. . . .—Nothingness is more original than chaos" (KA, 18: 77–78). Just as the origin of chaos lies in nothingness, the origin of the world lies in chaos. Nothingness, which is an "analytic concept," appears as "infinite agility," and this appearance belongs to the ana-lytic movement of nothingness, its movement of separation. The absolute origin of chaos and world must henceforth be thought as an infinite in nothingness, as a movement of its differentiation, as the nihilation of nothingness. In this, the original self-differentiation or retraction of nothingness, in this creation from nothingness lies, according to Schlegel, the essence of the modern: "The essence of the modern consists in creation from nothingness—such a principle was at the basis of Christianity—a similar one in the revolution, in Fichte's philosophy—and the same in modern poetry" (KA, 18: 315).[13] However creation from nothingness may be modified in religion, politics, philosophy, or poetry, its principle is a principle of unconditioned freedom and is, for Schlegel, not only the essence of the modern

and Oldenbourg, 1927–54], 4: 30). Furthermore, in the *Ages of the World,* after citing a line from Angelus Silesius—"Tender divinity is nothingness and over nothingness"— Schelling adds, "as pure freedom is a nothingness, like the will that wills nothing. . . . Such a will is nothing and everything" (*Werke,* 4: 610–11). Close to a remark on the self-positing of the not-I Schlegel expresses his doubts concerning the concept of positing in general: "Question about the concept of *positing.* Demand that it be justified" (KA, 18: 510). Such a justification would be difficult to achieve, for a pre-subjective nothingness can only be a pre-positional one, indeed a nothingness that never has a relation to position or a nothingness that only lets position arise from its own non-relationality. The later works of Schelling are devoted to precisely this movement.

13. One of the most famous *Athenäum* fragments—fragment 216, which "Über die Unverständlichkeit" (On Incomprehensibility) then takes up and comments upon—is obviously related to this notebook entry. The first two sentences of this fragment read, "The French revolution, Fichte's doctrine of knowledge, and Goethe's *Meister* are the greatest tendencies of the time. Whoever is offended by this juxtaposition, whoever finds a revolution unimportant unless it is noisy and material, has not achieved the lofty, wide-open standpoint on the history of humanity."

but, for this reason, the very focus of his attempt to bring philosophical clarity to its concept.

If the pure self-positing of the I in Fichte's original "enactment" is at the same time a positing of Being, it would involve the greatest conceivable inconsistency not to recognize in this self-positing also a positing from nothingness and, accordingly, to see this nothingness not as opposed to the I but prior to it and its Being. Nothingness is not, as Schlegel makes clear in his note, the opposite or the lack of Being that would, for its part, be an objective something, a subject or object; rather, it is the other appearance of Being that cannot be stabilized in any representation, even in the representation "I." Being and nothingness both give themselves as the sheer "that" of the freedom of existence—of an existence that is not already defined as a position of subjectivity, nor arrested and turned into a certain positivity, still less can it be made into one object among others. "Everything is distinguished from nothingness merely by being full" (KV 18: 271). But the concept of the fullness—or *pleroma*—of Being and the concept of nothingness in which the mere "that" of existence is asserted are, once again, "romantic categories" (LN, 1503), and as such they are categories of an interminable tendency. They mark a movement in which there is neither an emptiness nor a fullness, a movement in which there is not even—or not yet—a secure "that." What there is in the movement of the "romantic" tendency; what gives this movement its motility, if one can still speaking of giving here, is the project of a "that," the opening toward it. All talk of language—and therefore all talk and every language—must take part in this project and must be as much talk *about* as talk *from* this project of its Being or nothingness.

Schlegel thought of this parekbasic Being or this parekbasis of the Being or the nothingness of language as the movement of what he modestly and misunderstandably called "romantic literature." He characterized the novel—the genre of genres, the proposition and ex-position of genre—as a system of novellas and jotted down this note concerning the novella: "In the novella the story must be as *nothing* as possible. To be able to make a proper story epideixis of and from nothingness" (LN, 1900).[14] "Epideixis of and from nothingness": a

14. Something similar is found in the following entry, one of a long sequence of formulations like "novella from nothingness," "stories from nothingness," "poem from

de-monstration coming from nothingness and relating to nothingness, a non-demonstration of nothingness; a pure demonstration, a pure showing without object and without sign. Such is the novella from which the novel, the *Roman,* romantic literature, and thus literature as such are to come forth: in the novella, as in Flaubert's projected novel about nothingness, nothing is supposed to show itself but the showing, and nothing but the sheer movement of phenomenalization takes place, as it does in Mallarmé's *fleur! . . . l'absente de tous bouquets.*[15] Nothing yet is supposed to be said in it. *"Le blanc de l'ouvrage* in love is the plague against which one must create amusements" (LN, 1439). If these "amusements" follow the same logic as the "epideixis of and from nothingness," if, like Boccaccio's novellas—which were offered to distract from the plague—they are supposed to ward off and deflect *le blanc de l'ouvrage* as well, then this conclusion is inevitable: what shows itself in the amusements that come out of nothingness—out of the hole in the work, its pause or interruption—is not quite the other of this *blanc,* neither its fulfillment nor the work itself; rather, this very *blanc* shows itself in these amusements and shows itself as the deflection and resumption of *le blanc* itself. What resumes in literature, in language as such, is interruption, ex-position, and leprosy: *Aussetzung* and *Aussatz.* What shows itself in literature and language is the trajectory of what cannot

---

nothingness," "poetry from nothingness": "The idea of the novella is that they are—studies, reworking of old stories in a romantic spirit, mixing of all romantic forms. Furthermore, *epideixis* or stories from NOTHINGNESS" (KA, 16: 197, Nr. 40). In his essay "Reports on the Poetic Works of Giovanni Boccaccio" Schlegel develops one aspect of this formulation: "If the art of story-telling goes only a little higher, the story-teller will seek to show it either by deceptively entertaining with a pleasant nothingness, with an anecdote that, strictly speaking, would not even be an anecdote, and by knowing how to adorn so richly with the fullness of his art what is in itself a nothing, that we are willingly deceived and are indeed seriously interested in it" (KA, 2: 394). In the following note Schlegel makes the connection between the novella—and thus the figure from which the novel, the *Roman,* and (romantic) literature take their point of departure—and comedy, which is essentially characterized by parekbasis. This connection could also be described as that between the epideixis of nothingness and the parekbasis of nothingness: "Comedy nothing when it is not Aristophanic; this must let itself create out of nothingness" (LN, 1877). Just as parekbasis interrupts comedy, comedy comes from an interruption: it comes forth from nothingness, and this coming-forth, this parekbasis at its origin, its origin as parekbasis, repeats itself in its dramatic-paradramatic breaking of form.

15. Stephane Mallarmé, "Crise de vers" in *Oeuvres complètes* (Paris: Pléiade, 1945), 368.

be seen: *le blanc de l'ouvrage,* the empty, the workless spot of the work in its permanent deflection. Schlegel's philosophy of art and language is not, as his conservative contemporaries feared, an exaggerated version of nihilism. This philosophy is not concerned with nothingness but with creation from nothingness, with an autonomy without *autos,* and with a Being whose meaning cannot be reduced to the mere position of self-conscious subjectivity. Its concern is for language as the excess of saying beyond every assertion, for language as the surplus of demonstration beyond everything demonstrated, and thus for inconsistency itself: the inconsistency of every self.

This inconsistency—the leap in the fundamental proposition of the I, the freedom that first opens up and maintains the possibility of an I, and the possibility of freedom as a subjective position—does not leave nothingness untouched. As *le blanc de l'ouvrage* and as the "epideixis of and from nothingness," nothingness is articulated, different from itself, its own excess or its own remainder. As nothingness it has no constancy, but this lack does not then make it into an objective something. "Every self-annihilation," Schlegel notes, "annihilates itself. Much more gracious if someone shows *how little* he is than that he is nothing at all" (LN, 254). One can read these sentences as cues to an urbane, ironic self-relation. But one can also understand them as a commentary on the structure of the movement of a nothingness that, by annihilating itself, is the nothingness of a nothingness and, therefore, a generation of nothingness: it is the movement of a withdrawal that opens up a showing but withdraws this showing at the same time, an "epideixis of and from nothingness." The self-contraction of nothingness without beginning or end—a showing of withdrawal, showing from and in this withdrawal—is the only way that language as such, without presuppositions and this side of self-positing, can be: permanent eksemiosis, pareksemiosis from nothingness. This movement of language from the withdrawal, this nonpositional and presuppositionless language of freedom, is, according to one possible reading of Schlegel's note, "little." It does not show an object that would be little but shows "how little" its showing is and thus shows that there is language and, along with language, that there is "Being" and "nothingness"—that there is a "that"—only in the mode of being-little. Being, like nothingness, *is* not, but *is little.* And this "little" knows neither diminution nor addition; it is an absolute comparative in contrast to the romantic concepts "Being" and "nothingness"—concepts of infinite approximation that can find a point of support, and the condition of their possibility and impossibility in this absolute comparative alone, in being-little, and so in being-finite. Ontology lives on, and that means it outlives itself as microntology.

The fragment, the bagatelle—this little bit—is not simply a literary form: it is anything but simple; it is not a form, and it is not literary in a vague and inconsequential sense. At each and every moment, it is the singular way that being-little articulates itself as the unsurpassable and irreducible, indeed as the sole remaining modality of Being in the breaking down, the suspension, or the parekbasis of absolute subjectivity's position. *Nichts ist noch gesagt:* "Nothing is yet said"—this fragment or this note, this little bit, also means that nothingness is preserved in the "yet" of language, language in the "yet" of nothingness, and that language speaks only as the little of this "yet." Benjamin, alluding to Hofmannsthal's *Das gerettete Venedig* (Venice Saved), called art works *die gerettete Nacht,* "the night saved."[16] Schlegel's fragments suggest that the Idea of language is *das im Noch gerettete Nichts,* the nothingness saved in the "yet": ex-position and interruption of the work in and from *le blanc de l'ouvrage.* Finite permanence of setting free. Little.

16. Walter Benjamin, *Briefe,* ed. Gershom Scholem and Theodor Adorno (Frankfurt am Main: Suhrkamp, 1966), 1: 323; *The Correspondence of Walter Benjamin,* trans. Manfred Jacobson and Evelyn Jacobson (Chicago: University of Chicago Press, 1994), 223.

The Quaking of Presentation

Kleist's "Earthquake in Chile"

> Le monde n'est qu'une branloire perenne. Toutes choses y bran-
> lent sans cesse: la terre, les rochers du Caucase, les pyramides
> d'Aegypte, et du branle public et du leur. La constance mesme
> n'est autre chose qu'un branle plus languissant. Je ne puis
> asseurer mon object.
> —Montaigne, *Essais* III 2

Among the fundamental theses most generally respected by both hedonistic and critical modes of reading literary texts is the claim that these
texts present a specific reality in language. It is not important for this
consensus whether "reality" is understood as a content of social or individual experience or whether "presentation" is understood as a specific
form of imitation, construction, or expression. This thesis owes its un-
deniable attractiveness to its self-evident character; but this self-evidence
is purchased at a very high price, for it implies a disturbing hermeneutical consequence. The thesis makes literary texts into empirical objects
that are then supposed to be retranslatable into their corresponding
meanings through a more or less mechanical process of reduction. Under the direction of this thesis, all research into literature must conceive
of its task as systematic restitution: the restitution, more exactly, of those
realities to which the literary texts themselves are said to correspond; the
restitution of the specific means that are put into place so as to facilitate
an adequate presentation of reality; and the restitution of the transformations to which the experience was subjected in the course of its
literary articulation. When literary texts are considered experiences of
reality *sui generis,* the claim contained in such a conception of literature

and of reading literary texts is only moderated, not altered. For as problematic as the thesis of reducibility may become whenever literary works are themselves given ultimate authority and are granted the status of a *novum*, it nevertheless remains impossible to overlook the fact that this maximal thesis concerning the ontological character of literature— in flight from a poorly conceived tension between experience and its presentation—covers both literature and reality with a no less impoverished veneer of equality. Just as a straightforward attempt to refer literature as a mode of presentation to reality, even if this reality is preformed in a literary manner, frees itself from the scandal that is literature—and does so by way of a sociological, historical, psychological, and generally anthropological reduction to empirical data—the hypostasis of the literary text into an irreducible *novum* frees it from the exacting claims of comprehensibility in general. If the concept of presentation is, in one case, a license to cross the border into what literature is supposed to present, in the other case—the one in which literature appears to have purified itself to the point where it is the self-presentation of reality—the concept of presentation forbids all traffic between a literary reality and any other. In both cases, the text is interpreted according to a criterion drawn from an economy of signification, an economy through which either the stability of whatever is presented—be it a state of consciousness, an affective modification of the mind, or a historical fact—or the stability of the presentation itself *as* presentation—be it a creative process, a self-sufficient structure, or the immanent play of self-reference—is supposed to be secured once and for all. Both of these cases emerge as countervailing consequences from the common maxim that literature is the presentation of a specific reality, and in both cases a possibility is overlooked so as to safeguard the need for security inherent to any theoretical pursuit: the possibility, namely, that the point of literature is not to fulfill the concept of presentation but to bring into question— with no less rigor than a theoretical investigation—the implications and the very structure of this concept, and to do so through a specific form of linguistic praxis. As long as the point of literary scholarship is not to subject the texts it chooses to linguistic and aesthetic conventions foreign to them or to standards contested by these texts—as long as the point of literary knowledge is not therefore to sidestep its object—this at least logical possibility must be incorporated into the heuristic principles of its actual practice. This is not to say that literature is simply a form of linguistic praxis removed *toto coelo* from that of presenting reality; but it does mean that literature—and, above all, a series of its outstanding texts—can cast doubt on the methodological premises not only of literary scholarship but of philosophical aesthetics, instead of accommodating itself to these premises without reservation. Whenever literature does this, it is no longer the object of any science of literature, whether philological, historical, or critical; rather, literary scholarship is, *ordine inverso,* the object of a critique carried out by literature.

"An Accidental Archway"

The earthquake that in the works of Descartes functions as the methodic movement of cognition as it doubts itself, the earthquake that thus shakes the *terre mouvante*[1] of the representational contents of thought, the earthquake that alone was destined to find within itself a *fundamentum inconcussum* for self-certainty, solidity for cognitive objects, and legitimacy for the belief in God—this methodic earthquake, which relieves the intelligible I of its representations, forfeits the very function of securing and grounding when it is faced with the catastrophic consequences of an earthquake in the empirical world. This Cartesian earthquake shows *ex post facto* that the intelligible core of reason—a core that is supposed to establish a pure relation to itself in the tremors it unleashes—is empirically affected from the very start, if only by its need to articulate itself in the metaphor of quaking. The fact that the consequences of this metaphor for the efficacy of reason cannot be controlled by reason becomes clear even before the historical occurrence of an immensely destructive earthquake, for it already appears in the paradox toward which this metaphor drives every thought of the self: only the tremor remains firm; only in quaking does the self reveal its stability. Under the impression exerted by the Lisbon earthquake, which touched the European mind in one its more sensitive epochs,[2] the metaphorics of ground and tremor completely lost their apparent innocence; they were no longer merely figures of speech. In the texts that Voltaire de-

1. René Descartes, *Oeuvres philosophiques,* ed. F. Alquie (Paris: Garnier, 1963), 1: 599.

2. Harald Weinrich made a survey of philosophical and literary reactions to this event; see H. Weinrich, "Literaturgeschichte eines Weltereignisses: Das Erdbeben von Lissabon" in *Literatur für Leser* (Stuttgart: Kohlhammer, 1971), 64–76.

voted to the events in Lisbon (*Poème sur le désastre de Lisbonne* and *Candide*) and in Rousseau's letter to Voltaire of August 1756 as well as in Kant's three scientific studies of 1756,[3] the earthquake does not entirely escape the framework of its metaphoricity; it is, above all, a historical *datum,* a natural-historical and world-historical point of reference for a discourse that cannot contain the enormity of the fact and indeed acknowledges this failure not only in the theoretical consequences it tries to draw from the quake but also in an unmetaphorical naming of names and listing of numbers. The figure of the earthquake bears the marks of its irrational, uncontrollable, and unsurpassable character even in *Candide,* which makes it into its literary subject-matter and uses it to bolster an argument against teleology. But these marks are even more emphatic in the most significant text to play out the violence of the metaphor of the earthquake in all its ambiguity: Heinrich von Kleist's story, "The Earthquake in Chile" (1807). A philosophical metaphor that is also a metaphor for the process of philosophical thought becomes a border figure, and on this border any philosophy that seeks to secure its ground begins to crack. A metaphor for the possible consolidation of ideational structures, in view of their collapse, becomes a figure of the unreliability not only of the physical world but of the entire world of knowledge. A metaphor of representation through which the very form of an idea is supposed to be presented and objectified becomes a figure of the opaqueness of the world and the impossibility of translating its mode of appearance into a transcendent meaning. The metaphor becomes incapable of holding together a fact and its meaning, or an image and its reference, and of translating any of these into the other.

At the precise moment in which the metaphor of quaking begins to forfeit its metaphorical potency and become a recitation of documented

3. For the above, see Voltaire, *Oeuvres complètes,* ed. Beuchot (Paris: Garnier, 1877–1885), 9: 465–79; Jean-Jacques Rousseau's letter to Voltaire of August 18, 1756, in *Oeuvres complètes,* ed. B. Gagnebin and M. Raymond (Paris: Pléiade, 1959), 4: 1074ff; of Kant's three essays, the most important one is "History and Natural Description of the Remarkable Incidents of the Earthquake That Convulsed a Large Part of the Earth at the End of 1755" (*Kants Gesammelte Schriften,* ed. Königliche Preussische [later, Deutsche] Akademie der Wissenschaften [Berlin and Leipzig: Georg Reimer, later, Walter de Gruyter, 1900–]; 1: 456–61; hereafter, "Ak"). All citations of Kant again refer to the Akademie edition, except citations of the *Critique of Pure Reason,* which refer to the A and B editions of the work. Akademie edition pagination can be found in any currently available translation of the *Critique of Judgment.*

historical events that are no longer sanctified by a teleological perspective, the metaphor strengthens its tendency to present itself as a citation of certain conventional literary images and themes. And at its extreme, this tendency runs against the historical facticity and thus against the contingent character of the event itself. The double breach of the figurality of classical literary discourse comes to light in a particularly striking manner in Kleist's story. On the one hand, following a procedure that characterizes nearly all of his stories, Kleist is emphatic about the historical authenticity of the tale he tells. He thus begins with verifiable names and numbers: "In St. Jago, the capital of the kingdom of Chile . . . at the moment of the great earthquake in the year 1647 during which thousands of human lives found their end. . . ."[4] On the other hand, it is impossible not to notice—although it has up until now not been noted—that important aspects of the thematic content of Kleist's story can already be found in a series of scenes from *Candide* and that these scenes are themselves travesties of clichés Voltaire had encountered in contemporary literary productions.[5] Kleist's story is not only a variation on Voltaire's philosophical buffoonery, nor is it simply linked to certain aspects of Voltaire's novel—the accidental bewilderment by an earth-

---

4. See Heinrich von Kleist, *Sämtliche Werke und Briefe*, ed. H. Sembdner (Munich: Deutscher Taschenbuch Verlag, 1987), 2: 144. All citations of Kleist refer to this edition. English readers may consult *The Marquise of O—and Other Stories,* trans. David Luke and Nigel Reeves (Harmondsworth: Penguin, 1978), 51–67; hereafter, "M." All excerpts from Kleist are newly translated for this volume.

5. Candide's expulsion from the paradise of Thunder-Ten-Tronckh has its origin in a love affair between a tutor (the Leibnizian Pangloss) and a lady's maid and, as a consequence, an affair between Candide and the daughter of his host. The social motif that in Kleist's story unleashes the series of misfortunes for the tutor Jeronimo and his student Josepha is related not only to Rousseau's *Nouvelle Héloïse,* as has been hitherto supposed, but also to *Candide.* After participating in a war and experiencing its horror—"butchered wives, who still clutched their infants to their bleeding breasts. . . . Scattered brains and severed limbs littered the ground" (Voltaire, *Candide,* trans. Robert Adams [New York: Norton, 1966], 5)—and after having been rescued from a shipwreck by an improbable accident, Candide lands in Lisbon as the earth begins to shake the city. The *causa finalis* of the earthquake, according to Candide, is that "The Last Judgment is here" (10). The Inquisition then condemns those who have narrowly escaped the ravages of the earthquake to be executed in an auto-da-fé, "an infallible specific against earthquakes" (12). Contrary to custom, Pangloss is not burned but apparently hanged. Graced with luck, Candide finds his beloved, whom he believed to be dead, outside the now destroyed city of Lisbon.

quake that was soon interpreted as the beginning of the apocalypse, the transformation from one kind of death to another, the accidental rescue from a sacrificial execution, the accidental rediscovery of the lovers. Kleist's story is also closely related to *Candide*'s compositional means, including the use of parallel stories; and above all, it is bound up with the philosophical question posed by Voltaire's novel: the justification of evil in the world and the providential reason overseeing the fates of individuals as well as collectives. Kleist's story can thus be read as a rebuttal of the Enlightenment satire: what Voltaire treats episodically and in an almost frivolous manner comes to occupy the center and discards its playful costume. Kleist's exposure of the alliance between the various orders of power—the state, the propertied bourgeoisie, the Catholic clergy—and his unmasking of the philosophical thesis that this is the best of all possible worlds may be just as graphically exhibited as in Voltaire. But individual susceptibility to teleological explanations ceases to be a ridiculous tic from which the author and the public believe themselves immune; rather, this susceptibility to teleology turns into a compulsive self-deception from which no reader can ever be sufficiently distanced. The nonteleological accidents dramatized by Voltaire out of decidedly didactic motives become in Kleist the predominant form of events in a world that has lost its transparency. However much Kleist's story may be a "literary" response to Voltaire's novel, it is still, in sum, a critique of the distancing and protective gestures of the literature Voltaire writes. It is an attempt to produce *out of* language—and not merely with its *means*—the *factum brutum* of an earthquake in the world of established political, moral, and literary relations.

The collision of teleology and accidentality—a collision whose resolution requires the essentialization of everything contingent—is not merely Voltaire's theme in *Candide;* it is also the theme Leibniz pursues in his *Essais de Théodicée.* And the conception of a *faute heureuse*—evils that reciprocally cancel each other, *bina venena juvant*[6]—not only belongs to the ironic principle of composition in Voltaire's novel; in an entirely unironic manner it lays down the foundation for Enlightenment philosophy. And it is on this point that the idea attracted Kleist's atten-

---

6. See G. W. Leibniz, *Die philosophischen Schriften,* ed. C. J. Gerhardt (rpt. Berlin: Hildesheim, 1961), 6: 108; *Theodicy,* trans. E. M. Huggard (La Salle, Il.: Open Court, 1985), 129.

tion. During the time he most likely composed the earthquake story (November 1806), Kleist writes in a letter to Marie von Kleist that he senses "the truth of D'Alembert's principle that two evils, taken together, can become a consolation. For one distracts me from another."[7] Kleist's story presents itself as a systematic execution of this structural formula of *bina venena juvant* and thus appears not simply to retrieve a thought from the field of theodicy but even to take sides in favor of theodicy itself. Yet Kleist's story executes this structural formula to the point of its reversal: double luck brings disaster. And the story does not hesitate to relativize this formula, for it is deemed valid only from the ever-changing perspectives of the protagonists. The earthquake can thus be sanctioned as a divine manifestation from the perspective of Jeronimo's liberation, and his rescue by way of a natural catastrophe can thereafter be seen as a miracle: "He bowed so low that his forehead touched the ground, thanking God for his miraculous rescue" (2: 147; M, 54). But as soon as he reflects on the fact that he has lost the one he loves, everything changes: "the being that ruled above the clouds seemed terrible to him" (2: 147; M, 54). When the two lovers find each other after having escaped death owing to the same chance event, it is once again a "miracle of heaven" that saves them, and even the loss of "thousands of human lives" seems justified by the survival of these two and their child: "[they] were very moved when they thought how much evil had to enter the world so that they could become happy" (2: 150; M, 57). And when further developments show their happiness had been an illusion, their private teleological interpretation of the accidental occurrences that had once led to their happiness will again be shaken. Neither the philosophical thesis of the *faute heureuse* nor D'Alembert's principle is used as an ontological principle; they are both unstable explanatory figures that can be applied only to specific situations and that are immediately relinquished under the pressure of their alteration. The happy accident and the fortunate coincidence of evil accidents do not offer a secure ground upon which solid representations of the world and its relation to a highest Being could be established; on the contrary, they are everywhere exposed to chance. This story, like all of Kleist's stories, is not concerned with happy or unhappy accidents but with accidentality; not with contingent events but with unforeseeable contingency; and not with cases that do not fall under any rule but with something quite different: cases that do not even allow for the construction of a rule. They stage the process of a dialectic of contingency in which there is no moment of synthesis.

The word "accident" *(Zufall)* in Kleist does not simply refer to those events for which there is neither an adequate mechanical explanation nor an adequate representation in terms of an onto-theological principle of ordering; it is also to be understood as an irregular coincidence of events, each of which results from the collapse of rules. One of Kleist's favorite allegories ascribes this latter meaning to the term *Zufall* (accident, chance). The allegory appears for the first time six years before the letter in which he mentions D'Alembert's principle and which could be read as its conceptual abbreviation. In one of the pedagogical letters he wrote to his fiancée, Wilhelmine von Zenge, Kleist describes in November of 1800 an experience he had undergone "that evening, before the most important day of my life"—a day, he believed, on which a life-or-death decision would be made: "Turning inward, pondering, I went back into the city through the arched doorway. Why doesn't the arch fall down, I thought, since it has no support? It stands, I answered, because all the stones want to fall at once" (2: 593). No theory of self-preservation could be more free of illusions: the concomitant inclination of all elements towards a common center of gravity—a center that spells not life but death—momentarily preserves them by means of reciprocal blockage. "The Earthquake in Chile" combines this conception of a common collapse through which everything is held in place with the concept of accident as *Zu-fall* or *ad-cadere*. After referring to a rope that would "tear" Jeronimo from this world and that "chance [*Zufall*] had left him," Kleist writes:

> The ground swayed under his feet, all the walls of the prison fell apart, the entire structure was inclined to *fall* into the street, and only the *fall* of the neighboring building, encountering its slow *fall,* prevented, by means of an *accidental* archway, the complete collapse of both buildings. Trembling . . . Jeronimo slipped through the gap that had been torn through the front wall of his prison as the two buildings *collided*. (2: 145–46; M, 53; emphases added)

An accident is precisely an incident in which at least two cases of a rule run into such conflict with each other that they no longer even fall under this rule at all. But an accident is not an exception from the rule; it is an event in which the rule collides with itself and produces a new and highly ambiguous order—an order that corresponds to the laws of nature but at the same time does away with them. When two cases of a rule collide, not only is the case of a rule suspended; so, too, is the very rule under which this case was supposed to fall. In the accident of their collision, neither the rule nor its elements maintain the status that conceptuality—itself based on rules and cases—attempts to secure for them. The fall, which falls under the rule as the rule itself falls away, cancels, preserves, and arrests itself. The fall arrests itself in the sense that its downward tendency, which determines its identity, has been blocked; it is not "the fall" but—held up by parenthesis—"the fall, encountering its slow fall": *der, seinem langsamen Fall begegnende, Fall.* It preserves itself, since that which falls remains in the air, hovering by virtue of its very falling—and thus forms an "accidental archway." Finally, the fall cancels itself, since it remains a fall all along: the "accidental archway," once the second tremor strikes, again "falls down." The accident—in all its meanings: collapse, contingency, coincidence, convergence—thus sublates itself. Because of its collapse the accident holds itself up when it collides with another accident. Because the fall—but not its collision with another fall—corresponds to the laws of mechanics, the interruption of this falling down is not stabilized into an enduring synthesis but proceeds toward a resumption of the general collapse. The sublation of the accident—and here Kleist's logic of *Aufhebung* is different from that of Hegel[8]—is itself sublated.

Accidents assume an extraordinary significance in Kleist's story because everything within its framework stands under the sign of accidentality. Not only do neighboring walls accidentally fall down, hold each other up because of their combined fall, and thereby let Jeronimo slip through the archway they form; the earthquake that occasions their combined collapse shakes the city "exactly at the instant" when Jeronimo is about to hang himself and just as his beloved is "on her way to death, already near the place of execution" (2: 148; M, 55). Just as the collision of two buildings holds them up, the collision of both social and natural violence holds back the violent death prepared for Jeronimo and

---

8. On the sublation *(Aufhebung)* of accident in Hegel, see Dieter Henrich, "Hegels Theorie über den Zufall" in *Hegel im Kontext* (Frankfurt am Main: Suhrkamp, 1971), 157–86.

Josepha. This collision forms, as it were, an archway through which the pair and their child can flee, and—again like the neighboring buildings—it collapses on them when another tremor of social relations strikes. And in this latter case, too, the tremor does not fail to leave something accidentally behind: this time an opening through which their child escapes. The story is thus motivated and scanned by a long series of accidents whose stereotypical formula is found in the repeated use of the phrase "in the very same instant"; the succession of different phases in the story also presents the three determining moments of accidentality: the collision of two fatal incidents of violence in the first part of this triptych, the reciprocal suspension of these incidents in the second part, and the execution of their murderous tendency in the final one. In this way the story itself forms the "accidental archway" it describes: it sets up countervailing moments and thus delays the collapse inscribed in the rule of both natural and institutional law. The story is the presentation of the incidents it describes only to the extent that it itself presents the image of presentation collapsing.

Because the accident Kleist stages at the beginning of the story is a happy one, it has the character of a trap for cognition: it does not present itself to the protagonists in its contingency but exclusively in its relation to a necessary being who was supposed to guide the natural events in their favor. The fiction of a teleological order for Jeronimo and Josepha thus turns into objective knowledge of the foundation on which the world rests, while the contingency of nature turns into divine necessity according to their private sacred history. But the massive concentration of accidents to which Kleist exposes his protagonists does not simply appear to be regulated in their eyes; with an equal measure of systematicity and excess, this concentration dissolves the contingent character of these accidents as well as the normative character of the rules— and it does so to the point of doing away with the opposition between rule and case or regularity and accidentality. Both accident and rule are enlisted in a collapse in which there is both a suspension and a preservation: the cognitive value of "accident" and "rule" is suspended, whereas the generalizability of the exceptional cases he describes as well as the untranslatable singularity of these cases, the collapse of the rules on which experience is based as well as the continued validity of these rules, are all preserved—in collapsing. It is not only the architecture of Kleist's story that obeys the schema of collapsing stones holding themselves up in their collapse; so, too, does its procedure for dealing with concepts and rules. Presentation is—suspended—collapse.

The intentional dissolution of the conventions of experience corresponds on the linguistic level to the rupture of the unitary meaning of the word "accident" *(Zufall)*, the guarantor of which lies in the conventional rules of comprehensibility. For "accident" in Kleist's text does not simply mean whatever is comprehended under the term "accident" in conventionalized language. The conceptual value of "accident," which Kant defines in the "Remark to the Fourth Antinomy" as something "whose contradictory counterpart is possible,"[9] is just as significant as the metaphorical value of collapse. Both the conceptual and the metaphorical values undergo convulsions, lose their univocal sense, and both of their meanings are newly organized through their association with neighboring words and by virtue of their particular placement within the narrative structure. The series of falls in the text—*Zufall, einstürzte, versank, umzufallen, einzustürzen, Fall, Fall, zufällige, Zusammenschlag, zusammenfiel*[10]—weaves the word "accident" into a verbal net that grants it at least two other meanings beyond the conventional ones of chance and contingency: it comes to mean "convergence" and "collapse." The poetic logic of accident in Kleist's text is neither the linear one of natural causality nor the numinous one of divine disruption. It belongs neither to the logic of concepts nor to the logic of metaphor; rather, it accords with the logic of language. Words combine in such a way that they stand in a rigorous material and formal relation to one another but do not mix together to form a vague unity, nor do they simply stand isolated next to each other. Converging, running up against each other, reciprocally blocking their own semantic tendencies, these words constitute a latent syntagma whose elements, momentarily hovering, maintain themselves against the pull of conventional linguistic usage, just as the "accidental archway" braces its elements against the pull of gravity. The more burdensome the semantic weight of the word—and in the "case" of "accident," in the *Fall* of *Zufall*, this weight is extreme—the more tightly strung the bow of connotations. The more highly articulated the semantic and formal relations of contiguity, the more stubborn the resistance

9. Immanuel Kant, *The Critique of Pure Reason* (A: 459; B; 487).

10. This series can be translated as "accident," "collapsed," "sank," "to tumble," "to crash down," "fall," "accidental," "collision," "fell together."

of their elements to repeated reductions to isolated unities of meaning. The combination of "fall," "accident," "collision," "fell together," and so forth brings about a progressive emptying of meaning to the degree that each individual member of its chain is re-determined by this very combination. Not only does falling interrupt itself and thereby arrest itself; the condition of the allegory it presents—the semantic and formal unity of the word "falling"—is disfigured and disseminated.[11] In all its many shadings, this condition for the possibility of any figural presentation is dispersed and multiplied throughout the text, and it is thus robbed of its homogeneity, its linearity, and its univocal sense. In this way, Kleist makes good on his poetological maxim: "art can, in relation to [speech], aim for nothing but what makes it *disappear* as much as possible."[12] In Kleist's language "accident" does not designate something a discourse devoted to exposition could present; rather, it is a linguistic event in which the expository and presentational functions of discourse are themselves on the verge of falling but nevertheless remain in force because of their falling in unison, having been at once blocked and strengthened. "Accident" is a linguistic occurrence beyond concept and metaphor, an incident in which the linguisticity of language is articulated as the suspension of any meaning that is supposed to transcend language.

Kleist with Kant—Negative Presentation

The entire verbal field of "falling" and "rising" along with the corresponding antithetical movements laid out in Kleist's story obey a dynamic principle in terms of their organization: something rises only where it falls and falls as soon as it has reached the pinnacle of its height. This principle of permanent peripeteia—which organizes and regulates both the vocabulary and succession of events from the first to the last sentence—is constructed in accordance with the principle of the dynamically sublime as analyzed by Kant in the *Critique of Judgment*.[13] In

11. The "concept" of dissemination has been developed by Jacques Derrida in *Dissemination,* trans. Barbara Johnson (Chicago: University of Chicago Press, 1981).

12. This formulation is drawn from Kleist's "Letter from One Poet to Another," 2: 348.

13. The following analysis is not concerned with the question whether Kant "influenced" Kleist and still less with the so-called "Kant crisis" that Kleist was supposed

§ 28, "Nature as a Power," Kant explicitly names earthquakes alongside tempests, storms, volcanos, and hurricanes as powers that can awaken the feeling of sublimity in us, "because they raise the strength of the soul above its usual measure and allow us to discover within ourselves an entirely different kind of capacity for resistance, and this discovery gives us the courage to be able to measure ourselves against the apparently omnipotent power of nature" (Ak, 5: 261). No measure derived from the senses can grasp the absolutely great as manifested in nature. The infinite deficit of human sensibility when faced with such natural phenomena compels the imagination to seek help for its presentation of the absolutely great beyond the faculties of intuition and understanding, and so this deficit forces us to look for support in the moral Idea of "humanity in our person" (Ak, 5: 262). Yet the imagination does not achieve a commensurate presentation even in this Idea, for it only arrives at a "superiority over nature itself in its incommensurability" (Ak, 5: 261). The imagination cannot therefore correspond in any positive manner to the natural phenomena whose exhibition and presentation it aims to accomplish. Now, the "faculty" of presentation doubtless fails when it comes face to face with the sublimity of nature, but the imagination can interpret this failure in the face of an overwhelming phenomenon as the desertion of sensible intuition when confronted with an Idea superior to everything given to the senses. A presentation that is incommensurable with nature turns into the presentation of the incommensurability of every presentation with respect to the Idea. In this way, the imagination negatively relates to itself, and from the capacity to interrupt itself and to enter into a difference in relation to itself, it likewise produces *as* this difference respect for the moral law. The presentation of this law is a presentation of the inadequacy of presentation in

---

to have undergone. Rather, the issue at hand is to demonstrate the close systematic connection between Kant's Analytic of the Sublime and Kleist's investigation into the problem of a mode of presentation under conditions in which the dogmatic use of teleological concepts and therefore the logic of representation are convulsed. There is no space here for an examination of how the theory of the sublime is fundamental for all theoretical reflections on modern art and modernity in general, whether it—as in Benjamin and Adorno—explicitly links up with Kant or—as in Heidegger—avoids this recursive gesture. But this examination can be undertaken only when the theory of the sublime is seen as a critique of the concept of the aesthetic and of aesthetic theory as such.

itself.[14] But the difference of presentation in itself, which is without a sign of its own, can still designate at the limit of designation, and only when the objectifying re-presentation of things founders does the presence of the Idea give rise to respect as its effect.

Only when a power of nature humiliates the capacities of human subjectivity does the one power of human beings "that does not belong to nature" arise—a power that, for this very reason, no longer stands under its laws. Only when human beings, as physical entities, are subjected to the violence of nature do they rise up as moral beings and transcend the forces that could destroy their physical existence. The inability of human beings, as entities endowed with senses and understanding, to preserve themselves against the forces of nature is outweighed by a "self-preservation of an entirely other kind"—by a capacity on the part of the imagination to awaken respect for "the Idea of humanity in our subject" (Ak, 5: 257). In this rhythm of falling and rising, setting up and unsettling, the dialectic of the dynamically sublime not only corresponds to the events in Kleist's story; the theoretical reflections of its protagonists also respond in detail to this model: "And in fact, during these horrible moments in which all the earthly goods of human beings were devastated and nature was on the verge of being buried, the human spirit itself seemed, like a beautiful flower, to rise up" (2: 152; M, 60).

In the devastation of earthly goods—and life is among these goods for Kant as well as for Kleist—"the human spirit itself" seems to rise up. Thus arises what Kant calls with a certain formal precision "the Idea of humanity in our subject." In the convulsions of nature—and a nature still interpreted according to the principle of purposiveness—nature opens itself up in all its beauty and does so purposively but without any purpose. By formulating the arousal of "human spirit" in terms of a beautiful flower in bloom, Kleist, who seems to take his stand from the center of Kantian critique, not only speaks of a specific object in his story to which he, by way of metaphor, lends a poetic lustre; he also speaks of the rising up, the arousal, resurrection, erection, and opening up of

14. See Jacques Derrida's thorough analysis of this motif and related ones in the *Critique of Judgment;* Derrida, *Truth in Painting,* trans. Geoff Bennington and Ian McLeod (Chicago: University of Chicago Press, 1987), 119–47; see also Jean-Luc Nancy, "The Sublime Offering" in *Of the Sublime,* trans. Jeffrey Librett (Albany, N.Y.: SUNY Press, 1993), 25–54.

presentation itself. For the comparison of the human spirit with a beautiful flower associates the former with the Idea of beauty and its always fragile "purposiveness without purpose," which Kant, too, discusses with regard to an exemplary flower (Ak, 5: 236). In addition, Kleist's formulation compares "human spirit"—for the term "flower" is also a metaphor for metaphor itself—with the poetical presentation experienced by such spirit in precisely this comparison. The metaphor of "human spirit" is at the same time a metaphor of presentation; the rising up of "humanity in our person" is at the same time the genesis of language. Human spirit in its linguistic form arises in precisely the place where it can no longer be an object of designation. Only where it stops being a matter of presentation does it—"human spirit"—begin. This is the arrival of itself out of its difference from every positively determinated form.

As an antithetical result, the arousal of humanity and the arrival of language are bound up with an experience of the collapse of all normal and normative concepts of humanity and, moreover, with an experience of the unreliability not only of human nature but of the nature in which human beings find themselves. Language and "human spirit," as they are conceived by Kleist—and Kant—are effects of the negative self-affection of the imagination, not positions but immemorial processes of de-positioning, ex-position. As such, their products are, *strictu sensu,* not accessible to any literary scholarship whose cognitive claims depend on historical and rhetorical analyses. For these ex-positions are the origin of rhetoricity and historical experience. Only where the flower of human spirit arises does the possibility of a "flower" and a metaphorical employment of the word "flower" arise. Only in these "horrible moments" of Kleist's story, when sensible experience "is devastated," does an experience capable of escaping a reduction to the experiences of natural life find its foundation. There is no beauty that does not arise from horror and maintain itself there, just as there is no morality that does not break with external legality and preserve itself within such a breach. The immanent split of experience that is articulated in "The Earthquake in Chile"—the split into pleasure and displeasure, adequacy and inadequacy, intuition and the unimaginable—escapes any reduction to anthropological and psychological modes of explanation, for this split is itself the origin of the psyche and of the sole power—the human one— "that does not belong to nature." Insofar as Kleist's text describes the experience of the rational determination of humanity from the perspective of a collision with whatever is absolutely irrational in itself and in its reality, it can only be adequately read as a philosophical story: as a narrative analytic of the sublime.

In close connection with the rising up of the beautiful flower, the following event is recorded:

> On the fields, as far as the eye could see, people of all social classes could be seen lying next to each other, princes and beggars, wealthy matrons and peasant women, state officials and day laborers, clergymen and nuns; pitying one another, reaching out to help each other, joyously sharing with one another whatever they saved so as to keep each other alive, as if the general calamity had made *one* family out of those who escaped it. (2: 152; M, 60; Kleist's emphasis)

However clearly this description alludes to the social utopia of Rousseau—and, in particular, to the harvest festival proposed in *La Nouvelle Héloise*[15]—the accent in this description, down to the very typography of the text, lies in the *unity* that the "general calamity" and the mutual aid it occasions have brought to a society torn into different classes. But the unity does not then correspond to some vague, supposedly Rousseavian concept of natural relations within society but to the specific demand that, according to Kant, the imagination imposes on itself—the demand to bring the disparate elements of an apparently unmeasurable reality into the totality of a *single* intuition. The social relations Kleist describes in the valley below St. Jago constitute a metaphor for moral respect, now put into practice, which in turn corresponds to the feeling of the sublimity of *one* rational Idea—"the humanity in our person." The same goes for the "enormous deeds" (2: 152; M, 60) recounted within this society. As Kant claims in § 28 of the third *Critique,* the warrior demonstrates respect for the moral law by disregarding all danger and by holding in contempt every threat to merely sensible goods, including that of his own natural life. Heroic comportment in the face of natural catastrophe—Kleist speaks here of "Roman greatness"—thus obeys the law of the dynamically sublime as well: the greater the loss in the sphere of sensibility, the greater the gain for the negative presentation of the rational Idea.

15. See Jean-Jacques Rousseau, *Julie, ou la Nouvelle Héloise,* part V, letter 7.

"The divine sacrifice" (2: 152; M, 60) of which Kleist speaks—with an emphatic definite article—is a self-sacrifice of the imagination and a limitation of the principle of pleasure by which the imagination constructs its intuitions. Kant writes: "The pleasure in the sublime of nature is . . . only negative . . . namely, a feeling of being robbed [in the same context Kant also speak of 'sacrifice'] of the freedom of the imagination by the imagination itself" (Ak, 5: 269). The pain of being unable to achieve an adequate sensible presentation of the Idea—in an act of transcendental masochism—provokes a pleasure in the adequacy of precisely this inadequacy of sensibility with respect to the Idea of reason. Imagination does violence to itself and sacrifices itself in order to experience as a gain the pleasure of a negative adequation to the still unpresentable Idea of reason. This manner of presentation, as *praesentatio ex negativo* and as a measure breached by itself, not only leads to an indissociable mixture of pain and pleasure; its also brings about a categorial alteration in the status of presentation itself. For *Darstellung*—presentation, exhibition, performance, "placing there"—is no longer a making-present of a rigorously defined representational content or a determinate concept applied to an intuition, the aim of which is to secure the matter thus represented; rather, it is the unfixable movement in which a position deserts itself in order to follow a law whose place cannot be assigned to either conceptuality or intuition. Drawing on a significant comparison, Kant designates this movement as a "tremor," as a "quickly oscillating rejection and attraction of the same object." Not only does presentation lose its firm stance on an externally fixed foundation, but in every presentation, according to Kant's own formulation, an abyss opens up: "an abyss, as it were, in which it fears to lose itself" (Ak, 5: 258). Kant's Analytic of the Sublime is not so much concerned with the presentation of, for example, an earthquake as with an earthquake of presentation without which there would be no presentation at all. Kleist's "Earthquake in Chile" does not present this earthquake without at the same time being the quaking of presentation itself.

Kleist took over this consideration of the quakes and convulsions to which the experience of the self and of reality are subjected, but, in strict accordance with the Kantian conception of the incommensurability of knowledge and intuition to the determination of reason, his formulations concerning the indissociable ambiguity of losing and gaining, pleasure and displeasure, presentation and breach of presentation contain certain reservations: undecidability, possible illusion, "as if." He gathers some of the central motifs of the Kantian Analytic of the Sublime under these reservations. Those who are struck by the earthquake do not in fact enter into the harmonious unity of a family but, rather, do so only *as if* they were one. After mentioning "the divine sacrifice," the story continues:

> Indeed, since there was no one to whom, on this day, some touching kindness had not occurred or who had not done some magnanimous deed, the pain in every human breast was mixed with so much sweet pleasure that, as [Josepha] thought, *there is absolutely nothing that can indicate* whether the sum total of general well-being had not increased on the one side by as much as it had decreased on the other. (2: 152–53; M, 60; italics added)

As the counting of gains and loses fails, so too does the recounting of the story: Kleist does not recount; he writes what is recounted in a society that has, it appears, grown into a *single* family—"now stories were recounted of enormous deeds" (2: 152; M, 60)—but he writes what nevertheless cannot be adequately presented in any thought, any intuition, or any feeling. Kleist does not recount a story about events before whose immensity words—or judgments or sentences—fail; rather, he writes the text of the inadequacy of every attempt to recount such events so as, *modo negativo,* to write the measureless text of these events themselves.

Experimentum Crucis

Not only is Kleist's text embedded in the philosophical problems of theology that are at the root of Voltaire's and Rousseau's reflections on teleology and natural catastrophes; its connection to Kant's Analytic of the Sublime engages it in these problems in a way that far surpasses the typical Enlightenment critique of a morally corrupt clergy. In § 28 of the *Critique of Judgment* Kant writes: "This analysis of the concept of the sublime [as the sublimity of humanity's rational determination] . . . seems to conflict with the fact that we are accustomed to presenting God during tempests, storms, earthquakes, and the like not only in anger but also in his sublimity, while it would be foolish and sacrilegious to image a superiority of our mind over the effects and in particular, as it seems, the intentions of such a power" (Ak, 5: 263). Kant counters this hypothetical accusation of hybris by assigning it to the "superstitious" belief that it is in fact God who presents himself in earthquakes. What is presented is, rather, "the Idea of the humanity of our subject," which is then linked to the intuition of a natural catastrophe only by "a certain subreption"—by the "exchange," that is, "of our regard for an object" with "our respect for the Idea of humanity in our subject" (Ak, 5: 263).

If Kant's investigation into the sublime is understood as an analysis of both this aesthetic subreption and the transcendental subreption of regulative and constitutive concepts that it implies, Kleist's story can be characterized as the systematic pursuit of precisely these subreptions to the point where they dissolve. Every character in this story assumes either a vengeful or a redemptive God as the author of the earthquake—a "creator" who is supposed to have demonstrated "his incomprehensible and sublime power" in the earthquake itself. And furthermore, this God is also a "creator" in the sense that he "restored" (2: 148; M, 56) Josepha's son to her: Philipp is in her eyes a son of the God who, as the Father and as an absolutely necessary being, watches over him in the incognito of an accident. Accordingly—and with calculated ambiguity—Jeronimo greets Josepha with the cry, "Mother of God, you Holy One" (2: 148; M, 55). In this apostrophe and in Josepha's corresponding formulation, not only does one find the characters interpreting themselves according to the schema of the Holy Family; independently of any character's perspective, the details of the text also make the Christological model transparent. Unmistakable allusions are found in the names of the protagonists: the "Mother of God" bears the name of Christ's foster father, Joseph. The natural father bears a name that recalls the supernatural, indeed, the name of the holy one: the Holy Name, Hieronymous, Jeronimo. The name of the child whose conception and life are presented in Luke and Mark in strict parallel with the conception and life of Jesus is reserved for Philipp's counterpart and *Doppelgänger*—Juan. And even the name of the biblical John's mother, Elizabeth, is used to name the sister of Juan's mother.

In addition to the citations contained in the proper names, a further association with Christianity comes into play: Josepha gives birth to her son at the feast of the Corpus Christi and thus during the festival that, for the Catholic Church, celebrates the transsubstantiation of bread and wine into the body and blood of Christ.[16] By setting the birth of Philipp on the festival of the Eucharist, Kleist lays bare the secret connection between the ideas of transsubstantiation and incarnation, and he further indicates that in the figure of the illegitimate, despised, and exposed child nothing less than the Son of God is born.[17] By means of this reference, Kleist's story presents itself up to a certain point as a new dramatization of the life and passion of Christ. It is the history of the repeated revelation of God, but it is a history in an entirely unsanctimonious sense, indeed in a monstrous sense that manifests itself in the earthquake's power to induce birth: "immediately after the first major tremors the city was everywhere full of women who gave birth to children in full view of all the men" (2: 151; M, 59). The apocalyptic arrival of God announces itself in the dissolution of natural as well as social arrangements and in the destruction of the old religious order, as in the Christian Gospel. During the hour of Jesus' death and as a sign of his resurrection, the earth undergoes comparable tremors. And the Acts of the Apostles tell of Paul's liberation from prison in the city of *Philippi:* "But quickly a great earthquake arose that set the pillars of the prison in motion. And from that hour on all doors burst open and all bonds were broken" (Acts 16: 26).

The earthquake is a theophanic topos *par excellence*—and not only in the texts of the Christian tradition. It is also at work in one of the most significant dramas of antiquity, Euripides' *Bacchai*.[18] Dionysus *and* the

16. Kleist, who had amazingly accurate knowledge of what happened during the Chilean earthquake, may also have been aware that certain scenes from the Christian story of salvation were incorporated into celebratory processions during the *festum corporis Christi* in areas dominated by the Spanish crown. Among such *autos sacramentales* were the so-called *autos del Corpus Christi* and *autos del Natal*. Theatrical representations of Christ's birth were presented during the procession of the Corpus Christi.

17. Other texts of Kleist are, of course, equally indebted to this motif. *Amphitryon* ends with this paraphrase of the proclamation to Mary: "A son will be born to you whose name is Heracles" (1: 319; ll. 2335–36). Also, in the "Marquise of O. . . ." Kleist describes the mirror reverse of *Amphitryon:* the story of the disillusionment of a women to whom the origin of her child "appeared to be more divine than those of other people because it [its origin] was mysterious" (2: 126; M, 94). The only model she can find for her condition is that of the "Holy Virgin" (2: 124; M, 91).

18. Kleist was doubtless aware of Euripides' last tragedy. Like the story of the earthquake in Acts, the Greek play provides a model for Jeronimo's spectacular liberation from

Crucified One proclaim their power by making the earth tremble, by dissolving rational principles of order, by causing traditional religions to crumble, and by severing umbilical cords: a liberation from the fetters of codified conventions and a repetition of conception or birth in which the profane site of their appearance, consumed by divine fire, is turned to ashes. By drawing on the theme of a Parousia inaugurated during a liberating earthquake and by constantly referring to the fate of the messianic figures of the Christian and Greek myths, Kleist's story starts to present itself as a form of Holy Scripture, however subversive—a Holy Scripture that not only reports on certain divine figures but is itself the site of a literary Parousia. In this story, with only the slightest dissimulation, God once again becomes human: with a heretical literalness, the profane food in the story turns into the bodily form of the Redeemer; the bearer of the Holy Name is once again liberated by an earthquake from the tomb of his prison; and, with the reservations of an "as if," the Garden of Eden arises once again.

The new Holy Family feels itself transposed into a literary Eden—as an image contrasting with that of the Apocalypse—in which the social unity of hitherto competing classes and the aesthetic unity of poetry and reality, dream and actuality, are achieved along with the Holy Union of the God-man. The theme of the perfect transparency of the presentation in the thing presented culminates in the description of the Dominican cathedral and the congregation gathered there to celebrate the mass:

---

prison. Even the piece of rope makes an appearance in the *Bacchai*. As Pentheus, who contests the divinity of Dionysus, seeks to shackle his theatrical incarnation in the dungeon of the palace, he binds a steer instead, and at that very instant the new god makes the house quake and reignites the fire on the grave of his mother Semele: "as in this instant / The house quakes *[bebt]*, seized by Bacchus, and consumed by the fire of his mother's grave" (lines 552–54, in the translation Kleist probably read; *Euripides Werke*, trans. F. H. Bothe [Berlin: Stettin, 1800–03], vol. 3). Certain elements of the *Bacchai*'s dramatic composition, arrangement of material, and individual formulations are also incorporated into Kleist's *Penthesilea;* see also Jochen Schmidt, *Heinrich von Kleist—Studien zu seiner poetischen Verfahrensweise* (Tübingen: Niemeyer, 1974), 234–41; Bernhard Böschenstein, "Die *Bakchen* des Euripides in der Umstaltung Hölderlins und Kleists," in *Aspekte der Goethezeit*, ed. S. Corngold, M. Curschmann, and T. Ziolkowski (Göttingen: Vadenhoeck & Ruprecht, 1977). The earthquake as a theophanic topos can also be found in, for example, Virgil, *The Aeneid*, Book 3, lines 90ff.; Ovid, *Metamorphoses*, Book 9, lines 782–83; Longinus, *Peri Hypsous*, § 63.

"high on the walls, in the frames of the paintings, boys hung and held with expectant looks their caps in their hands" (2: 155; M, 63). It is no longer images but living human figures that hang in the frames and, as natural figures of art, replace the paintings. Furthermore, the church rosette does not break up the light of the sun but, instead, "glowed, like the evening sun that illuminated it" (2: 155; M, 63). And in perfect psycho-physical parallelism, the glow of the sun and the lustre of the artificial rose illuminating the sacral room correspond to the fervent glow of the entire congregation, a glow from a flame that soars upward toward the heavens. Heaven and earth, individual and community, nature and art, outside and inside, presentation and the thing presented permeate one another to the point of unbroken homogeneity.

That unity emerges most clearly—emphasized by the orthographical change—in the unity of the family that appears to give form to the society gathered in the valley below St. Jago. This unity is shown in a concrete connection between Fernando's and Jeronimo's families. Because Juan's mother is injured and cannot nurse her son, his father asks Josepha if she "would not for a short time extend her breast to this pure little thing," and Josepha "took the tiny stranger, gave her own child to its father and laid it on her breast" (2: 150; M, 58). The unity of the two families—the pariah family united with the representatives of the very society from which it had been excluded—takes place through a simple process of replacement and exchange: through the replacement of a breast that no longer nourishes by one that has suffered no injuries; through the exchange of one family's milk for another's breakfast; and through an implicit exchange that takes place when Fernando, on his way to the cathedral and inside its walls, is of service to Josepha, while Jeronimo helps Fernando's sister-in-law, an exchange that gains moral credit for one family as it wins the honor of unprejudiced magnanimity for the other. The healthy breast presents and produces what the injured one lacks; the breakfast one family lacks is compensated by the abundance of food the other possesses; the morality that was injured when one family condemned the other is restored in the orality of the acts of acknowledgment and exchange. What is lacking finds fulfillment; what is separated returns to unity by the acknowledgment that those who have suffered separation are equals and by the concomitant exchange of equivalents: "It was as if all minds, since the terrible stroke that resounded [*durchdröhnt*] in them, were reconciled [*versöhnt*]" (2: 151;

M, 59). But it is only because Jeronimo and Josepha are unable to hear the echo of the "resounding" stroke in their "reconciliation" that they can believe that they really form a *single* family and thus belong to the same society that condemned them to death. Only because their earlier fate has fallen prey to a certain amnesia and because they, in turn, believe themselves under the protection of an ever-present God whose fulfilled presence leaves them without a trace of the past do they set out on a path that leads them to the "entire congregation of Christianity gathered in the temple of Jesus" (2: 157; M, 65).

Even in this Temple they retain the positions they occupied during the exchange of children and breasts. They form a *chiasm;* indeed, each partner within a pair takes the corresponding place in the other pair. This chiasmic placement—the choreographic figure of social unity—constitutes the compositional schema of the entire story: the rescue stories of Jeronimo and Josepha, which parallel each other in time, lead to their meeting in the valley as their common point of intersection; after the pairs have regrouped and as the Passion story follows its course, their paths spread out once again; the perspective of the story, whose vanishing points in the first part are Jeronimo and Josepha, intersects in the second part with the focus on Fernando and his family, the result of which is, in the third part, a concentration on Fernando himself. In the exact middle of the story the idea of *chiliasm*—the apocalyptic arrival of the Kingdom of God—is evoked, and this idea is then linked not only with the *crucifix*—the sign of the crucified and resurrected *Christ,* King of the thousand year reign—but with the name *Chili* as well: "A story was told . . . how the monks ran around with crucifixes in their hands and cried, 'The end of the world is here! . . . There is no Viceroy of Chile any longer!'" (2: 151; M, 59). Kleist carefully choses his words for the very next sentence: "at an instant when stories intersected [*kreuzten*] one another in the most lively manner" (2: 151; M, 59). At this instant Elvire asks Josepha to recount her story and, scarcely before the main features had come to light, she bids silence. At the point where their stories cross—which also marks the middle point of Kleist's own story—sympathetic silence, like the silence in the corresponding scene of breast-feeding, takes place. Just as, for Hegel, a rose arises in the cross of the present, the "beautiful flower" of "human spirit" arises, for Kleist, at the story's point of intersection and appears as the silencing of narrative discourse altogether. In the chiliastic chiasm, in the sign of the cross which is not only named in the story and which is not only formed from its protagonists and their speech but constitutes the story itself—at this point, the story opens up the articulation between the different presentations as it likewise articulates the space between the act of presentation and the things presented. And it does all this by ceasing to be merely a linguistic presentation, by making room for silence at the very center of the latent graphic cipher as the structural formula of the story itself. "The Earthquake in Chile" recounts the story of chiliastic recounting, and it recounts the breaking down of counting and recounting. It is an *experimentum crucis* of a chiasm in which speaking and speechlessness fold into, intersect, and cross over into one another: the "crucifiction" of a communication at whose center the word expires. In the cipher of divine presence the story writes—and writes itself as this very cipher—the recounting of the story carries out the sacrifice of the living Logos without, however, being able to constitute its sign.

Redemption took place; but since it was redemption through the sacrifice of a representative, it did not allow for redemption from representation or from sacrifice. Having been truncated into a sign of remembrance and into a corresponding promise, this redemption must be repeated again and again in the representative sacrifice of the mass. The events of the third part of "The Earthquake in Chile" not only take place *during* the celebration of the mass; they *are* this mass executed with a perverse literalness.[19] On two counts the murders stand under the sign of re-presentation. On the one hand, the murders heed the imperative

19. Using a very significant comparison, Kleist twice warns his fiancée Wilhelmine von Zenge against placing unreserved trust in the conventional signs of morality. In his open letter "On the Enlightenment of Women" (of September 16, 1800), he writes: "And yet, all of this is only the *sign* of a feeling that could be expressed in an entirely different way. For when you take bread from the hand of the priest during Communion, you may feel the same thing the [native] Mexican felt when he strangled his brother before the altar of his idols" (2: 316–17). The only criterion of correct action that, according to Kleist, resists deception is the categorical imperative, for it is supposed to communicate itself by the voice of conscience. Yet one year later, in a letter written on August 15, 1801, a similar analogy between Christianity and barbarism puts this imperative into question: "Let no one say that a secret voice tells us clearly what is right. The same voice that calls on the Christian to forgive his enemy calls on the South Sea Islander to roast his, and he piously eats him up. If convictions can justify such acts, should one trust any conviction?" (2: 683). No doubt Kleist perceived in the Christian mass not only a religious convention but also its murderous and cannibalistic implications.

to fill the void that was left when God removed himself from his flock—a
lack of presence that was thought to have been the cause of the earthquake in the first place. And they execute this imperative by doing away
with those in whom this absence is personified: Jeronimo, Josepha, and
their child. On the other hand, not only are those who represent God's
absence struck down, but this act is itself a repetition of the sacrifice of
the Eucharist through which the latent analogy of the victims with the
founding figures of the Christian religion is finally brought to completion. Just as the murderous fury is both a lynching and a sacred act—
both spontaneous excess and ritual drama—the victims are simultaneously personifications of absence and incarnations of the highest divine
presence. But the ambiguities of the representatives and the equivoca-
tions of the murderous effort to restore presence emerge only by way of
naming and judging language. Silence stands at the center of the intersecting stories, and the unification of opposites during the first scene at
the cathedral—nature unified with art, individual with society—is associated with a certain speechlessness; by contrast, the agonal dispute, as
an attack on the body and life of the victims, begins with the words of
the priest. In the act of naming and judging, he "abandoned the souls
of the evil-doers, calling them by their names, to all the princes of Hell"
(2: 156; M, 64).[20] But the judging word does not simply strike them from
the outside, for the structure of representation and replacement is immanent to the two families and to the chiasm they constitute. The
language of judgment, itself a *quid pro quo,* strikes in *one* family a figure
already given over to a *quid pro quo:* in other words, family members
already present themselves as substitutions for one another. The confusion to which the discourse of identification falls prey results from this
intersecting of the very figures of substitution. The symbolic arrangement of the characters must appear within the language of judgment as

---

20. Not only does the judging word destroy, but so does the voice, as the privileged
medium through which judgment is objectified. With the announcement of its own
presence, of presence *tout court,* the voice destroys what it claims to have begotten. In a
mocking paraphrase of the baptism of Jesus in which a voice cries from heaven, "This is
my beloved son in whom I delight," Kleist writes: "a voice from the frantic mob . . . cried,
'this is Jeronimo Rugera, citizens, for I am his own father!' and with an enormous blow
. . . struck him to the ground" (2: 157–58; M, 66). It is the "voice" that strikes him to the
ground! Presence destroys its re-presentation, the origin strikes down what it originated.
The naming word is the murderer of the object named.

a conventional order that lets one deduce the name of one partner from that of the other. Given the public perception that Jeronimo and Josepha form a pair, one can infer that the man who accompanies Josepha, who happens to be Fernando, must be Jeronimo. Given the mob's judgment that Josepha and her son belong together, one can infer not only that the child on her arm must be her own son but that the inference concerning the identity of Jeronimo is confirmed when this child turns to the man who accompanies its supposed mother. Paradoxically, when the mob judges—and according to its own standards, misjudges by naming Fernando "Jeronimo" and Juan "Philipp"—they are doing nothing more than drawing the most extreme conclusion from the symbolic ordering of the two pairs in a chiasm. As the unity of a family makes allowances for—and the moral law demands—each member can be substituted for every other, just as Josepha places Juan at her breast instead of Philipp. However immoral the conclusions drawn by the crowd might be, they constitute the unconscious reverse-image of the moral judgment of a *single* family, a judgment in which all individuals are regarded as equal and the same demands are made on all. Within the structure of symbolic exchange, the emphatic "is" in the false statement "'He *is* Jeronimo Rugera!'" (2: 157; M, 65) is just as true as Fernando's correct—that is to say, morally justified—assertion that Jeronimo is only passing himself off as Jeronimo, which is not only false but is even immoral from the perspective of the subsequent murder of his sister-in-law. The logic of exchange, substitution, and representation leads without fail to confusion, to the perversion of good into evil, the inversion of morality into mere legality, the distortion and devaluation of the beautiful presentation of morality within the chiasm of the pair and their children. The vertiginous movement of exchange and confusion culminates in the scene where Juan instead of Philipp—the legitimate son instead of the "bastard" (2: 158; M, 66), the human child instead of the child who would be divine—is smashed against a wall.

Although he had been furnished with the attributes of Jesus and been designated a figure of redemption throughout the text, Philipp is spared when the crowd grabs Juan.[21] But it is not within Philipp's power to

21. Kleist could have found a similar confusion in the *Bacchai*. Pentheus' mother Agave, deluded into thinking that she is ripping apart a young lion, tears apart her own son, and thus prepares him for the fate to which Dionysus was consigned. Along with

save his own life, and he can hold onto his life only by relinquishing the messianic role to which he was first appointed. It is possible to perceive—and the structure of the story invites such an interpretation—the same transcendent power that once appeared to save the lives of Philipp and his parents during the earthquake at work in the accident that draws the contingency of judgment into the domain of events and allows Juan to occupy the sacrificial spot reserved for Philipp. But the shattering of the Christological paradigm, through which the story is organized until the murders on the cathedral plaza, undermines this theo-teleological interpretation. Unlike the events prescribed in the Gospel, it is the *parents* of Philipp who fall victim to the pogrom, whereas Philipp himself—the reincarnation of Christ—stays alive. His survival breaches the promise of salvation his figure offers, for this promise could come to pass only by the sacrifice of his own life. The savior is saved, but a saved savior is no savior at all.

At this point the logic of supplementarity elaborated in Kleist's text transgresses the limits of the Christological model which his references to Holy Family, the apocalyptic catastrophe, and the celebration of the mass have drawn.[22] And it transgresses these limits not on the basis of an arbitrary narrative decision but in response to the dynamics of supplementarity itself. Kleist shows that the unification of society in a single family depends on an act of exchange and thus on substitution, but he shows just as clearly the duplicity of the central objects of substitution as well as the ambiguity inherent to the mechanism of replacement: the breast is needed to save Juan's life, but it is also implicated in an exchange

---

the myth, Euripides' chorus points out the *quid pro quo:* "As a bull appear, or come, many-headed, to us, / A dragon, or fire-red lion, Eleleus!" (ll. 940–41, in Bothe's translation cited above). Pentheus suffers the *sparagmos* ordered by Dionysus, and he does so as the *Doppelgänger* of Dionysus himself. Both appear in the form of a lion, their *tertium comparationis,* and are in this way bound together. The sacrifice of Pentheus doubtless serves the establishment and propagation of the Dionysian domain and the *restitutio ad integrum* of his insulted divinity; but it is also the very form of his domination and a presentation of his divinity to overturn and tear apart the phenomenal word, including his "own." In the Euripidean tragedy the god is confused with his counterpart, but this confusion is itself the presentation of a god who is exposed to no further confusion.

22. On the logic of supplementarity, see Jacques Derrida, *Of Grammatology,* trans. Gayatri Spivak (Baltimore: Johns Hopkins University Press, 1978); "Plato's Pharmacy" in *Dissemination,* 61–171.

that results in death; the exchange between the individual family members doubtless leads to a homogeneous social formation, but it also produces a society in which confusion over the identity of individuals destroys its members; the notion that God revealed himself in the earthquake doubtless supports the conviction that a sacred unity of the divine and the human has given rise to a new Holy Family, but this notion also sanctions the ritual murder of these "blasphemers" (2: 157; M, 65). Every supplement—the other breast, the one family, the self-presentation of God—is required so as to make up for a deficiency in vitality, morality, or justification. Yet not only are all these supplements dangerous and corrupting; they increase the very deficit they were supposed to fill. This double character of substitution manifests itself most emphatically in the breast. For the breast to which Don Fernando takes his son so as to provide him with nourishment (2: 151; M, 58) is the same one from which at the end of the story his son is "torn," then "whirled around in a circle up in the air, and smashed to pieces on the corner of one of the pillars of the church" (2: 158; M, 67)—on a pillar that may recall the pillar where Jeronimo, in the first sentence of the story, wanted to kill himself. The *quid pro quo* is complete. Juan is nourished in place of Philipp, and he is struck down in his place. The nurturing breast turns into a deadly pillar. The mother into a father. The feeding into a killing. Life into death. What began on the festival of Corpus Christi, when bread and wine turn into body and blood ends with corpses "drenched in blood" (2: 158; M, 66). The logic of supplementarity inverts the gain into a loss, the presentation into a distortion, the repetition into a devaluation, and it attests to the fact that there is no presence without the ruinous trace of the absence representation inscribes into it.[23]

23. Kleist's story consumes itself in the tension between the desire for the restitution of pure presence—which is also the presence and completeness of the maternal body—and the fear lest such presence be destroyed by this very restitution. The beloved object—the mother and, *totum pro parte*, the maternal breast—is not one. In "The Earthquake in Chile" as in *Penthesilea*, Kleist shows this breast to be divided. There are two breasts: the injured one from which Juan can no longer receive nourishment and the healthy one from which Philipp is withdrawn. There are two children: one is nourished in place of the other and is killed instead of him. Two mothers and two fathers are exchanged and sacrificed for one another. Whoever desires *one* breast—and only one breast is *whole*—must be separated from *another* breast; the latter must be given up, distanced, ripped apart, struck down. Yet every stroke that strikes the other imparts itself to the one and parts it into two. In one place, it is said the breast is "imparted" *(mitgeteilt);* and such is

This aporetic logic makes it impossible for any representation, strictly speaking, to be a representation: every representation is in need of a substitute that repairs its lack. But the Christological semiotics excludes the representation of representation; there can be no representative of God's representative because only the uniqueness and irreplaceability of his presentation within the domain of finitude lets him maintain his own uniqueness and his power over everything finite. Once his uniqueness and irreplaceability are secured, the representative of God on earth can proclaim the nullity of the world by sacrificing his own life, and he can restore the presence of the divinity itself only by relinquishing the world and by simultaneously relinquishing his claim to represent God. Kleist's text ruptures the framework of this Christological schema of representation. Not only does it introduce, with Philipp, the representative of a representative of God—an innovation sanctioned by the tradition of the Christian mass, even if it does violence to the demand for a unique and irreplaceable sacrifice—but it also proposes in Juan a *Doppelgänger* who suffers the Passion instead of Philipp. The death of Juan saves the life of Philipp, but only Philipp's death would have perfected the analogy between him and Christ, between the massacre and the mass. And this death alone could bring about the restitution of the authentic, unique, and irrevocable relation to the divinity as a transcendent power. However heretical and disfigured, Philipp's death would have been the cultic counterpart to a methodical effort to secure an absolute ground and an

---

Kleist's language: this communication, this imparting, this parting with the "with" of the breast. The composition of the scene of nourishment in which children and breasts are exchanged is striking for another reason: Juan's mother is incapable of giving her son her *breast* on account of a *foot* injury. Breast and foot are obviously in a relation of substitution. Furthermore, through the mediating moment of the feet, an image of a Satanic father stands in a metonymic relation with the breasts—the image embodied in Pedrillo, who happens to bear the same name as the father of Juan's mother: "a cobbler who had worked for Josepha and who knew her at least as well as he knew her little feet" (2: 156; M, 64). The wound of Elvira, who is another Josepha and who, like Josepha, has been masculinized by her name into a *vir*, clearly lies deeper: it is between the breasts and the feet. Moreover, only one event will heal the unity of one "breast" and one "family" torn apart by her division—the blows of the one who mends shoes for a living, the murders instigated by the cobbler Pedrillo. The diaporetic logic of this configuration is also the aporetic logic of Kleist's story: every trait lives and dies by way of its counterpart. It is the logic of accidental arches formed in a common collapse.

illusionless self-relation of the subject to itself as substance. God should have presented himself in Philipp, and the divine presence should have been restored with his death. Juan, by contrast, represents only Philipp, and the death of Juan is not a means to cancel the limits of sensibility and restitute the infinite but is, instead, the senseless end of a human life—beyond which there is no divine one. The accident of Juan's death indicates not only the contingent character of the absolute ground and of the methods that are supposed to lead in this direction; it also shows the susceptibility of this ground and these methods to fictionalization. In this way the accident of Juan's death points toward the finitude of the thought of infinite substance. Every theological and every teleological explanation must renounce itself in the face of this accident. For it destroys the core of transcendent meaning on which these explanations depend for their support. God did not manifest himself in the one who promised to become his representative, since He has not died in him. "God is dead" would only be the consoling formula of an atheism that still insisted He once could have lived. For Kleist, who is more desolate, God is a proclamation whose conditions of fulfillment are undermined by the representational structure of this very proclamation. God is an object, in Kantian terms, that does not stand under the conditions of objectivity, a necessarily broken promise. The death of his prophet— John, Juan—leaves no *logos* behind, no spoken gospel, but only a motionless and stupefied child whose mouth has been shut by his father's "endless caressing": an infant, an *infans*.

If Philipp occupied the center of the unification of society into one family and if, at the silent intersection of society's stories, he was the symbol of this unity, he emerges no less mute from its collapse as an allegory of this symbol. If he still presents something, it is the failure of the intention with which his figure was invested—the intention of arriving at a symbol in which the unity of the Idea of humanity and the reconciliation with God would become visible in a paradise or an apocalypse. Philipp does not present something; rather, he presents the complete inability of his figure to measure up to what is presented in it. And this goes for the story itself. By allowing Philipp to escape death, the story disengages itself from the Christological paradigm of representation and does away with the very illusion it had brought to life: the illusion, namely, that it could offer a literary reincarnation of divine presence, of the Idea, of a solid ground, of the Logos. The literary subreption of the Kleistian text—it would be the new version of the Holy Scriptures, its figures the *dramatis personae* of a new story of salvation, and the events it recounts the revelation of the divinity—is destroyed by the critical power of the text itself. But this destruction does not take place during the process of an analysis that believes itself free of illusions and intends to penetrate illusions as if they were merely foreign substances. It is the immanent dynamic of the drama of presentation that precipitates the crisis in which the promise of presentation is breached. The *experimentum crucis* of the story crosses itself out. It does not form the beautiful symbol of morality but the figure of a self-destructive diremption from the illusion that it could ever do so. The story thus turns into an allegory of its own symbolic intention. Its meaning is critical: the impossibility of presenting a highest and final instance, a seat of authority capable of granting unity and meaning. The story of a transcendent truth is struck down along with the falsely identified child. And when the story is struck down, so, too, is the fundamental schema of a representation whose function is to maintain a necessary and irreplaceable relation to whatever is represented; so, too, is the schema of a substitution incapable of further substitution; so, too, is the schema of a homogeneity between the presentation and the object presented, a homogeneity that would make it possible for the presentation—seamlessly and without a breach—to bring the objects presented into view. The doubling of the presentation of a transcendental Ideal which is practiced by Kleist's story undoes both the uniqueness and the necessity of this presentation, and thereby undoes the certainty of the objects presented in it. Having become contingent, the presentation can no longer find a point of support either in itself or in the ideal it has abandoned to a merely contingent mode of knowledge. This now contingent presentation is not a self-sufficient presence; it is the figure in which a discourse concerned with presentation, restitution, and certainty foregoes its claims and discloses in the breakdown of its symbolization the difference which enabled the text to articulate itself in the first place. If a presentation still presents something after having passed from a necessary presentation to a contingent one—and from a presentation incapable of repetition to one susceptible to endless replacements—it can only present its own distance from itself. Yet Kleist's story nevertheless remains the articulation of an experience and indeed of a historical one. But it is not the experience of a determinate content of representation, nor is it the experience of a representational form; it is the experience of a difference—the difference that makes representation possible and destroys its form, its exclusivity, and its truth.

The collapse of representation does not leave interpretation unimpaired. An interpretation that wishes to see a certain necessity in the rescue of Philipp would not only be an implicit justification of Juan's murder; it would commit the same error as Jeronimo and Josepha, who interpret the accident of their rescue as an act of divine grace. Such an interpretation would essentialize the accident. And from another perspective it would commit the same "error" as the Christian congregation, which interprets the rescue of the proscribed and despised pair not as the sign of divine favor but as a divine demand for their execution. However fitting these teleological interpretations of contingency may appear to their respective defenders, the fact that they contradict one another proves their contingent character. Every essentializing interpretation of contingent events can attest only to the contingency it seeks to contest. The essentializing interpretation of Philipp's survival would be cynical, for he has gained nothing but a life that commemorates the death of another. According to the critical strategy of Kleist's text, Philipp's rescue ought instead to be interpreted as the result of the conflict between different theo-teleological interpretations of the earthquake; it is thus to be interpreted as an accident that is strictly analogous to the accident that allows Jeronimo to escape from the crumbling prison, since it, too, arises from a concomitant collapse—the collapse, this time, of competing interpretive systems. By staging the drama of presentation, Kleist's story also performs the drama of interpretations, each of which explicates certain facts with respect to their transcendent significance for the sake of the unity of experience. But the outcome of the conflict of interpretations recounted by Kleist removes the ground upon which that unity of experience would rest. And the narrative critique of interpretation—which constitutes the text itself—shows the untenability of every interpretation of the text that seeks to restore this unity of experience by embedding it in a historical, sociological, or psychological continuum. The only "method" of interpretation able to withstand the critique of the text itself is one that does not attempt to restore the already destroyed unity through the application of its own methodological rules. Only a "method" that is itself attacked by the accident perpetrated by the text and that neither denies nor transfigures its vio-lence—only a "method," therefore, that ceases to be a procedure accord-ing to rules or a procedure with a view toward a universal rule would be capable of an interpretive experience of this text.

What remains for an interpretation whose privileged object—a secure meaning—is withdrawn and which is thus left with nothing but a de-preciated meaning is just the impossible imperative that is forced upon Fernando when he sees Philipp in place of his own child. When Fer-nando "compares him [Philipp] with Juan and how he acquired the two of them, it seemed almost as though he had to rejoice" (2: 159; M, 67). Moral fatherhood ought to outweigh not only the loss of his own son but also the dashing of his hopes to live on in this child. But it can do so only up to a point. For the joy over the adopted boy would have to include the joy over the murder of his natural son. It is, therefore, only "*almost* as though he had to rejoice." But once again, as in the oscillation between pain and pleasure in the feeling of the sublime, it is "as though he *had* to rejoice" over something that cannot be greeted with joy. The ethics of reading—where the solid ground of knowledge gives way, all hermeneutic questions turn into ethical ones[24]—demands the same: to give up the apparently natural assurances of cognition offered by theo-teleo-logy and thus to surrender the solid basis that understanding, presentation, and representation seek for themselves; to continue the work of detachment and withdrawal undertaken in the text itself; and to turn toward the case of that which escapes every rule and yet all the same remains a case, a *casus* or *Fall*. This task of giving up expresses itself only in the subjunctive, not in a "he had to" but in an "as though he had to [*müßt*]"—in a form indicative of the forfeiture of cognitive certainty even in the domain of moral feeling. However uncertain, unproductive, or painful it may be, reading has to work on this task—of giving up—in interpretation and beyond every interpretation.

24. See "The Promise of Interpretation" in this volume.

The Gesture in the Name

On Benjamin and Kafka

Failure is generally considered one of the fundamental figures of modernity and especially of modern literature. Modernity and its literature are said to emerge from the collapse of traditional orders, from the corrosion of conventions, and from the loss of the social and aesthetic codes that were once able to secure a certain coherence and continuity for all forms of behavior and production. Modernity is regarded, however, not only as the result of this disintegration but also as its hero: because it recognizes itself in the collapse of the old, modernity must make failure into its principle. Modernity must fail in order to stay modern. This belief in the heroic negativity of the new and newest has become so much a part of theoretical and literary-theoretical investigations into modernity that no one who repeats this axiom, no one who says that the foundation of modernity is failure, could ever risk failing. Indeed, failure is considered a victory, and foundering is understood as a sign of historical necessity. From this perspective—although not, of course, in the evaluation of the view it opens up—champions of conservation and those of modernity are of like mind: it is the collapse of the old order that creates the new one precisely because this collapse prevents the new one from ever growing old. Fragility is sometimes censured and sometimes hoped-for, sometimes made into an enemy and sometimes greeted as a herald of good news; but in every case it becomes a sign in which the epoch contemplates, secures, and saves itself. Collapse is a mode of conservation. And modernity, which draws all its pathos from the fact that it preserves itself only by outdoing itself again and again, consists entirely in the project of conserving the collapse from which it emerges and which it drives ever onward. Or such is the perspective conservatives and modernists share. Considered as a domain of negativity, the logic of modernity cannot then avoid a conclusion as ironic as it is fatal: nothing could be more modern—and thus more ultra-modern or post-modern—than modernity's own conservatism.

In terms of its self-definition, modernity cannot be entirely serious about failure. Modernity is not serious about failure as long as it subjects itself to the principle of knowledge and links the experience of failure with the law of representational cognition. Unlike the theorists of modernity and its outdoing, the practitioners of modernity in this century— and in earlier ones—have contested the prerogative of knowledge and the representational forms determined by cognition whenever the historical severity of their experience was at stake. That they, too, were not entirely serious about failure may have—and nothing can yet be decided on this point—an entirely different meaning than the lack of seriousness on the part of theorists. One of Kafka's best-known formulations concerns precisely this issue: "only writing is helpless, does not dwell in itself, is frivolity and despair."[1] Despair, above all, over this point: writing can find no point of support in itself and none in the conventions of a life and a language to which it is continually bound without being able to derive from them a law for its presentations. Writing is neither autarkic nor economical: it does not submit to the law of the house, "does not dwell within itself," and it is "helpless" in the sense that it

---

1. Whenever possible, Kafka's writings will be cited according to the new critical edition, *Kritische Ausgabe: Schriften, Tagebücher, Briefe*, ed. J. Born, G. Neumann, H. G. Koch, M. Pasley, and J. Schillemeit (Frankfurt am Main: Fischer, 1990). The *Tagebücher* (diaries) will hereafter be designated by "T." An English translation of them can be found in a two-volume set, *The Diaries of Franz Kafka, 1910–1913*, ed. Max Brod, trans. Joseph Kresh (New York: Schocken, 1948); *The Diaries of Franz Kafka, 1914–1923,* ed. Max Brod, trans. Martin Greenberg with the cooperation of Hannah Arendt (New York: Schocken, 1949); hereafter, "D." The complete text of Kafka's entry for December 6, 1921, reads: "From a letter: 'During this dreary winter I warm myself by it.' Metaphors are one among many things which make me despair of writing. Writing's lack of independence from the world, its dependence on the maid who tends the fire, on the cat warming itself by the oven; it is even dependent on the poor old human being warming himself by the stove. All these are independent activities ruled by their own laws; only writing is helpless, does not dwell in itself, is frivolity and despair" (T, 875; D, 2: 200–01). All translations of Kafka have been prepared for this volume.

remains without a self and without a rule based on the self. The law of writing is that it has no law. But when writing no longer accedes to a norm, when every rational or transparent coherence is conspicuous by its absence, then despair over this absence is not despair after all; it must be experienced as errant "frivolity," as a mere joke. If it is no longer clear what is absent, what is lost, and what has missed the mark, then all talk of absence, losing, and missing the mark is not only hypothetical; it misses the mark in principle. It has forfeited the epistemic security that would have been able to provide a background for the pathos of failure and the pathos of salvation. "Despair" is not simply despair but is also "frivolity." Lack—"helplessness"—is the lack of lack, and is thus a merely cited lack, a so-called "lack," a so-called "name," a mis-nomer. This literature or this modernity is not only not at home with itself; it does not even dwell in the homelessness of its absence. It moves in a realm in-between, a hybrid realm that no longer bears a canonical or even a disposable name. Faced with this literature and this modernity, questions like "What is called literature?" and "What is called modernity?" must turn into redoubled questions: "What calls for calling?" "Does it call, calling?" "Does it call at all?" "What calls for naming?" "Does it name, naming?"

Alterations undergone by canonical forms of literary presentation testify to the dilemma reflected by these questions. Walter Benjamin, who was certainly not the first theorist and historiographer of modernity but was one of the most circumspect and most nuanced, devoted particular attention to these alterations in his essays and notes on Kafka. Some of the observations that worked their way into his essay "Franz Kafka: On the Tenth Anniversary of His Death" constitute a starting point for a discussion he had with Bertolt Brecht on July 6, 1934, in Svendenborg, Denmark. This discussion concerns the problem of the seriousness of presentation, and it takes issue with both the pragmatic and political sides of the problem. The point is to show—not only with respect to this discussion—that all the problems of presentation and its epistemological correlates exhibit not only a literary-historical and a linguistic-theoretical dimension but also a decisive political one. According to Benjamin's notes on this discussion, Brecht proceeds from the following fiction:

Confucius has written a tragedy or Lenin a novel. One would find this inadmissible, he [Brecht] declares, conduct unworthy of them. Let us assume that you read an excellent political novel and later find out that it is by Lenin; your opinion of both would change, and to the disfavor of both. Confucius would also not be allowed to write a play by Euripides; it would be regarded as unworthy. But his parables are not.[2]

This fiction boils down to a distinction between two literary types: "the visionary, who is serious," and the "reflective type, who is not altogether serious" (BK, 149; Ref, 205). Whoever speaks in parables is, according to the typology developed by Brecht and Benjamin, not altogether serious, for in the last instance such a speaker answers only to reason, and in the face of reason, all literary formulations of doctrine must dissolve into semantically transparent means of instruction. A parable is simply "unserious" because its linguistic forms and materials are insubstantial: they mean something other than themselves, and indeed, according to the rationalistic tradition of fables and parables, they mean in each of their elements and figures the universality of rational concepts. By contrast, the visionary and the mystic, according to Brecht's and Benjamin's typological assumption, are serious about literature, because they see in its linguistic forms something substantial; in every present circumstance they see something coming; to them a literary representation is not an ephemeral vehicle of the thing represented but this thing's own presence at work. Benjamin asks Brecht: to which of these two types does Kafka belong? They agree on an answer: "it cannot be decided" (BK, 150; Ref, 205). Benjamin continues: "And this very undecidability is, for Brecht, the sign that Kafka, whom he considers a great writer"—and whom he had called in an earlier discussion "the only genuine Bolshevik writer" (BK, 131)—"like Kleist, Grabbe, or Büchner, is a failure" (BK, 150; Ref, 205). Kafka is regarded as a failure precisely because it cannot be decided whether he is a visionary or a sage, whether he writes parables or novels, whether he means his literary production to be serious or not entirely so. With whatever suspicion the concept and practice of typology should

2. Benjamin's comments on Kafka are cited from the collection edited by Rolf Tiedemann, *Benjamin über Kafka* (Frankfurt am Main: Suhrkamp, 1981); hereafter "BK." An English translation of this passage can be found in *Reflections*, trans. Edmund Jephcott (New York: Schocken, 1978), 205; hereafter "Ref." Some of Benjamin's writing on Kafka have been translated in *Illuminations*, trans. Harry Zohn (New York: Schocken, 1968); hereafter "Il." Many of his other reflections on Kafka can be found in his letters to Scholem; see *The Correspondence of Walter Benjamin and Gershom Scholem, 1932–1940*, ed. Gershom Scholem, trans. Gary Smith and Andre Lefevere (New York: Schocken, 1989); hereafter, "Cor." All translations of Benjamin have been prepared for this volume.

be regarded and however questionable the criteria used in this case may be, Benjamin took them seriously enough to include them, with only slight alterations, in his Kafka essay of 1934: Lenin is replaced by the preacher Salomo; the visionary is renamed the enthusiast; and failure becomes incompleteness. But the concept of failure is acceptable to Benjamin only because he regards it as a historico-philosophical category; he does not view it, as does Brecht, as a term of disparagement.[3] Precisely because Kafka "failed"—or because the typology of visionary and parabolist "fails" when it comes to him—he is, like Kleist, Grabbe, or Büchner, a "great" writer of modernity. Only by failing does he become modern in the first place. But the criterion for this failure and for this modernity is not any "modern" standard of success; it is the undecidability of characterizing his work—or deciding whether it corresponds to any standard at all. The undecidable provides the decision: the ambiguous, the opaque, the cloudy.

In three of the four sections of his essay on Kafka, Benjamin speaks of a "cloudy spot." In connection with the opening anecdote about Potemkin he writes: "The enigma that beclouds it is Kafka's" (BK, 10; Il, 112). Concerning the parable "Before the Law," he writes: "The reader who encountered it in *The Country Doctor* was perhaps struck by the cloudy spot in its interior" (BK, 20; Il, 122). And Benjamin takes up this strange metaphor again in the third section: "Kafka could grasp some things always only in gesture. And this gesture, which he did not understand, forms the cloudy spot of the parables. From this gesture arises Kafka's fiction" (BK, 27; Il, 129).[4] In the text of the parable, the cloudy

3. Benjamin had come upon the concept of failure as a central category for the interpretation of Kafka long before his discussion with Brecht. In the notes dated before 1931, he writes the following about Kafka's "Faust fiction": "Even this fiction is in turn the fiction of a failure, like everything Kafkean. 'The way one does it is false.' But the new ear for new laws and the new eye for new relationships prepares itself in this failure" (BK, 121). Benjamin is just as emphatic in a letter he wrote to Gershom Scholem in July, 1934: "And for this reason insight into his production seems to me bound up, among other things, with the simple realization that he failed" (BK, 77; Cor, 128). In addition, in the essay of 1934 he writes, "His testament orders their [his writings'] destruction. This testament, which no examination of Kafka can avoid, says that they do not satisfy their author, that he regarded his efforts as a failure, that he counted himself among those who were bound to founder. He did founder in his great attempt to draw fiction into doctrine. . . ." (BK, 271; Il, 129).

4. These passages correspond to certain notes for his essay of 1934: "In Kafka this satire [of juridical institutions] does not constitute a breakthrough. For, just as a cloudy

spot about which Benjamin speaks is the dark moment that remains opaque to doctrine. The cloud does not present doctrine but rather conceals it. At best, it distorts doctrine and disavows the task of exemplary, instructive narrative: to make one aware of its moral without delay and without obfuscation. Rather than mediating between particular figure and universal significance, the cloud parasitically draws attention to itself, defers or frustrates the arrival of doctrine in the presentation, and in this murky, almost milky, intermediary domain, it allows the line of demarcation between literature and life to dissipate. Just as this cloudy spot lacks a pedagogical and moral function, it also lacks a positive semantic function within the economy of the text. The cloudy spot no longer presents anything, no longer mediates, and no longer instructs. In Benjamin's view it undertakes the transformation of a literary presentation into a literal life—a life that can only be mystically inhabited.

The formal consequence of this transformation is a generic shift from parable to novel—a shift, in other words, to the literary form of a virtually endless postponement that no longer serves as an introduction to a teaching, a doctrine, a moral, or a law but has the task of deferring what is coming. For this reason Benjamin can write: "In the stories he left us the epic regains the significance it had in the mouth of Scheherazade: to defer what is coming. In *The Trial* the deferral is the hope of the one accused if only the proceedings do not gradually turn into judgment" (BK, 27; Il, 129).[5] Since, however, this epic moment of de-

---

spot is implanted in the parable—the one about the guardian of the door shows it clearly—and this cloudy spot takes away from the parable its parable-character in order to elevate it into a symbol, so too is mysticism implanted in the satire. *The Trial* is in fact a hybrid between satire and mysticism" (BK, 167). Among the remarks Benjamin planned to insert into his 1934 essay after the statement "this organization resembles fate" (BK, 121), there is this sentence: "It [this organization] is the cloudy spot in his world-image, the spot where it stops being transparent" (BK, 172).

5. By saying this—"if only the proceedings did not gradually turn into a judgment"— he marks the catastrophe that threatens the epic tendency of Kafka's work: it could turn into a parable or a moral story; the deferral of the decision could be, for its part, a decision; the interruption of the judgment could be a judgment and could pass into a "gradual" decapitation of Scheherazade. But the catastrophe in the deferral of the catastrophe also affects the interpretation of Kafka's writings. His texts are made to avoid their interpretation: "Kafka had a rare ability to create parables for himself. Yet he never exhausted what is interpretable in them; rather, he took all conceivable precautions against the interpretation of his texts" (BK, 22; Il, 124). According to the logic of the epic procedures that gradually become parables, the frustration of interpretation is already a transition to

ferral, as semantic opaqueness, already settles into and distorts the parable, the novel entitled *The Trial* is, according to Benjamin, "nothing but an unfolding of the parable ['Before the Law']" (BK, 20; Il, 122). And before the law stands, for Benjamin, every one of Kafka's parables, not only the one that carries this programmatic title. Benjamin can speak of a "cloudy spot in its interior" for the precise reason that "Before the Law" is not about the law but about the "before" of the law. From this "before" and from its pre-positional structure this parable nevertheless speaks of the structure of the law itself: it is defined as what remains inaccessible to visitation and visualization. It stands open and, during the lifetime of its single visitor, it never ceases to stand open. Yet precisely this openness makes it impossible for anyone at any given moment to enter into it. "'It is possible,' the doorkeeper says, 'but not now.'"[6] It is the openness of the law that withdraws from the opposition between outside and inside, and it is this very openness that closes itself. This is the law: that there is always only a "before" of the law. The withholding and withdrawing structure of the law forbids the one for whom it is reserved from experiencing it in any other way than in the impossibility of its ever being experienced—to say nothing of forbidding anyone

---

interpretation; a hindered exegesis is itself an exegesis, a judgment, and indeed the slow execution of the text. Even the deferral of interpretation interprets. It is equally right—according to the same wrong—to say this about Kafka, his identity, and his name: "But who was Kafka? He did everything in order to block the way to an answer to this question" (BK, 40, cf. 121). This blockage, one could say, is Kafka's hope—if only it did not gradually turn into an interpretation, into another interpretation, of course, an interpretation that preserved in its postponement the chance for something other than interpretation. (It is clear that, for Kafka, as Benjamin reads him, readers belong to the assistants of the court: they must arrest the accused through the interpretation of his writings, present him to the court, deliver and execute the verdict. The precautions Kafka takes against the exegesis of his writings and against the answer to the question who he might be are precautions against a reader who operates as policeman, judge, and executioner. Among the precautions are the effort to drag out the proceedings by aggravating the reconnoitering [cf. BK, 40] and also simple corruption. For corruption is "the only hopeful thing" [BK, 31; Il, 132; on justice as corruption, cf. BK, 125; "corruption the emblem of grace," BK, 141]. Only a corrupted reading would be a just one—a reading that gazes into a world without a trial, a judgment, or an execution.)

6. Franz Kafka, *Die Erzählungen,* ed. Klaus Wagenbach (Frankfurt am Main: Fischer, 1961), 135; hereafter "E." There is an English translation of these stories in Franz Kafka, *The Complete Stories,* ed. N. Glatzer (New York: Schocken, 1971), 3; hereafter "CS."

from receiving a merely approximating concept of it. Just as the man from the country remains before the law, so, too, does the parable "Before the Law," and only in this way does it express its truth, the law of the law, and its very own law: namely, that the law is obstructed. The law is what withdraws from presentation. "Before the Law" presents the law as little as it formulates both less and more than this: the law of the law, which states that it never presents itself as such and never comes to light in the transparent form of the parable. Abiding by the law, "Before the Law" stands before the law of the parable, and it does so by not presenting a rule, a teaching, a doctrine, a moral, a law; by inhibiting itself and dissembling itself; and as a "cloudy spot," by placing itself before its own function of presentation, before itself as a parable. "Before the Law" is itself the "cloudy spot" of all parables that have treated the law—and the law of fiction—in the tradition of doctrinal, didactic fiction.

When Benjamin speaks of the "cloudy spot" in the "interior" of the parable "Before the Law," this reminiscence touches on the point in Kafka's text where he mentions the "interior" of the law. It brings the parable in close proximity with the law: the "cloudy spot" in the parable is the law that forbids its own presentation but is at the same time the forbidden law; it is the forbidden law and the forbidding law and thus the law that forbids itself and every self, the law as the retreat of the law, a law without law. Whatever is most interior to this law becomes, by virtue of this trait, absolute exteriority, an exile of the law from the law: an exile of the parable from its traditional function, and since there is no other, an exile of the parable from every function. "Cloudy spot" thus names the forbidding event (of the presentation) of forbidding and thus the impossibility of naming, of meaning, of speaking a language.[7] But the law of the "cloudy spot" must also be valid for any presentation of the "cloud" and the structure of its meaning—otherwise, it would not

---

7. Kafka repeatedly expressed himself in precisely this way in notes using a more abstract language. To cite only one example among many, there is a diary entry of January 21, 1922, in which the motif of "the task"—thus "the law"—and the motif of "impossibility" are closely connected with one other: "No one's task was as difficult, so far as I know. One might say that it is not a task at all, not even an impossible one, it is not even impossibility itself, it is nothing, it is not even as much of a child as the hope of a barren woman. But nevertheless it is the air I am meant to breathe, so long as I breathe at all" (T, 884; D, 2: 206).

becloud the "law." And so "cloudy spot" "means" that it does not mean, does not name, and does not designate anything. It is not a metaphor for something else but is a metaphor for the impossibility of metaphor itself, hence a figurative-defigurative hybrid: at once a symbol and the metafigurative self-denial of this symbol, an allegory that means something other than itself, something impossible to mean.[8]

The aporetic structure of the law and the discourse of law are clearly valid not merely for isolated advice about life nor for a particular law among other possible ones. This structure is the structure of the law insofar as it is a law and therefore determines the rational law of moral action no less than the law of historical transmission and the representational forms in which such transmission takes place.[9] Benjamin largely privileges this historical dimension of the law in his discussion of Kafka's parables. What, for Benjamin, arises from the opacity of the law in Kafka's stories and from the aporetic character of the forms in which these stories are told is, above all, the fact that the historical consistency of the law, the "consistency of truth" (BK, 87), has been lost. "Kafka presents tradition falling ill," Benjamin writes (BK, 87). Not simply a "falling-ill" of the tradition of the parable as a genre and a "falling-ill" of its canonical demand for transparency, but a "falling-ill" of tradition in general, a "falling-ill" of passing-on, of transmission, and

8. In an already cited passage from his notes on Kafka, Benjamin speaks of the "cloudy spot" as the one that "takes from the parable its parable character in order to elevate it into a symbol" (BK, 167); in another place he speaks of the "laws" as "allegorical objects" (BK, 142). In the essay "Franz Kafka: At the Building of the Chinese Wall," he writes: "everything that he [Kafka] describes asserts something other than itself" (BK, 41). Benjamin connects this formal condition in which he characterizes the rhetorical structure of Kafka's work as allegory—as *allo agoreuein,* saying something else—with the ontological, or allontological, condition that Kafka's "one and only object" is the "distortion of existence" (BK, 41). Benjamin's definition of allegory occurs at the end of *The Origin of the German Mourning-Play* where he writes that evil exists only in allegory and is allegory and therefore "means something other than it is" (Walter Benjamin, *Gesammelte Schriften,* 1: 406; *The Origin of German Tragic Drama,* 233). Benjamin never explicitly discusses this double characterization of Kafka's work as both symbolic and allegorical, but it corresponds to his general diagnosis of its hybrid character and the undecidability of its genres.

9. Jacques Derrida in particular has pointed out how close Kafka's law is to the Kantian moral law; see "Before the Law" in Jacques Derrida, *Acts of Literature,* ed. D. Attridge (New York: Routledge, 1992), 183–220. A reading that connects the open door of the law with "the open" in Heidegger has been undertaken by Massimo Cacciari in *Dallo Steinhof—Prospettive viennesi del primo Novecento* (Milan: Adelphi, 1980).

of history insofar as its structure is dependent upon the form of a doc-trinal, didactic story and upon the transmission of truths, rules, and laws: a "falling-ill," in sum, of presentation in its historical and cognitive dimensions. The law of history called for something to be transmitted and passed on. This law is gone, and with it, the prospect that what was valid in the past will no longer be so in the future. By losing the tradition and the literature that mediates this tradition, history has become para-doxical: it has turned into the transmission of the untransmissible and thus into a transmission without content. History is still written, but it is a history in which nothing happens. In Kafka's prose, literature and the historical continuum of transmission it helps produce transform themselves into an "ill" tradition, into a giving and a giving-over that no longer gives a content, no longer offers a gift, but only gives this giving itself. "He gave up truth," Benjamin writes, "in order to maintain its transmissibility" (BK, 87). What is maintained is a history without event, another law without law—and a history that is just as much loss as liberation: a history that releases itself from history as a normative continuum in which meaning is mediated and transmitted, and a history that opens itself onto another one—but not onto a history "for us." Having been freed from this continuum, history is likewise freed from its anthropological determinations and directions. Kafka's remark about hope, which Benjamin again and again cites in his notes, goes for litera-ture and for the law that is transmitted by and *as* this literature. There is, Kafka says, "plenty of hope, an infinite amount of hope—but not for us" (BK, 14, 141; Il, 116).[10] There is hope always only for another—and for "us" only when there is, so to speak, no "us," when "we" stop being "ourselves" and begin to be another. "Plenty of hope," therefore, "but not for us." Hope, rather, case by case, for others, for another literature and another history.

Benjamin's analysis of the formal structure of Kafka's stories is thus an analysis of the historico-philosophical diagnosis that these stories pro-pose and at the same time an analysis of the historical praxis at work in them. If Kafka's work presents an interruption of history—and indeed presents this only by interrupting the principle of presentation—then it

---

10. Benjamin may have read in Kafka's sentence a variation on the sentence with which he closes his own essay on Goethe's *Elective Affinities:* "Only for the sake of the hopeless is hope given to us" (Benjamin, *Gesammelte Schriften,* 1: 201).

not only suspends a regional, genre-specific tradition; it also boycotts the paradigmatic function this tradition claims for history in its entirety, including the future. If the model of figuration is itself "beclouded," if it is suspended, then so is its claim to be able to prefigure the future. This suspension, which Kafka's distorted parables do not passively register but actively undertake, has two sides: on the one hand, it still takes part in the tradition by referring in the manner of Enlightenment discourse to a specific doctrine, a rule, a law; on the other hand, it insists that this doctrine does not exist, that the rule cannot be formulated, and that the law—of the past and the future—cannot be presented. These two traits crisscross in Kafka's text and produce the condition in which the openness and thus the inaccessibility of the law appear as a law—and as a law of the law. As Kafka's texts infinitely hesitate on the threshold of meaning, even their own meaning, they likewise absorb into themselves the potential for meaning they have blocked and have indeed increased by blocking it. Unexpectedly, their presentation turns into the unpresentable. They transgress the law that makes the future unpresentable because this law consists in nothing but the limitless transgression into something else. They show the withdrawal from showing and thereby draw themselves into a cloud.

Benjamin called this side of Kafka's productions "magical." The "cloudy spot" at the core of the parable dissolves the distancing character of its art—and transforms it into life. If one of the criteria of the parable as a historically codified literary genre is that its characters are not taken altogether seriously—for they do not put up any resistance to being traded for their meaning—then the opacity of the parable, which in terms of the canonical tradition simply means its failure, has the effect that it, the parable, becomes the seriousness of life. The failure of literature, according to this schema, can be interpreted as the success of a vague, uncomprehended life. Wherever the text annuls its distancing function, the boundary separating it from life falls away, and it becomes one of life's ghostly figures. Benjamin notes this trait in Kafka's work with a certain critical uneasiness. He explicitly links it with another of Kafka's programmatic stories, a story Max Brod entitled "On Parables" *(Von den Gleichnissen)*. In it those who bemoan the sage's invitation to make the transition into a "legendary yonder" receive the reply: "Why do you resist? If you would only follow the parables, you would have become parables yourself and would thereby already be free of your daily toil" (E, 328; CS, 457). There is no talk here of doctrines, only of parables. But the parable raises a claim to being absolute. Even to recognize it as a mere parable already means that one has removed oneself from its demand. The demand is that the reader become a parable and stop reading. At one point in his notes Benjamin cites the story of an old Chinese painter who, in front of his friends, stepped into his last and most perfect picture and disappeared into the interior of a painted pagoda. Benjamin comments: "But thereby his picture achieved a magical character and wasn't a picture any longer. Kafka's work participates in its fate" (BK, 170). Benjamin recounts the same story in a central section of his *A Berlin Childhood Around 1900* entitled "Die Mummerehlen," with this addition: when he painted as a child, he too would have "distorted [himself] into the picture. I resembled the porcelain in which I entered along with a color cloud."[11]

The magical transformation recounted in the Chinese story is not accomplished in Kafka's text; it is a theme and a problem within a particular conversation. But this magical metamorphosis—which led Benjamin to the observation that Kafka did "not always . . . avoid the temptations of mysticism" (BK, 22; Il, 124)—this magical mimesis is not simply a theme and a problem; as a procedure, it remains a part of Kafka's production. Even the dialogue "On Parables" nowhere denies it. But if a magical motif gains entrance into the didactic presentation, if the cloud brings along an obfuscation of the Enlightenment and its pedagogical as well as moral intentions, then the task of historical criticism is not to censure this in some moralistic fashion but to read it first and foremost—and therefore before any attempt at intervention—as an index of what is happening, what has happened, and what may yet happen. The task is not, then, simply to diagnose it as a symptom of collapse and certainly not to recommend a return to the old values; it is to take into account the possibility—at least the possibility—that in the disintegration of the presentation something else, something hitherto unknown and unprecedented, is preparing itself. That is how Benjamin reads the trait of mystical opacity in Kafka's prose. His pieces, he writes,

11. Benjamin, *Gesammelte Schriften*, 4: 263. I have further traced the motif of the cloud in this and other texts of Benjamin in "The Word *Wolke*—If It Is One," trans. Peter Fenves in *Studies in Twentieth-Century Literature* 11 (Fall 1986), 133–61; *Benjamin's Ground,* ed. R. Nägele (Detroit: Wayne State University Press, 1987), 147–76.

are not parables, and yet they do not want to be taken at face value either. . . . But do we have the doctrine that accompanies Kafka's parables and is elucidated in K.'s gestures [*Gesten*] and the gesticulations [*Gebärden*] of his animals? It is not there; at most we can say this or that alludes to it. Kafka would have perhaps said: as relics they hand down the doctrine. But we could just as well say: as precursors they prepare this doctrine. (BK, 20; Il, 122)

The doctrine, the law, the order on whose doorstep Kafka's parables founder—or deny themselves—belong, for Benjamin, to the future as much as to the past. But neither the law of the past nor that of the future is presented, reproduced, symbolized, allegorized, or otherwise figuralized according to some codification of literary procedures. All these figures belong to orders that have become obsolete, and by not corresponding to any of them, Kafka's texts bear witness to their insufficiency. The "cloudy spot" in his prose forms, the incomprehensible gestures, and the enigmatic figures that populate them are to be read as witnesses of this refusal or this impossibility of anticipating what is coming and of subordinating it to past forms of presentation. The transformation of the parable into magic is thus not merely a phenomenon of regression into the aesthetic unity of image and life; on the contrary, it belongs to the paradox of the magical character of Kafka's images that they stop being images, copies, or models. Their magic comes about by making themselves similar to the absolutely dissimilar, the unknown, the incomparable, the things that cannot be anticipated. This absolute dissimilarity is an aspect of the future, but only one aspect—for the other is the sheer opposite: one can already tell that what announces itself as the future of social life and its communicative and cognitive forms will also appear as an order and appear in the form of laws.

The "cloudy spot" of the parable is, as an answer to the ambiguity of the future, itself an ambiguous phenomenon: it opens up the historical forms of representation to the future and resists anything in this future that would amount to a regression into a mythical past; it marks the site of the future and protects it from whatever might impair its futurity, its unprogrammatic alterity. The distortion that gains ground in the forms of Kafka's prose is thus a place-holder for a *novum,* for anything that would have a place in no other recognized order of presentation and would not itself be any such order. And this could be defined as its "modernity": not that it lines a new order up alongside an old one so as to continue the homogeneous expansion of all ordering powers but that in all orders—and first of all in the order of presentation—it opens up whatever relates itself in a homogeneous manner to these orders and these ordering powers. In this way, all art, even the oldest, has a dimension that could be called "modern" whenever it exposes in the presentation of historical experience a caesura, a "cloudy spot," or the incomprehensible gesture that opens itself to the alterity of the future. The minimal political program of "modernity" is a resistance to the assimilation of the future to the past and, accordingly, a refusal to submit itself to the claims of universality made by the tradition of presentation, a tradition that always carries out this assimilation. Old orders do not fail so that newer ones can succeed; it is the very principle of presentation that fails, for this principle founds the continuity between "old" and "new" and thereby establishes the continuity of hitherto prevailing historical time. This failure strikes at the traditional image of history as a continuum of experiences. But only in the interruption of the continuum of presentation, in the "falling-ill of tradition," does history open up—history no longer as a merely normative structure but in an emphatic sense, as occurrence.[12] For the Benjamin who wrote "Toward the Critique of Violence," the political complement of this history was the proletarian general strike—the refusal, without violence, to work under the laws established by State power.[13] The "cloudy spot of the parables" may have been, for Benjamin, the strike against the tradition of presen-

12. Compare the following note from the *Arcades Project:* "In every true work of art there is a spot at which anyone who plunges into it will feel it blowing toward him like the cool wind of the coming morning. From this arises the insight that art, which one often regards as a deflection from every relation to progress, can give the latter its genuine determination. Progress does not take up residence in the continuity of the temporal flow but in the moments that interfere with this continuity: where the truly new first makes itself felt with the sobriety of the morning" (*Gesammelte Schriften*, 5: 593; N 9a, 7). The "spot" about which Benjamin speaks may be that "cloudy spot" in Kafka's parables—the place, that is, in which the parables remove themselves from the continuum of their tradition and are for this reason not so much indications of something coming but rather this very coming itself, each time anew, for the first time.

13. It is Benjamin himself who makes the link to his earlier text "Toward the Critique of Violence": "The 'Critique of Violence' is to be compared with respect to the demonic nature of the legal order *[das Recht]* that Kafka constantly had in view and that is doubtless the ground of his cautiousness" (BK, 139). The emphasis Benjamin placed on the "mythi-

tation and against presentation as tradition—a *politicum* in which an other future topples literary and aesthetic, positive and mythical orders alike.

The refusal of presentation practiced by Kafka's stories makes them useless for the very order whose emergence they announce. They prepare for something and at the same time prevent its arrival; indeed, they prepare *by* preventing. Kafka's stories are the messengers of a doctrine they boycott. Benjamin formulates their dual character in the following manner: "Kafka's fictions are parables from beginning to end. But this is their misery and their beauty, that they had to become *more* than parables. They do not modestly lie at the feet of doctrine, as Haggadah lies at the feet of Halachah. When they have crouched down, they unexpectedly raise a mighty paw against it" (BK, 87; Cor, 225). And so Kafka's work stands "under the sign of the opposition between the mystic and the parabolist, the language of gesture and the language of instruction, the visionary and the sage" (BK, 169). This opposition is, as Brecht and Benjamin recognize, undecidable in Kafka's case; indeed, the logic of the opposition between mysticism and rationality becomes obsolete precisely when a presentation makes itself similar to the unpresentable and thus becomes dissimilar to itself.

Just as Kafka's stories are hybrid creatures that incline toward self-obliteration, so too are the figures that enter into them. Benjamin calls them "monstra" (BK, 123, 133, 135, 138). Four of these creatures are repeatedly mentioned by Benjamin as well as by subsequent authors writing about Kafka: they are the bug, the ape, the cat-lamb, and

---

cal" character of the legal order in Kafka is obviously to be understood in connection with his earlier study; see, for example, the sentence in which Benjamin states that "the legal order in Kafka's work has the character of a mythical construction" (BK, 141). The "cloudy spot" at the core of the law is the place where its mythical violence break down. It undertakes the demythologization of the mythical power of positing. See also my essay, "Affirmative, Strike," trans. Dana Hollander, *Cardozo Law Review* 13 (December 1991): 1133–57; *Walter Benjamin's Philosophy,* ed. A. Benjamin and P. Osborne (London: Routledge, 1994), 110–138. See also the rather differently accented texts of Jacques Derrida, "Force de loi—Force of Law" in *Deconstruction and the Possibility of Justice,* special issue of the *Cardozo Law Review* 11 (July/August 1990): 919–1045; and Alexander García Düttmann, "Die Gewalt der Zerstörung" in *Gewalt und Gerechtigkeit,* ed. A. Haverkamp (Frankfurt am Main: Suhrkamp, 1994).

Odradek. What Benjamin said about them can essentially be grouped around the motifs of forgetting, the body, debt, and guilt. Having called the body "the strangest, most forgotten region," Benjamin continues:

> Odradek is the form things assume in forgetfulness. They are distorted [*entstellt*]. Distorted are the "Cares of the Family Man," which no one can identify; distorted is the bug, of which we know all too well that it represents Gregor Samsa; distorted is the large animal, half-lamb and half-kitten, for which "the butcher's knife" would perhaps be "redemption." (BK, 31; Il, 133)

In the texts to which Benjamin refers, Kafka does in fact write about distorted bodies, but not in every case does he indicate the means by which this distortion took place, least of all in the case of Odradek. Yet Benjamin's discussion of distortion proceeds from the general assumption that it encroaches upon the natural and normal model of animal or human bodies. Although Benjamin's theory of poetry and history examines ideal types only to show their imperfections, certain aspects of his reading of Kafka's stories of metamorphosis and hybridization suggest that he fell prey to a certain normative realism. This is especially noteworthy considering the fact that the concept of distortion is central for Benjamin's view of Kafka's work and of "modernity" in general. But the distortions in Kafka's texts can be read otherwise. More exactly, they can be read as distortions related not to a natural body but to a name or a complex of names. This reading is not meant to demonstrate that Benjamin, one of the most important philosophers of the name, missed something; rather, its aim is to reconsider his reflections on the structure and technique of Kafka's prose, to bring these reflections to bear on certain details he neglected, and to specify the movement of distortion from which they proceed.

The publication of Kafka's diaries and letters has demonstrated the almost obsessive attention he paid to investigating the meaning of his own name. That he investigated the meaning of his name means, first of all, that it had a meaning for him and was not simply consigned to the function of designation. And the meaning of this name was not readily apparent in the language of his stories, for in German the name "Kafka" awakens no more than onomatopoetic associations. By contrast, in Czech, which was the language he used in his business and his daily affairs throughout almost his entire life, the meaning of his name is immediately recognizable: *kavka* means "jackdaw," and a jackdaw served as the company emblem on the stationary of Kafka's father, who dealt with both German and Czech-speaking customers. Besides Yiddish, Franz Kafka was exposed to at least these two languages all his life, and one must account for the fact that he not only had a command of both languages but that this dual command gave rise to a problem: a problem of bi- and multi-lingualism, a problem of translation, and a problem of the translatability of proper names. For if a proper name, as a singular term that functions as a mark of identity within a system of social classification and is closely connected with the constitution of the bearer as a subject in both his conscious and unconscious life—if such a name is translated, then it is never translated as a singular name but only as a general one, never as a name of a person but only as a name for an entire class of objects in which the singularity of the name and the inalienable attributes of the person are affected along with the identity of the object named. Not only does antonomasia—the transformation of the proper name into a concept—wipe away the singular traits marked by the name, but antonomasia also takes away the transparency of the concept that is supposed to correspond to this name in the translation, and it further-more renders this concept useless as an instrument of a clear and distinct denotation. Wherever names and nouns, singular and general terms, can be generated from one another through antonomasia, critical distinc-tions in the domain of concept are no longer possible without qualifica-tion. And the same can be said of the production of concepts, the transparency of the particular within the general, and the subsumption of an individual under a universal law—all of which are demanded by conceptual thought. Virtually all words, not only nouns, construct a gloomy court around themselves by means of antonomasia, a court that becomes impenetrable once antonomasia spins out an entire story. If, for example, the name "Franz" becomes *Franse* (fringe, fray) by way of paranomasia, and the latter turns into *Faden* (thread); if "Kafka" is translated into "jackdaw," and this translation is then extended by in-tralinguistic transmutations into "raven," "crow," "blackbird," "vul-ture," "stork," and so forth—and all these *nomina genera* do indeed appear in Kafka's texts—then one will no more recognize "Franz Kafka" in the combination of "thread" and "crow" than one would recognize

Baudelaire in the epithet "the beautiful of the air." Now, the effect of such onomastic distortions is no less striking for translations within a particular idiom than for translations between different national languages, especially when it is not the entire name but only its constituent parts—salient phonetic groups, syllables, or complexes of letters—that are transformed in this way.

Kafka explicitly comments on the mechanism of such distortions, which resembles that of the dream-work, in a famous diary entry related to his story "The Judgment." Concerning the name of its protagonist, he writes: "Georg has the same number of letters as Franz. In Bendemann 'mann' is only an amplification of 'Bende' intended to provide for all the as yet unknown possibilities in the story. But Bende has exactly the same number of letters as Kafka, and the vowel 'e' is repeated in the same places as the vowel 'a' in Kafka" (T, 492; D, 1: 279). If this method of deciphering, which Kafka repeats almost word for word in a letter to Felice Bauer four months later,[14] can be seen as an approximate key for the interpretation of the proper names of this story and indeed for the interpretation of nouns and words of all kinds in Kafka's texts, then it is plausible to read "Gregor Samsa" not only as a further cryptonym for "Franz Kafka" and as *ego sum* ‹*Sarg*›—"I am a coffin, I am a crypt"—but also to read the entire story of "The Metamorphosis" as the story of Kafka's metamorphosis into his distorted name: the transformation of *Kafka* into *Käfer*—into a "bug."[15] Furthermore, it will not seem implausible to interpret "A Report to an Academy" as a displaced inversion of this metamorphosis: as a transformation, that is, of *Kaf*ka's *af*—or *Aff*,—into what is called a talking-name, into the metaphor of a talking *Affe,* a speaking ape. The case of the hunter Gracchus is well-known: *gracchio* in Italian means the same as *kavka* in Czech, "jackdaw." The third story frequently cited by Kafka's interpreters, including Benjamin, as an example of a monstrous deformation, is "A Crossbreed," which tells of a cross between a lamb and a cat. Here it is worth recalling an entry in Kafka's diary which begins: "In Hebrew my name is Anschel,

14. Franz Kafka, *Briefe an Felice,* ed. E. Heller and J. Born (Frankfurt am Main: Fischer, 1967), 394; cf. *Letters to Felice,* trans. James Stern and Elizabeth Duckworth (New York: Schocken, 1973), 265.

15. The French "cafard," almost a homonym of Kafka, means "cockroach," "sneak," and "gloomy."

like my mother's maternal grandfather. . . ." (T, 318; D, 1: 197).[16] For not only does the *Amsel* (blackbird), a paranomasia of Amschel, belong to the family of the jackdaw—or the *kavka* family—and thereby anticipate the ornithonym in the maternal lineage; the name "Amschel" also contains the anagram *Lamm* (lamb), just as Kafka's mother's maiden name, Löwy, leads with a slight shift to *Löwe* (lion) and then to the generic name "cat." Whatever else it may be, the cat-lamb is also the literalization of the fatal crossbreeding of Kafka's metamorphosized family names. But this monstrosity of double naming is fatal for at least two reasons: because its two halves strive in opposite directions—"it flees cats, it wants to assault lambs"—and because its execution at the hands of the butcher appears to be the only solution to its aporetic existence: "Perhaps the knife of the butcher would be a redemption for this animal." But such a redemption is impossible, for "as it is an heirloom, I must deny it that" (N, 2: 374; CS, 427).

The unresolvable conflict of names does not play itself out in the often-cited "monsters" alone. The story "Jackals and Arabs" also stages a desperate struggle within the name "Kafka": a struggle between the *Ka* of *Schakale* (jackal) and the jackdaw-like *Raben* (raven) of the *Araber* (Arabs), a struggle for *Aas* (carrion)—or the two *a*'s of Kafka's name—and for the *Kadaver* (cadaver) of a *Kamel* (camel) from a *Karawane* (caravan).[17] And the nomads whose incursion into the Chinese metropolis is recounted in "An Old Manuscript" are also "onomads" of Kafka's name. Although they do not carry his name, they act under his law and under the law of the name, the name of the law. For nomads are the bearers of the name "name." As *nomeus*, the nomad stands under the *nomos*, the law of the name, *onoma*, and the law as a taking,

16. The editors of the critical edition refer to the following remark of Harmut Binder: "Adam Porias (1794–1862), whose name in Yiddish is 'Amschel Brias'. . . ." (T, Kommentarband, 82). "Anschel" in Kafka's diary entry thus refers to an "Amschel," and the desperate hybrid of a lamb and a cat, this paradox of naming, goes back to an Adam Porias, an A. Porias with whom all aporias of his existence begin. It is explicitly said of the cat-lamb that it is "an heirloom from my father's possessions"—from the possessions of a forefather who bore, perhaps, the name Adam. See Franz Kafka, "Eine Kreuzung" in *Nachgelassene Schriften und Fragmente: Kritische Ausgabe* (Frankfurt am Main: Fischer, 1993), 2: 372; hereafter "N." "A Crossbreed" can be found in CS, 426–27.

17. See Kafka, "Schakale und Araber" (E, 136–40; CS, 407–11).

nemein.[18] "One cannot speak with the nomads. They do not know our language; indeed, they hardly have one of their own. They make themselves understood among themselves much as jackdaws do. Always one hears this cry of jackdaws" (N, 2: 359; CS, 416). The nomadizing name Kafka—the name "name" and the "noun" *kavka*—means to him that he has no language. Kafka's language, by contrast, means that he has no name that could correspond to him. Every Cratylism, every attempt to fantasize some substantial affinity between the name and the thing named, between the reference of the name and the character of the one who bears it, founders upon this experience—a dual experience and an experience that, since it puts language itself into question, is not merely contra*dictory* but aporetic. For the name here insists that language itself—and thus the forms of its correspondence—be exposed, interrupted, suspended. At issue is not only what a name means but *whether* it can say anything at all, whether it belongs to language, whether, in sum, a language of names is a language at all and indeed whether a name is a name at all—and not, as Kafka's "nomads" suggest, a monstrous power that takes away every name that can be spoken. A *Namens-Sprache* (language of names) would not then be a gift of language but the taking away of language, a *Sprach-Nahme*.

"One cannot speak with the nomads." In Kafka's staging of his name, a certain trait makes itself known that marks every name in its singularity: the name does not belong to a system of language that communicates something but to the markings in this system whose only function is to secure communicability itself. These markings do not "say" anything, they mark. In this sense, they are the places most resistant to meaning in any system generally disposed toward meaning. However much a name may be inclined toward the pure denotation of an unmistakable and nontransferable singularity, it nevertheless remains caught in a network of connotations, and contrary to certain claims made by analytic philosophy, these connotations do not allow us to find the

18. On the philological reconstruction of widely known connection between *nemo, nomos, nemizō, onoma*—a connection to which Plato often refers—see Max Pohlenz's three studies in *Kleine Schriften* (Hildesheim: Olms, 1965), 2: 314–360; see also Emmanuel Laroche, *Histoire de la racine NEM en Grec ancien* (Paris: Klincksieck, 1949). Cf. the citations and remarks in Thomas Schestag, *Parerga* (Munich: Boer, 1991), esp. 108 (where he refers to Kafka's "Old Manuscript").

logical model of the name in a pure demonstrative that would immediately refer to an object at hand or would *posit* a name with a view toward the named object—and nothing else—in some original act of nomination. Both Bertrand Russell, who conceives of the name as a simple deixis, and Saul Kripke, who sees it as the result of a "baptism," forget that deixis and baptizing are always already absorbed in an open system of differential relations, and this system erases the absolute singularity they propose as it inevitably joins each singularity to a codex of classifications.[19] For it is precisely this joining that opens denotation to connotation and introduces into the core of a proper name its transformation into a general term. Such a term no longer must refer to already constituted objects, generally recognized identities, or universal representations; it could also refer to fictions and thus to constructions that do not belong to any already familiar class of phenomena or forms of life. Whenever the name is translated—whether it is the name "name" or the name "Kafka"—the jackdaw cry of the nomads interrupts the ordered world of intentions and expropriates the proper name, which is supposed to name and preserve the most proper thing; it makes the proper into an inevitable and unassailable foreigner, and displaces the borders of every class whose function was to secure the singular and specific status of every term in the first place. The term de-termines itself. The proper name expropriates. By lending a particular identity, the proper name takes away whatever belongs to this identity and at the same time lays claim to—or takes charge of—this very identity. Every name is such a taking-charge; every *Name* (name) is a *Nahme* (taking). The name in Kafka's "Old Manuscript" again and again presents itself according to this close connection between *nomos, nomeus, nemein, onoma*—and therefore between dividing up into parts, nomadic herds-

19. Both Russell and Kripke's theories of naming deserve detailed presentation and discussion. They are cited here only in reference to their orthodox traits. Less limited and more useful is the psychoanalytic work on naming and the linguistic structure and function of the name—one example is Serge Leclaire, *Psychanalyser: Essai sur l'ordre de l'inconscient et la pratique de la lettre* (Paris: Seuil, 1968). See also the comprehensive and wide-ranging analyses of Jacques Derrida, particularly *Glas,* trans. John P. Leavey and Richard Rand (Lincoln, Neb.: University of Nebraska Press, 1986); *Signéponge/Signsponge,* trans. Richard Rand (New York: Columbia University Press, 1984). For a discussion of the name in Hegel, see my *"pleroma"*; in Heidegger and Adorno, see Alexander García Düttmann, *Das Gedächtnis des Denkens* (Frankfurt am Main: Suhrkamp, 1991); in Kierkegaard, see Peter Fenves, *"Chatter"* (Stanford: Stanford University Press, 1993).

men, taking, and naming: "One cannot speak with the nomads. . . . They hardly have a language of their own. . . . Whatever they need, they take [*nehmen*]. One cannot say that they do so by force. In the face of their attack, one simply stands aside and leaves them everything. From my provisions, too, they have taken [*genommen*] many good pieces" (N, 2: 359; CS, 416).

If names, nouns, and nomads offer a nominal and political order, if they give labels to possessions and lend substantial meaning, they do so only by taking away everything that has hitherto—or up until the incursion—been considered an established order, a possession, a life. And they even steal the "provisions" for the future as well. The semanticization of a name has traditionally aimed at overcoming its resistance to meaning and at integrating it into a homogeneous corpus of intentional discourse; but in Kafka this semanticization gives birth to monsters that flay the symbolic order of the "fatherland"—the order *tout court*—and tear apart the law, just as the nomads tear into the living flesh of an ox: "an ox . . . that the nomads were leaping on from all sides so as to tear pieces from its warm flesh with their teeth" (N, 2: 360; CS, 417).[20] The name is a field of slaughter. In its translation in the "Old Manuscript" story, the name "Kafka" does not represent a denomination of a singular substance or a marking of an indivisible and incommunicable individu-

---

20. It is not easy to understand the "ox" about which "An Old Manuscript" speaks. We cannot, however, ignore the fact that Kafka, who paid close attention to the composition of the collection of stories that appeared under the title *A Country Doctor* (a volume that includes "An Old Manuscript"), placed at the beginning of the volume, as a frontispiece, so to speak, the story entitled "The New Advocate." The name of this advocate, who was once "Alexander's battle charger," is Bucephalus: in English, "Ox-head." This advocate, Bucephalus, is presented as a reader of law books and especially of "our old books." By the placement of the text in which he appears, Bucephalus is thus presented as a reader of the very book in which he appears, *A Country Doctor*, and is indeed presented as a reader of himself, of his "own" book, his own "Buc": "So perhaps it is really best to absorb oneself in law books, as Bucephalus has done. Free, his flanks unhampered by the thighs of a rider, under a quiet lamp, far from the clamor of Alexander's battles, he reads and turns the pages of our old books *[die Blätter unserer alten Bücher]*" (E, 125; CS, 415), which include "An Old Manuscript," *Ein altes Blatt*. Bucephalus reads a law-*Buc* . . . and reads therefore *bous*, an ox. His reading, far from the slaughter of "battle," is no longer the tearing apart of an ox—or of the law—but is the reading, "under a quiet lamp," of this tearing apart. Yet it can be such a reading only if he tears himself open: in Bucephalus and his book. (Benjamin cites the same sentences from "The New Advocate" in his essay of 1934; see BK, 37; Il, 138–39.)

ality without at the same time introducing the transference of this singularity and the division of its markings. In every name a ruinous antonomasia is at work. Just as every language means too much, every name names too much, overnames, and thus de-names. Every name anonymizes. Regardless of whether it is a "civil" or a "literary" name, each one is a distortion that escapes fixity in any civil or literary order, in any order whatsoever. It is not, therefore, a demonstrative; it is a monster that shows neither the particular nor the universal but always shows precisely what was not intended and, *a limine,* shows nothing and corresponds to no possible sense. The name is a monster of language in which it is said that language does not properly speak: a *monstrum* without *monstratum.*

Lessing could still justify his choice of animals for a fable according to the doctrine of "intuitive cognition": each animal is supposed to allow the particular to be immediately transparent within a generally accessible language and a universal moral order. There could be conflicts—and indeed fatal ones—among the creatures who inhabited the fable, but such clashes would give rise to a rule or a piece of advice sanctioned by a universally practical and epistemological order. By contrast, in Kafka's animals—in the animals of his name—the gate of language opens up to a blind, if not altogether arbitrary power. Because names are distorted, there is no longer a language that could serve as a medium of a general order, and because there is no such order, this blind power dismembers semantic generality and moral universality. The protagonists of Kafka's parables are no longer the species-beings that inhabit Lessing's fables; they are *hapax legomena* of his proper name, entities that can enter into the generality of language—and that also means: come to themselves—only by abandoning their classificatory and socializing function. The name no longer appears as a nominal unit but as a virtually asemantic bundle of markings that further decomposes into particular letters and syllables. Kafka's name and Kafka's names are no longer ultimate, irreducible, linguistic unities but are, instead, effects of a movement that cannot condense at any substantial point. As effects of the translation and collision between at least two linguistic and social orders, they cannot be appeased or "sublated" into a higher, more encompassing order. Like all other linguistic elements, the name is subject to a dissemiosis in which language, as an agent of classification and social identification, proves to be a medium of dissociation and de-identification, a medium in which the individual falls away from all classes—and even from the class of the unclassifiable. Apostate of the name, it is suspended into a mere gesture of naming. Only by traversing, blocking, dispersing this transition into a generality, a rule, or a law does the name hold on to the possibility of another praxis of language and under-standing—a praxis no longer given over to the function of identification and no longer dedicated to the subsumption of singularity.

In his brief study of Proust's onomastics Roland Barthes ascribes to the Proustian name a "Cratylean character" and describes the proper name as "un signe toujours gros d'une épaisseur touffue de sens"—"a sign always pregnant with a dense thickness of meaning," hence a sign in whose material form the essence of the thing would reproduce itself.[21] However questionable this conclusion may be in the case of Proust, it clearly does not apply to Kafka, for the crossbreeding of meaning marked by his names and his texts constitutes a crossing-out of their meaning and of the very marks that are supposed to carry it. For this reason, Benjamin was able to use the same metaphor as Barthes when he says of Kafka's stories that they "are pregnant with a moral, but never give birth to it" (BK, 42).[22] Using Benjamin's other metaphor, one could say that Kafka's parables, by mobilizing his own name's resistance to meaning, form the "cloudy spot" that obstructs their significance and aborts any specification of the exemplary point toward which they strive. If literature is the communication or even the constitution of a meaning, as Barthes indicates, then Kafka's texts miss the meaning of literature. But they do not simply miss it as one can miss a target; missing is for them the medium of another success: "Once he was certain of eventual failure," Benjamin writes to Scholem, "everything succeeded for him on the way as in a dream" (BK, 88; Il, 145). Failure failed him—this is also

21. Roland Barthes, "Proust et les noms," in *Le Degré zéro de l'écriture, suivi de Nouveaux essais critiques* (Paris: Seuil, 1972), 125; cf. "Proust and Names," in *New Critical Essays,* trans. Richard Howard (New York: Hill and Wang, 1980), 59. Barthes speaks of the "Cratylean character of the name (and of the sign) in Proust" as a "motivated relation" between signifier and signified, "one copying the other and reproducing in its material form the signified essence of the thing" ("Proust et les noms," 133; "Proust and Names," 67).

22. Kafka saw his own life under the metaphor of delayed birth. In a particularly prominent diary entry (from January 24, 1922), he writes: "Delay before birth. If there is a transmigration of souls then I am not yet on the bottom rung. My life is a delay before birth" (T, 888; D, 2: 210).

what failure can mean. And only in this way did the transformation of literature into a mere gesture succeed for him, a success that is always only "on the way." It is a gesture that no longer bears out, no longer gives birth; it gives and brings nothing but this very bearing forth, carrying out, and bringing on. Just as only the messenger remains from the "imperial message," only the gesture that is supposed to carry the law remains of the law itself.

The reading of Kafka's texts is affected in turn. If the name resists its transposition and transference into transparent concepts, then the anamorphoses of the name offered in the stories cannot simply be translated back into the "proper" or "original" "meaning" of the name "Kafka"—not, in any case, without taking into account the distortion and blockage of translation and, therefore, not unless incomprehensibility and unaccountability have been accounted for. "Jackdaw," "bug," "ape," or "Gracchus" do not actually mean "Kafka" but are emblems in which the transformation of his name into another breaks down halfway, so to speak. These words—like *kavka*—"mean" "Kafka" only from afar; they mean something other than "Kafka," and they always do something other than "mean." Just as these names are doubled, any effort to understand them is a dual effort, and every reading of them is always a double reading: a reading in which they are understood as translations and another in which they are understood as failed translations; a reading in which something is understood and another in which it retreats from comprehensibility—a reading that is no less a hybrid creature than the creatures Kafka writes about in his stories. It will have to be a reading in the subjunctive, an interpretation that slips away from itself: an inter-pretation, interrupted.

Kafka's "Cares of a Family Man" concerns just such a reading of a name and just such an attempt to account for its incomprehensibility. The story first appeared in *The Country Doctor,* the same volume of 1919 that contains "An Old Manuscript," "Before the Law," "Jackals and Arabs," and "A Report to an Academy"—that is, all the stories in which Kafka's onomastics and its law of dispersal, the *nomos* of *onoma,* and the anomy of anonymity are under discussion. As a monologue from the perspective of a "house father" *(Hausvater),* "Cares of a Family Man" first takes issue with a word that, it soon becomes apparent, is a name: "Odradek." The family man's worries about this name prompt certain etymological speculations concerning its formation and meaning, speculations that ironically anticipate some of the hermeneutic efforts subsequently devoted to this text by professional critics. Interpretation—whether it be "spontaneous" or "critical"—appears in Kafka's story as a form of care, hence as a relation to something whose meaning can never be an object of rational calculation.[23] The report of the family man begins as follows:

> Some say the word Odradek comes from the Slavic, and on this basis they seek to ascertain the formation of the word. Others again say it comes from the German and is only influenced by the Slavic. The uncertainty of both interpretations, however, allows one to conclude with justice that neither hits the mark, especially since one cannot find a meaning of the word with either of them.   (E, 144; CS, 427–28)

The family man thus adopts the position of a hermeneut for whom a formal or genetic derivation of a word is unsound if it fails to provide certainty and meaning. Max Brod's interpretation of this word accordingly belongs among the uncertain ones, and the family man would presumably consider it unsound for this reason. In an essay on Kafka that was published during his lifetime, Brod maintains that in Odradek "an entire scale of Slavic words meaning 'deserter' or 'apostate' is evoked: deserter from the kind, *rod;* deserter from *Rat* [counsel], the divine decision about creation, *rada.*"[24] Another uncertain interpretation of "Odradek" is suggested by Wilhelm Emrich, who writes:

> In Czech . . . there is the verb *odraditi,* meaning to dissuade or deter someone from something. This word etymologically stems from the German (*rad = Rat:* advice, counsel, teaching). The subsequent Slavic

23. In the diary entry of August 27, 1916, Kafka makes this remark: "Cares, that is, impossibility of making calculations. . . . Start seeing what you are instead of calculating what you should become" (T, 803; D, 2: 164).

24. Max Brod, "Der Dichter Franz Kafka" in *Juden in der deutschen Literatur: Essays über zeitgenössische Schriftsteller,* ed. S. Krojanker (Berlin: Welt, 1922), 60. In "Ermorderung einer Puppe namens Franz Kafka," which is Brod's critique of Günther Anders's book on Kafka, he repeats a part of his commentary about Odradek: "(Slavic etymology: having defected from counsel [*Rat*]—*rada = Rat*)" (Max Brod, *Über Franz Kafka* [Frankfurt am Main: Fischer, 1974], 385). One may wonder what this interpretation of "Odradek" as the apostate from the *rod,* the "kind," says about the one who interprets it in this way, namely Brod.

"influence" is embodied in the the prefix *od,* meaning *ab,* "off," away from," and in the suffix *ek,* indicating a diminutive. . . . Odradek . . . would therefore mean a small creature that dissuades someone from something, or rather, a creature that always dissuades in general.[25]

And among the uncertain readings of "Odradek" which "the family man"—this economist of meaning who is always concerned with certainty in matters of interpretation—would have to refuse, there are also those that recall certain other connections in Czech: *rada* means not only *Rat* (counsel) but also series, row, direction, rank, and line; *rád* means series, order, class, rule as well as advisable, prudent; *rádek* means small series, row, and line.[26] Odradek would thus be the thing that carried on its mischief outside of the linguistic and literary order, outside of speech, not only severed from the order of discourse *(Rede)* but also outside of every genealogical and logical series: a *Verräter,* a "betrayer" of every party and every conceivable whole. If, then, "the family man" rejects the genetic interpretation of "Odradek" as uncertain and unsound for the sake of the genealogy and economy of meaning, he does so, as he says, "with justice," for "Odradek" means apostate—apostate from the continuum of generation, line, rights, discourse, *ratio,* logic. Any interpretation of "Odradek" that lays claim to certainty, conclusiveness, and meaning—and these are the hermeneutic principles of both "the family man" and the etymologists he criticizes—must miss

25. Wilhelm Emrich, *Franz Kafka* (Bonn: Athenäum, 1958), 92–93. Emrich thus skips over the connection that Brod showed between *rod, rada,* "species"—or (although Brod avoids the word) "race"—and *Rat* (counsel), *Ratschluß* (decision). Wilhelm von Humboldt suggests that this connection may rest on an etymological affinity: "One derives *Race* from *radix, radius* (as *linea propagionis*) and *ratio.* . . ." See Humboldt's 1830–1835 *Über die Verschiedenheit des menschlichen Sprachbaues,* in *Werke in fünf Bänden,* ed. A. Flitner and K. Giel (Berlin: Rütten & Loening, 1963), 3: 247; § 79. Humboldt's suggestion is confirmed by Leo Spitzer, "Race" in *Studies in Historical Semantics* (New York: Vanni, 1948), 147–69. Once again, this connection, which is supposed to be found not only in German or Slavic but also in Latin, consists in the affinity among *ratio, radius,* and *radix.* It also corresponds to the connection between *Rat* and *Rede* (speech, discourse) and *Geschlecht,* both in the sense of the (male) sexual member and the genealogical series or the "species."

26. I have consulted the following works in connection with Czech etymology and usage, *Cesko-Nemecky Slovník,* ed. Frantisek Stepan Kott (Prague: Kolar, 1878–1893), vol. 2; and *Slownjk Cesko—Némecky,* ed. Josefa Jungmanna (Prague, 1835–1839; rpt. Prague: Academia, 1989).

"Odradek" because "Odradek" means dissidence, dissense, and a defection from the order of meaning. "Odradek" thus "means" that it does not mean. His discourse says that he denies this discourse, that he runs off course, that he de-courses; his name says that he has no name.

Even the remark that "Odradek" can also be read as "Od-rade-K" and "Od-Rabe-K"—or "Od-raven-K"—and thus contains a double reference to the name "Kafka" misses this "word," a word moving outside of the order of the word, outside of natural, national, and rational languages. Not even the name "Kafka," its contraction into the letter K, and its transformations into "jackdaw" and "raven" could be a source of meaning, an origin of discourse, or a root of reference, for "Kafka" separates itself in "Odradek" precisely from its roots, its *radix*. Odradek is the "od-radix": the one "without roots"; in Czech, *odrodek*, the one without its own kind, the one who "steps out of the lineage" (*odroditi*—to degenerate, to be uprooted). "Odradek" is, in short, the one who belongs to no kind and is without counsel, the one with neither a discourse nor a name of his own.[27] *Odradek* is a word from at least two languages, *between* at least two languages, and thus a "word" belonging to neither— a hybrid word and a hybrid between a word and a non-word: "often he is silent for a long time, like the wood he seems to be." The word belongs as little to German literature—or any other national literature—as the words and sentences of *Finnegans Wake* belong to English literature. The

27. According to Kott's dictionary, *odraditi* means "to alienate," "to entice away"; *odranec* means "rags"; *odranka* means "a piece of paper," "patchwork of a text"; *odrati* means "tear off"; *odrbati* means "scrape off," "rub away"; *odrek* means "the renunciation"; *odrh* means "reproach," "reproof"; *odrod* and *odrodek* mean "the one without a kind." Kafka may have connected pieces from all of these with *Odradek*. They support the remark of Malcolm Pasley that Kafka would always speak of his writings as "patchwork," fragments soldered together, little bits of a story running around without a home. On the other hand, this hardly supports Palsey's conclusion that Odradek is a meta-fiction whose actual referent is "The Hunter Gracchus" (see Malcolm Pasley, "Drei literarische Mystifikationen Kafkas" in *Kafka-Symposium*, ed. Jürgen Born et al. [Berlin: Wagenbach, 1965], esp. 26–31). Kafka translates certain aspects of Odradek (*odranec, odrati*) into German and puts them in a description of the spool of thread: "it does in fact seem to have thread wound upon it; to be sure, it may only be broken-off, old bits of thread, knotted up with one another but also tangled in each other, of the most varied kinds and colors" (E, 144; CS, 428). "Kind" (*Art*) and "color" (*Farbe*)—and indeed Kafka's favorite, "but" (*aber*)—can be read in this text as mutations of *rat*, i.e., *rad*, and *Rabe*, "raven," his emblematic bird. According to the information in Jungmanna's dictionary, *Odráček* means "draconicus (monstrum)," and Benjamin, presumably unaware of this, speaks of Odradek as a monster.

name—"Odradek"—is an apostate from the order of language and from the order, the *rád* or *archē* in general; it is the an-archist in miniature. If one follows the interpretation that "the family man" and, in turn, every economist of meaning rejects as uncertain and senseless, then one can say of Odradek—and one can say this because he "says" it himself precisely when he remains "silent"—that he leaps out of the "row," out of the "murderers' row," a feat that only writing can do for Kafka: "The strange, mysterious, perhaps dangerous, perhaps redemptive consolation that there is in writing: it is a leap out of the murderers' row . . ." (T, 892; D, 2: 212).[28] Odradek is the leap from the series of rationality's normative positionings; he is nothing but ex-position.[29]

28. The continuation of this diary entry of January 27, 1922 again takes up the motif of the "series"—therefore of *rádek*—and links it to the calculability that was important for the determination of "care" (see footnote 23): "Deed-observation, in that a higher kind of observation is created, a higher, not a keener kind, and the higher it is and the less within reach of the 'row,' the more independent it becomes, the more obedient to its own laws of motion, the more incalculable, the more joyful, the more ascendant its course" (T, 892; D, 2: 212). The thought of independence in the sense of freedom, of absolution from guilt, and "perhaps" of redemption is thus connected, for Kafka, with the thought of aseriality—or singularity—and of incalculability. The discussion of a "perhaps" dangerous, "perhaps" redemptive consolation of writing does not indicate an empirical uncertainty that would somehow be resolved; it points toward an incalculability for which there is never certainty and which must announce itself in a "perhaps." There is only "perhaps" redemption, release, or emancipation, and in this "perhaps" it already shows itself—but only in such a way that "perhaps" is also dangerous; it is not emancipation, not redemption, and not a "leap out of murderers' row." One could say that "perhaps" is the syncategorical word for "Odradek"—or for writing as Kafka experienced it. Another diary entry of the same day concerns a name change, presumably the change of Kafka's name into that of the protagonist of *The Trial*. The entry reads: "Despite my having clearly written down my name at the hotel, despite their having correctly written to me twice already, they still have Joseph K. on the ledger. Should I enlighten them, or should I let them enlighten me?" (T, 893; D, 2: 213). No one will be able decide whether this is a report or a fantasy. What is decisive is the concession Kafka makes in his "or": "or *(oder)* should I let them enlighten me. . . ." With this *oder* he admits the possibility that a false or even fictive name could be the right one and that a name could also be no name at all. In the space of this *oder*—of disjunction, of the open decision—is where Odradek moves.

29. And their expropriation: Odradek does not *belong*, since he moves between at least two incompatible orders; he is owned by no one and has no property other than that of an aporetically determined "self." Every attempt to transpose "Odradek" into

The shape of "Odradek" shows what this name—or this off-name and odd-name, this anonym—says: "It appears at first to be a flat star-like spool of thread. . . . But it is not only a spool, for a small crossbar sticks out of the middle of the star, and another small rod fits into this one at a right angle. By means of this latter rod on one side and one of the points of the star on the other, the whole thing can stand upright as if on two legs." What first appears as a realistic description of a home-made homunculus can also be read as a description of a word-object, a rebus generated from the individual pieces of the word "Odradek" and the "translated" name Kafka. The words for "spool" and "bobbin" in Czech are *cívka* or *cevka,* which are similar enough orthographically and phonetically to the name Kafka to function as its paronyms. And "star" in combination with *rade-Rabe* from "Odradek" can be read as an allusion to the star Algorab in the constellation of the Raven and also to the hexagram, the signet-star that was used for the first time in Prague as the Magen David, the "official" sign of the Jewish community.[30] This hexa-

another word, another name or term—call him "Kafka," "kavka," "Kaka," *Unrat* (garbage), or *Un-Rat* (absurd advice)—must fail, because the outcome of such a translation would always be a term, a concept, or a name that, as such, belonged to a linguistic or symbolic order the value of which is disavowed by the other translation, the translation "outside of all orders." That "Odradek" does not belong to an order means, above all, that he belongs to no order of nameability or translatability. If, however, his name "Without-Name" is still always a name, then "name" means disaster of the name, for the name no longer names anything but is nothing other than an empty speaking that refers to emptiness—or to everything. It does nothing more than "perform" the naming itself and has lost every propositional or designative content. The name "Without-Name" thus introduces a true monster into the order of the name, into the order *kat exochen,* for it marks in this order sheer speaking, without object and without content, unlimited non-intentionality. And it marks this not only for the "exceptional case" of "Odradek" but— since the exception is always a name, the *Ausnahme* always a *Name*—for every name without exception. Every name is immediately an exception from the law of designative, classifying, and identifying acts of naming; every name is the expropriating appropriation of a mere speaking, a speaking that says nothing but "itself." Odradek, a "star-like spool of thread" that is not like anything, is the disaster of every language that still has something to say. But this disaster is also what makes it possible for something to be said in the first place.

30. See Gershom Scholem, "Das Davidschild" in *Judaica* (Frankfurt am Main: Suhrkamp, 1963), 75–118, esp. 107–108; "The Star of David: History of a Symbol," in *The Messianic Idea in Judaism,* trans. Michael Meyer (New York: Schocken, 1971), 257–81.

gram then lets one read in Kafka's name all the letters organized in a ring around an empty middle: the letters K A K A.[31] And the middle letter F appears in Odradek's figure as "small crossbar" that "sticks out of the middle of the star" to which a second rod is attached at a right angle, which, together with one of the other "rays" (or radii) makes it possible for the whole thing to stand. The crossbar and rod form the (incomplete) letter F, which completes the sequence of letters in the hexagram, spelling the name KAFKA. According to this reading, what the family man describes as Odradek's shape appears as the name "Kafka" distorted into a thing—a name in which pictographic, phonographic, and idiographic features are combined into an emblem that denies every "natural" or conventional affinity with the name or its meaning: "the whole thing appears meaningless, to be sure, but self-contained in its own way. In any case, nothing nearer the mark can be said, since Odradek is *extraordinarily* nimble and cannot be caught" (E, 145; CS, 428; emphasis added).

Inside and outside the house, inside and outside the lines and the series, inside and outside any order, any counsel, any language, wandering like a nomad around stairwells, hallways, and corridors, a creature of transition, the allegory of a metaphor, Odradek—both the word and

---

31. ✡ If one reads the Star-of-David hexagram as an ordering of letters, one will decipher a K in the left side of the triangle resting on the hexagram's basis line and traversed by two other lines. The two sides of this same triangle, together with the line of the second triangle that traverses them forms an A. A collapsing K can also be formed on the right side from the two traversing lines. And a corresponding, up-side-down A can be formed out of the triangle's sides. Since a V can be read in every combination of two sides, the complete text of the hexagram would be KAVKA, and the F composed out of the "crossbar" qualifies as the beginning letter of Franz. It goes without saying that the "family man" would reject such a reading. And "with justice," for it is not only uncertain but discovers no "meaning" for the word *Odradek,* since *kavka* or even "Kafka" does not mean anything but is only a name for a creature that can at best ask about meaning or expose itself to this question. But the same goes for the "family man": he, too, is not a final instance of certainty concerning meaning or even a demand for meaning. Regardless of whether one understands him as a merely literary figure or an emblem of hermeneutics, he has just the generic name of "Haus-*vater.*" And despite this name he is banished from the position he claims to occupy—the position of guaranteeing a symbolic order—by the negation of *rat* and thus by the negation of his *ater (rate, rat);* he is even exiled from his "own" house, from his "own" name. The deracination and profanation that grow in the vicinity of Odradek also affect the otherwise always "justified" principles of understanding.

the name, both the name and the thing—belongs neither to German nor to Slavic, neither to language nor to the world of mere things, neither to an order nor to its negation, and yet, in transition, as a transition, Odradek belongs to all these—without, however, forming a new order of his own:

> Of course you do not pose difficult questions to him but treat him like a child—already his tininess seduces you in this way. "So what's your name?" you asks him. "Odradek," he says. "And where do you live?" "Undetermined address," he says and laughs; but it is only a laugh as one can produce without lungs. It sounds like the rustling of fallen leaves. With this the conversation is usually at an end. Even these answers are not always obtained; often he stays mute for a long time, like the wood he seem to be.[32]

"Od-adresa," without address, between body and language, laughter and rustling, living organism and dead writing on "fallen leaves" or "fallen pages" *(Blätter),* always "undetermined"—and undetermined whether it is "without a destination" *(Bestimmung)* or "without a voice" *(Stimme)*—Odradek, an anarchist before all laws, wanders everywhere, even on the border between life and death. Ever concerned—and here again, cares and worries, according to Kafka, always concern the incalculable—"the family man" asks himself:

> Can he even die? Everything that dies once had some kind of goal, a kind of activity, and has ground itself down on this; that does not apply in the case of Odradek. Is he then supposed to roll down the stairs once

---

32. As something set off from every kind, belonging to nothing and no one, "Odradek" must be tiny, almost nothing. One example of the important motif of "tininess" in Kafka, thus of things that are almost nothing, is the 90th aphorism from Kafka's "Considerations of Sin, Suffering, Hope, and the True Way": "Two possibilities: making oneself infinitely small or being so. The second is perfection, that is to say, inactivity, the first is beginning, that is to say, action" (N, 2: 78; *The Blue Octavo Notebooks,* ed. Max Brod, trans. Ernst Kaiser and Eithne Wilkins [Cambridge, Mass.: Exact Change, 1991], 95). Odradek, "meaningless, to be sure, but self-contained in its own way," would have to be regarded as perfection. But a diary entry of January 20, 1922 notes how a "trifle" brings torment as much as life: "Seized by the collar, dragged through the streets, pushed through the door. In abstract, this is how it is; in reality, there are counterforces, only a trifle less violent than the forces they oppose—the trifle that keeps life and torment alive. I the victim of both" (T, 882; D, 2: 205).

more at the feet of my children and children's children, with threads trailing behind? He clearly does no harm to anyone; but the idea that he is supposed to outlive me is, for me, almost painful. (E, 145; CS, 429)

As name and writing, as literary name and the name taken literally, Odradek—Kafka's signature—withdraws from every order, including the one between life and death. Whatever has never completely belonged to the system of significance, purposiveness, and meaning cannot take up residence in a logical or teleological construction and has never "actually" lived: it was always already more or less than living and has always already "survived" without being able to live or to die. It has outlived itself and, along with the self, outlived all forms of self-identity. "Odradek"—outside of the genealogical and logical series, a bastard offspring of speech and silence—is Kafka's ex-proper name for "the survivor proper"—Kafka's name for himself (T, 867; D, 193)—who, like the hunter Gracchus, is dead and yet unable to die, who only "lives in a certain sense" (E, 272; CS, 228).[33] For such "survival" or such "outliving" there is no future that could be dictated solely by the laws of genealogy or of meaningful speech. The "name" that outlives in this way contains no program for the future; it withdraws—or clouds over—its law. This "name" and, with it, the language it affects, the languages of Kafka's text, and the languages of its readers have no determinate address, no destination, no definition, no language except "Odradek" and "od-adresa." Since this language is without any address, goal, or site and does not even reside within itself, it presents itself as a speaking outside of the discursive, genealogical, and logical consistency of speaking, as a

33. One could take the word *kollern* (to roll) in the formulation "roll down the stairs . . . with threads trailing behind" for a peculiar vulgarism. Yet the Czech word for *kollern*, which does not mean *rollen* (to roll) but *kaudern* (turkey calling), is *kâvdrati*, and the word for "gobble" in Czech is *puran kavdra*. Since *kavka* not only means "jackdaw" but also "crudely drawn character," "scribbling," "making crow's feet," there is a suggestion that it is Kafka's distorted name, his mutilated signature, his "scribblings" that roll down the stairs with threads trailing behind. They not only "outlive" the "family man" but are absolved from him, "translated" into "another" language—into "the same one"—and from the very beginning they also "outlive" the author who publishes them under the name Franz Kafka.

transition of language into that which has no language and thus as a speaking of mere language—as its *gesture*.

Odradek, Benjamin notes, is the form that things assume in forgetfulness. One can also say—and argue on better philological grounds—that "Odradek" is the name that withdraws from the law of meaning, escapes familiarized and teleological bounded history, and defects from advice, counsel, doctrine, and obligatory morals. It promises its universalization and translation into the language of a transparent fable by taking back its promise in the very same gesture; it is a hybrid whose two halves are locked in a struggle with each other. Benjamin noticed this double trait in Kafka's stories and in the names of their characters without, however, relating it to Kafka's experience of his proper name or showing it in his texts. One of Benjamin's earliest notes on Kafka says: "A crack goes through the names of his characters; they belong in part to the guilty world and in part to the redeemed one" (BK, 130). This crack is also the distance separating the tradition in Kafka's work from the experience of modernity: "Kafka's work is an ellipse whose widely separated foci are determined by mystical experience (which is the experience of tradition, above all) on the one hand, and by the experience of the modern big-city dweller, on the other" (BK, 84; Il, 141).[34] This dual experience, which imparts to Kafka's text the form of an ellipse, is doubly aporetic: an

34. This is what Benjamin wrote in his letter to Scholem of June 12, 1938. In his edition of the correspondence Scholem notes: "W. B. appropriated this identification [of mystical experience and the experience of tradition] from the technical term 'Kabbalah,' which literally means 'tradition,' as Benjamin knew" (Walter Benjamin and Gershom Scholem, *Briefwechsel,* ed. G. Scholem [Frankfurt am Main: Suhrkamp, 1980] 269, 273; Cor, 223).— By characterizing Kafka's work as an ellipse, Benjamin takes up a concept of romantic literary criticism and linguistic philosophy, which represented a critical transformation of the Fichtean self-reflection, and gives it a certain historical-philosophical twist. Friedrich Schlegel uses the example of *Don Quixote* to comment upon his theory of the "two centers" of romantic poetry and his theory of their elliptical and hyperbolic forms: "The central character in the second part of *Don Quixote* is the first part. Such is the thorough-going reflection of the work on itself" (*Literary Notebooks,* nr. 1727; on Schlegel's theory, see "Position Exposed" in this volume). Of all of Kafka's writings on Don Quixote, the following comes closest to Schlegel's note and at the same time marks the distance separating his "ellipse" from that of the romantics: "One of the most important deeds of Don Quixote, more imposing than the fight with the windmill, is suicide. The dead Don

experience of an unavailable past and of a future that does not yet exist. However real it may be, the ellipse in Kafka's work is an impossible ellipse, for neither of its two foci is given; neither can be reached, and only the imaginary connection of the two—and thus of two impossible experiences—can be experienced. Benjamin indicates this logic of double aporia in comments that concern the obfuscation not only of the boundaries between genres but of the very movement of language: "Kafka's work thus stands under the sign of the opposition between the mystic and the parabolist, the language of gesture and the language of instruction, the visionary and the sage. An opposition that is a crossing [*Verschränkung*]" (BK, 169). This opposition is a "crossing" because every one of its polar determinations encroaches on every other one and literally sets up a border *(Schranke)* for the others, making them inaccessible, opaque, and incomplete, cutting off each one from every other and indeed from itself. Not only are the names of his characters subordinated to the logic of (border) crossing that rules over Kafka's language; since his own name also belongs there, it too submits to this logic of *Verschränkung*. All these names are traversed by a crack that splits them up, makes them incomplete and incomprehensible. What Benjamin says about the parable is then equally true of them: in the name—and even in the name "name"—there is a "cloudy spot" that makes them opaque and annuls their naming or marking function. Just as "gestural language" sets itself down as a border in the "language of instruction" and thus defers the arrival of doctrine, something that remains without a name sets itself into the name as a border. This (border) crossing of the name with the unnamable is never so apparent as in "Odradek." His name means that it does not mean; that it has no language other than the one that says "without language"; that his name is "Without Name." His "name"—and Kafka's too—is "distorted": distorted, *entstellt,* not only in the sense that it is disturbed and disfigured but in the sense that it is dis-placed, is without a place, and is in this way, strictly speaking, incomprehensible, readable only in its unreadability. What is exposed in the name "Without Name" is the law-without-law, the self-crossing of

Quixote wants to kill the dead Don Quixote; in order to kill, however, he needs a spot that is still alive. His search for this with his sword is just as ceaseless as it is useless. Thus occupied, the two dead ones, as an indissoluble somersault, roll through all time" (N, 2: 38–39).

the law, and the aporia structuring Kafka's text. In this "name," one could also say, the name falls into forgetfulness.

This self-crossing—or self-hindering, deferral, crack, distortion—carries in Benjamin's essays on Kafka a far-reaching name. He speaks of it as *gestus* or gesture, pointing, first of all, to certain gestures of which Kafka's writings are the inventory: carrying a leaf in the palm of the hand, a head sunk down, the readiness of a waiter, even the shrill tone of a doorbell that resonates beyond the street and into the sky. But these terms also point toward what Kafka found graspable and yet incomprehensible, what was present before his eyes and yet inconceivable—everything, therefore, that was aporetic about his world. Because Benjamin knows that "Kafka's entire work presents a codex of gestures that from the outset had absolutely no secure, symbolic meaning for the author" (BK, 18; Il, 120), he could write: "Kafka could grasp some things always only in gesture. And this gesture, which he did not understand, forms the cloudy spot of the parables. From this gesture arises Kafka's fiction" (BK, 27; Il, 129). The spot of incomprehensibility and the "distortion of existence" (BK, 131), the spot without spot—which is u-topia as abandonment—this placeless place from which, according to Benjamin, Kafka's fiction originates is thus occupied by gesture. But gesture here has neither a secure symbolic nor a purely mimetic meaning (BK, 171); rather, it is the hesitation before every meaning and every doctrine, and is nothing but such hesitation. Benjamin aligns it with Haggadah, those "stories and anecdotes of rabbinical writing that serve to clarify and confirm doctrine, namely Halachah." Gesture bears a resemblance to this form of compliant and simultaneously refused presentation—a form of presentation that "continually interrupts itself [and] lingers on, always in the hope and with the fear that the Halachic order and form, the doctrine, could occur to it in passing" (BK, 42). It is peculiar to the gesture in Kafka's stories that it does not allow this order—this ordering and this imperative—to occur, that it clouds over any relevant clarification and frustrates the very interpretation it initiates. It carries something without carrying it out. In this sense, it is an irreducible remainder, a leftover not only of doctrine and of law but of language as such: "The inclination in a certain sense to drain the meaning out of the incidents is very remarkable in Kafka. . . . Nothing is left here but gesture, which is absolved of all affective connections" (BK, 127). Gesture is what remains of language after meaning is withdrawn from it, and it is gesture that withdraws from meaning. The rest of language—and so language itself, language irreducible to meaning—is gesture. Just as the horse Bucephalus, whose function was to carry Alexander, remains after the warrior is gone, just as the reader is left over from the text, gesture is left over from language, from its law. This gesture carries the mere possibility of language and at the same time holds back its actual arrival.

However irreducible and resistant to meaning it may be, gesture thus remains ambiguous. It proclaims something whose arrival is prevented by this very announcement. It is not only a remainder but a threshold: it appears before the decision between meaning and meaninglessness or between oppression and redemption. "There is no gesture in Kafka," Benjamin writes, "that would not be struck by this ambiguity before the decision" (BK, 170). This ambiguity leads to the impossibility of deciding whether Kafka was a visionary or a sage, and one can also read this ambiguity in "Odradek," who does and does not bear a name. Yet in an extremely odd sentence Benjamin nevertheless insists that gesture remains "the decisive thing": "Kafka, like El Greco, tears open [*reißt auf*] the sky behind every gesture, but as with El Greco, who was the patron saint of Expressionism, gesture remains the decisive thing, the middle of the event" (BK, 19; Il, 121). Gesture is decisive insofar as it "tears open" the heavens as a "prospect" of the world-theater. But the verb "to tear open" *(aufreißen)* has at least two meanings here: on the one hand, to draft a drawing and thus to open up a prospect of a future and, on the other, to tear this drawing or prospect apart—and to do both at the same time. *Aufreißen* means to project a prospect and to rip it simultaneously apart. Gesture is "the decisive thing" since it is this twofold *Aufriß:* a ripping up and a tearing open, a drafting and a laying-out. And gesture is "the decisive thing" because it is the *Aufriß eines Aufrisses,* the tearing open of a draft, the laying out of a tearing open, the plan for a ripping apart and the ripping up of a plan. The draft—the gesture—draws itself, tears itself open; the decision taken in the gesture separates it from itself. In this internal doubling and self-crossing of decision, gesture is a pure performance of self-departure; it is an unconditional parting and imparting, dividing and communicating in itself—unconditional because it conditions parting and imparting, dividing and communicating in the first place. Gesture is not a decision in the sense that it decides *about* or *for* something, nor in the sense that it makes a judgment, establishes a law, or provides an example. For it would then belong to the domain of predicative language; it would refer to something other than mere speaking and would already thus presuppose what can be disclosed only in it. Thought as *Aufriß*—as a drafting and a ripping open—decision and thus gesture is, above all, the projection and disclosure of the event to which it could refer; it is, for this reason, a pure decision, a decision that decides nothing and thereby tears into its intentional content, into the meaning that it and its concept may come to have.

The decision taken by the gesture expresses nothing and indicates nothing, and if a mimetic or a semiotic moment still clings to it, this is not because it imitates or shows something other than itself but because it shows the showing itself and because it decides the decision itself. Showing *itself,* deciding *itself,* the gesture of decision—and every gesture is a decision—is an emancipation from all presuppositions, even from the presupposition of the "itself." For "itself" does not here refer as a reflexive to a being who would be given before the gesture; it is itself the decision. Benjamin can thus write of the actors in the Natural Theater of Oklahoma: "they may play *themselves;* they are freed from imitation" (BK, 171). And after a similar formulation he continues: "It is excluded from the realm of possibility that they could *be* in an emergency what they play" (BK, 22–23; Il, 124–25). Gesture is the decisive thing because in it nothing happens but itself; the distinction between playing and being is, for gesture, just as pointless as the distinction between meaning and the object meant or between annunciation and deferral. Because it is merely itself and merely plays itself, the decisive thing—the difference—is the point of indifference for all oppositions that could arise from it. Gesture is the difference. But it is not a difference between pregiven objects or acts; it is the original scission—Benjamin calls it "the middle of the event"—that first releases distinct acts and objects. Yet this also means that gesture does not belong to the repertoire of acts or things. Nothing is done in gesture; no object, no affect, and no meaning is represented in it. Free from all semiotic and psychic contents, free from intention above all, the decision taking place in gesture concerns itself alone. Gesture is the difference that, before anything could be differentiated, de-fers *itself:* it carries itself, carries itself asunder, and occurs in this carrying. It is the *gerere,* the "ference," that by merely carrying *itself* asunder is always something other than itself. As difference, as "the decisive thing," and as "the middle of the event," gesture is the place—the displaced place—in which the aporias of proclamation and prevention, of projection and interruption, of *Aufriß* as draft and *Aufriß* as tearing open meet; it is the place where the different, the ambiguous, and the undecidable carry themselves to themselves—to difference. In this "decisive thing," in gesture, only gesture itself is carried. The hope that "the burden [would be] removed from the back" (BK, 38; Il, 140) thus goes along with every gesture, especially with the one Benjamin emphasizes at the end of his essay, the gesture of a bent and burdened back, a hunchback.[35]

The decision—as a pure caesura in the language of predication, as an exposure of that which says without saying something—lies in what Benjamin calls gesture. And it thus lies in the "crack" that traverses Kafka's name. It occurs as a saying that says nothing but itself and must therefore say *of* itself that it says nothing. And precisely this—"the middle of the event" in which the event is interrupted, the middle of language in which it says nothing—happens in "Odradek." He is pure gesture, for his name, the threshold between language and muteness, says that he is without a name and that he is thus the difference of the name from itself. "Odradek" is the Haggadah of the name, the gesture—or the cloud—in the name; having nothing to do with the name understood as a sign of a representational unity, "Odradek" is precisely a pure name; it is the name as sheer decision, a decision that tears itself open. But the name of the name, the name without name, is a name and no name, a name and a nothingness—hence, perhaps, the "tininess" of Odradek. The theme of one of Kafka's most important reflections, which is cited in Benjamin's essay, is precisely this impossible and yet very real bond between something and nothing in literature—and not only in Kafka's. The reflection comes from Kafka's collection of aphorisms called "He." Benjamin's comment follows:

This is what Kafka was after, with his desire to hammer a table together with painstaking craftsmanship and at the same time to do nothing,

35. Benjamin's interpretation of gesture as the "decisive thing" and as the "middle of the event" resumes a train of thought he first formulated in his theory of the caesura and in the theory of choice and decision he elaborated in his essay on Goethe's *Elective Affinities*. His essay "Two Poems of Friedrich Hölderlin" presents the caesura as the "middle of the poem" and "unapproachable middle of all relations" (*Gesammelte Schriften*, 2: 124–25).

and indeed not to do nothing in such a way that someone could say "Hammering is nothing to him," but "To him, hammering is a real hammering and at the same time also nothing." In this way hammering would have become even bolder, even more resolute, even more real, and, if you like, more insane. (BK, 35; Il, 136–37)

The reality of hammering, hammering itself, owes its existence to a bond with nothingness. Whatever makes hammering into a "resolute gesture," to use Benjamin's phrase, lies in nothingness, and what makes gesture into "the decisive thing" lies in nothingness as well. Gesture is non-action in action, exile of the deed from the deed, ex-action; it is a nothing that is the basis for anything. In speaking—and not only in the speaking of literature—gesture is the nothingness of speaking and the moment in speaking that first makes it possible for something to be spoken *about*. In naming—whether in the name "Odradek" or in the name "name"—gesture is the nothing of naming that makes it possible for it to name something and still to participate in the language from which it withdraws.

This nothingness of language and of the name, their gesture, becomes clearest in reading. Studying the law—not practicing it, not legislating, not executing it—forms, for Benjamin, "the gate of justice," the gate that leads out of the mythical realm of judicial legalisms (BK, 37; Il, 139). Studying the law "stands very close to that which alone makes it possible for something to be useful. . . ." (BK, 35; Il, 136).[36] This nothingness is

36. This sentence of Benjamin's is an unacknowledged—and unrecognized by his editors—paraphrase of a sentence from Franz Rosenzweig's *Star of Redemption*. Along with the writings of Bachofen, Rosenzweig's work is the most important point of reference for Benjamin's essay on Kafka, and without it, his theory of prehistory, myth, and redemption is scarcely comprehensible. The Rosenzweig passage is as follows: "The Tao is this: effecting without acting; only deedlessly; this god who keeps 'quiet as a mouse' so that the world can move around it. It is entirely without essence; nothing exists in it. . . . Rather, it itself exists in everything . . . as the hub exists in the spokes, as the window exists in the wall, as the cavity exists in the vessel: *it is that which, by being 'nothing,' makes a something 'useful'*; it is the unmoved mover of the movable. It is the non-deed as the original ground of the deed" (Franz Rosenzweig, *Der Stern der Erlösung* [Frankfurt am Main; Suhrkamp, 1988], 40; cf. *The Star of Redemption,* trans. William Hallo [South Bend, Ind.: University of Notre Dame Press, 1985], 37; emphasis added). This citation from Rosenzweig is reproduced correctly in one of Benjamin's early notes (BK, 123). There is good reason to suppose that Rosenzweig's work and, in particular, the conception of "nothingness as the origin of something" he developed in conjunction with

a nothingness of praxis, a nothingness of the action that, as an action, is already subordinate to the law of identity and thus to the positive power of everything factual.[37] The nothingness exposed by gesture, by the study of law no longer practiced and no longer applied, by action no longer undertaken, suspends its validity and opens it—it is a gate, a door—to something other than itself. Gesture in language makes it useful for the future of language—even when, and precisely when, this future never finds it of any use. Kafka's names and Kafka's stories—and with them at least a part of modern literature, modernism, and modernity—tear open with a single gesture the nothingness in naming and in acting, the nothingness through which, as name, language, and action they become at once "more resolute," more *entschlossen,* more open; once they are in this way exposed to the ground torn open, they likewise become non-name, non-language, and non-action and so "more insane." They forge, in short, an escape route out of the order of legislative, judicial, and executive discourse; they make an opening to an

---

Hermann Cohen's theory of infinitesimals looms in the background of Benjamin and Scholem's controversy over "the nothing of revelation" in relation to Kafka (cf. *Stern der Erlösung,* 23; *Star of Redemption,* 21). Benjamin also has recourse to certain thoughts developed in the *Star of Redemption* when he reflects on the nature of gesture. "Nothing teaches us more clearly that the word is unredeemed than the multiplicity of languages. . . . It is for this reason that the supreme component of the liturgy is not the communal word but the communal gesture. Liturgy releases gesture from the fetter of awkward servitude to speech and makes it into something more than speech" (*Stern der Erlösung,* 328–29; *Star of Redemption,* 295–96). And in another context: "[T]he art of poetry . . . would have to have become gesture. For only gesture is beyond deed and discourse—not, of course, the gesture that wants to say something . . . but the gesture that brings humans to the completion of their Being, to their human-ness, and thus to their humanity" (*Stern der Erlösung,* 413; *Star of Redemption,* 371–72). The explosion of space and the erasure of time, which Rosenzweig assigns to liturgical gesture and to poetry (*Stern der Erlösung,* 414; *Star of Redemption,* 372), finds its counterpart in Benjamin's characterization of the gestures to which Kafka's figures were inclined: they are, he writes, "too sweeping for the accustomed environment and break into a more spacious one" (BK, 18; Il, 121).

37. In his very fine essay "Notes on Gesture," Giorgio Agamben has pointed out something similar—something like the *epochē* of praxis in gesture—with reference not only to Benjamin but also to Averroes and Albertus Magnus' commentaries on Aristotle. See Giorgio Agamben, "Noten zur Geste," in *Postmoderne und Politik,* ed. J. Georg-Lauer (Tübingen: edition diskord, 1992), 97–107; abridged as "Notes on Gesture" in *Infancy & Experience,* trans. Liz Heron (New York: Verso, 1993), 135–40.

always other, always futurial language, and at the same time prevent this future from ever becoming an order in its own right. Already now, disburdened, they carry nothing but themselves.

If one interprets modernity as the process of a universalized and accelerated rationalization—and in many ways there is good reason to interpret it so—then Odradek is what "outlives" this process, not as an irrationality but perhaps as "odrationality." He thus stands for another dimension in the literature of modernity—for a dimension that does not offer laws, morals, or universalizable images and indeed withdraws from any role assigned to it under their grasp and their concepts. Kafka's modernity has no proper name. It deserts naming and names this desertion with the misnomer "Odradek." The cloud in the parable in which the protest of singularity against its subsumption under the myth of the whole, including the myth of an entire epoch, is articulated, and thus the gesture in every one of Kafka's stories, is always again Kafka's distorted signature; it is "Odradek," the strange little thing that "outlives" every kind, every *rad,* every mode, every "modernity," and every "modernism"—and "outlives" them by suspending the principle of subjection to principles and forms, to names and their rationality. It is the dissimulated singularity that sabotages the industrial production of the future so as to hold open the possibility of another one.

If rhetoric is the organon of linguistic forms, then Kafka's figures and prose forms deviate from their canon: they withdraw from the system of rhetoric in the same way Odradek does—retreating from rhetoric into, one might say, "odrhetoric." "Odrhetoric" would be Kafka's law of literature: the law of a singularity through which no universal law shines, a law that is exemplary only in its nonexemplarity. It is a different law, a law of indeterminable otherness and of an essentially inapproachable openness of the law. In this law outside of law, in this exile from law, *nomos,* and name, in this parable that diverges from the parable—in this paraparable—it is no longer possible to dwell poetically, to reconstruct rationally, to reproduce along genealogical lines, or even to name without the name containing within itself the motto "without destination," "without address," "without name." It is Odradek when it writes. Whatever presents itself under his name is for this very reason displaced. Kafka's prose registers the pain of this displacement to which no rhetorical figure can correspond, and registers it as the pain of the finitude of the law, of language, and of the calculations of rhetoric. "Almost painful," says the family man. In this bated gesture, which shamefully takes distance from pain, the law is, almost, de-posed.

This is the experience Kafka undertook with himself, with his writing, and with his name: belonging to no order and no epoch—and yet always belonging to at least two at the same time—between at least two languages, at least two cultures, as a Jewish intellectual in nationalist Prague, living as a "useless" writer in a family of merchants, capable only of writing and yet always unable to write, bearing a name that in one place meant something—although not anything good—and in another was hardly more than an empty mark. This aporetic position, this ex-position of language and experience—whether historical, social, or political—no longer allows for a linear, unbroken presentation. This ex-position presents itself as a repetition of the prohibition against images. Benjamin correctly remarked: "No writer followed 'Thou shalt make no graven images' with greater exactitude" (BK, 28; Il, 129). But even Kafka's repetition of the Mosaic commandment, even his citation of the law, was doomed to fail. One of his notes captures the fragmentation of the citation in a micro-parable. It reads: "Thou shalt—no image . . ." (N, 2: 360). The prohibition that the sentence is about to express intervenes into this very sentence and makes it into the fragment of a language that would correspond to the prohibition. By adhering to the prohibition, however, the only sentence in which it could present itself as law is interrupted. This sentence no longer speaks, or does not yet speak, as a law that language—purely linguistic, imageless language— installs in the enactment of an original act. The sentence no longer speaks—or does not yet speak—as a performative speech act that inaugurates a convention of speaking or speech in general. It speaks, rather, as the opening up of a mere possibility of such speaking, as an adformative; it speaks as a making-possible that cannot find its fulfillment in any form, as a making-possible and a making-impossible, as an action and at the same time a non-action: as an afformative of language. What remains is not a sentence announcing the law of language but the ellipse—the gesture—that opens up this law and lets it remain open.

The Second of Inversion

Movements of a Figure through Celan's Poetry

Under the sign of the semantic function to which language, according to the classical doctrine formulated by Aristotle, should reduce itself in the course of its only veritative mode of expression—predicative assertions—language appears caught in an aporia that admits only an aporetic solution: it is explained away as an empty gesture that must evanesce before the power of the factual, or it is accorded all the weight of the only ascertained reality, whose types are stamped onto the entire region of objectivity and constitute objectivity itself. In the first case, language is destined to disappear before the presence of the world of things and their movements; it is nothing in itself, a mere instrument, in the crudest instance an instrument of deixis, a means of reference that should disappear whenever the things themselves appear. In the other case, language is exalted into the schema of all reality, and so it encounters in reality only itself; it employs objects to confirm the efficacy of its figures and runs through a virtually endless process of repeating, without resistance, its preestablished types. In one case, language makes statements about reality to which it cedes all rights in order, as the shadow-like image of reality, to recede before its light, whereas in the other case reality only retains the rights of language in whose image it was created. The infinitude of the real in one case confronts the infinitude of language in the other. In both cases, language and its inherent epistemological forms are denied the power to be a reality with its own rights and its own structure, a reality that could not be exhausted by any relationship of analogy, of representation, or of typifying other realities. Both interpretations of language, which essentially define it according to its semantic and referential functions, must therefore end up in a paradox: once language reaches its ends and thus the site of its definition, it no longer means anything and no longer refers to anything; on this destined site, it would make room for whatever has been meant by language, or it would only be purely itself in whatever has been modeled after its image. At the end of every semantic theory of language and its truth stands the aporetic verdict: language does not speak; it has nothing to say, only itself or its disappearance. But the basis of this aporia lies in the assumption that reality only shows itself as objectivity, that this objectivity fulfills itself in its being present and that, under the conditions of its absence—an absence projected according to the image of objectivity fulfilling itself in presence—language, as either substrate or prototype, intercedes in order to preserve or reserve the possibility of objectivity. According to this idea of a transcendental semantics, which organizes not only classical philosophical systems but also the most unreflective linguistic theories, language would be the proper place of origin for reality interpreted as objectivity.

But the very notion that reality takes its lead from language—and not the other way around—will be construed by the naive, normal, and natural understanding of the world as a malicious presumption. Once this notion is accepted, the world appears upside-down, perverted, stood on its head. In the texts of Kant and Hegel, as the culmination of the theories of absolute subjectivity, the metaphors of turning, of overturning and transforming, of perverting, reverting, and returning make their entrance together with those of reflection and speculation, and they do so with unprecedented density. Joining the Platonic figure of *epistrophē* and the evangelic one of *metanoia,* they gain an obligatory power that was to become mythical for subsequent philosophical and literary texts.

The Kantian "revolution in the mode of thought" attempts experimentally, as it were, and with an explicit appeal to the Copernican turn, to make a plausible argument that if there is *a priori* knowledge, objects must first be stamped by the forms under which they are known. In such knowledge the subject, as a form of representation, gives its objects the rule according to which they can be objects of knowledge in the first place. The inversion of the traditional mode of thinking that Kant sets into motion thus secures access to reality, since it assigns to knowledge the form of objectivity and thereby brings the entirety of the given under the epistemic premises of subjectivity. The *ordo inversus* induced by Kant's critique—an induction in which this critique is by no means exhausted—is the figure of totalized subjectivity. On this point Hegel appointed himself the executor of the legacy of Kant's critique, for he saw not only the world of nature but equally that of history placed under the principle of representing, conceptualizing, and thinking spirit. The *locus classicus* of his corresponding formulations refers once again to a revolution, the one that took place in France, and imparts to this revolution a significant turn of speech whose fragility deserves a detailed analysis. It is to be found in his *Lectures on the Philosophy of History:* "Never since the sun stood under the firmament and planets revolved around it had it come to pass that human beings stood on their heads, that is, in their thoughts, and built reality according to such thoughts. . . . This was indeed a glorious dawn."[1] If human beings and their reality stand on their heads when the light of reason first arises, it is because their life and history attain a stable foundation for their significance only in the head. Only in thought do reality and the historical process come into their own, and only by standing on its head does reality reach its first true stance, the stance of truth in which nothing alien opposes it any longer; on the contrary, the other shows itself to be the other of its *self*. In taking its stand on the principle of subjectivity, historical reality stands up and stands upright: it thereby shows that the objectivity of finite spirit is already inhabited by the infinite self-relation of subjective spirit.

But Hegel's speculative inversion does not simply bring the objective reality of history to itself and thus to reason. Inversion Hegelian style performs its greatest feat—and does so against the deepest intentions of the Kantian inversion—in the arena of nonreality, in death as the abstract negation of entities as such. Spirit shows itself as substantial subjectivity by turning its own nonreality—its dismemberment and absence—into

---

1. G. W. F. Hegel, *Werke in zwanzig Bänden,* eds. Eva Moldenhauer und Karl Markus Michel (Frankfurt am Main: Suhrkamp, 1970), 12: 529; cf. *The Philosophy of History,* trans. J. Sibree (New York: Dover, 1956), 447. All translations, including those of Celan, were prepared for this volume.

being. In the preface to the *Phenomenology of Spirit* Hegel writes: "Death, if that is the name we want to give this unreality, is the most dreadful thing of all, and the greatest strength is required to hold fast what is dead." Spirit is the power in which absolute dismemberment finds itself again, "only when it looks the negative in the face and dwells there. Such dwelling is the magical force that turns the negative into Being.—It is the same as what was earlier called the subject, . . . the true substance . . . that does not have mediation outside itself but rather is this mediation itself."[2] Death, "if that is the name we want to give to this unreality," can only be held fast, looked in the face, and turned into Being if it has been transformed from death into something dead, from an unreality— by prosopopoeia—into a face, from the negation of the I into the pure energy of the I. It can only be turned into being after it has been assigned a determinate place in the circle of speculative inversion. The point is not to censure a *petitio principii*—but this petition, this *petitio principii,* is perhaps *the* problem of philosophy. The point is, rather, to make clear that the life of spirit can turn the unreality of death into objective reality only because its absence comes into view as the hollow mold of its own shape, as a death in the image of life, as a negative according to the model of "absolute position or positing," as Kant defines Being. Meaning can only be affixed to a death for which subjectivity has lent an aspect, a countenance, a face according to the pattern of its own shape. The process of prosopopoeia—the lending of a face or a mask—and thus the roots of possible meaningfulness in finite life became a problem for Kant—most clearly so in the paragraphs of the third *Critique* devoted to the Analytic of the Sublime—but turned into a problem for Hegel only in those places that he himself considered peripheral to the system. The dominant figure of Hegelian philosophy—negation of the negation, speculative inversion—holds sway over a domain already sheltered by the principle of subjectivity against the abyssal shapelessness of death, "if that is the name we want to give this unreality." Only because nothingness, as Hegel writes in his critique of skepticism, always figures as the "nothingness of something" and thus already assumes the figure of

2. G. W. F. Hegel, *Phänomenologie des Geistes,* ed. J. Hoffmeister (Berlin: Ullstein, 1973), 29; preface, § 32. Cf. *Phenomenology of Spirit,* trans. A. V. Miller (Oxford: Oxford University Press, 1977), 19.

objective being, can the figure of inversion be brought to bear against it, and only then can it—or "nothingness"—be returned to Being. Turning in this way, the Being of the subject is mediated with its nonbeing and is itself nothing other than the movement of this mediation with its other as itself. By virtue of the mediating and converting character of the substantial subject, a meaning attaches itself to each linguistic sign it posits—we indeed "want to name" this unreality (even after a certain pause) death—and this meaning remains indispensable for the interaction between the sign, what it signifies, and the communicative interaction between different speakers, because the very thing signified is already drawn into the shape of subjectivity as a moment of mediation. To the degree that everything falling under the domain of language becomes, through the movement of mediation, a means of semiocentric inversion, everything also—or at least this is Hegel's intention—steps into the middle of its meaning: it no longer means anything but is itself the process of meaningfulness; it not only refers to something absent but is itself the process of its presentation, pure energy of subjectivity as it presents and thereby objectifies itself.

One could demonstrate the efficacy and determining power of the figure of inversion, here sketched only with reference to two standard philosophical texts, over a wide range of philosophical and literary texts from romanticism and classicism to Feuerbachian and Marxian materialism as well as in so-called poetical realism and into neo-romanticism. And one could show the efficacy of this figure in the macrostructure of the *Bildungsroman* as well as in the syntactical details of lyric poetry.[3] However diverse the intentions controlling it may be, inversion remains—with the great exception of the Hölderlinian inversion, which sets the resistance to the meaning of finite linguistic material against the universalization of its semantic energy[4]—the dominant rhetorical and

---

3. Manfred Frank and Gerhard Kurz have begun to carry out a portion of this task, though not with uniform persuasiveness; see "Ordo Inversus: zu einer Reflexionsfigur bei Novalis, Hölderlin, Kleist und Kafka," in *Geist und Zeichen, Festschrift für Arthur Henkel* (Heidelberg: Winter, 1977), 75–97.

4. These thoughts are given theoretical formulations in a series of notes bearing the title "Reflexion" in Friedrich Hölderlin, *Sämtliche Werke,* ed. F. Beißner (Stuttgart: Kohlhammer, 1961), 4: 233–36. Here one finds the sentence: "One has inversions of words in the period. Yet the inversion of the periods themselves, then, must prove greater and

epistemological figure for the consolidation of meaning and for the universalization of subjectivity.

In this sense inversion is also the canonical shape of the lyric. It reaches its culmination in Rilke's *New Poems*.[5] In the "Archaic Torso of Apollo," which is placed as an emblem at the opening of its second part and thus occupies roughly the center of the entire book, the remains of Greek plastic art turn into precisely what time has taken away from it: they turn into eyesight, *Augenlicht*.

> Wir kannten nicht sein unerhörtes Haupt,
> darin die Augenäpfel reiften. Aber
> sein Torso glüht noch wie ein Kandelaber. . .
>
> [We did not know its unheard-of head,
> in which its pupils ripened. But
> its torso still glowed like a candelabrum. . .][6]

Contrary to the impression awakened by the prosaic temporality of "still," the torso's blinding brilliance does not radiate as a residue of shape that was whole at its origin; rather, this brilliance arises only by virtue of its fragmentation. Only because this God of phenomenality lacks eyesight, does that which is absent wander into its torso and bring the mutilated body to light as an extinguished one, thus making the "stone" into a "star," material obscurity into the foundation of the phenomenal world of objectivity and the poetic one of sound—the world, that is, in which Rilke's poetry installs itself as its own stele and presents itself in its melodious perfection. Just as the viewer of Apollo's torso becomes something seen because this torso itself has become its missing "unheard-of head"—"denn da ist keine Stelle, / die dich nicht sieht" [for there is no place / that does not see you]—so this "unheard-

---

more effective" (cf. Hölderlin, *Essays and Letters on Theory*, trans. Thomas Pfau [New York: SUNY Press, 1988], 45).

5. Paul de Man has shown this in his text on Rilke; see "Tropes (Rilke)," in *Allegories of Reading* (New Haven: Yale University Press, 1979), 20–56.

6. Rainer Maria Rilke, *Sämtliche Werke*, ed. E. Zinn et al. (Frankfurt am Main: Insel, 1955), 2: 557.

of head" becomes in the poem something heard: in its place the poem states the imperative of the glance that falls from the torso to the reader: "Du mußt dein Leben ändern" [You must alter your life]. But how alter your life other than according to the canon of inversion—an inversion, moreover, that the reader, having come under the imperative of art, has experienced in the shape of an Apollo turned into sound and appearance through his fragmentation? The language of the poem and its object have so thoroughly permeated one another that the one, in a further inversion, has taken the place of the other: the object of the poem has turned into the poem, the poem into its object. "You must alter your life." Alter life you must—and the imperative is here at the same time a constative of necessity—because the resonant glance of the poem has itself become the subject of life blinded in its finitude, and its finitude turns into the fulfillment of sound and shape. The poem is imperative, because it is *strictu sensu,* by virtue of the figure of inversion that it describes and runs through, *not-wendig:* nimbly turning away misery. It transforms its misery of being merely fragmentary into the virtue of presenting by itself the law of the whole. Only where the artwork is ruined can its sheer shape, *ordine inverso,* come forth. With this turn, the ethical mandate of the poem has been established. For the life of that which is seen—apostrophized in the "you"—already stands, as finite, under the law that the poem establishes for its object: having to be, as a broken piece, already another, namely the generation of the whole. The imperative that states the necessary consequence of the figure of inversion is therefore also the *restitutio ad integrum* of the center of the "Archaic Torso of Apollo"—"jener Mitte, die die Zeugung trug" [the center that bore procreation]. That it was once there, although as little known as the "unheard-of head," and that only a smile the torso aims at the place that "bore" it still remains—this is what lends the entire text a nostalgic trait; but the fact that this center captures undistorted hearing in the imperative to regenerate the whole and guarantees the whole energy of subjectivity turned into sound and appearance precisely in its absence lends Rilke's inversion-poem the pathos of a finitude that knows itself capable of virtually endless procreative acts. In this poem, the phallic substrate of subjectivity emerges in an almost compulsive fashion. The archaic torso of Apollo is the *archē* of a *whole* generation of art. Only the very last poems of Rilke turn toward a finitude that no longer allows for pathos, toward an absence that cannot be inverted into a pure presence and so withstands its transformation into shape and resounding meaning.

Paul Celan, whose precise familiarity with Rilke's poetry has been copiously documented, adheres to this tradition. Hardly a figure of his early and middle lyrics asserts itself with such open insistence as inversion. But it is characteristic for the historico-philosophical position of this poetry—if it is still possible to speak in an unaltered way, with reference to Celan, of history, philosophy, and position—that it radicalizes this figure to an abstract purity, no longer tolerating any ornamental glow, and seeks ultimately to surpass and abandon this figure by means of a procedure to which the formulation "inversion of inversion" scarcely does justice. In the early collection of aphorisms and parables Celan published in 1949 in the Zürich journal *Die Tat* under the programmatic title *Gegenlicht* (Counter-light), the sentence "Their embrace lasted so long that love despaired of them"[7] takes up a position against the concept of unification on behalf of its concrete realization, and this realization has the power to drive the general concept into despair and division. In the sentence "The day of judgment had come, and in search of the greatest of desecrations the cross was nailed to Christ,"[8] the apocalypse appears as that turnabout in which the cross—mere instrument of desecration—becomes itself the object of desecration and the human being becomes irredeemably devalued through instrumentalization; furthermore, in the sentence " 'Everything flows': even this thought, and does it not bring everything again to a standstill?"[9] the Heraclitean dictum is turned against itself: if everything flows, then so does this thought, and this thought, having now turned into another, can only maintain the flow of all things if at the same time it lets this flow stand still: this dictum can be a universal statement only when its performance

---

7. "So lange währte ihre Umarmung, daß die Liebe an ihnen verzweifelte." Quotations are drawn from Paul Celan, *Gesammelte Werke,* ed. Beda Allemann, Stefan Reichert in association with Rolf Bücher (Frankfurt am Main: Suhrkamp, 1983), 3: 163. All further references of Celan's work will be to this collection.

8. "Der Tag des Gerichts war gekommen, und um die größte der Schandtaten zu suchen, wurde das Kreuz an Christus genagelt" (3: 163).

9. "'Alles fließt': auch dieser Gedanke, und bringt er nicht alles wieder zum Stehen?" (3: 165).

denies the universality of what it states. In this inversion and in the other ones that *Gegenlicht* pursues, the possibility and the constancy of general sentences and concepts in which a truth, an insight, or even just a stable meaning is supposed to be preserved are drawn into doubt by their own inner logic. If murder and movement present themselves as negations of constancy and dignity, then Celan's inversions negate the positive remainder that inhabits their negativity and thus prevents every harmonizing mediation. In this respect, they do not amount to inversions of inversions in the sense of a dialectical setting aright of a perverted world, and they are not a return to its authentic form. As the thought of the cross nailed to Christ bears witness, Celan's world is one of perfect desecration, and the light that his texts cast on the world is there thanks to this world: it is only light as counter-light, and that means darkness as well. In a meditation that recalls the Kabbalistic theory of *zimzum*, the self-limitation of nothingness, Celan writes: "Don't confuse yourself: this last lamp no longer gives off light—the enveloping darkness has absorbed itself into itself."[10] If there is still a light and if there is still a language in which this light imparts itself, then it is not as positive phenomenality and not as a remainder of the original logos but, rather, as a lucidity out of emptiness, out of the space left by the self-absorption of darkness. There is no light that would not be in this sense—and against ordinary representations of naive consciousness, even if it is given a dialectical spin—merely the lack of darkness. Linguistic signs are not referential indicators coordinated by autonomous subjects with their representations, nor are they the self-presentation of their objectivity. In the ellipsis of Celan's inversions, they are only the barren space opened up by a muteness lost in itself. Like the site of language, so their presence—even the apocalyptic presence of its last instant—is not a primary fact of reason but the secondary effect of a self-contraction of absence.

The second to the last cycle in Celan's second volume of poems, *Mohn und Gedächtnis* (Poppy and Memory), bears the same title as the early collection of aphorisms: *Gegenlicht*, Counter-Light. The last poem in this cycle, a love poem, concerns the very site of the language of love:

---

10. "Täusche dich nicht, nicht diese letzte Lampe spendet mehr Licht—das Dunkel rings hat sich in sich vertieft" (3: 165).

Der Tauben weißeste flog auf: ich darf dich lieben!
Im leisen Fenster schwankt die leise Tür.
Der stille Baum trat in die stille Stube.
Du bist so nah, als weiltest du nicht hier.

Aus meiner Hand nimmst du die große Blume:
sie ist nicht weiß, nicht rot, nicht blau—doch nimmst du sie.
Wo sie nie war, da wird sie immer bleiben.
Wir waren nie, so bleiben wir bei ihr. (1: 61)

[The whitest dove flies off: I can love you!
In the soft window swings the soft door.
The still tree stepped into the still room.
You are so near as though you did not linger here.

From my hand you take the great flower:
it is not white, not red, not blue—yet you take it.
Where it never was, it will always remain.
We never were, so we remain with it.]

The poem describes in a relatively classical fashion and, with regard to
its lay-out, in a rather didactic way the linear progression of convergence
and joining. Following the seemingly late-romantic metaphor of eleva-
tion (the flight of the dove), the poem, with the image of reflection in
the windowpane, first brings together two spatial openings (window
and door) and then outer and inner space, nearness and distance, so as
to address in the last line of the first stanza the nearness of the beloved
as the appearance of a distance: "You are so near as though you did not
linger here." The law of inversion—the greater the distance, the nearer
the figure—finds no less pronounced formulations in *Niemandsrose* (No
One's Rose) than in *Mohn und Gedächtnis*. In "Chymisch" (Chymous)
the large, gray shape of the sister is said to be "wie alles Vorlorene nahe"
[near as all things lost] (1: 227); in "Stumme Herbstgerüche" (Mute
Autumn Smells) the second stanza runs:

Eine fremde Verlorenheit war
gestalthaft zugegen, du hättest
beinah
gelebt (1: 223)

[A strange forlornness was
present as shape, you might have
almost
lived]

Whereas a severity in tone is produced in these later texts by abstractions, by the adversative connotations of *zugegen* (present) and the mere *beinah* (almost) of the living shape—a tone indicating a change in the figure of inversion—the harsh distance in the text from "Gegenlicht" is dissolved into the obliging *melos* of its plain language. Yet the flower the beloved receives from the hand of the speaker becomes by virtue of its thoroughly negative attributes—at least on the semantic level of the poem— almost a nothing flower, a no one's flower. In this flower, the inversion of distance into nearness is radicalized to the point where absence turns into presence, and this radicalization manifests itself in the line "where it never was, it will always remain," even if it appears to have been softened by the tense shift from "was" to "will remain." The poem reaches the extreme of radicality in its final line, where it asserts the nonexistence of the "we" and draws the consequence from this assertion—in accordance with the law of inversion—that we remain in the flower that always remains: the annihilated "we," analogous to the nothing flower, has changed into the ever-lingering constancy: "We never were, so we remain with it." If the "blue flower" of Novalis was still a symbol of the universal poeticization of the world, this early flower of Celan—which is not blue and indeed, having no other color, could dazzle by its absence like no other flowers but those collected by Mallarmé—is no less a symbol: it is a symbol of the poeticization of lack. In the best symbolic tradition, the remaining presence of poetry and the unification of I and You into We climbs out of the *flos rhetoricus negativus*. In the language of this flower, which is indeed not metaphorical in the traditional sense but meta-metaphorical, laying bare the carrying-over mechanism of imagistic language at its extreme, thus trope, turn, and reversal *par excellence*—: in the language of this flower, separated things have been brought together and what never was has turned into ever-remaining existence, for this very language came from a nothing and became something that remains. But this change is indebted to the categorical certainty of being perceived, received, and retained, and only in this perception that institutes the unity between giver and receiver does the gift of nothingness change into substantial being: "From my hand you take the great flower: / it is not white, not red, not blue—yet you take it." If this per-ception, this taking-in, were to remain outstanding, if the gift were not to arrive at its destined site, there would be no language, no change, no remaining. If the nothing of language were not received and perceived, its inversion into being would not be possible. This possibility of the impossibility of its own existence breaks open in Celan's poem only in the dash before the *doch* (yet), in the interruption of tropic language, in the mute hesitation of receiving and perceiving. This graphic pause—Celan later found for a similar moment the word *Verhoffen,* a state of expectancy to which the alternatives of hope and despair do not apply, as in the alarm of animals when faced with a hunter—opens in poetic speaking a hole that cannot be closed by the logic of inversion; it opens a distance that cannot be transformed into a nearness, a difference that cannot turn into a unity, a mute site that cannot change into a topos of an eloquent image. This is the site of an absence that must still remain unreachable to every absence that could change into our own, into the presence of our language.

However small this hole in the tropological system of Celan may be, it makes clear a danger that threatens many of his early texts: the danger of making nothingness into a positive, the danger of allowing for absence merely as the negative of presence, and thus the danger of wanting to change absence, by virtue of language, into ever-lasting Being. However desperately and mockingly certain texts may at times deny the possibility of such a reversal, they still remain unquestionably committed to its idea. The emphatic closing lines of "Spät und Tief" (Late and Deep) show this:

> es komme . . .
> der geharnischte Windstoß der Umkehr,
> der mitternächtige Tag,
> es komme, was niemals noch war!
>
> Es komme ein Mensch aus dem Grabe. (1: 35–36)
>
> [let come . . .
> the armored gust of reversal

the midnight day,
let come what never yet was!

Let come a man from the grave.]

This commitment is shown in oxymorons of the "rostgeborenen Messern [rust-born knives]" (1: 68), the "gesteinigten Stein [lapidated stone]" (1: 51) and the "Flor der abgeblühten Stunde [bloom of withered hour]" (1: 55). All these oxymorons, paradoxes, and inversions have—and they thus take up in a radicalized manner the problem of subjectivity in philosophy and literature since romanticism—the movement of time as their subject. The transcendental-aesthetic foundation for the figure of inversion is given in time, as the formal unity of contradictory predicates. The rhetoric of inversion is the rhetoric of temporality to the extent that temporality is represented as the finite form of unity for whatever differs from itself. This concept of time permeates the lyrics of the young Celan even in those passages that drive it to its utmost limit.

Under the Nietzschean title "Lob der Ferne" (Praise of Distance) Celan weaves an entire mesh of antinomian formulations whose intention is not simply the presentation of unity but, dialectically, the presentation of the unity of unity and division:

> Abtrünnig erst bin ich treu.
> Ich bin du, wenn ich ich bin.
> [. . .]
> Ein Garn fing ein Garn ein:
> wir scheiden umschlungen.
>
> Im Quell deiner Augen
> erwürgt ein Gehenkter den Strang. (1: 33)

> [Only disloyally am I faithful.
> I am you when I am I.
> [. . .]
> A net caught a net:
> we part entangled.
>
> In the depths of your eyes
> a hanged man strangles the rope.]

Only apostasy, betrayal, and separation bind together; only the dynamic of difference gives force to unification, and only in the sundering of itself that characterizes time do the separated parts come together. "Im Quell deiner Augen / hält das Meer sein Versprechen" [In the source of your eyes / the sea holds its promise]. The promise, once delivered to its redemption in temporal distance, is "held" by the sea in the eyes of the beloved; it is already fulfilled and is the—oxymoronically—fulfilled speaking of the poem in which everything subjected to temporal disso-ciation stands together in the formula of a negative unity. Celan's poem attempts to speak from the negativity of time itself, but this negativity, however deeply it may have buried the traits of transience in the words spoken and distorted them into a mere allegory of speaking, nevertheless remains the center of mediation between source and sea, presence and past, I and you, the promise and its redemption in the poem. The promise holds because past and presence are held together by the threads that run through time and that split them asunder. Because time—by virtue of its negativity, not in spite of it—is the most powerful force of synthesis, it is also the foundation for all figures of inversion that are collected in Celan's early volumes of poetry and that find their greatest concentration in *Mohn und Gedächtnis*. For inversion is nothing other than the negative positing of the negative and, by virtue of its negativity, the strict binding together of that which has been separated: it is the movement of time itself to the extent that time—as with Hegel but not only with him—is determined as the continuum of negativity referring to itself and, furthermore, as the negative unity of difference. The language of inversion is the language of time represented as a continuum of negativity. In it, the I becomes the You at the precise moment when it disavows its loyalty to the You; the I departs from the You at the precise moment when they become entangled in one another: I and You in their relation to one another and in their self-relation are conceived as temporal moments, as moments of time for which a posi-tive unity is as unreachable as the negative unity of their binding sepa-ration is compelling. The same negativity also stamps the speaking that the poem helps to express: in this speaking a promise is held only in such a way that the corresponding oath is breached: "Hier werf ich / [. . .] / von mir [. . .] den Glanz eines Schwures" [Here I cast / . . . / from me . . . the glow of an oath]. Only apostasy from the already given word can fulfill it; only the breached word holds the promise of language. And so the central metaphor of the "Garne der Fischer der Irrsee" [Nets of the Fishermen of the Sea of Error], which organizes the entire texture of the poem, may be read as the spinning out of the metaphor of the "seaman's yarn," a turn of speech that stands for lying, fraud, and fantastical fabrication. The promise of which Celan's poem speaks and which it gives itself is a fraudulent one—a promise that, like the Sea of Error, leads into errancy, a promise that only fulfills what it betrays and is only fulfilled in revealing itself as a fraud.

The language of time is not that of simple reference, which, because of its own consistency, could then refer to constant substances. Nor is it that of deception, which allows one to maintain the illusion that there is a region free from deception. The language of time is one that denies to itself the denial of its truth-content and fulfills the false promise in its very breach.[11] It is, in sum, the language of a temporality that—because of the negation it can repeat infinitely and on the basis of the continuity secured by such negation—remains in a position to speak the truth under the conditions of deception and to speak of this remaining under the conditions of disappearance: the remaining of time and its language. To become one with the movement of time—of negativity—in such a way that it would become the continuum of time itself was probably among the deepest intentions of Celan's language in *Mohn und Gedächtnis*. The loving unification of time and language can only succeed because both, as a result of their negativity, are energies of unification. The exhausted, the failed, the buried: "blind wie der Blick, den wir tauschen, / küßt es die Zeit auf den Mund" [blind as the gaze we exchange, / it kisses time on the mouth] (1: 57). It is time itself that sings and speaks; it is no longer an object of discourse but a subject that speaks: "Die Zeit, aus feinem Sande, singt in meinen Armen: / . . . / noch einmal mit dem Tod im Chor die Welt herübersingen" [Time, from fine sand, sings in my arms: / . . . / once again in the chorus with death to sing the world hither] (1: 69). The imago of the beloved that Celan's poems project bears the traits of time as much as it bears all the other subjects that find their way into his texts. But this very temporal structure suits them only because time is the subject and form of the process of the language in

11. In this connection see Paul de Man, "The Rhetoric of Temporality," in *Blindness and Insight: Essays in the Rhetoric of Contemporary Criticism,* 2nd rev. ed. (Minneapolis: University of Minnesota Press, 1983), 187–229.

which these subjects are presented: ". . . ein Wort, von Sensen gespro-
chen, . . ." [a word, spoken by scythes] (1: 70). With every word spoken,
the time of the things this word means not only passes away; but the
word—or the name—is also itself the cut with which time does away
with the consistent subsistence of representations. And yet, in its negativity, the language of time is essentially positive: it brings what is said
into a finite world and into earthly life. The death that the word brings
about belongs to the conditions of life:

> Aus Herzen und Hirnen
> sprießen die Halme der Nacht,
> und ein Wort, von Sensen gesprochen,
> neigt sie ins Leben. (1: 70)

> [Out of hearts and brains
> sprout the blades of night
> and a word, spoken by scythes,
> bends them into life.]

The semantic potential of language which lets it refer to objects and
objective relations in the world of experience is as indebted to its temporalization as the world of experience itself. A ripening and temporalizing function accrues to language even before its referential function.
What Kant said of time is no less valid for temporal language in Celan:
it is the formal condition *a priori* of representation in general. In this
way, Celan's poems speak—in a transcendental manner like only those
of Hölderlin and, to a lesser degree, those of Rilke—of the conditions
of their own possibility. They do not name something determinate but
bring the very determining ground of speaking into language: its temporalizing character. In a significant departure from Kant, however,
temporalizing language in Celan is not the form of representation that
makes possible the projection of world-pictures and of particular representations but is, rather, the form of transformation that makes subjects
themselves into figures of time and thereby robs them of the possibility
of relating themselves, as stable subjects of language, to the world and
its appearances: "Stumm wie . . . [die Halme der Nacht] / wehn wir der
Welt entgegen: / . . ." [mute as . . . (the blades of night) / we waft toward the world] (1: 70). We *have* no language we could utilize as an
instrument; rather, we *are* only that which has been spoken, wafted into

a world by the cut of language—a world in which we must remain mute because, here too, time takes the words out of our mouths:

[. . .] was wir jetzt sind,
schenken die Stunden der Zeit ein.

Munden wir ihr? Kein Laut und kein Licht
schlüpft zwischen uns, es zu sagen. (1: 70)

[. . . what we now are,
the hours pour into time.

Does it savor us? No sound and no light
slips between us to say so.]

The word of time does not refer to objective data or abstract meanings; it *is* only as the withdrawal of objectivity and meaning. The language of finitude is the chronic retreat of the referential and semantic functions of language, because with each one of its words—all of which bend representations into life—the world and the very being of the things thus spoken are brought to the point of disappearance. In turning to speak to its own ground, Celan's poetry can assert the condition of its possibility only as the condition of the impossibility of its stable semantic subsistence, and so it opens up the abyss of its own futility. "Poetry," as Celan will say in his 1960 "Meridian" address, "poetry, ladies and gentlemen—: this pronouncement of the infinite of sheer mortality and in vain!"[12]

The temporalization of language—and of everything able to enter into its domain—shakes the place of the subject and the stability of discourse, although these were supposed to be secured by the transcendental turn. If it can be said and must be thought that the scythe—this allegorical prop of death and time—wields language, the *ordo inversus* that was supposed to give a foundation for the order of subjectivity and that had already fallen into difficulties with Kant's discovery of finitude and his demonstration of a merely finite faculty of human presentation no longer offers any reliable guarantee for the presentation and the linguistic fixation of a world and its possible meaning. The only unity and the only continuum that, from now on, can yield to speech are those

12. "Die Dichtung, meine Damen und Herren—: diese Unendlichsprechung von lauter Sterblichkeit und Umsonst!" (3: 200).

of disappearance, of a negativity without center and without sublation. Still, the lyrics in Celan's *Mohn und Gedächtnis* draw their formal unity from this structure of negativity. A figure of inversion such as "Blicklos / schweigt nun dein Aug in mein Aug sich" [sightless / your eye now goes silent in my eye] (1: 70)—despite the negation of language and appearance expressed in it—nevertheless holds onto the rigorous relation between my eye and yours, and in their intimate unity the inversion maintains that communication beyond language and sight reaches its mark. While the figure of the inverse order along with the form of communication persists, its substance, as sheer transience, is consumed: its content is emptied, and its basis is turned into an abyss. The inverted world is not, as in Hegel, a world stood on its head as its unshakable ground but is a world held in the abyss of temporality, a world so held that no one can hold onto it any longer. In his "Meridian" address Celan lays open this same abyss in a formulation drawn from Büchner's *Lenz*, which, like many lines in his dramas, takes aim at Hegel, by giving a spin to a trifling turn of speech that had already become a "classical" figure of inversion during Büchner's own time. Büchner says of Lenz: "He went forward with indifference; nothing stood in his way, now going up, now going down. He had no trace of weariness; only he sometimes felt irritated that he could not walk on his head."[13] Celan's justly famous comment on this turn of speech runs: "he who walks on his head, ladies and gentlemen,—he who walks on his head has the sky beneath him as an abyss."[14] This abyss—not the bottomlessness of heaven, not what a deteriorating philosophy would like to perceive in

---

13. See Georg Büchner, *Werke und Briefe*, ed. F. Bergemann (Wiesbaden: Insel, 1958), 85. Cf. *Lenz*, trans. Michael Patterson, in Georg Büchner, *The Complete Plays*, ed. M. Patterson (London: Methuen, 1987), 249. One can assume that Büchner was familiar with the "Walpurgis Night's Dream" in the first part of Goethe's *Faust*, where the following words are put into the mouths of the "clever ones"—and, as the text suggests, the changed ones—: "Going by foot doesn't work any more / so we go by our heads" (ll. 4369–70).

14. "Wer auf dem Kopf geht, meine Damen und Herren,—wer auf dem Kopf geht, der hat den Himmel als Abgrund unter sich" (3: 195). Celan's commentary on Büchner's sentence once again recalls Hölderlin's "Reflexionen": "Man kann auch in die Höhe fallen, wie in die Tiefe" [One can fall upwards as well as downwards] (*Sämtliche Werke*, 4: 233; cf. *Essays and Letters on Theory*, 45). Without referring to Hölderlin, Heidegger took up this thought in his first study of Trakl, "Die Sprache" (Language) and used it for the determination of his gnomon, "Die Sprache spricht" [Language speaks]. We may

the inverted sky and call transcendence but, instead, the untenability of the transcendental forms of our representation itself—opens up with ever less concealment in Celan's linguistic mode of procedure and his poetological reflection during the late fifties and sixties.

If language is nothing more than the articulation of the withdrawal of the world, then it becomes itself a figure of falling, no longer able to designate this withdrawal as an object. If it is unable to stand the world on the head of its poetic presentation, if it is, instead, nothing more than the cut and strut of an incessant passing away, then it is itself drawn into the turnings and becomes the vertiginous vortex of disfiguration in which nothing can any longer mean what it says. Just as the functions of the sign break down in the face of an "object" such as the abyss, death, or nothingness, conventional units of meaning—words and sentences, strophes, which are also turns—likewise dissolve, having been infected, as it were, with this death, and they thus leave room for an altered form of speaking and for the interruption of speaking itself. One of the destructuring figures Celan privileges in his poetry is paranomasia.[15] In explicit instances of paranomasia—as when "Zangen" [forceps] is placed

---

assume that Celan knew Hölderlin's text as well as that of Heidegger. In "Die Sprache" (Language), Heidegger writes: "We fall upwards. The height of this fall opens up a depth. Together, they measure out a site in which we would like to become at home, so as to find the dwelling-place for the essence of man" (Martin Heidegger, *Unterwegs zur Sprache* [Pfullingen: Neske, 1971], 13; cf. *Poetry, Language, Thought,* trans. Albert Hofstadter [New York: Harper & Row, 1975], 191–92).

15. Peter Szondi was the first to recognize it as such. See "Poetry of Constancy—Poetik der Beständigkeit," in *Schriften,* ed. J. Bollak et al. (Frankfurt am Main: Suhrkamp, 1978), esp. 2: 338; "The Poetry of Constancy: Paul Celan's Translations of Shakespeare's Sonnet 105," in Peter Szondi, *On Textual Understanding and Other Essays,* ed. Michael Hays, trans. Harvey Mendelsohn (Minneapolis: University of Minnesota Press, 1986), 165. Although, not unjustly in this context, Szondi places paranomasia as "phonological near-identity" under the rubric of unification and constantiation, I read in paranomasia, as it is used by Celan, a mode of the diversification of linguistic units (syllables, words, syntagms) through which they open themselves to a multiplicity of other—and indeed, *a limine,* indeterminable—unities, hence under the appearance of correspondence, making room for a limitless play of alteration. Ferdinand de Saussure, in his search for a suitable concept for the principle of construction for "saturnine" verses, which he finally called "anagrammatic," considered the term "hypogram" and made the fragmentary remark: "Paranomasia comes so close with its principle that . . ." Jean Starobinski comments: "It is curious that Saussure . . . should not have fixed his attention more closely on para-

alongside "Zungen der Sehnsucht" [tongues of longing], the "Verbran-nte" [incinerated] alongside the "Verbannten" [exiled], "Schläfe" [tem-ples] alongside "schlaflos" [sleepless], "Erzväter" [patriarchs] alongside "Erzflitter" [the glitter of ore], and "das blutende Ohr" [bloody ear] alongside "blühselige Botschaft" [blessed tidings]—the phonetic prox-imity of the words whereby one affects the other with its semantic potential sets a verbal unity into oscillation. In "Huhediblu" the lines themselves tell how they came into being and how they are to be read:

> [. . .] du liest,
> dies hier, dies:
> Dis-
> parates—: . . . (1: 275)
>
> [. . . you read,
> this here, this:
> Dis-
> parates—: . . .]

The lines come into being and are read as *disparation:* as the diversifica-tion and dispersal of the monosemic body of the word. In implicit instances of paranomasia, a minimal alteration of the phonetic or graphic form of a word that does not itself appear produces another word, and this other word acts as the distorted echo of the first: "rauch-dünn" [smoke-thin] thus replaces "hauchdünn" [filmy] (1: 288); "Mor-gen-Lot" [morning plumb-line] stands in for "Morgenrot" [dawn]; "Ferse" [heels] for "Verse" [verses] (2: 25); "Pestlaken" [plague shroud] for "Bettlaken" [bed sheet] (2: 153); and "Datteln" [the dates one eats] for "Daten" [the dates of a calendar] (2: 134). If in explicit paranomasia the alteration is manifest and the semantic destabilization is confined to

---

nomasia. Perhaps he feared . . . that this 'figure of speech' might imperil the aspect of *discovery* which, for him, was attached to the theory of anagrams" (*Les Mots sous les mots* [Paris: Gallimard, 1971], 32; *Word upon Word: The Anagrams of Ferdinand de Saussure,* trans. Olivia Emmet [New Haven, Ct.: Yale University Press, 1979], 19). Paul de Man has extensively commented and expanded on Saussure's considerations of the hypogram in "Hypogram and Inscription" (*The Resistance to Theory* [Minneapolis: University of Min-nesota Press, 1986], 27–63).

the localized zone of the word as it appears in the text, the corresponding word in implicit paranomasia remains latent, its shape uncertain, and so it exposes every word in the text to the possibility of being an alteration of some lost paradigm, which stubbornly withdraws from rational or divinatory reconstruction. Each of these words presents itself—if not exclusively then at least primarily—as the disfiguration of what has gone silent, *a limine*, as the translation of what does not give rise to voice, as the carrying over of everything muted. What Celan writes elsewhere of a forgotten word goes for these words as well: "Dies ist ein Wort, das neben den Worten einherging, / ein Wort nach dem Bilde des Schweigens" [This is a word that walked along with the words, / a word in the image of silence] (1: 92).

In the programmatic opening sequence of the volume *Sprachgitter* from which Celan, in his "Meridian" address, cited the second section— "Komm auf den Hände zu uns" [come on your hands to us]—as a parallel to the abyssal maxim drawn from Büchner's *Lenz*, the first text reads:

> *Stimmen,* ins Grün
> der Wasserfläche geritzt.
> Wenn der Eisvogel taucht,
> sirrt die Sekunde:
>
> Was zu dir stand
> an jedem der Ufer,
> es tritt
> gemäht in ein anderes Bild. (1: 147)
>
> [*Voices,* into the green
> of the water surface etched.
> When the kingfisher dives,
> the second buzzes:
>
> What confronted you
> on each of the banks,
> it steps,
> mowed into another image.]

The figure of inversion that the next text of the sequence will explicitly make into an image is latent in this one as well: the objective world of the embankment whose image has benevolently turned toward the "you" addressed in the poem enters, like the voices that have etched the surface of the water, into the image of the water-mirror; it enters inadvertently, averted and unfamiliar, having been inverted and stood on its head. This transformation—a metamorphosis like the one Alcyone undergoes when she is turned into a "kingfisher" during her dive after her drowned husband[16]—is occasioned by a cut: what is trusted and familiar is "mowed" into another image—mowed, that is, by the cut of the *Sekunde* understood now in its etymological sense, as the *secare* of time. Time transforms the voices into the writing of the water-mirror and turns the trusted image of the objective world into the averted, inverted, and afflicted images of the literary text, which no longer offers them a ground beyond that of an *unda* in which they sink. But the same displacement underlies the language in which the poem articulates this transformation of a stable image into one that is overturned. Not only is the metaphor of reaping drawn from a metaphor lying dormant in a foreign word (in the *secare* of *Sekunde*)—a procedure Celan abundantly employs[17]—but this word, *die Sekunde*, is itself cut and read as *diese Kunde*, "this message," "this conduit of communication."[18] The possibility of reading *die Sekunde* in this way is suggested by the phonetic combination of *s* and *i* in *sirrt*, which provokes a corresponding contamination of the *ie* and *Se* that follows, and it is also suggested by the very colon after *Sekunde*, which allows the second quatrain to appear as

16. See Ovid, *Metamorphoses*, trans. Mary M. Innes (New York: Penguin, 1955), XI, ll. 720–48. In this connection one is reminded of Celan's remark (September 1966) that naming takes place in the depth of language, that *taufen* ("baptize") and *tauchen* ("dive") stand in an intimate relation to one another (reported by Dietlinde Meinecke in *Wort und Name bei Paul Celan* [Bad Homburg: Gehlen, 1970], 189).

17. See, for example, the informative studies of Elizabeth Petuchowski, which are devoted to the polylingual word-play in Celan: "A New Approach to Paul Celan's 'Argumentum e Silentio'" and "Bilingual and Multilingual *Wortspiele* in the Poetry of Paul Celan," both in *Deutsche Vierteljahrsschrift für Literaturwissenschaften und Geistesgeschichte* 52 (1978): 111–36 and 635–51, respectively. The young Celan's proclivity for word-play with inversion is well documented by Peter Solomon, "Paul Celans Bukarester Aufenthalt," in *Zeitschrift für Kulturaustausch* (Stuttgart: Institut für Auslandsbeziehungen), 3 (1982): 222–26.

18. One finds a comparable treatment of words in "Ein Tag und noch einer" (A Day and One More), also in the volume *Sprachgitter:* the expression "der Ast, / rasch an den

the content of a message, indeed as a conduit. *Die Sekunde—diese Kunde;* the second—this conduit: it is time, the cutter, that conducts its message in the inversion of the world of images, but this message accomplishes the inversion only by subjecting the second itself—the temporal atom— to its own principle of fission, by splitting the unity of the message, cutting off the conduit. The very principle of separation by which "an- other image" is generated brings together whatever stands on separate banks—"on each of the banks"—and so *DieSeKunde* is not simply a metamorphosis but also a metaphor, the very movement of metaphori- zation: conducting across and carrying over. All images and all turns of

---

Himmel geschrieben" [the branch, / quickly scrawled on the sky] (1: 179) contains the word *Astra,* written apart and dismembered by the line break and the comma. Before it finds in "Leuchter" [chandelier] a relatively unambiguous semantic equivalent, it is again repeated in disguise: "ein Morgen / sprang ins Gestern hinauf" [a tomorrow / leapt up into yesterday]: "Gestern" can also, in this context and with its reference to "hinauf," be read as "Ge-Stern," collective of stars. Cf. Celan's pun *per c-aspera ad astra,* reported by Israel Chalfen in *Paul Celan: Eine Biographie seiner Jugend* (Frankfurt am Main: Suhrkamp, 1983), 96. In a poem from *Fadensonnen,* Celan gave the poetic recipe for the preparation and reading of his texts, and not just his own: "Kleide die Worthöhlen aus / mit Pantherhäuten, // erweitere sie, fellhin und fellher, / sinnhin und sinnher, // gib ihnen Vorhöfe, Kammern, Klappen / und Wildnisse, parietal, // und lausch ihrem zweiten / und jeweils zweiten und zweiten / Ton" [Dress the wordcaves / with pantherskins, // expand them, infur and outfur, toward sense and away from sense, // give them vesti- bules, chambers, shutters / and wildernesses, parietal, // and overhear their second / and each time second and second / tone] (2: 198). Here, too, we have an inversion of familiar ideas. Aside from the duplicity of the word *auskleiden,* which by itself can mean both "dress" and "undress," the outside—the skin, the pelt—is displaced as sense into the inscape of the word; sense is only one—and indeed an alien, second—skin, an inner mask. Tone, as "that which is always second," is in each case distanced further than the audible tone, infinitely secondary; it too is a second. Celan's later poems are written out of this second and for its sake; they are dated, as finite language, on the second. The inversion of the secondary into the "primary," of the outer into the "inner," is always effected in them so that they expand the character of the secondary, *in fine,* instead of domesticating it. Thus, as Celan himself stressed, we can only "understand" his texts "from a distance."

In addition, *Auskleiden* is one of the possible meanings of *Auslegen* (to interpret, to lay out). Insofar as the poem takes on this—second—sense in the image, in the clothing, in the pelt, it itself practices the "hermeneutic" operation it recommends: the whole becomes feline, *fellhin und fellher,* although not without falling into what would count as failure for a normative understanding.

speech in Celan's text follow the alteration dictated by its eccentric center—*dieSeKunde,* the second, this conduit: they are not metaphors for representations but metaphors for metaphorization, not images of a world but images of the generation of images, not the transcription of voices but the production of the etched voices of the poem itself. They inscribe themselves as the script of alteration when they let themselves be exposed to this very alteration: they write, they are *dieSeKunde,* this second, this conduit; the incisive word-exchange in which the phenomenal and linguistic world is opened onto a caesura that not a single shape of this world can exorcize, since each of these shapes results from it. The second—this conduit—of Celan's poem is the self-interrupting, self-dismembering, distributing and redistributing, communicating and imparting speaking of language. The differentiation and varying distribution of linguistic segments do not so much articulate a particular meaning or nexus of meaning—although they do this, too, by expressing the rigorous connection between linguisticity and temporality—nor do they turn toward an earlier and primary meaning that, being secondary, they would help bring to light; rather, this differentiation and distribution articulate the condition of possible meaning—language—by opening themselves to that which does not correspond to themselves. The privative *se* of *SeKunde* cuts this conduit—this *Kunde,* the word for language—and takes from it the indubitable capacity to mean something that it, as a conduit of a communication, could still claim, dividing its language as it divides language from itself. *SeKunde* is the secession of *Kunde* from itself, the rift or etch in the conduit at which point its language interrupts and exposes itself as finite, as not in agreement with itself. *Die Sekunde*—this second, this conduit—dictates the law of "originary" secondariness; it is the cut that precedes everything primary, the rift that opens in every principle, including that of universal linguisticity, and it disperses every unit and every condition that makes unity possible. *DieSeKunde* is, from the start, second in relation to itself: "Sekunde"—it "buzzes"—in the musicological sense of interval, an interval between different meanings, an interval between different languages, an interval in language itself that first gives the speaking of language space and time. Whatever steps into it, into this interval, this speaking, becomes other than it is.

The conduit—*ordine inverso*—is not one; it has no message to impart.

It asserts nothing more than this: that it has nothing to assert but its own secession from itself and is, as self-revocation, the movement of turning about. In so turning, it does not turn toward an empirical or transcendental other but rather steps, itself "mowed," into another image, one that no longer stands in for a You and no longer belongs to anyone. Nothing could be more foreign, for it is the etched image of a fundamental alteration, the alteration of every basis into an abyss.

If the semantic function of language, which the figure of inversion was supposed to secure under conditions of finitude, is suspended, and if this suspension, as the radicalization of inversion, implies that language turns into the image of its own interruption, then the very communicative performance of language is likewise put into question. It can no longer be conceived as an exchange between two or more already constituted subjects of a linguistic community. On the contrary, since there can be language only because of its division from itself, communicative performance must be thought as the im-parting of language through which its subjects, however unstable they may be, are first constituted. The fact that this im-parting[19] can no longer be a mediation at a midpoint held in common and cannot be a communication in an already given common medium; the fact that there is no place in such im-parting either for the substantialization of language or its instrumentalization into a means—all this comes into language in one of the longer texts of *Die Niemandsrose*, "Radix, Matrix." Precisely what distance lies between this text and the earlier ones becomes evident when one reflects on the attribution in *Mohn und Gedächtnis* of an instrumental character to lan-

19. Helpful indications for the problem of language as a *Mit-teilung* (im-parting) that precedes every reduction and idealizing into communication—indications, however, that have to be elaborated—are given in Walter Benjamin, "Über Sprache überhaupt und über die Sprache des Menschen," in *Gesammelte Schriften*, 2: 142 ("On Language as such and on Human Language" in *Reflections* trans. E. Jephcott [New York: Schocken, 1978], 315–16); in Martin Heidegger, *Sein und Zeit*, § 34, 160–64; and in the untitled introductory text to Maurice Blanchot, *L'Entretien infini* (Paris: Gallimard, 1969), ix–xxvi. The problem of *Mit-Teilung* is also developed masterfully by Jean-Luc Nancy, *Le Partage des voix* (Paris: Galilée, 1982); and *La Communauté desoeuvrée* (Paris: Galilée, 1986); "Sharing Voices" in *Transforming the Hermeneutic Context,* eds. Gayle L. Ormiston and Alan D. Schrift (Albany, N.Y.: SUNY Press, 1990), 211–59; *The Inoperative Community,* ed. P. Connor, foreword Christopher Fynsk (Minneapolis: University of Minnesota Press, 1991).

guage and indeed to the language of the mother, to the mother-tongue[20]—the character, that is, of help and protection. Celan is most outspoken in the poem "Reisekamerad" (Traveling Companion):

> Deiner Mutter Seele schwebt voraus.
> Deiner Mutter Seele hilft die Nacht umschiffen, Riff um Riff.
> Deiner Mutter Seele peitscht die Haie vor dir her.
>
> Dieses Wort ist deiner Mutter Mündel.
> Deiner Mutter Mündel teilt dein Lager, Stein um Stein.
> Deiner Mutter Mündel bückt sich nach der Krume Lichts. (1: 66)
>
> [Your mother's soul hovers on ahead.
> Your mother's soul helps navigate the night, reef after reef.
> Your mother's soul whips the sharks in front of you.
>
> This word is your mother's ward.
> Your mother's ward shares your bed, stone by stone.
> Your mother's ward stoops for the crumb of light.]

This poem—"this word"—stands under the guardianship of the mother, who helps it to steer clear of the danger of being struck dumb, helps to turn it away from darkness, and helps it to preserve the remnants of light. It is one of the most lucid poems Celan ever wrote. But it is also one of the most spellbound, for the maternal tutelage of which it speaks is realized by the mastery of a single syntactical paradigm, and this paradigm only allows the most minimal variation. Such a paradigm—the matrix of language that guarantees the strength of coherence and mutual comprehension—is given up in "Radix, Matrix." It is a poem devoted to the loss of the mother tongue, of the middle, and of the capacity of the mother tongue and middle to mediate.

20. Israel Chalfen writes in his biography that for Celan's mother, "the German language was the more important, and throughout her life she made sure that a correct, literary German was spoken in her house. She had no patience with the everyday language of Bukovina" (*Paul Celan,* 40). And "she especially liked to read the German classics, and in later years she would compete with her son Paul in citing from the authors they most loved" (31).

RADIX, MATRIX

Wie man zum Stein spricht, wie
du,
mir vom Abgrund her, von
einer Heimat her Ver-
schwisterte, Zu-
geschleuderte, du,
du mir vorzeiten,
du mir im Nichts einer Nacht,
du in der Aber-Nacht Be-
gegnete, du
Aber-Du—:

Damals, da ich nicht da war,
damals, da du
den Acker abschrittst, allein:

Wer,
wer wars, jenes
Geschlecht, jenes gemordete, jenes
schwarz in den Himmel stehende:
Rute und Hode—?

(Wurzel.
Wurzel Abrahams. Wurzel Jesse. Niemandes
Wurzel—o
unser.)

Ja,
wie man zum Stein spricht, wie
du
mit meinen Händen dorthin
und ins Nichts greifst, so
ist, was hier ist:
auch dieser
Fruchtboden klafft,
dieses
Hinab
ist die eine der wild-
blühenden Kronen. (1: 139–40)

[As one speaks to the stone, as
you
to me from the abyss, from
a homeland, con-
genial, cata-
pulted, you,
you to me long ago,
you to me in the nothingness of a night
you in the counter-night encountered, you,
counter-you—:

Then, since I was not there,
then, since you
paced off the plow land, alone:

Who,
who was it, that
race, the murdered one, the one
standing black in the sky:
rod and testicle—?

(Root.
Root of Abraham. Root of Jesse. No one's
root—o
ours.)

Yes,
as one speaks to the stone, as
you
with my hands over there
and into nothingness grasp, so
is what is here:
even this
receptacle gapes:
this
Downward
is one of the wild-
blooming crowns.]

"Radix, Matrix" describes the figure of an impossible dialogue. The attempt undertaken in the first clause to determine the speaking by placing the impersonal "one" in relation to the anorganic "stone," is already suspended with the insertion of the second part of the sentence, and this suspension is accomplished by an almost luxuriating digression in which the lyrical I apostrophizes this "you" in a series of pronominations that all touch on the forms of relation between the I and the "you," until the I inverts the direction of speaking: whereas at the beginning of the clause it still ran from the "you" to an indeterminate addressee, at its end it runs—inverted—along the line of illocution from the I to that "you." The second clause—"as / you," and with it, the determination of the addressee of the discourse of the "you"—remains open even after the end of the first strophe: the sentence it begins finds no conclusion. One finds only implicit indications of the possibility that the I could itself be the addressee of the discourse of the other. For the series of apostrophes speaks of this "you" as congenial, catapulted, and encountered exclusively in its relation to the I. But this virtual addressee, I, this virtualized I is characterized by its parallelism with the stone—the other addressee of the discourse—as mute, as voiceless and without determination: not something that can be the subject of the poem's discourse. In "Gespräch im Gebirg" (Dialogue in the Mountains), which may have originated contemporaneously with "Radix, Matrix," Celan writes of the stone: "It does not engage in discourse, it speaks, and whoever speaks, cousin, engages in discourse with no one; that one speaks, because no one hears it, no one and No one. . . ."[21] Since the determination of the discourse of the "you" remains suspended in the first stanza, something can be read in the second stanza that jumps, as it were, into the gap of the first—a new attempt at determination undertaken by the I, which at the same time expresses the reason why this I did not become the addressee of the discourse of the "you": "Then, since I was not there, / then, since you / paced off the plow land, alone: . . ." The "you" that paces off the plow land according to an archaic form of measurement and that accomplishes the determination of its site with this pace is without an addressee, without the I to whom it could turn its discourse. Yet the second stanza could be read as a continuation of the discourse of the I, who, without a voice or at least with an indeterminate voice, asserts its own absence, and it could also be read—with equal justification, especially if

---

21. "Er redet nicht, er spricht, und wer spricht, Geschwisterkind, der redet zu niemand, der spricht, weil niemand ihn hört, niemand und Niemand. . ." (3: 171).

one considers the colon at the end of the first sentence—as the discourse
of the "you" who "then . . . was not there" and who left the I alone
during its attempt at determination. This double character of discourse,
being both continuation and alteration; this double character of the two
points of the colon, signaling both continuity and interruption; these
two double characters not only have as their consequence the wandering
and diffusion of the "you" and the I of this text, they also yield the
ineluctable indeterminacy in the structure of speaking—a structure with
which the very discourse of the text is concerned and thus an indeterminacy in the discourse of the text itself that strikes its subject and its
addressee as well as its illocutionary character. Nothing of this discourse
is certain any longer, nor can anything in the discourse be subjected to
logical rules or their linguistic correlates, especially since the reciprocal
determination of the "you" and the I, which appeared to classical metaphysics and even to dialogics to be possible as an intersubjective event,
is referred to its lack of an object by means of interruption and immanent muteness. The ineluctable ambiguity of Celan's formulation
whereby the absence of the "you" suspends the I and the absence of the
I suspends the "you" and, accordingly, suspends discourse itself—this
unsublatable ambiguity realizes on the level of composition what the
apostrophe says about the "you" when it links up with the terminology
of dialogistics: namely, that it is the one encountered "in the nothingness of the night." But this nothingness is just as much the space in
which the "you" encounters the I as it is whatever, as the "you", encounters the I: nothingness encountered; nothingness speaks, and it speaks—
the I is also a form of that "you"—to nothingness. As one speaks to the
stone, so too does the stone speak: to no one and to nothing. But then
so does the poem make itself into the stone and into nothingness.

This, the most radical version of inversion whereupon language no
longer turns its own nothingness into the substantial Being of appearance, sound, and consciousness, as in Hegel and Rilke, but rather turns
its literary existence, compositionally and semantically, into nothingness
is grounded in the third stanza's questioning after the murdered race,
the murdered *Geschlecht*. This question, opened once again by the colon
of the preceding stanza, could pertain just as well to a "you" asking the
I or asking after the I as it could pertain to the I asking the "you" or
asking after the "you." This question questions, undecidably, from each
to each and asks for the ground of their commonality, inquiring after
that "race," after that *Geschlecht*, in which familial, genealogical, social,

sexual, and linguistic unity would be given and, in this gift of unity, the reciprocal determination of the subjects of speaking in dialogue as well as the determination of speaking and of language would first be made possible. But this question is not only undecidable in the sense that neither its subject nor its addressee can be discerned; it is also unde-cidable in the sense that it is an impossible question, a question not possible to answer, for it asks after the essence of a race—of a *Geschlecht*—that was murdered, destroyed, annihilated, and stands "black" in the sky like the "nothingness of a night." The question itself reacts to the inde-terminacy of its object, to its virtual loss of an object, and does so by ending up once again after a colon—"who was it, that race"—in an explicit apposition that could very well be the attempt at an answer that it itself has put into question: "Rute und Hode—?" Rod and testicle isolate the sexual aspect of the *Geschlecht* but not, as it might appear, its phallic aspect. For *Rute* is the word for the *radix*, which stands in Latin not only for vegetable root, for origin, source, firm ground, and soil, but also, as in *radix virilis* for the masculine member. *Hode,* on the other hand, derives from the Latin *cunnus,* the pudenda, and so corresponds to *matrix,* which just as much as *radix* means source, origin, and stem, but in its feminine aspect as progenitrix, womb, uterus.[22] Only together, as *Rute* and *Hode,* and brought still closer in the asyndeton of the title, as *radix, matrix:* as the coupling of the masculine and feminine sexes are they "that *Geschlecht,* that murdered one, the one / standing black in the sky." Only in this coupling do they fulfill the figure of immanent inver-sion that the erected abyss presents.

The question directed at this *Geschlecht,* at this coupling of *Geschlechter*—and it cannot be concluded from the text of the poem whether this coupling is not itself its murder—does not allow for an answer, because it is without an object, because the murdered *Geschlecht* after which it asks is not an object of possible presentation, even though it and it alone demands its presentation. For only in the *radix, matrix* would language have gained an object and an addressee as well as its own ground, its origin and its source, its provenance and the possibility

22. In this connection it is not unimportant that in the mystical speculations of Jacob Böhme, a few of which may have been known to Celan, *matrix* is given outstanding significance. See, in particular, *"De tribus principiis matrix* oder Beschreibung der Drei Prinzipien Göttlichen Wesens,"* chapters 5–13, in Jacob Böhme, *Sämtliche Schriften,* fac. of 1730 edition, ed. Will-Erich Peuckert (Stuttgart: Frommann, 1955–61), volume 2. See also further references in volume 11 (index).

of a future, and only by means of the *Geschlecht* and the commonality guaranteed in it could there be a dialogical mediation between "I" and "you" along with a communicating, determinate, and determining language. In asking after *radix, matrix,* the poem asks after its own ground. In presenting its question as objectless, it delivers itself up to the abyss of possible meaninglessness, indeterminacy, and incomprehensibility. With the open question whose openness is not incidental but indeed structural, the one who questions—"I" or "you" along with their two languages—places itself in question and wrenches open something that could have counted as a ground: opens itself as an abyss. In the open question, the poem makes itself into that speechless stone whose muteness is renounced by every community of language—of every *Geschlecht*—and announces nothing more than this renunciation. The language of this poem is *die Sekunde des Geschlechts*—the second of the race, this conduit of the sex—in which it, cut, murdered, no longer communicates nor mediates but, instead, im-parts that which, along with the *Geschlecht,* is cut in its nothingness. This "second" itself is the mark of castration, and in its historical, its most intolerable form, it is the mark of the murdering of European Jewry in the extermination camps of the Nazi regime. If, according to Adorno's dictum, "After Auschwitz . . . it became impossible . . . to write poems,"[23] and if Szondi made this more precise with the dictum that "after Auschwitz no poem is any longer possible except on the basis of Auschwitz,"[24] then, faced with "Radix, Matrix," it is necessary to add that this basis of the poem is an abyss, that it is not the condition of its possibility but of its impossibility, and that the poem can still speak only because it exposes itself to the impossibility of its speaking. It no longer speaks the language of a race or a sex, which could be the ground, center, origin, father, and mother; it speaks—deracinated, dematricated—the language of the murdered *Geschlecht.* For this reason, Auschwitz does not become for it a historically limited fact, the murder does not become an unproblematical object of speaking, but the objection of a question that concedes its muteness and thereby admits that it itself has been struck by that murder.

23. "Kulturkritik und Gesellschaft," in *Prismen* (Frankfurt am Main: Suhrkamp, 1955), 31; cf. "Cultural Criticism and Society," in Theodor W. Adorno, *Prisms,* trans. Samuel and Shierry Weber (Cambridge, Mass.: MIT Press, 1981), 34.
24. Peter Szondi, "Durch die Enge geführt," *Schriften,* 2: 384.

Not even the fourth stanza offers an answer. It stands—the parentheses around it indicate this—outside the discourse; it is the very discourse of the eradicated root, its parentheses having retracted and curtailed its significance and its determinacy. "No one's / root—o / ours." No one's root is not a root and at the same time the root of personal nonexistence. In the doubleness of this root—being both no root and the root of no one—the doubleness of "radix, matrix" refracts the doubleness of the nothingness of night that is a counter-night *(Aber-Nacht)*, of the You that is a counter-You *(Aber-Du):* an again-You and an against-You, a You and a not-You. So, as the immanent revocation of its name, its concept, and its linguistic sign, the nothingness at the root of language asserts itself within language, but against it and its semantic function. As the You always doubles and reduces itself to a counter-You for the I, so the root is our own only so long as it is no one's root, and it is no one's root only so long as it is ours. The commonality of the I and the You that first finds its word—"ours"—in this (parenthetical) place; this commonality, which is that of the sexes and is thus the race, is attained only where it is suspended in the loss of personal, generic, sexual, and historical existence. Only in their separation from one another and from the *Geschlecht,* as the ground of secure Being and of stable communication, can they be and be open to one another; only in the dispersal, dismemberment, and destruction of language's historical continuity and of the *Geschlecht*'s homogeneity does language—abandoned to its finitude, to its nothingness—impart.

This im-parting no longer underlies the figure of inversion, however little it can renounce it, for this figure is itself struck by division: "(Root. / Root of Abraham. Root of Jesse. No one's / root—o / ours.)" The terse genealogical catalogue, which contains an infinite genealogical promise, is—after "Jesse"—no longer subject to a chiasmus alone, to an inversion of the syntactical elements that sets "no one" in the place of "root," but this chiasmus is itself subjected by the line-break to an interruption that opens in the place of "root" an empty place—a "pause," a "hiatus," a "lacuna."[25] It is the pause in the meaning of the *Geschlecht*'s

25. *Pause, Wortlücke,* and *Leerstelle* are concepts employed by Celan in "Gespräch im Gebirg": ". . . es schweigt der Stock, es schweigt der Stein, und kein Schweigen, kein Wort ist da verstummt und kein Satz, eine Pause ists bloß, eine Wortlücke ists, eine Leerstelle ists, du siehst alle Silben umherstehn" [the stick goes silent, the stone goes silent, and no silence, no word is struck dumb here, nor any sentence; it is only a pause, a lacuna, a hiatus, you see all the syllables stand about] (3: 170). One encounters the

language—a pause that can no longer be characterized according to morphological oppositions. Only by virtue of such morphological oppositions, however, are linguistic signs and their meaning generated. This pause could be characterized as a zero-opposition, to use a concept Jakobson develops, and it could thus be understood as a linguistic event whose distinguishing mark consists in presenting no opposition to already established linguistic forms but which nevertheless—and indeed against Jakobson's definition of this concept[26]—persists in *not* neutralizing these oppositions. The lacuna between "no one's" and "root" cannot be brought down on either side of the opposition between meaning and meaninglessness: it maintains itself between the poles of this opposition, as it likewise maintains itself between the negative pronoun "no one's" and the noun "root," which—and here is a remarkable convergence between the formal and semantic structure of this line— designates the root of meaningfulness as such. Neither semantically nor asemantically cathected, the lacuna—and not only this one—holds open the space between negation and the negated, keeps it open for their relation and at the same time for the possibility of non-relation. Thus the pause between "no one's" and "root" stands between the nothingness of the *Geschlecht*'s language, which can still be asserted and thus become the negative referent of this language, on the one hand, and its sheer absence, on the other: between mere muteness and the possibility of saying or writing "mute." In the pause there is nothing and there is not nothingness. This pause is "the weight that holds back emptiness," as the text that precedes "Radix, Matrix" in *Niemandsrose* puts it: it holds the emptiness up, detaining and delaying it; the pause holds the emptiness fast and exorcises it; this pause hampers—be it only for the second of writing or reading—its arrival and its disappearance. The second of emptiness interrupts the inversion of the genealogical discourse of *radix, matrix* and holds it back. So held back is the "root" that it neither disappears *into* the discourse of origin nor *out* of it. Root: it becomes a

---

"same" inversion and the "same" hiatus between "Wurzel Jesse. Niemandes Wurzel" to "Wurzel—o / unser," where the "o"—placeholder for the "Wurzel"—is to be read not only as a plaintive sound but also as the graphic sign of the annulment of the root and of ours.

26. See "Sign Zéro," in *Selected Writings* (The Hague and Paris: Mouton, 1971), 2: 219.

root of no one's *Geschlecht* and of no one's language only by traversing its pause and therefore only as a suspended root. Only when this lacuna and loophole separate language from itself does language impart as ours; as language held in common, it only imparts as one held back by the collapse of communication.

Once this commonality is articulated in the suspension of commonality, the speaking of the poem again takes up the attempt at determination that was already interrupted in its second line, and it does so with the paradoxical amplification that, just as one speaks to a stone, so "you / with my hands over there / and into nothingness grasp." Speaking is grasping with the hands. In his letter to Hans Bender, Celan had written of poetry as hand-clasping[27] and had thereby taken up once again the dead metaphor of grasping a concept, of making oneself capable of being grasped and, held in this grasp, of being understood. Because of its parallelism with nothingness *(Nichts)*, the stone *(Stein)* shows itself to be anagrammic inversion: *Niets.* Just as the language of the murdered race gropes into nothingness and says nothing to no one, so "is what is here:" here, in the very *hic et nunc* of the poem; here is neither the site of sheer *nihil negativum* nor the locus of its reversal into fulfilled being of present language. Here the linguistic being is articulated—and being *is* only thus articulated—in which language reaches out to its own nothingness, to the nothingness of its reference, its meaning, and its determination. Language refers to nothingness as to its own no-longer; it is—and this is its *thus,* its mode, its genre, its kind, and its *Geschlecht*—the already-there of its no-longer, the reference to its nothingness in which the reference that makes it into language withdraws from itself. As the withdrawal of reference, however, it still is this draft of the possibility of its own impossibility; as the already-there of its no-longer, it is at the same time the still-there of its no-longer, so that the gap it opens up in itself, as the gap of its own nothingness, is also—while it holds open the *possibility* of this impossibility—the gaping of the vegetative receptacle. The collapse of the poem into the abyss of its impossibility is the *summum* of the possibilities of its speaking. Thus, cut by a caesura, speaking with the lacuna between its words, as its impossible You and its impossible I, the poem—deracinated and robbed of the matrix of its determi-

27. "Only true hands write true poetry. I see no difference in principle between handclasping and poetry" (Letter to Hans Bender dated 18 May 1960; 3: 117).

nations, without ground and without a law that would stand above it—imparts as "one of the wild- / blooming crowns."

> even this
> receptacle gapes:
> this
> Downward
> is one of the wild-
> blooming crowns.

Two impulses may have had a hand in the elevated pathos of this metaphor, the content of which still remains perfectly discreet. The first is Psalm 132:18: "His [David's] enemies will I clothe with shame: but upon himself shall his crown bloom." The other is a formulation from the *Book of Bahir*, which Celan may have known through Scholem's work on the symbolism of the Kabbalah; according to this book, "holy Israel" forms the "crown" of the tree of both the world and God.[28] From the same work of Scholem it emerges that, according to the *Zohar*, with which Celan must have been familiar, the "root of all roots" from which the tree draws nourishment is the nothingness that, as an aura, surrounds *En-Sof*: the non-basis and abyss of God.[29] However influential these biblical and kabbalistic metaphors may have been with regard to "Radix, Matrix," they are altered when they enter into Celan's text. In the poem there is no longer a root about which it could be absolutely said that it is nothingness, for nothingness appears only in a verbal form breached by a pause, as counter-nothingness, as non-nothingness and double-nothingness, as a vacancy and a holding back of its linguistic presentation. But the crown that is announced to David and his *Geschlecht* is here no longer one that blooms over him and that could be imparted to him from outside. The poem itself—"what is here . . . this / downward"—is one, but it is only one, not *the only one;* one but not the only wild-blooming, insubordinate, insubstantial crown.

There is—where no matrix remains—no longer any poem that could claim the privilege of being able to articulate the lacuna that the loss of

---

28. See Gershom Scholem, *Zur Kabbala und ihrer Symbolik* (Frankfurt am Main: Suhrkamp, 1973), 124; *On the Kabbalah and Its Symbolism,* trans. Ralph Manheim (New York: Schocken, 1965), 92.

29. See *Zur Kabbala,* 138; *On the Kabbalah,* 103.

this matrix opens up. For there is no longer the one lacuna that could stand alone at the end of the attempt to determine it. At the point where the support that speech could find in its object or in its own figures fails, speaking itself steps forward, altered. No end and no aim, no object—not even a negative one—and no subject—not even if this subject is said to be absent—organizes the poem; organization comes only from what it, here, *is:* a path, a movement *downward,* without further determination, destination or definition. This downward *without* ground is the crown. Where, however, the ground fails—and even the ground of *a* nothingness objectified, the ground of nothingness determined as *one*—there is also no longer the one, no longer *the* crown, and no longer *the* poem that could correspond to this failure. Not only the subject and figure of speaking but also this speaking itself loses its totalizing power. The inversion, which is no longer merely a rhetorical figure that this speaking would employ to present its objects but is, rather, the procedural form that is supposed to secure its own possibility, is disempowered. There is no longer the one and only inversion, no longer *the* inversion whereby the poem's descent could turn into a climax and its objectless question after the *Geschlecht* could become its highest pronouncement. The version the poem passes through is one of the inversions: one of two. Just as the grasp of the You, "with my hands," blossoms as one of the crowns into the nothingness of the I and its *Geschlecht,* so the other one blossoms in the grasping of the I, with your hands, into the nothingness of the You. I and Thou, which, according to dialogical theories, should reciprocally constitute each other, deconstitute each other in the chiasmus—it, too, an inversion—of their crossed attempts to get a grip on themselves and to make themselves capable of being grasped, until this deconstitution makes them into figures of an encounter with nothingness. Each one encounters in the other its own nothingness, and the discourse of the other opens itself to each one as the abyss of its own. "What is here" does not therefore only mean the poem in which "you / with my hands over there / and into nothingness grasp," and so does not only mean the chiastic crossing of I and You in the foundering and, by its foundering, the blooming grasp for the commonality of the *Geschlecht:* "what is here" acknowledges in the almost imperceptibly minor detail of the phrase *"one of the* crowns" that it is still the discourse of the I, that the poem thus remains bound to its primacy, and "what is here" also refers, in turn, to the missing complement that would be the *other* one of the crowns: the crown that does not bloom *here* and that does not blossom out of the I. The inversion does not offer itself as the entire inversion, as a total one. "Wurzelkrone: / gescheitelt" [crown of roots: / parted] (2: 196) — thus is the movement of "Radix, Matrix" expressed with extreme concentration in a later text from the volume *Fadensonnen*. One crown remains separate from the other, because there is no You for which the I would not once again be a You, no other whose strangeness the poem respects by declining to speak in its place. Its alterity remains insusceptible to sublation in the inversion. Only what is rootless — and is even without the root of the one nothingness — can be a crown. And only that other for whom even this crown is no root is itself a crown.

There are always at least two crowns. They do not submit to a common matrix by way of inversion. The inversion that was for a long phase of Celan's lyric production the very form of movement with which the I and its language could claim to mediate whatever eluded their grasp has ceased to be its rhetorical and epistemological matrix. It no longer constitutes the commonality of the one language of *Geschlecht* but — itself merely one of two, partial — only institutes the commonality of the reciprocal indeterminacy of I and You as they fail to encounter one another. Being-with-one-another is a gaping — of at once the abyss and the receptacle — which rips open the gap of being-oneself and its inversion into a thematic You. The parting of the two crowns that hold themselves together and apart no longer has a positive figure in the poem. The poem is the movement in which I and You im-part each other without being able to gather together in the one crown that is the positive figure of *this* poem. The poem — and, with it, the logic of inversion — imparts itself: to that which (it) cannot be. Only as the im-parting and this parting of speaking in which it exposes (itself) does the poem carry out the *encounter* with the alterity of the You, which is at the same time its own alteration. It speaks as the movement of alteration and thereby stops being merely *this* poem and merely a *poem*. It is the carrying out of the difference between itself and the other — not the carrying out therefore of the difference between its Being and its non-being no longer spoken in the voice of subjectivity; not the carrying out therefore of the difference between its determination by the one *Geschlecht* and its indeterminacy written from the position of objectified Being; no longer therefore fixed to the arche-teleological line of communication. It is rather the carrying out of the difference between its meaning and the incapacity of meaning in view of nothingness—and it is therefore a poem that withdraws from the schematisms of semantics, and only by virtue of its parasemantic character does it attain the peculiar gravity of its speaking. "Radix, Matrix" is a poem that departs from the radix and the matrix of every provenance and parts ways with itself.[30] Only as a movement of its deracination, dematrication, dissemination is it a speaking that has nothing above it, nothing about it, and does not speak *about* anything. It is the experience of freedom from its own language. And only in giving up the grounding figure that organizes its movement— that of inversion—and in crossing out its own trope, is it on a path that neither it itself nor its basic figure dominates. The radicalization of inversion leads to the giving up of inversion as a matrix.

Since the time of the transcendental turn in philosophy and literature at the very latest, the figure of inversion has been tied to the idea of turning back, of returning and restoring the self. The immanent reversal of history, represented as a process of disintegration, is supposed to allow the subject to grasp once again its authentic shape and to attain an undistorted understanding of itself and its language. Inversion can thus be characterized as the figure of the historical, aesthetic, and hermeneutic self-relation of the subject, as the privileged trope of subjectivity in general. In this figure, language not only relates to itself and refers to itself; in it and as it, it *is* real and effective in the first place. Szondi has spelled out the consequences of this theory of subjectivity for one part of Celan's lyrical production, without, of course, committing himself to this theory. In "Poetry of Constancy—Poetik der Beständigkeit," at the end of his analysis of Celan's translation of a Shakespeare sonnet, he writes that Celan has "replaced the traditional symbolist poem, which is concerned only with itself and which has itself as its subject-matter, with a poem that is no longer concerned with itself but that is itself."[31] Szondi's formulation has the merit of insisting on a trait of Celan's lyrics that threatens to be concealed by the theories of negativity advanced by

30. Bernard Böschenstein's fine comment on "Sperrtonnensprache" points in a similar direction: "The poem has outlived and survived itself" (*Leuchttürme* [Frankfurt am Main: Insel, 1977], 305).

31. Peter Szondi, *Schriften*, 2: 344; "The Poetry of Constancy," 178.

much of the scholarship devoted to his poetry. Conversely, Szondi's formulation has the disadvantage of disregarding the specific constitution of the poem so as to affirm its selfhood. Celan's texts do not part ways with subjectivity by adhering to the sphere of sheer objectivity located in their linguistic being, to find there a new home and a guarantee for their constancy, as so-called concrete poetry tries to do through the technical organization of language reduced to material; rather, they depart from subjectivity by articulating the structure of self-relation and self-reference as that of a linguistic act which, once dissolved from the self and the logic of its positing, attains an altered relation to itself in the very movement of dissolution. Language is not posited but projected: in accordance with a graphic paranomasia, a paragraphism that corresponds to the one in Greek between λογος and λογχη, "word" and "javelin"—the word *(Wort)* is a throwing stick *(Wurf-holz);* a boomerang, a projectile with the ability to turn on itself and return to its place of departure if thrown in the right way. In Celan's poem "Ein Wurfholz" (A Boomerang), which describes the movement of the word to itself, the point of departure is no longer taken up in the discourse, as it had been in the poem "Aber" (But) from *Sprachgitter,* where, relying on the classical poetic emblem of the swan, he has the boomerang to which it is compared whiz by "from nothingness":

> die Schwäne,
> in Genf, ich sah's nicht, flogen, es war,
> als schwirrte, vom Nichts her, ein Wurfholz
> ins Ziel einer Seele: . . . (1: 182)

> [the swans,
> in Geneva, I didn't see it, flew, it was,
> as if, from nothingness, a boomerang whizzed by
> into the target of a soul: . . .]

The reference to this initial nothingness first installs itself in a later text from *Niemandsrose* at the site where the word arrives—in its relation to itself:

> EIN WURFHOLZ, auf Atemwegen,
> so wanderts, das Flügel-
> mächtige, das

Wahre. Auf
Sternen-
bahnen, von Welten-
splittern geküßt, von Zeit-
körnern genarbt, von Zeitstaub, mit-
verwaisend mit euch,
Lapilli, ver-
zwergt, verwinzigt, ver-
nichtet,
verbracht und verworfen,
sich selber der Reim,—
so kommt es
geflogen, so kommts
wieder und heim,
einen Herzschlag, ein Tausendjahr lang
innezuhalten als
einziger Zeiger im Rund,
das eine Seele,
das seine
Seele
beschrieb,
das eine
Seele
beziffert. (1: 258)

[A BOOMERANG, on breath-ways,
so it wanders, the wing-
powered, the
true. On
astral
orbits, by world-
splinters kissed, by time-
kernels grained, by time-dust, co-
orphaned with you,
Lapilli, be-
littled, dwarfed, an-
nihilated,
deported and thrown away,
itself the rhyme,—
thus it comes
flown, thus it comes

back and home,
for a heartbeat, for a millennium,
to pause as
a lone hand on the dial,
by one soul,
by its soul
inscribed,
by one
soul
ciphered.]

Thrown, a boomerang—this word—is already on its way with the first word of the poem, thus not at home but grasped in the flight of its displacements and transformations, "on breath-paths." It is under way along not one but several elliptical or circular orbits which traverse the domains of the living (*Atemwege* also means "respiratory ducts"), the mythical ("the wing- / powered" not only contains an allusion to Hermes, the winged messenger-god of Greek mythology, but also to angels, the messengers of God in Judaic and Christian mythology), and the cosmic ("astral / orbits"), and, as it wanders through these domains, it turns into another: from the collisions with the shards of the world and of time that it undergoes on these orbits, it is increasingly diminished, "be- / littled, dwarfed," in order finally to be "an- / nihilated." Only thus—"an- / nihilated, deported and thrown away"—only in such a way that it is brought to the point of disappearing, brought away from the path of living breath, de-ported, despised, not made familiar and, thrown in the wrong direction, not brought to the target for which it was destined—: only in this way does it come, "it comes / back and home." Not by corresponding to something else, to another *Wort* (word) or another *Ruf* (call); not by reaching the intentions bound up with its throw or by reaching out to the intended addressee, but by corresponding to nothing and to no one, by speaking to nothing and to no one as to itself; only therefore by being "itself the rhyme," can it be said of the *Wurfholz,* this boomerang, that "it comes / flown . . . it comes / back and home." But it does not come to itself as if it were a given, objective being; annihilated, it comes to a nothingness whose place is not the grounding point of departure of its movement nor the target of its meaning but is, instead, the false, the failed, the site of failure

reached only in the displacement and distortion of the general topogra-
phy of intentions by way of its de-portation and its throwing away. This
is not the site of a positive nothingness, for *ver-* / *nichtet* does not simply
mean *vernichtet* but, as the severing of the *ver-* brings out its intensifying,
digressive, and dissimulative connotations (as in *verschreiben*, "mis-
write," or *versetzen*, "displace"), it also means the failure of this annihilation; it is not the site of a nothingness that corresponds with itself. The
site to which the word, the call, the topos come back and come home is
the u-topos found wherever it does not itself arrive as word, call, and
topos. The word comes to itself as to nothing. In "Deine Augen im Arm"
(Your Eyes in the Arm), from *Fadensonnen* (2: 123), Celan makes it clear
that the negation of "where" *(wo)* is at the same time the negation and
the stupefaction of the "word" *(Wort)*, when he writes this negation as
entwo.[32] This poem—itself the word, "a boomerang"—does not write
this coming-to-itself by positing itself as an objective entity that it itself
grasps, but writes it by exposing itself to the movement of its disappearance. It exposes itself to damage, to being thrown away, to annihilation;
it sets out to disrupt itself by exposing itself to the distance from its
destination and to the rejection of its form; and it ex-poses itself by
interrupting its discourse. In every one of its word-breaks and line-
breaks, in every one of its alterations of images, in its central line, it so
ex-poses itself that it characterizes its linguistic self-reference not as identity but as paranomasia, as *Reim* (rhyme), and it makes this outcome
even more precise through the rhyme-word *heim* (home), thus by way
of a further alteration. And in its central line it ex-poses itself even more:
this pivotal line is interrupted with a dash that disrupts the discourse
precisely where it comes to itself. Celan's poem, where it comes to itself,
is the rhyme, the paranomasia of its an-nihilation. Its word is the ex-posure—the interruption and breakdown—of its being. "La poésie," as it
is said in the sole French maxim of Celan that has so far been transmitted, "la poésie ne s'impose plus, elle s'expose."[33]

The return and the homecoming of the word to itself, traditionally
regarded as the awakening of the potencies exhausted by conventional
usage or as the "metapoetic" reflection of its content and thus, once

---

32. Cf. Winfried Menninghaus's analysis in *Paul Celan: Magie der Form* (Frankfurt am
Main: Suhrkamp, 1980), 62–67.

33. "Poetry no longer imposes, it exposes itself" (3: 181).

again, as the inversion that sets things in order, takes a strange turn in Celan's poem, for it does not return in restituted form to its authentic and proper site but returns, instead, in a scarred, dismembered, and finally an-nihilated form at a site that is not its own, at site where it is not itself. The word is just as little itself here as it means itself. It refers only in orphaning: its *Verweisung* (reference) is always a *Verwaisung* (orphaning). It separates itself from its provenance and from the intentions to which it is bound; it mortifies what is meant by it and addressed with it, and it is therefore the movement of infinite singularization. The sole connection it maintains is the link—expressed in a lapidary fashion, like everything in Celan—with what is likewise on the way to becoming an orphan: "co- / orphaned with you, / Lapilli." This "Lapilli," the only apostrophe in this poem, evokes the whole series of stones and rock-formations with which Celan's texts, true lithographs, calculate; the philosopher's alchemical stone, *der Stein der Weisen,* as well as that of the orphans, *des Steins, den der Waisen* (1: 283); the white stone of the apocalypse, which resembles the hidden manna and in which a new name is written, a name that no man knows save he who receives it (Rev. 2:17); the voting stones of Artemis that save Orestes; the white stones of Hänsel and Gretel which failed to show them the way home; "The Stone" from Mandelstam's first volume of poetry; and the pebble that—like "language," the "three-year-land of your mother" and the "bud on her breast"—"your thoughts carried to Prague, / to the grave, to graves, into life" (1: 285).[34] With all these and many other memorials and head-stones, the poet invokes in particular the black ballot-pebbles called *lapilli,*[35] from the fifteenth book of Ovid's *Metamorphoses,* which condemned the one named Myscelus—not so far from Celan—to death and which later, having been transformed into a white stone under the influence of Hercules, freed him and allowed him to leave his fatherland to found a new city at the site designated by God, at the grave of Croton. This absolving and expiating trait of Ovid's *lapilli* is even more pointed in Celan's poem, since the orphaning of its "Lapilli" knows neither a God nor a homeland beyond its own nothingness.

---

34. Cf. Israel Chalfen, *Paul Celan* (Frankfurt am Main: Suhrkamp, 1983), 30.

35. "Mos erat antiquus niveis atrisque lapillis, / his damnare reos, illis absolvere culpa" (It was the practice, in days of old, to condemn prisoners with black pebbles, to acquit them with white); Ovid, *Metamorphoses,* XV, 336; ll. 41–42.

Following the syntactical ambiguity of the lines "by time- /kernels grained, by time-dust, co-/ orphaned with you,/ Lapilli, be-/ littled, dwarfed," this orphaning can be an orphaning *by* the boomerang, or it can be a boomerang whose object is the boomerang itself. The orphaned word becomes that from which it was orphaned. It becomes a kernel of time: the smallest segment of time and the seed of time, isolated as the "lone hand on the dial" which points, isolated as the graphic atom of the elapsing of time (the form of the boomerang in fact resembles that of the hands of the clock); it becomes an index, a script, and a cipher of time and history, which marks its own passing away (the crooked figure of the boomerang, like a "C," presents not only a Roman numeral but also the first letter of Celan's name: one can read the entire poem as a "C élan", as a hypogram, a signature, an autobiographical stenogram).[36] The word—the poem—is, as self-orphaning, "the second" in which it

36. Among the palimpsests of "EIN WURFHOLZ" may be the "Speech of Christ, after Death, from the Cosmos, that there is no God," the "First Flower-Piece" from the *Siebenkäs* of Jean Paul, whom Celan held in high esteem. Its central theme is that the atheist is orphaned: "No one is so much alone in the universe as a denier of God. With an orphaned heart, which has lost the greatest of fathers, he stands mourning" (Jean Paul, *Werke,* ed. N. Miller [Munich: Hanser, 1971], 2: 270; cf. *Flower, Fruit and Thorn Pieces,* trans. Edward Henry Noel [Leipzig: Tauchnitz, 1871], 1: 279). This also means that the son of God who denies God has ceased to be himself (a son of God) and is in fact fatherless: "'We are all orphans, I and you; we are without a father'" (2: 273; 1: 282). The path the dead Christ traverses in search of his father is not unlike the one taken by the boomerang: "'I traversed the world. I ascended into the suns, and flew the milky ways through the wilderness of the heavens; but there is no God'" (2: 273; 1: 281–82). The "I" finds itself annihilated, in "frozen, dumb Nothingness" (2: 274; 1: 283). It is the fate of the particular poetic figures in Jean Paul's "Speech," like that of the boomerang, to announce their own dissociation and destruction. They are allegories in the strict sense, the sense given by Benjamin: they signify the non-being of what they present. See Walter Benjamin, *Der Ursprung des deutschen Trauerspiels* in *Gesammelte Schriften,* 1: 406; cf. *The Origin of German Tragic Drama,* trans. John Osborne (New York: Verso, 1985), 233. The closeness as well as the distance between Jean Paul's "Speech" and Celan's poem emerge with the greatest clarity in noting that, in Celan's Democritean universe, orphaning no longer refers to God but only to itself, thereby annuling its own indexical function; the "dial" which the boomerang—"its / soul"—"described" and whose "solitary hand" it is displays the same O, the same untimely conditioning of time and of the sign as does the "dial-plate" of eternity in Jean Paul: "Aloft, on the church-dome, stood the dial-plate of Eternity; but there is no figure visible upon it, and it was its own index [*Zeiger,* hand]; only a black finger pointed to it, and the dead wished to read the time upon it" (2: 273; 1: 281).

separates itself from itself. As an orphaning that is itself orphaned, it lacks every semantic or communicative reference; as an orphaned, objectless orphaning that has become selfless, its coming to itself, its homecoming, and return stand under the sign of non-arrivability. The boomerang comes to itself, to language—but, orphaned by itself, it does not arrive. Only because and as long as it does not arrive, does it come home. Its homecoming and return are this: not arriving. Being, being-oneself, being-with-one-another is a coming without arrival. "A Boomerang," however much it turns on itself and describes its trajectory as a circle, is not and cannot mean—metapoetically—itself; rather, it refers, out of the distance necessary for this referral, to itself as a distancing reference that can never reach home—its literal sense, intended meaning, the thing meant, the desired word—without confronting therein that distancing, that referring altered into an orphaning, and thus confronting the fact that the orphaning is not present in the reference itself. The relation of every reference to itself writes itself necessarily—and so the "boomerang" is not called true but "the/ true"—as the spatiotemporal distancing and drafting of reference, as its self-withdrawal. As language without language. Its speaking of itself is this conduit, the second in which it departs from itself and is with itself, with the parting, the difference. Its being—being is orphaning. Its inversion is the trope that, traversing itself, gapes open.[37]

37. At the end of the "Meridian" address, Celan writes: "Ich finde etwas—wie die Sprache—Immaterialles, aber Irdisches, Terrestrisches, etwas Kreisförmiges, über die beiden Pole in sich selbst Zurückkehrendes und dabei—heitererweise—sogar die Tropen Durchkreuzendes—: ich finde . . . einen *Meridian*" [I find something—like language—immaterial yet earthly, terrestrial, something circular, returning to itself over the two poles and thereby—cheerfully—even traversing the tropics. I find . . . a *meridian*] (3: 202). Marlies Janz has stressed the possibility that the address about the "meridian" could represent a greeting to Adorno, who refers to a meridian, if only very casually, at the outset of his essay "Valérys Abweichungen" (Valéry's Deviations), published in 1960 and dedicated to Celan in gratitude for his "Gespräch im Gebirg." See *Vom Engagement absoluter Poesie: Zur Lyrik und Ästhetik Paul Celans* (Frankfurt am Main: Syndikat, 1976), 115–16. With equal—if not more pertinent—justification, one could venture the conjecture that the address on the "meridian" refers to Heidegger's text, "Zur Seinsfrage" (in *Wegmarken*, 2nd and rev. and enl. ed. [Frankfurt am Main: Klostermann, 1987], 379–419), which was first published as a response to Ernst Jünger's "Über die Linie" (in *Sämtliche Werke* [Stuttgart: Klett-Cotta, 1980], 7: 239–80; Essays vol. 1) with the title "Über 'Die Linie.'" This text, like the one of Jünger, characterizes the "line" as the *Nullmeridian*, "the

For a better understanding of "A la pointe acérée," Celan reported in a conversation[38] that he borrowed the title of the text from a note by Baudelaire, cited in Hofmannsthal's journal under the date June 29, 1917: "Il est de certaines sensations délicieuses dont le vague n'exclut pas l'intensité, et il n'est pas de pointe plus acérée que l'Infini."[39] Celan's poem, as its ambiguous title indicates, is written *on* this point of the infinite and *with* it. Immediately before this citation from Baudelaire, Hofmannsthal quotes from Paul Claudel's *Les Muses,* as follows: "O mon âme! Le poème n'est point fait de ces lettres que je plante comme des clous, mais du blanc qui reste sur le papier."[40] Hofmannsthal adds this remark: "Here is the very image of the emptiness that persecutes me," and follows with a stylistic observation about Claudel's "highly peculiar prose," which ties down the rush of the sentence by a "sudden freezing." In Celan's poem, it is not the overflowing of language but the "blanc qui reste sur le papier" that crystalizes itself; it is the "unwritten" that hardens into language in accordance with another saying of Hofmannsthal, the final words Death speaks in *Der Tor und der Tod* (Death and the Fool): human beings are the ones "who interpret the uninterpretable,/ Who read what was never written."[41] With the pointers Hof-

---

prime meridian." These two references are not mutually exclusive; in accordance with Celan's usual procedure, they may be thought as concentrated into the single word "meridian." As far as I know, the only serious discussion devoted to the problem of Celan's relation to Heidegger is to be found in Philippe Lacoue-Labarthe, *La Poèsie comme expérience* (Paris: Bourgois, 1986), 11–58.

38. The conversation was with Dietlinde Meinecke; see *Wort und Name bei Paul Celan* (Bad Homburg: Gehlen, 1970), 229–30.

39. "There are certain delicious sensations whose vagueness does not exclude intensity, and there is no sharper point than Infinity" (Hugo von Hofmannsthal, *Aufzeichnungen,* ed. H. Steiner [Frankfurt am Main: Fischer, 1959], 181). Hofmannsthal quotes from the third piece in Baudelaire's *Spleen de Paris,* entitled "Le confiteor de l'artiste." "The sharpest point of the Infinite" is quoted again in Hofmannsthal's 1924 prose poem "Erinnerung" (Remembrance), as "the point of a lance" that destines the one whose heart is hit— Hofmannsthal speaks here of his own experience—to be a poet (*Gesammelte Werke,* ed. B. Schöller [Frankfurt am Main: Fischer, 1979], 7: 155).

40. "O my soul! The poem is not at all made of these letters that I plant like nails but of the white that remains on the paper."

41. "Die, was nicht deutbar, dennoch deuten, / Was nie geschrieben wurde, lesen" (Hofmannsthal, *Gesammelte Werke,* 1: 297–98; cf. "Death and the Fool," in Hofmannsthal, *Three Plays,* trans. Alfred Schwarz [Detroit: Wayne State University Press, 1966], 65)

mannsthal gave him, Celan reads in the opening lines of his poem the "pointe acérée de l'Infini" about which Baudelaire speaks as the "clous plantés de ces lettres" to which Claudel refers; against Claudel's intentions, however, he reads them as the high point in which the unwritten, instead of remaining outside of writing, contracts into writing. Writing concentrates the *blanc*. The infinite emptiness that crystalizes into language remains effective in language and through language as the intermittent movement of laying bare and setting free.

> Es liegen die Erze bloß, die Kristalle,
> die Drusen.
> Ungeschriebenes, zu
> Sprache verhärtet, legt
> einen Himmel frei.
>
> (Nach oben verworfen, zutage,
> überquer, so
> liegen auch wir.) (1: 251)

> [The ores are laid bare, the crystals,
> the druses.
> The unwritten, into
> language hardened, sets
> a sky free.
>
> (Rejected upward, into daylight,
> crisscross, so
> we too lie.)]

However much Celan's poetry may be quoting in these lines, it always quotes only the unwritten, the empty, the holes, the *blanc*. No topos, not even the topoi it employs, determines the site, none of its tropes determine the movement, and no method defines the path of the poem. The *loci communes* of "ore" and "crystals" open in the hollows of the "druses" an emptiness that no writing, however hardened, can capture except in circum-scription and trans-scription; the metaphor of petrifying the unwritten into language, itself written, brings to light that it misses the unwritten; the "Wege dorthin./ . . . der blubbernden Radspur entlang" [the ways hither . . . along the spluttering wheel track] (1: 251) follow, by paranomasia, "der Spur einer Rede" [the trace of a discourse] that lays bare in the explosion of its bubbles something it conceals. These are the ways of the poem—"spluttering ways hither." Something is under way along these ways, not in order to come into language but to lay bare what must remain vacant in its petrifaction, unwritten in the poem, and unattainable in its progress toward the "unrepeatable": it is under way toward that which has not come into language, on its way to the indeterminable, along a trace, as a reading:

Auf-
gelesene
kleine, klaffende
Buchecker: schwärzliches
Offen, von
Fingergedanken befragt
nach—
wonach? (1: 251)

[Col-
lected, read
open,
small, gaping
beech nuts: blackish
Open, by
finger thoughts questioned
after—
after what?]

The seed capsule "col-/ lected" from a beech—from a book—is, with respect to its "Open," that which is read open *(offen-gelesene):* interpretation is setting free, *Auslegung* is *Freilegung.* Reading, as *lectio* and *Lesen,* is not so much a collecting and storage, a recollecting and a sublation, as an opening of language onto what remains unsaid in it, what indicates itself in it of the unrepeatable bygone, what merely announces itself as coming. This co-lectio is the questioning movement of thought along a way that cannot lead to the unrepeatable as long as it is a way cleared by conventions of discourse and reading. Insofar as it relates to the unrepeatable, the reading of the poem does not give back a pregiven reality; it does not detain any hidden or remote sense in the house of language; rather, it opens itself onto a coming that no intentional act can bring about. The poem therefore takes a turn in its last stanza and no longer speaks of its going or the goings-on of a reader but, inversely, of a coming.

> Etwas, das gehn kann, grußlos
> wie Herzgewordenes,
> kommt. (1: 252)

> [Something, that can go, without greetings
> like a heart transformed,
> comes.]

What comes here can, however, be double. From the viewpoint of the reading that gropes along, what comes is the unwritten, that which is interrogated in all reading, and the unwritten must impart from itself to interpretation by way of its coming, since it could not otherwise become an object even of the most abstract thought. On the other hand, from the vanishing point of the unwritten, what comes is the poem with its questioning reading.

> Etwas, das gehn kann, grußlos
> wie Herzgewordenes,
> kommt.

As the movement of writing, the poem approaches itself as the unwritten—the unwritten comes to the poem as the experience of the interruption of its writing. Its going is the coming of the unrepeatable. It comes as the disfiguration of the figures into which writing has conjured its language. Selfless, it writes itself only in writing the coming of an other, of the poem; it writes itself only in writing itself otherwise and in ascribing itself to another. As for the poem, what is coming in its writing is not itself but that which it does not write. It is always the other that comes. This two-turned coming—the implicit inversion of writing and the unwritten, of reading and the unreadable, in every poem, every speaking and reading—is itself the movement of alteration in which even the most hardened and petrified self opens itself toward an other. The "ores" *(Erze)* of the beginning are then "transformed into a heart" *(Herzgewordenes)*.

What comes, always the other, must be able to set out on a way, to go and also to go away. It has not been said that what is coming also arrives. But the possibility that whatever comes goes away belongs to the conditions of coming—of the poem and of what it does not write, of reading and what it does not read. Without greetings, without a word, in a going even prior to the alternatives of coming and going, in the linguistic movement prior to the choice between the word "come" and the word "go," it is there and gone away. It writes itself, it reads itself—it comes—free.

Sources

"Premises" was written for this volume.

"Hermeneutic Ellipses: Writing the Hermeneutic Circle in Schleiermacher" first appeared as "Hermeneutische Ellipsen: Zirkel und Schrift bei Schleiermacher" in *Texthermeneutik,* ed. Ulrich Nassen (Paderborn: Schöningh, 1979). A slightly revised English version, translated by Timothy Bahti, appeared in *Transforming the Hermeneutic Context: From Nietzsche to Nancy,* ed. Gayle L. Ormiston and Alan D. Schrift (Albany, N.Y.: SUNY Press, 1990).

"The Promise of Interpretation: Remarks on the Hermeneutic Imperative in Kant and Nietzsche" was first delivered in March, 1983, at the University of California at Santa Barbara. That early version was published under the title "Das Versprechen der Auslegung: Überlegungen zum hermeneutischen Imperativ bei Kant und Nietzsche" in *Spiegel und Gleichnis: Festschrift für Jacob Taubes,* ed. N. W. Bolz and W. Hübener (Würzburg: Königshausen & Neumann, 1983) and translated by Jane O. Newman and John H. Smith for *Looking After Nietzsche,* ed. Lawrence A. Rickels (Albany: SUNY Press, 1990). This is a revised version.

A version of "'Disgregation of the Will': Nietzsche on the Individual and Individuality" was written in January 1984 for the Colloquium "Reconstructing Individualism" at the Humanities Center of Stanford University. It was revised in December 1984 and published under the title "'Disgregation des Willens': Nietzsche über Individuum und Individualität," *Nietzsche-Studien* 15 (Berlin: de Gruyter, 1986), and in the English translation of Jeffrey Librett in *Reconstructing Individualism,* ed. Thomas Heller, Morton Sosna, and David Wellbery (Stanford: Stanford University Press, 1986). The present version was completed in July 1991.

An earlier version of "'Lectio': de Man's Imperative" was translated by Susan Bernstein for *Reading de Man Reading,* ed. Lindsay Waters and Wlad Godzich (Minneapolis: University of Minnesota Press, 1989), 171–201.

"Position Exposed: Friedrich Schlegel's Poetological Transposition of Fichte's Absolute Proposition" was delivered in Strasburg as an address to an international colloquium on genre (July 4–8, 1979), organized by the Université de Strasbourg, the State University of New York at Buffalo, and the Johns Hopkins University. The address was published in *Modern Language Notes* 95 (1980) under the title "Der Satz der Gattung: Friedrich Schlegels poetologische Umsetzung von Fichtes unbedingtem Grundsatz." This is a revised version.

"The Quaking of Presentation: Kleist's 'Earthquake in Chile'" was drawn from a longer study completed in May 1982 and published under the title "Das Beben der Darstellung" in *Positionen der Literaturwissenschaft,* ed. D. E. Wellbery (Munich: Beck, 1985).

"The Gesture in the Name: On Benjamin and Kafka" was delivered first in a series of lectures on literary modernity for the German Department at Yale University (1991) and in another version, a year later, as the tenth Reinhard Kuhn Memorial Lecture sponsored by the Department of Comparative Literature at Brown University.

"The Second of Inversion: Movements of a Figure through Celan's Poetry" was written in 1984 and first published in the translation of William Jewett for *Yale French Studies* 69 (1985). It appeared in German under the title "Die Sekunde der Inversion: Bewegungen einer Figur durch Celans Gedichte" in *Paul Celan,* ed. Werner Hamacher and Winfried Menninghaus (Frankfurt am Main: Suhrkamp, 1988). A new version was translated by Peter Fenves for *Word Traces,* ed. Aris Fioretos (Baltimore: Johns Hopkins University Press, 1994). This is a revised translation.

Index

Adorno, Theodor, 39–40, 158n, 368, 382n
Agamben, Giorgio, 32n, 334n
Aristotle, 5–6, 18, 50
Ast, Friedrich, 47–48

Barthes, Roland, 317
Bataille, George, 39n
Baudelaire, Charles, 383
Benjamin, Walter, 254, 260, 308, 294–336, 361n; *Arcades Project*, 307n; *A Berlin Childhood Around 1900*, 305; *Illuminations*, 298–300, 303, 305-06, 309, 317, 327, 329–333, 336; *Origin of the German Mourning-Play*, 197n, 302n; *Reflections*, 297–98
Blanchot, Maurice, 361n
Böhme, Jacob, 367n
Böschenstein, Bernhard, 281n, 375n
Bourget, Paul, 164, 165n
Brecht, Bertolt, 296–98
Brod, Max, 319
Büchner, Georg, 354

Cacciari, Massimo, 302n
Celan, Paul, 21, 337–87; "Chymisch," 346; *Fadensonnen*, 359n; *Gegenlicht*, 344–45; "Gegenlicht," 345–46; "Gespräch im Gebirg," 365; "Huhediblu," 356; "Lob der Ferne," 349–51; "The Meridian," 41–43, 353, 354, 382n; *Mohn und Gedächtnis*, 345–46, 351, 354; *Niemandsrose*, 346; "A la pointe acérée," 383–86; "Radix, Matrix," 363–75; "Reisekamerad,"

362; "Spät und Tief," 348–49; *Sprachgitter*, 357; "Stumme Herbstgerüche," 346–47; "Ein Wurfholz," 376–82
Chalfen, Israel, 362n, 380n

d'Alembert, Jean Le Rond, 267–68
de Man, Paul, 181–221, 342n; "Allegory (*Julie*)," 184, 192–93, 198–203, 207; "Excuses (*Confessions*)," 212, 219; "Hypogram and Inscription," 356n; "Promises (*Social Contract*)," 203, 215, 217; "Reading (Proust)," 183, 185–88, 190, 191, 211; "Resistance to Theory," 207-08; "The Rhetoric of Temporality," 215, 351n; "Self (*Pygmalion*)," 211n; "Semiology and Rhetoric," 188–90; "Shelley Disfigured," 213
Derrida, Jacques, 32n, 54n, 64n, 104n, 159n, 160-01n, 215n, 221n, 272n, 274n, 287n, 302n, 308n, 314n
Descartes, René, 232, 263
Dilthey, Wilhelm, 22–25
Düttmann, Alexander García, 308n, 314n;

Emrich, Wilhelm, 319–20
Euripides, 22, 280–81, 286–87n

Fenves, Peter, 314n
Fichte, Johann Gottlieb, 12, 13, 146, 230–43, 257; "Foundations for the Entire *Wissenschaftslehre*," 232–33
Fischer, Kuno, 109
Flaubert, Gustave, 258

Förster, Eckart, 12n
Frank, Manfred, 59n, 64n, 341n

Gadamer, Hans-Georg, 49–51; *Truth and Method*, 37n
Goethe, Johann Wolfgang von, 9n, 20, 145, 251

Hamann, Johann Georg, 66, 252
Hardenberg, Friedrich von (Novalis), 108, 230, 238
Hebel, Peter, 22
Hegel, G. W. F., 13, 60, 108, 146, 269, 338–40; *Lectures on the Philosophy of History*, 5–11, 339; *Phenomenology of Spirit*, 115, 340; *Science of Logic*, 13
Heidegger, Martin, 26–38, 39n, 50, 218, 382–83n; *Being and Time*, 26–38, 100n, 149–50n, 361n; *Introduction to Metaphysics*, 20n; "Kant's Thesis on Being," 98n, 231n; *Nietzsche*, 138n, 140n; "On the Essence of Truth," 38; "The Origin of the Work of Art," 197–98n; "Die Sprache," 354–55n
Henrich, Dieter, 235n, 269n
Hintikka, Jaakko, 236–37n
Hobbes, Thomas, 96n
Hofmannsthal, Hugo von, 383
Hölderlin, Friedrich, 20, 66, 85n, 341–42n, 354n
Humboldt, Wilhelm von, 320n
Hume, David, 96n

Jakobson, Roman, 72n, 191, 370
Janz, Marlies, 382n
Joyce, James, 21

Kafka, Franz, 20, 140n, 294–336; "Before the Law," 298, 300–01; "Cares of a Family Man," 318–26; "A Crossbreed," 311–12; *The Diaries of Franz Kafka*, 295, 301n, 311, 312, 322, 325n; "The Judgment," 311; "The Metamorphosis," 311; "The New Advocate," 315n; "An Old Manuscript," 312, 314–15; "On Parables," 304–05;

"A Report to an Academy," 311; *The Trial*, 299–300
Kant, Immanuel, 11, 39n, 67, 85–108, 111, 112, 117, 124, 129, 141, 145, 175, 188, 245, 264, 302n, 338–40; *Critique of Judgment*, 12n, 85n, 102–03n, 272–79; *Critique of Practical Reason*, 93, 94n; *Critique of Pure Reason*, 11–12, 94n, 271; *Groundwork for the Metaphysics of Morals*, 88n, 90n, 93, 96, 97n, 98n; *Metaphysics of Morals*, 103, 105; "On the Failure of All Philosophical Attempts at Theodicy," 85, 91n, 107-08; *The One Possible Basis of Proof for a Demonstration of the Existence of God*, 11, 98, 231n; *Opus postumum*, 14n
Kierkegaard, Søren, 20, 22, 39n, 128n, 146
Kleist, Heinrich von, 20, 261–93; "Earthquake in Chile," 264–72, 274–93
Kripke, Saul, 314

La Bruyère, Jean de, 224n
Lacoue-Labarthe, Philippe, 147n, 383n
Laroche, Emmanuel, 313n
Leclaire, Serge, 314n
Leibniz, Gottfried Wilhelm, 143–44, 151, 232n, 266; "Principles of Nature and Grace," 126, 244n
Lessing, Gotthold Ephraim, 316
Lévinas, Emmanuel, 42n
Locke, John, 96n

Mallarmé, Stéphane, 66, 258
Menninghaus, Winfried, 379n
Meuli, Karl, 61n
Montaigne, Michel Eyquem de, 261

Nancy, Jean-Luc, 9n, 274n, 361n
Nietzsche, Friedrich, 72, 79, 108–42, 143–80, 188; *Beyond Good and Evil*, 109, 155–64, 176–77, 179; *The Birth of Tragedy*, 153; *The Case of Wagner*, 164–66, 178; *Ecce Homo*, 159; *The Gay Science*, 39n, 135–36, 168, 171–

72, 174–75; *A Genealogy of Morals,*
109–30, 134, 149, 169; *Human, All
Too Human,* 148; "On Ethics," 109;
"On Truth and Lying in an Extra-
Moral Sense," 73n, 109, 173–74;
"Teleology Since Kant," 109, 179;
Thus Spake Zarathustra, 139–40; *Twi-
light of the Idols,* 131–32, 138, 180;
Untimely Meditations, 146–47, 149–
53; *Will to Power,* 130, 133, 134,
137

Ovid, 380

Pasley, Malcolm, 321n
Petuchowski, Elizabeth, 358n
Plato, 49, 51, 54–55
Pohlenz, Max, 313n
Ponge, Francis, 66
Proust, Marcel, 187, 220–21

Richter, Jean Paul, 381n
Rilke, Rainer Maria, 342–43
Rosenzweig, Franz, 333–34n
Rousseau, Jean Jacques, 192–94, 197,
252, 264, 276, 278
Russell, Bertrand, 314

Saussure, Ferdinand de, 56, 355n
Schelling, F. W. J., 15, 102n, 108, 255–
56n
Schestag, Thomas, 313n
Schlegel, August Wilhelm, 225n

Schlegel, Friedrich, 15–18, 20, 44, 79,
83n, 108, 146, 205n, 219, 222–30,
242–60, 327–28n; *Athenäum,* 226–
28, 230, 238, 240, 242–45, 254; *Literary Notebooks,* 223, 229, 244–50, 253,
255, 257–59; "On Incomprehensibility," 17–18; "On Lessing," 224
Schleiermacher, Friedrich, 25–26, 44–80,
81–85, 108, 142; *Hermeneutics: The
Handwritten Manuscripts,* 72–73; *Hermeneutik und Kritik,* 45–49, 51–54,
56–58, 60–80; "Outlines for a System
of Moral Doctrine," 55
Schmidt, Jochen, 281n
Scholem, Gershom, 323n, 327n, 372
Schopenhauer, Arthur, 105-06n, 109,
152, 153n
Solomon, Peter, 358n
Spitzer, Leo, 320n
Starobinski, Jean, 355–56n
Sternberger, Dolf, 32n
Szondi, Peter, 215–16, 355n, 368, 375–
76

Theunissen, Michael, 36n
Tieck, Ludwig von, 251, 253

Voltaire (François M. Arouet), 263–64,
278; *Candide,* 265–66

Wagner, Richard, 165–67, 178
Weinrich, Harald, 263
Wolff, Christian, 144

MERIDIAN

Crossing Aesthetics

Giorgio Agamben, *Potentialities: Collected Essays*

Jacques Derrida, *Adieu to Emmanuel Levinas*

E. S. Burt, *Poetry's Appeal: Nineteenth-Century French Lyric and the Political Space*

Werner Hamacher, *Premises: Essays on Philosophy and Literature from Kant to Celan*

Aris Fioretos, *The Gray Book*

Deborah Esch, *In the Event: Reading Journalism, Reading Theory*

Winfried Menninghaus, *In Praise of Nonsense: Kant and Bluebeard*

Giorgio Agamben, *The Man Without Content*

Giorgio Agamben, *The End of the Poem: Essays in Poetics*

Theodor W. Adorno, *Sound Figures*

Louis Marin, *Sublime Poussin*

Philippe Lacoue-Labarthe, *Poetry as Experience*

Jacques Derrida, *Resistances of Psychoanalysis*

Ernst Bloch, *Literary Essays*

Marc Froment-Meurice, *That Is to Say: Heidegger's Poetics*

Francis Ponge, *Soap*

Phillipe Lacoue-Labarthe, *Typography: Mimesis, Philosophy, Politics*

Giorgio Agamben, *Homo Sacer: Sovereign Power and Bare Life*

Emmanuel Levinas, *Of God Who Comes to Mind*

Bernard Stiegler, *Technics and Time, 1: The Fault of Epimetheus*

Werner Hamacher, *pleroma—Reading in Hegel*

Serge Leclaire, *Psychoanalyzing*

Serge Leclaire, *A Child Is Being Killed*

Sigmund Freud, *Writings on Art and Literature*

Cornelius Castoriadis, *World in Fragments*

Thomas Keenan, *Fables of Responsibility: Aberrations and Predicaments in Ethics and Politics*

Emmanuel Levinas, *Proper Names*

Alexander García Düttmann, *At Odds with AIDS: Thinking and Talking About a Virus*

Maurice Blanchot, *Friendship*

Jean-Luc Nancy, *The Muses*

Massimo Cacciari, *Posthumous People: Vienna at the Turning Point*

David E. Wellbery, *The Specular Moment: Goethe's Early Lyric and the Beginnings of Romanticism*

Edmond Jabès, *The Little Book of Unsuspected Subversion*

Hans-Jost Frey, *Studies in Poetic Discourse: Mallarmé, Baudelaire, Rimbaud, Hölderlin*

Pierre Bourdieu, *The Rules of Art: Genesis and Structure of the Literary Field*

Nicolas Abraham, *Rhythms: On the Work, Translation, and Psychoanalysis*

Jacques Derrida, *On the Name*

David Wills, *Prosthesis*

Maurice Blanchot, *The Work of Fire*

Jacques Derrida, *Points ... : Interviews, 1974–1994*

J. Hillis Miller, *Topographies*

Philippe Lacoue-Labarthe, *Musica Ficta (Figures of Wagner)*

Jacques Derrida, *Aporias*

Emmanuel Levinas, *Outside the Subject*

Jean-François Lyotard, *Lessons on the Analytic of the Sublime*

Peter Fenves, *"Chatter": Language and History in Kierkegaard*

Jean-Luc Nancy, *The Experience of Freedom*

Jean-Joseph Goux, *Oedipus, Philosopher*

Haun Saussy, *The Problem of a Chinese Aesthetic*

Jean-Luc Nancy, *The Birth to Presence*